Register Now for to Your

SPRINGER PUBLISHING COMPANY
CONNECT™

Includes Student Data Files and A3 Template

Your print purchase of *Healthcare Quality Management: A Case Study Approach* **includes online access to the contents of your book**—increasing accessibility, portability, and searchability!

Access today at:

http://connect.springerpub.com/content/book/978-0-8261-4514-7 or scan the QR code at the right with your smartphone and enter the access code below.

H8VC8MWB

Scan here for quick access.

SPRINGER PUBLISHING COMPANY

View all our products at springerpub.com

Zachary Pruitt, PhD, MHA, CPH, is assistant professor and director of community practice at the University of South Florida College of Public Health. He holds a Master of Health Administration (MHA) and PhD in health services research from the University of South Florida College of Public Health. Dr. Pruitt teaches graduate and undergraduate courses in health administration, public health, and medicine. In addition to quality management, he teaches courses in strategic planning, marketing, and consulting practices. Dr. Pruitt has published research in *The Journal of Health Administration Education, Journal of Nursing Administration, Advances in Medical Education and Practice, American Journal of Managed Care*, and *Population Health Management*. Prior to academics, he directed Medicaid operations for a small government-sponsored health plan and managed policy and compliance projects for a large publicly traded managed care organization.

Candace S. Smith, PhD, RN, NEA-BC, is chief nursing officer at Manatee Memorial Hospital. She holds a board certification in advanced nursing executive from the American Nurses Credentialing Center and a PhD in education with a specialization in organizational leadership. A nationally known speaker with over 30 years of healthcare experience, Dr. Smith regularly presents on such topics as clinical excellence, exemplary leadership, and The Joint Commission's Speak Up™ patient safety program. Dr. Smith is an adjunct professor at State College of Florida Health Services Administration Program where she teaches quality management in healthcare and contemporary issues in healthcare.

Eddie Pérez-Ruberté, MS, is senior Lean project manager at BayCare Health Systems who leads the deployment of the Lean management system and culture. Eddie is a certified Lean expert and a certified Six Sigma Black Belt from the American Society for Quality. He is a nationally known speaker on applications of Lean in healthcare, employee engagement, healthcare quality, and performance improvement. He also helps organizations implement Lean programs through his consulting company, Areito Group. Eddie is an instructor for the Institute of Industrial and Systems Engineers where he teaches Lean and Six Sigma and certifies students in these methodologies at multiple universities and healthcare organizations across the United States. Eddie formerly held an appointment as instructor of healthcare systems engineering for the College of Medicine at Mayo Clinic.

HEALTHCARE QUALITY MANAGEMENT

A Case Study Approach

Zachary Pruitt, PhD, MHA, CPH

Candace S. Smith, PhD, RN, NEA-BC

Eddie Pérez-Ruberté, MS

SPRINGER PUBLISHING COMPANY

Springer Publishing Company, LLC
11 West 42nd Street
New York, NY 10036
www.springerpub.com
http://connect.springerpub.com/home

Acquisitions Editor: David D'Addona
Compositor: S4Carlisle Publishing Services

ISBN: 978-0-8261-4513-0
ebook ISBN: 978-0-8261-4514-7
DOI: 10.1891/9780826145147

Qualified instructors may request supplements by emailing textbook@springerpub.com
Instructor's Manual: 978-0-8261-4515-4
Instructor's PowerPoints: 978-0-8261-4516-1
Instructor's Data Files: 978-0-8261-4517-8
Instructor's A3s: 978-0-8261-4518-5
Student Ancillary Data Files and A3 template are available from: https://www.springerpub.com/hqm
Student Ancillary Data Files: 978-0-8261-4517-8
Student Ancillary A3 template: 978-0-8261-4524-6

20 21 22 23/ 5 4 3 2 1

The author and the publisher of this Work have made every effort to use sources believed to be reliable to provide information that is accurate and compatible with the standards generally accepted at the time of publication. The author and publisher shall not be liable for any special, consequential, or exemplary damages resulting, in whole or in part, from the readers' use of, or reliance on, the information contained in this book. The publisher has no responsibility for the persistence or accuracy of URLs for external or third-party Internet websites referred to in this publication and does not guarantee that any content on such websites is, or will remain, accurate or appropriate.

Library of Congress Cataloging-in-Publication Data

Names: Pruitt, Zachary, author. | Smith, Candace (Candace S.), author. |
  Pérez-Ruberté, Eddie, author.
Title: Healthcare quality management : a case study approach / Zachary
  Pruitt, Candace S. Smith, Eddie Pérez-Ruberté.
Description: New York : Springer Publishing Company, [2020] | Includes
  bibliographical references and index.
Identifiers: LCCN 2019047920 | ISBN 9780826145130 (paperback) | ISBN
  9780826145147 (ebook) | ISBN 9780826145154 (Instructor's Manual) | ISBN
  9780826145161 (PowerPoints) | ISBN 9780826145178 (Data Files)
Subjects: MESH: Health Services Administration | Quality Assurance, Health
  Care | Quality Indicators, Health Care | Case Reports
Classification: LCC RA971 | NLM W 84.41 | DDC 362.1--dc23
LC record available at https://lccn.loc.gov/2019047920

Contact us to receive discount rates on bulk purchases.
We can also customize our books to meet your needs.
For more information please contact: sales@springerpub.com

Publisher's Note: **New and used products purchased from third-party sellers are not guaranteed for quality, authenticity, or access to any included digital components.**

Printed in the United States of America.

CONTENTS

PREFACE

THE GOAL

We heard from you, our students of healthcare quality management. You strongly prefer active learning. You complain that the lecture-and-exam style of learning in the classroom drives you to distraction. When we teach quality management in hospitals and clinics, you tell us that you are too busy to learn theory. You would rather get back to caring for patients. No matter the setting, our students want to apply practical quality improvement methods to real-life scenarios.

Many textbooks offer in-depth coverage of the theoretical principles and technical tools of quality management. In our experience teaching quality management, though, you seek a different kind of textbook, one with numerous in-depth case studies that require you to apply your newly acquired problem-solving skills. We wrote this casebook for you, the undergraduate or graduate student in health administration, nursing, medicine, or other health professions. We wrote this casebook for you, the performance improvement team and frontline staff in hospitals, clinics, and other healthcare organizations. We wrote this casebook for instruction in the classroom or online formats.

Competency-based education requires a different kind of textbook. These days, education accreditation bodies, such as the Commission on Accreditation of Healthcare Management Education (CAHME) and the American Association of Colleges of Nursing (AACN), require that programs assess your professional competency in varying degrees of cognitive complexity. In other words, your instructor needs to evaluate not just what you know, but what you can actually do. Not only should you understand the material (a lower competency level), but you should show that you can apply knowledge, analyze complex situations, and evaluate alternative courses of action (higher levels of competency). Assessment of your high-level competency through the traditional lecture-and-exam method to teaching is impossible. Instead, you need a quality management textbook that engages you in active, problem-based learning. This casebook will enable you to demonstrate, at the highest level of cognitive complexity, your professional competency.

THE STORY

Part One of this casebook tells the story of how you can meet the challenge of fixing our broken healthcare system by adopting the right mindset, learning the basic skills, and obtaining your organization's support. Appropriate for students with no experience in healthcare quality management, these six chapters describe—in an easy-to-read, narrative style—the quality management fundamentals needed to analyze the case studies in Part Two.

Chapter 1, The Challenge explains how the U.S. healthcare system delivers comparatively low-quality, inefficient care. Despite highly trained, hard-working people, the system fails patients in all categories of healthcare quality management, including process improvement, patient safety, patient experience, and performance improvement. This chapter defines healthcare quality management and emphasizes the various quality issues that lower the value of the U.S. healthcare system.

Chapter 2, The Innovators describes the history of renowned manufacturing pioneers whose quality management approaches have been adopted by high-performing healthcare organizations. You will learn how these rigorous, yet simple quality management principles can be transferred to your healthcare organization.

Chapter 3, The Mindset describes the way of thinking you need to fix healthcare quality problems. This mindset is neither revolutionary nor complicated. It is necessary. This chapter describes, in simple language, the important quality management philosophies and methodologies, such as Lean, Six Sigma, and evidence-based management.

Chapter 4, The Culture describes how a supportive organizational culture enables better care, more efficient processes, and improved health outcomes. Because system-related problems are usually to blame for low quality of healthcare, you will learn the value of creating a just culture in your organization. This chapter also explains the numerous barriers you will face to implement your quality management mindset and skills. To help you overcome these obstacles, you will gain an understanding of noteworthy change management models that will enable you to build a culture responsive to healthcare quality management.

Chapter 5, The Casebook will teach you how to apply quality management through the case study method. A form of problem-based learning, the case study method favors active, team-based learning using realistic and challenging scenarios. You will learn a systematic approach to analyzing the case studies that encourages independent learning, application of knowledge, and team-based collaboration. In addition, this chapter will guide you to match case studies to the applicable professional competencies, such as leading patient-safety initiatives, analytical skills, community collaboration, interpersonal relations, and more.

Chapter 6, The Template describes the A3 problem-solving template, a common quality improvement tool that follows popular continuous quality improvement cycles (i.e., Plan-Do-Study-Act [PDSA] or Define, Measure, Analyze, Improve, and Control [DMAIC]). Termed the Case Application Exercise in this casebook, this chapter explains how to use the A3 as a single-page activity sheet for step-by-step problem-solving. We recommend that you apply the A3 problem-solving template to each case study in Part Two.

THE CASES

Part Two of this casebook features complex, realistic scenarios to prepare you to solve real-world problems. Inspired by real events, each case study includes the essential storytelling elements: character, plot, setting, and conflict. The stories connect the emotional with the logical to make your case study analysis memorable in addition to challenging.

The 25 case studies in Part Two are separated into four major sections: (a) process improvement, (b) patient experience, (c) patient safety, and (d) performance improvement. Introductions to each of the four sections provide brief summaries to the case studies for easy reference. Each case study contains competency-based learning objectives and discussion questions. Reflection and discussion of the characters and scenarios will support the development of professional competency in domains such as change management, accountability, and team leadership. The discussion questions are appropriate for either the classroom or online format.

Appendix A, Glossary, defines key terms and concepts related to healthcare quality management.

Appendix B, Case Study to Data File Matrix, lists the Excel-based data files provided in spreadsheet format for 15 of the 25 case studies. Some case assignments will require extensive analysis, such as pivot tables, IF–THEN statement, and scatter diagrams. Multiple case files provide thousands of lines of patient-level data, such as surgery timestamp data and inpatient encounters with length of stay. You will find that the data files are easily accessible by visiting the following url: https://www.springerpub.com/hqm.

Appendix C, Case Study to Healthcare Setting Matrix, lists the healthcare settings for each case study, including various inpatient sizes and types, emergency departments, post–acute care facilities, managed care organizations, outpatient clinics, and home care agencies.

Appendix D, Quality Management Tools and Approaches Matrix, illustrates how the 25 commonly used quality management tools or approaches included in Part Two, such as value stream maps, spaghetti diagrams, and control charts, connect to the relevant case studies. You will learn to apply these newly introduced quality improvement tools and approaches to case studies throughout the text. This approach reinforces understanding of the tools and approaches through their application to the analysis of the case study.

Appendix E, A3 Problem-Solving Template, provides a blank A3 problem-solving template with step-by-step problem-solving instructions.

Podcasts feature short interviews with healthcare managers who share their personal experiences with quality management related to each of the 25 case studies. Access the podcasts by following this url to Springer Publishing Company Connect™: https://connect.springer pub.com/content/book/978-0-8261-4514-7/front-matter/fmatter2.

THE RESOURCES

Your instructor will be the facilitator who will guide you through the problem-solving process. To support your efforts, qualified instructors have access to extensive casebook resources, including:

- Complete PowerPoint presentations for all chapters and case studies
- Teaching notes with summaries, Excel-based activity descriptions, tool/approach applications, and discussion of competencies for each case study
- Multiple solutions to A3 problem-solving template for each case study (students only receive access to the template file with instructions)

- Fully realized solutions to the Excel-based analyses with instructions (students only receive access to raw data and data dictionaries)
- Answers to discussion questions for all chapters and case studies

Qualified instructors can obtain all casebook resources (Instructor's Manual, PowerPoints, data files, and A3s) by emailing Springer Publishing Company at textbook@springerpub.com.

THE SUMMARY

You learn by doing. No other healthcare quality management textbook provides you with extensive, relevant, and realistic case studies that will enable you to expand your knowledge, practice your mindset, and apply your skills. Part One includes six chapters on the background of quality management needed to analyze the case studies. Part Two includes 25 extensive, realistic, story-based case studies that support development of your professional competencies.

If you have any feedback or ideas for future editions of the casebook, please let us know at zpruitt@usf.edu.

Zachary Pruitt
Candace S. Smith
Eddie Pérez-Ruberté

ACKNOWLEDGMENTS

We wish to thank Anthony Kovner and Cindy Jimmerson whose work and guidance served as inspiration for this casebook.

We would also like to express our gratitude and admiration to Natalie Wrightson for her work in reviewing the casebook and acting as our test case student for all of the Case Application Exercises. We were summarily impressed with her talent and expect great things from her as a future healthcare leader.

We would also like to convey our special thanks to the healthcare experts who supported this casebook. Thank you to Terri Ashmeade, Bill Auxier, Susan Benardo, Lea Ann Biafora, John Botsko, Kate Chapin, Steven Chew, Jim Cote, Lorelei De La Cruz, Valerie Franks, Daniel Gregg, Joseph Haider, Christine Hardin, Mel Hollis, Heather Ingram, Megan Lucas, Stephanie Minter, Kay Perrin, Steven Pino, Brian Pogue, Becky Pruitt, Edward Rafalski, Jody Rain, Gail Ryder, Laura Silvoy, Susan Sportsman, James Wengerd, and Carol Whitmore. We appreciate their participation in the podcasts and their help in making the case studies as realistic as possible.

LIST OF AUDIO PODCAST INTERVIEWS

Access the podcasts by scanning the QR code or following this link to Springer Publishing Company Connect™: https://connect.springerpub.com/content/book/978-0-8261-4514-7/front-matter/fmatter2

Process Improvement

1. **A Summer Internship Journal**
   Interview with Lorelei De La Cruz

2. **Claims Payment Processing**
   Interview with Brian Pogue

3. **Return-to-Work at a Home Healthcare Agency**
   Interview with Heather Ingram

4. **The Ophthalmologist Who Could Not See (The Waste)**
   Interview with Jim Cote

5. **Building a New IR Suite**
   Interview with Laura Silvoy

6. **Emergency Department Heroes**
   Interview with Jody Rain

Patient Experience

7. **Hurricane Mia Hits the Patient Access Call Center**
   Interview with Daniel Gregg

8. **The Cowboy Doctor's Patient Experience**
   Interview with Bill Auxier

9. **Patient Navigation at the Orthopedic Clinic**
   Interview with Lea Ann Biafora

10. **HCAHPS and the Quiet-at-Night Measure**
    Interview with Stephanie Minter

## PART ONE

Foundational Principles in Quality Management

CHAPTER SUMMARIES

Chapter 1: The Challenge

U.S. healthcare system delivers comparatively low-quality, inefficient care. The problem is not the people; it is the system.

Chapter 2: The Innovators

High-performing healthcare organizations adopt the quality management approaches of manufacturing innovators.

Chapter 3: The Mindset

The mindset needed to improve the healthcare system is neither revolutionary nor complicated. Embrace a mindset that clarifies, simplifies, and streamlines.

Chapter 4: The Culture

Organizational culture can empower improvement, but barriers to quality management will impede progress. Without individual change, organizational change is impossible.

Chapter 5: The Casebook

Apply the mindset, practice the skills, and build a culture responsive to healthcare quality management through the case study method.

Chapter 6: The Template

Powerfully simple, the A3 problem-solving template transforms a single page into a collaborative, systematic approach to healthcare quality management.

CHAPTER 1

The Challenge

OBJECTIVES

1. Identify quality management challenges associated with the U.S. healthcare system.
2. Define healthcare quality management.
3. Explain how the quality management mindset and skills can improve healthcare quality.
4. Describe healthcare quality problems related to process improvement, patient safety, patient experience, and performance improvement.

PERFORMANCE OF THE U.S. HEALTHCARE SYSTEM

The low-quality performance of our U.S. healthcare system will not surprise you. According to a recent survey, most Americans are troubled by the state of our healthcare system, with three-quarters saying that the healthcare system is "in a state of crisis" or "has major problems" (Reinhart, 2018). Our healthcare system fails to meet our expectations.

Although the most expensive healthcare system in the world, U.S. healthcare ranks below comparable high-income countries in many quality measures, such as infant mortality, maternal mortality, life expectancy, and number of medical errors (Bradley & Taylor, 2013; OECD, 2017; Sawyer & McDermott, 2019). Based on a set of metrics used by the Commonwealth Fund to compare healthcare system performance, the United States ranks last in administrative efficiency, last in access to healthcare, last in health equity, and next to last in overall health **outcomes** (Table 1.1; Schneider, Sarnak, Squires, Shah, & Doty, 2017).

We are not getting our money's worth. We spend more on healthcare—one-and-a-half times the next most expensive country in the world (Bradley & Taylor, 2013; OECD, 2017)—but we fail to deliver satisfactory health outcomes (Schneider et al., 2017). The best solutions to our healthcare performance problems do not include hiring more people or spending more money (McGinnis et al., 2016). The healthcare system employs more people than any other U.S. industry (Thompson, 2018), yet the healthcare workforce lags behind in productivity (Carnevale, Smith, Gulish, & Beach, 2012).

Why does the United States perform so poorly even with the most people and most resources? Because the problem is neither the people nor the resources, it is the system.

Table 1.1 Commonwealth Fund Rankings of Healthcare System Performance

	AUS	CAN	FRA	GER	NETH	NZ	NOR	SWE	SWIZ	UK	US
Overall ranking	2	9	10	8	3	4	4	6	6	1	11
Care process	2	6	9	8	4	3	10	11	7	1	5
Access	4	10	9	2	1	7	5	6	8	3	11
Administrative efficiency	1	6	11	6	9	2	4	5	8	3	10
Equity	7	9	10	6	2	8	5	3	4	1	11
Healthcare outcomes	1	9	5	8	6	7	3	2	4	10	11

Source: Reproduced with permission from Schneider, E. C., Sarnak, D. O., Squires, D., Shah, A., & Doty, M. M. (2017). *Mirror, Mirror 2017: International comparison reflects flaws and opportunities for better U.S. health care.* Retrieved from https://interactives.commonwealthfund.org/2017/july/mirror-mirror

We perform as well as our current system design allows. According to the Institute for Health-care Improvement (IHI) founder **Don Berwick**, the central law of quality improvement is defined as follows: "Every system is perfectly designed to achieve the results it achieves" (Berwick, 1996, p. 619). He joked that this adage should be "tattooed on the body" of people working in healthcare quality management to remind us that the quality-related problems stem from our processes, not our people (Donahue, 2015).

Why do we need to improve healthcare quality? First, patients deserve high-quality healthcare. Our healthcare quality management efforts should be focused on the views and experiences of the patient (Balik, Conway, Zipperer, & Watson, 2011). Next, healthcare professionals, including nonclinical managers, have an ethical duty to assure high-quality medical care (Baily, Bottrell, Lynn, & Jennings, 2006). From this ethical perspective, healthcare quality management should simply be thought of as a necessary part of normal healthcare operations. Finally, organizational survival depends on it. Where competition is most intense, healthcare quality management implementation is highest (Weiner, Alexander, Baker, Shortell, & Becker, 2006). In other words, quality management creates competitive advantage for healthcare organizations that improve quality; those organizations that fail to perform will cease to exist.

HOW YOU CAN HELP

Imagine you could fix the U.S. healthcare system. If you adopted the right mindset, learned the basic skills, and obtained the organizational support, where would you start? Would you improve health outcomes, safer healthcare, more efficient work processes, or higher patient satisfaction? Would you increase the value of healthcare for your community?

With so many opportunities for improvement, you may think that a complicated approach will be required to solve these difficult healthcare problems. In fact, the opposite is true. To improve healthcare quality, you must embrace a mindset that clarifies, simplifies, and streamlines. This mindset is not revolutionary. In fact, the approach is based on hundreds of years of scientific thinking. Asking questions, making predictions, measuring, observing, analyzing, and controlling are fundamental to both the scientific method and quality management.

If you combine the quality improvement mindset with fundamental management skills, you can solve some of our toughest healthcare quality challenges (Field, Heineke, Langabeer, & DelliFraine, 2014). You can improve broken processes, medical errors, dissatisfied patients, and lackluster performance. The quality management skills are neither difficult nor radical. These skills, when applied correctly, will empower you to identify root causes of problems, analyze dirty data, define new ways to work, recommend solutions, measure the outcomes, and sustain the changes.

You will find that the casebook contains realistic (but entertaining) case studies on an assortment of healthcare quality problems in a variety of management settings. However, the case study method is not for the passive learner. This casebook will require that you actively examine messy healthcare problems. There is no one "right" answer; each case will have more than one interpretation. Of course, this increases the level of difficulty but will better prepare you to confront the real-world healthcare quality challenges.

HEALTHCARE QUALITY MANAGEMENT DEFINITION

What do we mean when we say healthcare quality management? First, we start with the definition of quality. According to renowned quality management expert **W. Edwards Deming**, quality can be defined as "a predictable degree of uniformity and dependability with a quality standard suited to the customer" (Deming, 1982, p. 229). This definition accepts that some kind of standard has been set and that the system can produce to that standard reliably, without variation. In addition, using this definition, the standard-bearer of quality is the customer.

Like the general definition of quality offered by Deming, the definition of healthcare quality includes both a standard and a standard-bearer. The Institute of Medicine (IOM) follows Deming's logic and defines healthcare quality as "the degree to which health services for individuals and populations increase the likelihood of desired health outcomes and are consistent with current professional knowledge" (IOM, 1990 as cited in IOM, 2001, p. 44). The "consistent with current professional knowledge" component reflects the standard of care set by the community of healthcare practitioners based on the best available medical evidence. The "desired health outcomes" element represents the standard of quality determined by the patients or their families.

However, what the IOM definition does not address is what Deming terms, "a predictable degree of uniformity and dependability." Tellingly, the old healthcare quality adage of "the right care for the right patient at the right time" also reveals this oversight. As quality expert **Carolyn M. Clancy**, MD, advocates, "every time" should be added to this axiom (Clancy, 2009). Healthcare does not deliver a standard of care reliably, without variation. In other words, variability of healthcare delivery stands out as a major problem with our healthcare system. Therefore, healthcare quality management should aim to achieve the right care for the right patient at the right time, *every time*.

To achieve highly reliable healthcare quality, you must engage in systematic management practices. Management practices, according to one definition, are the "processes, composed of interrelated social and technical functions and activities, occurring within a formal organizational setting for the purpose of accomplishing predetermined objectives through utilization of human and other resources" (Longest & Darr, 2014, p. 255). In other words, managers must organize human and nonhuman resources to execute activities according to some planned goal.

Combining these concepts, we offer our working definition of healthcare quality management for this casebook. **Healthcare quality management** is the application of systematic practices that guide the formation of reliable processes in healthcare organizations in order to increase the likelihood of delivering evidence-based care and achieving the health outcomes expected by patients, their families, and their caregivers.

REVISITING THE PERFORMANCE OF THE U.S. HEALTHCARE SYSTEM

According to the standard of healthcare quality set by the Commonwealth Fund, the United States ranks dead last in the world in health system performance (Schneider et al., 2017). They created their assessment using dozens of quality metrics used to objectively calculate a composite performance scoring system. Their ranking system features many metrics for which the U.S. healthcare system disappoints, such as the preventive care measure, "avoidable hospital admissions for asthma," and the affordability measure, "cost-related access problem to medical care in the past year." The Commonwealth Fund also considers the quality of the medical care delivery by examining a measure called "mortality amenable to healthcare." This measure is defined as "deaths under age 75 from specific causes that are considered preventable in the presence of timely and effective health care." In 2014, the medical care provided in the United States trails the worldwide counterparts by a wide margin (Figure 1.1).

Of course, these negative results do not explain the whole story of U.S. healthcare system performance, as the Commonwealth Fund acknowledges. The United States tops the other countries in other measures of quality. For example, the United States excels at measures of the provider–patient relationship, such as "talked with provider about healthy diet, exercise and physical activity in the past 2 years" and "women aged 50-69 with mammography screening in the past year." This makes sense; the U.S. educational system is highly regarded around the world. Many U.S. medical schools are excellent, with 28 of the top 50 in the world located in the United States in 2018 (*U.S. News and World Report*, 2019). In addition, our physicians perform remarkably well in treating breast and cervical cancers, heart attacks, and ischemic stroke—all highly skilled interventions—where the mortality rates from these diseases are lower in the United States than those in comparable countries (Sawyer & McDermott, 2019). Success with sophisticated, technology-supported interventions by our well-trained providers supports the notion that our healthcare quality challenges are caused by our processes, not our people.

Think again about our definition of healthcare quality management. Depending on the standard-bearer perspective, the U.S. healthcare system performs well in some standards and poorly in others. When you seek to improve healthcare quality through management practices, you must first define the standard of quality. Definitions of quality must be specific

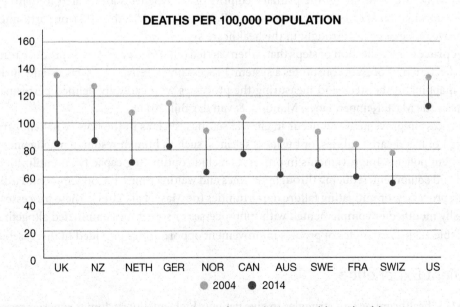

FIGURE 1.1 Commonwealth Fund's analysis of mortality amenable to healthcare.

Source: Reproduced with permission from Schneider, E. C., Sarnak, D. O., Squires, D., Shah, A., & Doty, M. M. (2017). *Mirror, Mirror 2017: International comparison reflects flaws and opportunities for better U.S. health care.* Retrieved from https://interactives.commonwealthfund.org/2017/july/mirror-mirror

and scientific. The practice of defining quality scientifically is called **operationalization**. This is not as easy as it seems. For example, "consistent with current professional knowledge" changes constantly based on new medical evidence. Furthermore, the standard-bearer of quality can change. The patient's opinion of "desired health outcomes" can be dramatically different from that of his or her doctor. Therefore, to conduct effective healthcare quality management, you must clearly identify the standard-bearer and objectively define the standard of quality. This means that many of the metrics used to evaluate performance of the U.S. healthcare system can and should be debated.

COMMON CHALLENGES IN HEALTHCARE QUALITY MANAGEMENT

Nevertheless, by most measures accepted by most stakeholders, the quality of healthcare in the United States—uneven and unreliable—can be improved dramatically (Jha, 2017; McGlynn et al., 2003). In this casebook, we provide you with realistic scenarios and detailed data on healthcare quality issues that regularly vex healthcare quality management practitioners. We divided the types of healthcare quality management problems into four groups: **process improvement, patient experience, patient safety,** and **performance improvement.**

Process Improvement

Chaotic, redundant, and unexamined work processes cause underperformance of the U.S. healthcare system. Inefficiencies in healthcare are easy to identify—from confusing hospital layouts to excessive patient waiting times—but the fixes are not so simple (Glied & Sacarny, 2018). Although the primary culprits of inefficiencies are related to delivery of care, coordination of care, and overtreatment (Berwick & Hackbarth, 2012), opportunities to improve processes exist throughout the healthcare system.

A **process** is a collection of steps that, when carried out in a specific order, produce results. A collection of processes constitutes a system. Process improvement projects usually include the mapping of the steps and measuring the processes with carefully defined performance metrics (de Mast, Kemper, Does, Mandjes, & van der Bijl, 2011).

Process improvement can occur in clinical settings, such as in the flow of patient care or design of healthcare facilities, or business settings, such as human resource management or payment policies. Improvements in processes include optimizing capacity and utilization of staff and equipment, reducing throughput times and waiting times, introducing standardized work processes, or mitigating failure opportunities (de Mast et al., 2011). These processes are usually modified or complemented with subprocesses or sometimes eliminated altogether.

Table 1.2 lists examples of process improvement opportunities provided in this casebook.

Patient Experience

The U.S. healthcare system struggles to give patients high-quality customer experiences seen in other economic sectors (Needham, 2012). Patient experience is the judgment, attitude, or perception of all interactions in a healthcare environment. Patient experience is related not only to the concept of patient satisfaction but also encompasses whether patients' expectations

Table 1.2 Process Improvement Case Studies

CASE STUDY	PROCESS IMPROVEMENT ISSUE
Case 1: A Summer Internship Journal	*Inefficient patient flow* can cause problems throughout the hospital, including unsafe delays in admissions from the emergency department, PACU, and cardiac catheterization lab (Destino et al., 2019).
Case 2: Claims Payment Processing	Delays in payments from managed care organizations to healthcare providers can be caused by unclear communication processes. Effective management of the *revenue cycle processes* can increase patient revenues and profitability (Hodges, 2002).
Case 3: Return to Work at a Home Health Agency	Patient care activities commonly cause injuries to clinicians, which may force them to take time off work, a benefit covered under the FMLA. *Return-to-work process* administration is one of the three top priorities for 91% of healthcare risk managers (Mercer, 2010).
Case 4: The Ophthalmologist Who Could Not See (The Waste)	Shrinking payments from Medicare and other payers require healthcare operations to cut costs. Healthcare service delivery is fraught with unnecessary *operational inefficiencies* that are not obvious to medical providers (de Koning, Verver, van den Heuvel, Bisgaard, & Does, 2006).
Case 5: Building a New IR Suite	Inefficiencies in the physical layout of healthcare facilities increase effort and costs of delivery health services. Improved workflow can be achieved through *optimized hospital design* (Reijula, Nevala, Lahtinen, Ruohomaki, & Reijula, 2014).
Case 6: Emergency Department Heroes	*ED crowding* and patient throughput challenges (Schwarz, Hasson, & Athlin, 2016) are caused by inefficiencies related to triage processes and other issues (Arbune, Wackerbarth, Allison, & Conigliaro, 2017).

ED, emergency department; FMLA, Family and Medical Leave Act; IR, interventional radiology; PACU, postacute anesthesia care unit.

about their experiences were met (Agency for Healthcare Research and Quality, 2017). Another related concept is patient centeredness, which has been defined by IHI founder Don Berwick as "the experience (to the extent the informed, individual patient desires it) of transparency, individualization, recognition, respect, dignity, and choice in all matters, without exception, related to one's person, circumstances, and relationships in health care" (2009, p. w560). Whether you call it "patient experience," "patient satisfaction," or "patient centeredness," these concepts seek to understand the quality of healthcare from the patient's perspective.

Improving patient experience requires a shift in thinking about healthcare delivery. The measurement of patient experience is not universally accepted by clinicians (Manary, Boulding, Staelin, & Glickman, 2013) who may bristle at the idea of "patient satisfaction" scores, feeling that patients assess only trivial items, such as wait times, or worse, that they encourage bad medicine, like prescribing unneeded pain medicines (Nash, 2015). Also, some clinicians fear that by refusing patients' specific requests for care, irrespective of its benefit, their performance rating will suffer (Manary et al., 2013). Despite this ongoing debate, research consistently indicates positive associations between patient experience measures and clinical effectiveness, especially patient adherence to recommended medical treatment (Doyle, Lennox, & Bell, 2013).

Consumers and purchasers increasingly demand information about their healthcare experience (Lake, Kvam, & Gold, 2005). The U.S. government—the Agency for Healthcare Research and Quality (AHRQ) and the Centers for Medicare and Medicaid Services (CMS)—responded in 2006 with the final version of the series of consumer surveys Consumer Assessment of Healthcare Providers and Systems (CAHPS; Giordano, Elliott, Goldstein, Lehrman, & Spencer, 2010). The **CAHPS** (pronounced "caps") surveys ask patients about their willingness to recommend, interactions with doctors and nurses, timeliness of their care, facility cleanliness, and more (Giordano et al., 2010). The government publishes results of the surveys, adjusted for patient-level factors, to the Hospital Compare website and the CAHPS Online Reporting System, for the purposes of consumer shopping comparisons and various pay-for-performance programs (Anhang Price et al., 2014). In response to the drive for improved patient experience from consumers and government purchasers, healthcare organizations have made big investments in work processes and workforce training (Burrill & Kane, 2018).

The case studies in Table 1.3 illustrate a range of patient experience challenges.

Table 1.3 Patient Experience Case Studies

CASE STUDY	PATIENT EXPERIENCE ISSUE
Case 7: Hurricane Mia Hits the Patient Access Call Center	Inefficient call center scheduling processes can cause unnecessary *delays in care* for patients, which negatively impact patient experience ratings (Brandenburg, Gabow, Steele, Toussaint, & Tyson, 2015; Rohleder et al., 2013).
Case 8: The Cowboy Doctor's Patient Experience	Although some physicians resist the notion of assessing patient experience (Nash, 2015), communication training can *change physician behaviors* and improve patient satisfaction (Boissy et al., 2016).
Case 9: Patient Navigation at the Ortho Clinic	Patient consent obtained by the surgeon may not be adequate to assure patient satisfaction (McGaughey, 2004). Navigators can improve communication and significantly improve *outpatient patient experience scores* for orthopedic surgery (Goldsmith et al., 2017; van Eck, Toor, Banffy, & Gambardella, 2018).
Case 10: HCAHPS and the Quiet-at-Night Measure	Critics argue that patient experience scores measure inconsequential aspects of healthcare (Jha, 2017), such as whether the hospital is *quiet at night*, but the patient satisfaction may strongly relate to health outcomes (Isaac, Zaslavsky, Cleary, & Landon, 2010).
Case 11: Discharge Phone Calls (En Español)	*Automated inpatient discharge communications* can improve health outcomes (Olsen, Courtemanche, & Hodach, 2016), but the lack of cultural competence in healthcare operations may lower overall patient experience scores (Weech-Maldonado et al., 2012).
Case 12: Patient Experience in Home Care	The competitive home healthcare market requires patient referrals from satisfied clients to increase growth in revenues (Abusalem, Myers, & Aljeesh, 2013; Kunz, 2018). The HH-CAHPS *Net Promoter Score* asks, "How likely is it that you would recommend our company to a friend or colleague?"

HCAHPS, Hospital Consumer Assessment of Healthcare Providers and Systems; HH-CAHPS, Home Healthcare Consumer Assessment of Healthcare Providers and Systems.

Patient Safety

Unreliable healthcare work processes fail to keep patients safe. According to the IOM (Kohn, Corrigan, & Donaldson, 2000), between 44,000 and 98,000 people were dying in the United States each year due to preventable medical errors. These mistakes are most likely to occur in hospitals, specifically in intensive care units, operating rooms, and emergency departments, but errors such as adverse drug events, falls, burns, pressure ulcers, and mistaken patient identities can happen throughout the healthcare continuum (Kohn et al., 2000). The IOM called for a comprehensive medical error prevention strategy to identify errors, raise performance standards, and implement safety systems (Kohn et al., 2000).

More than 20 years have passed since the first estimates were published on the extent of medical harm occurring in U.S. hospitals. Despite sizable time, money, and effort allocated to patient safety initiatives, the risk of death associated with medical error is still too high—about the same as dying from diabetes, which is the seventh highest cause of death in the United States (CDC National Center for Health Statistics, 2017; Sunshine et al., 2019).

Table 1.4 lists medical errors addressed in this casebook.

Table 1.4 Patient Safety Case Studies

CASE STUDY	PATIENT SAFETY ISSUE
Case 13: Reducing Patient Falls: The Sleuth Resident	In the United States, between 700,000 and 1 million patients fall in the hospital each year (Ganz et al., 2013). *Patient falls* are a leading cause of both fatal and nonfatal injuries among the elderly (Bergen, 2016).
Case 14: Sustaining Hand Hygiene	Sustaining even the simplest quality improvement intervention can be challenging. In 1847, Hungarian physician Ignaz Semmelweis demonstrated that hospital-acquired infections were transmitted via the hands of clinicians (Kadar, 2019). Even today, it is difficult to sustain adherence to disciplined *handwashing* routines (World Health Organization, 2009).
Case 15: A Warning Letter From the State Regulator	*Patient misidentification* errors can lead to serious harm or even loss of life (Hall, 2008). A variety of situations may contribute to patient identification errors within complex healthcare environments.
Case 16: Failure-to-Rescue	Not following existing clinical protocols can lead to patient death, a phenomenon known as *failure-to-rescue* (Garvey, 2015). Consequences of medical errors can create a "second victim" where clinicians experience stress, anxiety, depression, denial, and withdrawal (Seys et al., 2013).
Case 17: CLIF's Medication Errors	Nearly 5% of all hospitalized patients experience an adverse drug event, making *medication errors* one of the most common types of inpatient safety issues in U.S. healthcare (AHRQ Patient Safety Network, 2019; Hauck, & Zhao, 2011). Technology can not only help reduce medical errors but can also cause unintended patient safety consequences (Campbell, Sittig, Ash, Guappone, & Dykstra, 2006).
Case 18: A Mom's Story of Sepsis	*Sepsis infections* are a leading cause of death in the United States (Cohen et al., 2015). Avoiding deadly delays in sepsis treatment depends on early recognition (Kumar et al., 2006; Lynn, Gupta, Vaaler, Held, & Leon, 2018).

Performance Improvement

"Performance improvement" is a term often used interchangeably with "quality improvement." For the purposes of this casebook, we define performance improvement as quality issues related to demands made from outside your organization. Healthcare organizations, isolated from the community needs, governmental policies, and competitive pressures, must respond to a variety of externally generated quality management imperatives. For example, the opioid addiction epidemic profoundly affects communities throughout the United States, where overdoses lead to stress on hospital emergency department capacity (Vivolo-Kantor et al., 2018). In addition, continuous reductions in payments from health insurance companies motivate health services organizations to reexamine care processes for inefficiencies (Balzer, Raackow, Hahnenkamp, Flessa, & Meissner, 2017).

No other change has challenged healthcare organizations to improve their performance like value-based purchasing, also called "pay-for-performance" (VanLare & Conway, 2012). Value-based purchasing is the idea that healthcare payers, such as Medicare and insurance companies, replace payments for the number of services provided with the incentives for keeping patients healthy (Blumenthal & Jena, 2013). "Value" is defined as the quality of health achieved per dollar spent (Porter & Teisberg, 2006). In other words, healthcare organizations are given financial incentives to improve quality and reduce costs. This is a transformative change to the healthcare system incentive **structure** (Porter & Kaplan, 2017). Health services organizations must now control costs while at the same time invest in healthcare quality management initiatives, tasks that the U.S. healthcare system is largely unprepared to tackle.

To encourage the shift to value-based incentives, the U.S. government has implemented many policies that reward providers for value of care (Blumenthal, Davis, & Guterman, 2015). For example, Accountable Care Organizations (ACOs), under a Medicare program called the "Medicare Shared Savings Program," encourage a range of specialists, hospitals, and other providers to collaborate and reduce the overall costs of providing care. If the ACO reduces the overall costs below the predetermined expenditure benchmarks, then the savings are split between Medicare and the ACO. There's a catch, though. The ACO receives a bonus only if it meets the quality measure targets. The program tracks dozens of measures, such as breast cancer screening and depression remission at 12 months (CMS, 2019). Therefore, the intention of the ACO is to increase the value of the Medicare program—improved quality at a reduced cost.

Medicare does not just reward with carrots; it punishes with sticks. The Hospital Readmissions Reduction Program is a value-based purchasing program that reduces payments to hospitals with "worse-than-expected" rates of readmission within 30 days of discharge (CMS, 2014). CMS will withhold up to 3% of Medicare payments to hospitals if they have high 30-day readmission rates for six specific conditions. For a hospital industry whose profit margins are typically less than 3%, a revenue reduction that size on all of their Medicare patients would be a big stick, indeed (Ellison & Cohen, 2018; Mulvany, 2016).

In our conceptualization for this casebook, performance improvement involves effective quality management responses to inevitable changes in external environment. Consider the performance improvement case studies listed in Table 1.5.

Table 1.5 Performance Improvement Case Studies

CASE STUDY	PERFORMANCE IMPROVEMENT ISSUE
Case 19: Operating Room Recovery	Tightening budgets in hospitals requires better planning of operating room use. Improved performance in *operating room efficiency* requires analysis of complex surgical operations (Balzer et al., 2017).
Case 20: Opioid Overdoses in the Emergency Department	Failure to follow established clinical protocols can lower measures of community health performance, such as is seen in the *opioid overdose epidemic* (Califf, Woodcock, & Ostroff, 2016).
Case 21: The Lunchroom: Physician Engagement at a PCMH	A new model of healthcare delivery, called the PCMH, incentivizes performance measures (NCQA, 2014). Such organizational innovations can psychologically strain providers and lead to burnout (Swensen, Kabcenell, & Shanafelt, 2016), so efforts to *engage physicians* in performance improvement should be carefully implemented (Lee & Cosgrove, 2014).
Case 22: The Fulfillment Affair	Behavioral and social factors—not scores on quality measures—may predict *high-cost patients* (Sterling et al., 2018), so performance improvement requires close examination of patients' environments.
Case 23: Composite Quality Measures	*Composite quality measures* provide a useful summary of quality across several dimensions and are increasingly used in value-based purchasing programs to evaluate healthcare organization performance (Friebel & Steventon, 2019; Shwartz, Restuccia, & Rosen, 2015).
Case 24: Both/And Thinking in Readmission Prevention	The multifaceted causes of *inpatient readmissions* require interprofessional collaboration to prevent financial penalties levied by Medicare (Auerbach et al., 2016).
Case 25: Community Collaboration for Suicide Prevention	Federal law requires nonprofit hospitals to assess community health needs and set strategies for improved *population health*, including mortality associated with suicides. Ineffective performance could result in loss of tax-exempt status (Rosenbaum, 2015).

NCQA, National Committee for Quality Assurance; PCMH, patient-centered medical home.

SUMMARY

The United States is the most expensive healthcare system in the world and trails comparable high-income countries in many quality measures. The low value of the U.S. healthcare system makes adopting the quality management mindset and mastering the basic skills an imperative. Healthcare quality management is the application of systematic practices that guide the formation of reliable processes in healthcare organizations in order to increase the likelihood of delivering evidence-based care and achieving the health outcomes expected by patients, their families, and their caregivers. However, the U.S. healthcare system does not deliver a standard of care reliably, without variation. Healthcare quality management practices target the central problem with our healthcare system—the variability of healthcare delivery. This casebook divides healthcare quality management challenges into four categories: process improvement, patient experience, patient safety, and performance improvement. You will face a variety of quality management issues, from inefficient patient flow to patient harm, and this casebook will prepare you to meet these challenges.

DISCUSSION QUESTIONS

1 Why does the U.S. healthcare system have lower value than other comparable high-income counties?

2. How does U.S. healthcare fail to meet W. Edwards Deming's definition of quality?

3. Why is healthcare quality management an imperative in today's healthcare environment?

4. Why is measuring quality difficult in healthcare?

5. Choose the top three most important examples of low healthcare quality from this chapter. Explain why you chose these examples.

REFERENCES

Abusalem, S., Myers, J. A., & Aljeesh, Y. (2013). Patient satisfaction in home health care. *Journal of Clinical Nursing, 22*(17/18), 2426–2435. doi:10.1111/j.1365-2702.2012.04211.x

AHRQ Patient Safety Network. (2019) *Medication Errors and Adverse Drug Events.* Retrieved from https://psnet.ahrq.gov/primer/medication-errors-and-adverse-drug-events.

Agency for Healthcare Research and Quality. (2017). *What is patient experience?* Retrieved from https://www.ahrq.gov/cahps/about-cahps/patient-experience/index.html

Anhang, P. R., Elliott, M. N., Zaslavsky, A. M., Hays, R. D., Lehrman, W. G., Rybowski, L., . . . Cleary, P. D. (2014). Examining the role of patient experience surveys in measuring health care quality. *Medical Care Research and Review, 71*(5), 522–554. doi:10.1177/1077558714541480

Arbune, A., Wackerbarth, S., Allison, P., & Conigliaro, J. (2017). Improvement through small cycles of change: Lessons from an Academic Medical Center Emergency Department. *Journal for Healthcare Quality, 39*(5), 259–269. doi:10.1111/jhq.12078

Auerbach, A. D., Kripalani, S., Vasilevskis, E. E., Sehgal, N., Lindenauer, P. K., Metlay, J. P., . . . Schnipper, J. L. (2016). Preventability and causes of readmissions in a national cohort of general medicine patients. *Journal of the American Medical Association Internal Medicine, 176*(4), 484–493. doi:10.1001/jamainternmed.2015.7863

Baily, M. A., Bottrell, M. M., Lynn, J., & Jennings, B. (2006). *Special report: The ethics of using QI methods to improve health care quality and safety.* Retrieved from https://www.thehastingscenter.org/publications-resources/special-reports-2/the-ethics-of-using-qi-methods-to-improve-health-care-quality-safety

Balik, B., Conway, J., Zipperer, L., & Watson, J. (2011). *Achieving an exceptional patient and family experience of inpatient hospital care.* Retrieved from http://app.ihi.org/Events/Attachments/Event-2346/Document-2437/IHI_Patient_Family_Experience_of_Hospital_Care_Whi.pdf

Balzer, C., Raackow, D., Hahnenkamp, K., Flessa, S., & Meissner, K. (2017). Timeliness of operating room case planning and time utilization: Influence of first and to-follow cases. *Frontiers in Medicine, 4,* 49. doi:10.3389/fmed.2017.00049

Bergen, G. (2016). Falls and fall injuries among adults aged ≥ 65 years—United States, 2014. *MMWR. Morbidity and mortality weekly report, 65.*

Berwick, D. M. (1996). A primer on leading the improvement of systems. *BMJ, 312*(7031), 619–622. doi:10.1136/bmj.312.7031.619

Berwick, D. M. (2009). What 'patient-centered' should mean: Confessions of an extremist. *Health Affairs, 28*(4), w555–w565. doi:10.1377/hlthaff.28.4.w555

Berwick, D. M., & Hackbarth, A. D. (2012). Eliminating waste in US health care. *Journal of the American Medical Association, 307*(14), 1513–1516. doi:10.1001/jama.2012.362

Blumenthal, D., Davis, K., & Guterman, S. (2015). Medicare at 50-Moving Forward. *New England Journal of Medicine, 372*(7), 671–677. doi:10.1056/NEJMhpr1414856

Blumenthal, D., & Jena, A. B. (2013). Hospital value-based purchasing. *Journal of Hospital Medicine*, *8*(5), 271–277. doi:10.1002/jhm.2045

Boissy, A., Windover, A. K., Bokar, D., Karafa, M., Neuendorf, K., Frankel, R. M., . . . Rothberg, M. B. (2016). Communication skills training for physicians improves patient satisfaction. *Journal of General Internal Medicine*, *31*(7), 755–761. doi:10.1007/s11606-016-3597-2

Bradley, E. H., & Taylor, L. A. (2013). *The American health care paradox: Why spending more is getting us less.* New York, NY: Public Affairs.

Brandenburg, L., Gabow, P., Steele, G., Toussaint, J., & Tyson, B. J. (2015). *Innovation and best practices in health care scheduling.* Retrieved from https://nam.edu/wp-content/uploads/2015/06/SchedulingBestPractices.pdf

Burrill, S., & Kane, A. (2018). *Deloitte 2017 survey of US health system CEOs: Moving forward in an uncertain environment.* Retrieved from https://www2.deloitte.com/us/en/pages/life-sciences-and-health-care/articles/health-system-ceos.html

Califf, R. M., Woodcock, J., & Ostroff, S. (2016). A proactive response to prescription opioid abuse. *New England Journal of Medicine*, *374*(15), 1480–1485. doi:10.1056/NEJMsr1601307

Campbell, E. M., Sittig, D. F., Ash, J. S., Guappone, K. P., & Dykstra, R. H. (2006). Types of unintended consequences related to computerized provider order entry. *Journal of the American Medical Informatics Association*, *13*(5), 547–556. doi:10.1197/jamia.M2042

Carnevale, A. P., Smith, N., Gulish, A., & Beach, B. H. (2012). *Healthcare.* Retrieved from https://files.eric.ed.gov/fulltext/ED533705.pdf

Centers for Disease Control and Prevention: National Center for Health Statistics. (2017). *Leading causes of death and numbers of deaths, by sex, race, and Hispanic origin: United States, 1980 and 2016.* Retrieved from https://www.cdc.gov/nchs/data/hus/2017/019.pdf

Centers for Medicare & Medicaid Services. (2014). Hospital readmissions reduction program (HRRP). Retrieved from https://www.cms.gov/medicare/medicare-fee-for-service-payment/acuteinpatientpps/readmissions-reduction-program.html

Centers for Medicare & Medicaid Services. (2019). *Shared savings program: Program guidance & specifications.* Retrieved from https://www.cms.gov/Medicare/Medicare-Fee-for-Service-Payment/sharedsavingsprogram/program-guidance-and-specifications.html

Clancy, C. M. (2009). Ten years after to err is human. *American Journal of Medical Quality*, *24*(6), 525–528. doi:10.1177/1062860609349728

Cohen, J., Vincent, J. L., Adhikari, N. K. J., Machado, F. R., Angus, D. C., Calandra, T., . . . Pelfrene, E. (2015). Sepsis: A roadmap for future research. *Lancet Infectious Diseases*, *15*(5), 581–614. doi:10.1016/s1473-3099(15)70112-x

de Koning, H., Verver, J. P. S., van den Heuvel, J., Bisgaard, S., & Does, R. J. M. M. (2006). Lean six sigma in healthcare. *Journal for Healthcare Quality*, *28*(2), 4–11. doi:10.1111/j.1945-1474.2006.tb00596.x

de Mast, J., Kemper, B., Does, R., Mandjes, M., & van der Bijl, Y. (2011). Process improvement in healthcare: Overall resource efficiency. *Quality and Reliability Engineering International*, *27*(8), 1095–1106. doi:10.1002/qre.1198

Deming, W. E. (1982). *Out of the crisis.* Cambridge, MA: MIT Press.

Destino, L., Bennett, D., Wood, M., Acuna, C., Goodman, S., Asch, S. M., & Platchek, T. (2019). Improving patient flow: Analysis of an initiative to improve early discharge. *Journal of Hospital Medicine*, *14*(1), 22–27. doi:10.12788/jhm.3133

Donahue, C. (2015). *Learning from healthcare's use of improvement science.* Retrieved from https://www.carnegiefoundation.org/blog/learning-from-healthcares-use-of-improvement-science

Doyle, C., Lennox, L., & Bell, D. (2013). A systematic review of evidence on the links between patient experience and clinical safety and effectiveness. *BMJ Open*, *3*(1), e001570. doi:10.1136/bmjopen-2012-001570

Ellison, A., & Cohen, J. K. (2018). *224 hospital benchmarks—2018.* Retrieved from https://www.beckershospitalreview.com/lists/224-hospital-benchmarks-2018.html

Field, J. M., Heineke, J., Langabeer, J. R., & DelliFraine, J. L. (2014). Building the case for quality improvement in the health care industry: A focus on goals and training. *Quality Management in Health Care*, *23*(3), 138–154. doi:10.1097/qmh.0000000000000036

Friebel, R., & Steventon, A. (2019). Composite measures of healthcare quality: Sensible in theory, problematic in practice. *BMJ Quality & Safety*, *28*(2), 85–88. doi:10.1136/bmjqs-2018-008280

Ganz, D. A., Huang, C., Saliba, D., Shier, V., Berlowitz, D., VanDeusen Lukas, C., . . . Neumann, P. (2013). *Preventing falls in hospitals: A toolkit for improving quality of care.* Retrieved from https://www.ahrq .gov/sites/default/files/publications/files/fallpxtoolkit_0.pdf

Garvey, P. K. (2015). Failure to rescue: the nurse's impact. *MedSurg Nursing, 24*(3), 145.

Giordano, L. A., Elliott, M. N., Goldstein, E., Lehrman, W. G., & Spencer, P. A. (2010). Development, implementation, and public reporting of the HCAHPS survey. *Medical Care Research and Review, 67*(1), 27–37. doi:10.1177/1077558709341065

Glied, S., & Sacarny, A. (2018). Is the US health care system wasteful and inefficient? A review of the evidence. *Journal of Health Politics Policy and Law, 43*(5), 739–765. doi:10.1215/03616878-6951103

Goldsmith, L. J., Suryaprakash, N., Randall, E., Shum, J., MacDonald, V., Sawatzky, R., . . . Bryan, S. (2017). The importance of informational, clinical and personal support in patient experience with total knee replacement: A qualitative investigation. *BMC Musculoskeletal Disorders, 18,* 127. doi:10.1186/ s12891-017-1474-8

Hall, L. W. (2008). *Mistaken identity.* Retrieved from https://psnet.ahrq.gov/web-mm/mistaken-identity

Hauck, K., & Zhao, X. (2011). How dangerous is a day in hospital? A model of adverse events and length of stay for medical inpatients. *Medical care,* 1068–1075.

Hodges, J. (2002). Effective claims denial management enhances revenue: Claims denial management has become a critical component of a hospital's strategic effort to offset the adverse impact of Balanced Budget Act payment reductions. *Healthcare Financial Management, 56*(8), 40–50. Retrieved from https://go.gale.com/ps/anonymous?id=GALE%7CA90317285&sid=googleScholar&v =2.1&it=r&linkaccess=fulltext&issn=07350732&p=AONE&sw=w

Institute of Medicine. (2001). *Crossing the quality chasm: A new health system for the 21st century.* Washington, DC: National Academies Press. Retrieved from http://www.nationalacademies.org/ hmd/Global/News%20Announcements/Crossing-the-Quality-Chasm-The-IOM-Health-Care-Quality-Initiative.aspx

Isaac, T., Zaslavsky, A. M., Cleary, P. D., & Landon, B. E. (2010). The relationship between patients' perception of care and measures of hospital quality and safety. *Health Services Research, 45*(4), 1024–1040. doi:10.1111/j.1475-6773.2010.01122.x

Jha, A. K. (2017). Payment power to the patients. *Journal of the American Medical Association, 318*(1), 18–19. doi:10.1001/jama.2017.7533

Kadar, N. (2019). Rediscovering Ignaz Philipp Semmelweis (1818-1865). *American Journal of Obstetrics and Gynecology, 220*(1), 26–39. doi:10.1016/j.ajog.2018.11.1084

Kohn, L. T., Corrigan, J. M., & Donaldson, M. S. (Eds.). (2000). *To err is human: Building a safer health system.* Washington, DC: National Academies Press. doi:10.17226/9728

Kumar, A., Roberts, D., Wood, K. E., Light, B., Parrillo, J. E., Sharma, S., . . . Cheang, M. (2006). Duration of hypotension before initiation of effective antimicrobial therapy is the critical determinant of survival in human septic shock. *Critical Care Medicine, 34*(6), 1589–1596. doi:10.1097/01.ccm.0000217961.75225.e9

Kunz, C. (2018). *A home care agency owner's guide to net promoter score.* Retrieved from https://www .homecarepulse.com/articles/home-care-agency-owners-guide-net-promoter-score

Lake, T., Kvam, C., & Gold, M. (2005). Literature review: using quality information for health care decisions and quality improvement. *Cambridge, Mass.: Mathematica Policy Research.*

Lee, T. H., & Cosgrove, D. (2014, June). Engaging doctors in the health care revolution. *Harvard Business Review,* pp. 104–111. Retrieved from https://hbr.org/2014/06/engaging-doctors-in-the-health-care -revolution

Longest, B. B., Jr., & Darr, K. (2014). *Managing health services organizations and systems.* Baltimore, MD: Health Professions Press.

Lynn, N. B., Gupta, C., Vaaler, M., Held, J., & Leon, L. (2018). Severe sepsis 3-hour bundle compliance and mortality. *American Journal of Infection Control, 46*(11), 1299–1300. doi:10.1016/j.ajic.2018.04.228

Manary, M. P., Boulding, W., Staelin, R., & Glickman, S. W. (2013). The patient experience and health outcomes. *The New England Journal of Medicine, 368*(3), 201–203. doi:10.1056/NEJMp1211775

McGaughey, I. (2004). Informed consent and knee arthroscopies: An evaluation of patient understanding and satisfaction. *Knee, 11*(3), 237–242. doi:10.1016/s0968-0160(03)00107-8

McGinnis, J. M., Berwick, D. M., Dascle, T. A., Diaz, A., Fineberg, H. V., Frist, W. H., . . . Lavizzo-Mourey, R. (2016). *Systems strategies for health throughout the life course* [Discussion Paper]. Washington, DC: National Academy of Medicine. doi:10.31478/201609g

McGlynn, E. A., Asch, S. M., Adams, J., Keesey, J., Hicks, J., DeCristofaro, A., & Kerr, E. A. (2003). The quality of health care delivered to adults in the United States. *New England Journal of Medicine, 348*(26), 2635–2645. doi:10.1056/NEJMsa022615

Mercer. (2010). *US survey on absence and disability management.* Retrieved from https://www.imercer.com/ecommerce/products/absence-disability-survey

Mulvany, C. (2016). Margins under pressure. *Healthcare Financial Management, 70*(4), 30–33. Retrieved from https://go.gale.com/ps/anonymous?id=GALE%7CA451940253&sid=googleScholar&v=2.1&it=r&linkaccess=abs&issn=07350732&p=AONE&sw=w

Nash, I. S. (2015). Why physicians hate "patient satisfaction" but shouldn't. *Annals of Internal Medicine, 163*(10), 792–793. doi:10.7326/m15-1087

National Committee on Quality Assurance (2014). *Patient-centered medical home (PCMH).* Retrieved from http://www.ncqa.org/programs/recognition/practices/patient-centered-medical-home-pcmh

Needham, B. R. (2012). The truth about patient experience: What we can learn from other industries, and how three Ps can improve health outcomes, strengthen brands, and delight customers. *Journal of Healthcare Management, 57*(4), 255–263. doi:10.1097/00115514-201207000-00006

Organization for Economic Cooperation and Development (2017). *Health at a glance 2017: OECD indicators.* Retrieved from https://www.oecd.org/unitedstates/Health-at-a-Glance-2017-Key-Findings-UNITED-STATES.pdf

Olsen, R., Courtemanche, T., & Hodach, R. (2016). Automated phone assessments and hospital readmissions. *Population Health Management, 19*(2), 120–124. doi:10.1089/pop.2015.0014

Porter, M. E., & Kaplan, R. S. (2017). Managing healthcare costs and value: Interviewed by M. L. Frigo (Vol. 98), *Strategic Finance.* Retrieved from https://sfmagazine.com/post-entry/january-2017-managing-healthcare-costs-and-value

Porter, M. E., & Teisberg, E. O. (2006). *Redefining health care: Creating value-based competition on results.* Boston, MA: Harvard Business School Press.

Reijula, J., Nevala, N., Lahtinen, M., Ruohomaki, V., & Reijula, K. (2014). Lean design improves both health-care facilities and processes: A literature review. *Intelligent Buildings International, 6*(3), 170–185. doi:10.1080/17508975.2014.901904

Reinhart, R. (2018). *In the news: Americans' satisfaction with their healthcare.* Retrieved from https://news.gallup.com/poll/226607/news-americans-satisfaction-healthcare.aspx

Rohleder, T., Bailey, B., Crum, B., Faber, T., Johnson, B., Montgomery, L., & Pringnitz, R. (2013). Improving a patient appointment call center at Mayo Clinic. *International Journal of Health Care Quality Assurance, 26*(8), 714–728. doi:10.1108/ijhcqa-11-2011-0068

Rosenbaum, S. (2015). Additional requirements for charitable hospitals: Final rules on community health needs assessments and financial assistance. *Health Affairs Blog.* Retrieved from https://www.healthaffairs.org/do/10.1377/hblog20150123.044073/full

Sawyer, B., & McDermott, D. (2019). *How does the quality of the U.S. healthcare system compare to other countries?* Retrieved from https://www.healthsystemtracker.org/chart-collection/quality-u-s-healthcare-system-compare-countries/#item-in-hospital-mortality-rate-for-acute-myocardial-infarction-ischemic-stroke-and-hemorrhagic-stroke-2015

Schneider, E. C., Sarnak, D. O., Squires, D., Shah, A., & Doty, M. M. (2017). *Mirror, Mirror 2017: International comparison reflects flaws and opportunities for better U.S. health care.* Retrieved from https://interactives.commonwealthfund.org/2017/july/mirror-mirror

Schwarz, U. V., Hasson, H., & Athlin, A. M. (2016). Efficiency in the emergency department—A complex relationship between throughput rates and staff perceptions. *International Emergency Nursing, 29,* 15–20. doi:10.1016/j.ienj.2016.07.003

Seys, D., Scott, S., Wu, A., Van Gerven, E., Vleugels, A., Euwema, M., . . . Vanhaecht, K. (2013). Supporting involved health care professionals (second victims) following an adverse health event: A literature review. *International Journal of Nursing Studies, 50*(5), 678–687. doi:10.1016/j.ijnurstu.2012.07.006

Shwartz, M., Restuccia, J. D., & Rosen, A. K. (2015). Composite measures of health care provider performance: A description of approaches. *Milbank Quarterly, 93*(4), 788–825. doi:10.1111/1468-0009.12165

Sterling, S., Chi, F., Weisner, C., Grant, R., Pruzansky, A., Bui, S., . . . Pearl, R. (2018). Association of behavioral health factors and social determinants of health with high and persistently high healthcare costs. *Preventive Medicine Reports, 11,* 154–159. doi:10.1016/j.pmedr.2018.06.017

Sunshine, J. E., Meo, N., Kassebaum, N. J., Collison, M. L., Mokdad, A. H., & Naghavi, M. (2019). Association of adverse effects of medical treatment with mortality in the United States: A secondary analysis of the global burden of diseases, injuries, and risk factors study. *JAMA Network Open, 2*(1), e187041. doi:10.1001/jamanetworkopen.2018.7041

Swensen, S., Kabcenell, A., & Shanafelt, T. (2016). Physician-organization collaboration reduces physician burnout and promotes engagement: The Mayo Clinic Experience. *Journal of Healthcare Management, 61*(2), 105–127. doi:10.1097/00115514-201603000-00008

Thompson, D. (2018). *Health care just became the U.S.'s largest employer.* Retrieved from https://www.theatlantic.com/business/archive/2018/01/health-care-america-jobs/550079/

U.S. News and World Report. (2019). *Best global universities for clinical medicine.* Retrieved from https://www.usnews.com/education/best-global-universities/clinical-medicine

van Eck, C. F., Toor, A., Banffy, M. B., & Gambardella, R. A. (2018). Web-based education prior to outpatient orthopaedic surgery enhances early patient satisfaction scores: A prospective randomized controlled study. *Orthopaedic Journal of Sports Medicine, 6*(1). doi:10.1177/2325967117751418

VanLare, J. M., & Conway, P. H. (2012). Value-based purchasing—National programs to move from volume to value. *New England Journal of Medicine, 367*(4), 292–295. doi:10.1056/NEJMp1204939

Vivolo-Kantor, A. M., Seth, P., Gladden, R. M., Mattson, C. L., Baldwin, G. T., Kite-Powell, A., & Coletta, M. A. (2018). Vital signs: Trends in emergency department visits for suspected opioid overdoses—United States, July 2016-September 2017. *Morbidity and Mortality Weekly Report, 67*(9), 279–285. doi:10.15585/mmwr.mm6709e1

Weech-Maldonado, R., Elliott, M., Pradhan, R., Schiller, C., Hall, A., & Hays, R. D. (2012). Can hospital cultural competency reduce disparities in patient experiences with care? *Medical Care, 50*(11), S48–S55. doi:10.1097/MLR.0b013e3182610ad1

Weiner, B. J., Alexander, J. A., Baker, L. C., Shortell, S. M., & Becker, M. (2006). Quality improvement implementation and hospital performance on patient safety indicators. *Medical Care Research and Review, 63*(1), 29–57. doi:10.1177/1077558705283122

World Health Organization. (2009). *WHO guidelines on hand hygiene in health care: First global patient safety challenge clean care is safer care.* (p. 9) Geneva, Switzerland: Author.

The Innovators

EARLY HEALTHCARE QUALITY MANAGEMENT

Early innovators applied the scientific method to healthcare quality management in order to save patient lives. By asking questions, making predictions, measuring, observing, analyzing, and controlling, these visionaries created reliable processes for delivering quality. Like today, however, these heroes encountered strong resistance to their recommended improvements. To overcome barriers to quality improvement, these pioneers had to develop the right mindset, hone their quality management skills, and garner organizational support. Their groundwork shaped the modern healthcare quality management era.

Ignaz Semmelweis

Ignaz Semmelweis envisioned preventing mothers from contracting puerperal fever during childbirth, an often deadly condition. Semmelweis, a 19th-century Hungarian obstetrician, observed that medical students conducting autopsies contaminated their hands with "cadaveric particles" and then passed on the causative agent with their hands to the birth canal of mothers in labor (Jarvis, 1994). Equipped with irrefutable statistical evidence that maternal mortality could be prevented through disinfection, Semmelweis championed the importance of handwashing in medical care (Kadar, 2019). His 1847 discovery reduced maternal mortality dramatically in the clinics in which he worked.

If healthcare quality management were easy, Semmelweis would have been recognized as a hero in his lifetime. Sadly, most leading obstetricians in the 1850s rejected Semmelweis's handwashing idea because they thought his intervention did not fit with the current professional knowledge of the day. Because germ theory had not yet been developed, few in the medical establishment believed that "cadaveric particles" could be passed between a cadaver and mother on different wards (Kadar, 2019). Handwashing was still largely ignored by clinicians when Semmelweis died ignominiously in an asylum in 1865 (Jarvis, 1994). Despite his brilliance, the culture of medicine of the day hindered the adoption of handwashing in obstetrical care (Best & Neuhauser, 2004).

Florence Nightingale

Like Semmelweis, legendary 19th-century British nurse **Florence Nightingale** used statistically incontrovertible proof to change medical care. And yet, Nightingale succeeded where Semmelweis failed. The miserable, unsanitary conditions of the Crimean war zone hospitals were associated with extremely high mortality rates among soldiers (Marjoua & Bozic, 2012). Nightingale eventually improved the hospital living conditions, but her efforts were strongly resisted by army medical authorities whose prevailing culture was bureaucratic, hierarchical, and resistant to change. In part, her success was due to the fact she did not directly challenge the contemporary conception of the cause of disease. In fact, Nightingale herself doubted germ theory on which Semmelweis's intervention depended until late in her life (Steele, 2017).

Most importantly, though, Nightingale prevailed with her healthcare quality innovations because she recognized that effective management skills were necessary to implement her changes (Ulrich, 1992). When her boss, the chief medical officer of the war zone hospital, forbade her nursing staff to perform any medical tasks, she set about to improve nonclinical hospital processes, such as supply chain and food preparation (Meyer & Bishop, 2007). Nightingale focused on small projects, achieved small victories, and continuously built on these successes to affect significant change. In addition to this incremental approach, Nightingale believed in experimentation. She wrote, "Do not be fettered by too many rules at first. Try different things and see what answers best" (Barritt, 1975, p. 14). Her management skills earned Nightingale great renown, and she eventually shared her innovations throughout Europe.

TWENTIETH-CENTURY U.S. HEALTHCARE QUALITY

Most 19th-century medical practice in the United States lagged behind European countries in the level of scientific rigor, quality of trained physicians, and the standardization of care (Starr, 1982). In the 20th century, a new wave of American revolutionaries sought to improve healthcare quality by creating a set of standards brought about by medical education and performance evaluation reforms.

The Flexner Report

In 1910, an education scholar named **Abraham Flexner** conducted a quality inspection of many U.S. medical schools (Flexner, 1910). What he discovered was so alarming that he wrote the now-famous **Flexner Report**. The reaction to his scathing report transformed medical education and medical practice (Duffy, 2011). Stringent professional licensing standards soon followed, and by mid-20th century, physicians became one of the most respected professions in American society (Starr, 1982).

Healthcare Quality Standards

An early 20th-century hospital standardization movement also transformed the U.S. healthcare system (Roberts, Coale, & Redman, 1987). **Frank Gilbreth** published *Scientific Management in the Hospital* (1914) and *Motion Study in Surgery* (1916) that applied scientific management principles to healthcare, including the idea of standardization. Gilbreth's friend, the physician **Ernest Amory Codman**, advocated the "End Result Idea," which meant that physicians should track patients over time to determine the outcomes of their treatments (Baumgart & Neuhauser, 2009). Based on a combination of outcomes management and standardization, the American College of Surgeons published the *Minimum Standard for Hospitals* in 1917 (The Joint Commission, 2017). This medical society eventually evolved into the nonprofit, nongovernmental organization, **The Joint Commission**, that today accredits or certifies 21,000 healthcare organizations and programs in the United States (The Joint Commission, 2016).

A Framework for Measuring Healthcare Quality

These early 20th-century innovations in medical care and public health produced astounding improvements in the health of the population. In the years between the Flexner Report in 1910 and the passage of the landmark Medicare and Medicaid legislation in 1965, the life expectancy at birth increased an astounding 20 years—from under 50 to over 70 years (Centers for Disease Control and Prevention, 2010). These successes were due largely to sanitation, antibiotics, and surgical techniques (Cutler & Miller, 2005; Mackenbach, 1996). Although the expansion of health insurance through Medicare and Medicaid certainly improved the access to care, the modern healthcare quality movement had not yet begun (Chassin & Loeb, 2011).

Not until the 1966 classic paper by **Avedis Donabedian** did the United States begin assessing the quality of healthcare in a systematic way (Ayanian & Markel, 2016). Donabedian created the first conceptual framework for measuring healthcare quality—by assessing *structures*, *processes*, and *outcomes* of care—that remains the foundation today (Table 2.1). Donabedian advised us to ask, "What goes on here?" instead of, "What is wrong; and how can it be made better?" That is, we should not focus solely on health outcomes, such as mortality and morbidity, but we should shift our "concentration on understanding the medical care process itself" (Donabedian, 1966). What Donabedian did, for the first time, was urge the development of **operational definitions** of quality within these categories. Creating operational definitions is the process of defining an ambiguous concept in tangible, representational, measurable, quantifiable terms. To Donabedian, the metrics were essential to healthcare quality management (Ayanian & Markel, 2016).

INDUSTRIAL QUALITY MANAGEMENT

Quality management did not begin in healthcare. Using the scientific management approach, industrial quality management pioneers developed principles and techniques for quality improvement that revolutionized manufacturing, making quality management possible for healthcare organizations decades later (Laffel & Blumenthal, 1989).

Table 2.1 Donabedian's Healthcare Quality Measurement Domains

DOMAIN	DEFINITION	QUESTION ASKED	EXAMPLE METRICS
Structure	Settings, qualifications of providers, and administrative systems through which care takes place	"What is the capacity of the system to support and direct care?"	Number of hospital beds per 1,000; ratio of providers to patients; percentage of staff who completed hand hygiene staff training course
Process	Things providers do to maintain or improve health	"Was medicine properly practiced?"	Percentage of beta-blocker use following myocardial infarction; percentage of people with diabetes who had their HbA1c tested
Outcomes	Recovery, restoration of function, and survival	"What happened to the patient's health as a result of medical care?"	Mortality; morbidity; patient satisfaction; readmissions within 30 days of discharge

Frederick Winslow Taylor

Frederick Winslow Taylor is considered by many as the first efficiency expert, as he performed the first documented **time-and-motion studies** in the early 20th century (Kanigel, 2005). He famously applied scientific methods to management practices to obtain maximum output from a process or operation. Taylor reduced job complexity so that it became easier to train individuals to accomplish these tasks to the desired level of quality. The application of these scientific methods by management is sometimes referred to as **Taylorism**. Against Taylor's intentions, Taylorism principles were abused by unscrupulous managers to exploit and continuously monitor workers, robbing them of their independence (Kanigel, 2005).

Henry Ford

Henry Ford is probably most famously known for his moving assembly line, but it was Ford's obsession with eliminating waste in the manufacturing process that secured his place in quality improvement history (Wilson, 1995). Ford used Taylor's principles of scientific management to shrink the **cycle time** in the manufacturing process. For example, Ford created a steel mill within his factory to avoid wasting time waiting for delivery of sheet metal from outside producers. Ford's genius for efficiency, quality improvement, and waste reduction was such that he is said to have taught and inspired other quality improvement leaders around the world (Wilson, 1995).

Walter A. Shewhart

In 1924, while working at the Western Electric Company, **Walter A. Shewhart** examined the concept of variation in manufacturing to help us recognize when a process is out of control. Shewhart introduced the **control chart** and, ultimately, the concept of **statistical control**.

Based on Shewhart's philosophy for quality improvement, Motorola developed a statistical process control methodology called "Six Sigma" (Best & Neuhauser, 2006). Later, many other organizations started using Six Sigma, most notably CEO **Jack Welch** of General Electric Company (Best & Neuhauser, 2006). You will learn more about Six Sigma in Chapter 3, The Mindset.

Shewhart is also credited with developing the **Plan-Do-Study-Act** (PDSA) cycle of improvement, an integral part of the Lean quality improvement methodology. The PDSA cycle, sometimes called the "Shewhart cycle," brought structure to processes sometimes viewed as chaotic and aimless (Best & Neuhauser, 2006). The PDSA cycle will be presented in more detail in Chapter 3, The Mindset.

W. Edwards Deming

His biographer named **W. Edwards Deming** "The Man Who Discovered Quality" (Gabor, 1990). Deming is often credited with starting the quality revolution of the industrial world and publishing hundreds of original papers, articles, and books that cover a wide range of interrelated subjects—from statistical variance, to systems and systems thinking, to human psychology (The Deming Institute, 2018). Deming led the quality turnaround in postwar Japan, a contribution that created perhaps the world's greatest economic recovery story (Magnier, 1999). Although he was an American, mid-century Japan welcomed Deming's ideas—such as treating workers as associates, not hired hands—at a time when America did not (Magnier, 1999). After returning to the United States years later, Americans finally adopted Deming's ideas, especially after he published his most celebrated book in 1982, *Out of the Crisis*, in which he offered 14 key principles for management (Deming, 1982).

Joseph M. Juran

Joseph M. Juran worked with Walter A. Shewhart and W. Edwards Deming at Western Electric's Hawthorne plant outside Chicago in 1924 (Best & Neuhauser, 2006). Juran is known for his *Quality Control Handbook*, in which he defined the **Juran Trilogy** (Juran, 1951). The Juran trilogy guides managers and leaders to achieve breakthrough improvement through (a) quality planning, (b) quality control, and (c) quality improvement.

Phillip B. Crosby

In the early 1970s, ITT Corporation created one of the first corporate vice president of quality positions in the United States for **Philip B. Crosby** (Crosby, 1990). As a businessman first and foremost, Crosby could effectively communicate quality in the language of executives. Crosby believed that senior managers and executives should claim ultimate responsibility for quality. In his most famous book, *Quality is Free*, Crosby defined four absolutes of quality management: (a) quality is defined as conformance to requirements, not goodness, and requirements are defined by the customer; (b) quality comes from prevention, not detection; (c) quality performance standard is zero defects, not acceptable quality levels; and (d) quality is measured by the price of nonconformance (Crosby, 1990).

Taiichi Ohno

Taiichi Ohno, along with Eiji Toyoda, a descendant of the founding Toyoda family, studied Ford's methods for increasing manufacturing speed and efficiency. Ohno is generally recognized as the father of the Toyota Production System (TPS®; Womack, Jones, & Roos, 1990). For the purposes of this casebook, the TPS is synonymous with Lean manufacturing. In the Toyota community, employees are highly engaged in problem-solving, creating a highly motivated workforce (Womack et al., 1990).

Masaaki Imai

Masaaki Imai, founder of the **Kaizen** Institute, is a quality management consultant in executive development, personnel management, and organizational studies. Imai introduced the concept, mindset, and practice of ongoing improvement activities involving everybody (kaizen) at the place where employees have direct contact with customers (*gemba*; Quality Control International, 1997). Imai emphasized the idea that to change the results, we must change processes (Imai, 1986).

James Womack and Daniel Jones

Most of what is known today about Lean thinking was first introduced by **James Womack** and **Daniel Jones** based on their original research on the automobile industry. They discovered a 3-to-1 productivity ratio for Japanese versus American automakers and documented the reasons for the powerful differences in their book *The Machine that Changed the World* (Womack et al., 1990). This book coined the term "Lean" for quality management when one of the researchers, John Krafcik, wrote, "lean production is 'lean' because it uses less of everything compared with mass production—half the human effort in the factory, half the manufacturing space, half the investment in tools, half the engineering hours to develop a new product in half the time" (Womack et al., 1990, p. 13). After the incredible success of *The Machine that Changed the World*, Womack and Jones went on to define how to create and deploy a Lean operating and management system in their book *Lean Thinking: Banish Waste and Create Wealth in Your Corporation* (Womack & Jones, 1996). You will learn more about Lean thinking in Chapter 3, The Mindset.

QUALITY MANAGEMENT: FROM INDUSTRY TO HEALTHCARE

Early quality management innovators were in the manufacturing industry. Despite struggling with patient flow, long wait times, delays, hospital-acquired conditions, duplicate orders, medication errors, and the ever-increasing complexities of care, many healthcare leaders doubted whether the methods of manufacturing would work in patient care (Laffel & Blumenthal, 1989). However, some trailblazing healthcare organizations recognized the power of industrial quality management methodologies.

Mayo Clinic

The Mayo Clinic is based in Rochester, Minnesota, with additional locations in Florida, Arizona, Wisconsin, and Iowa. Mayo Clinic's reputation as a top-performing health system began in its earliest days (*U.S. News and World Report*, 2018). At the dawn of the 20th century, the young physician **Henry Plummer**, MD, joined Mayo as a practicing physician, but he was also an engineer, scientist, and inventor. With the encouragement of Mayo's leadership, Plummer's most renowned innovation, the numeric registration system and unified medical record, became a core infrastructure of Mayo Clinic (Berry & Seltman, 2008). Before this, physicians would make notes about patients in ledgers owned by each physician and were highly inconsistent in what and how much information to record. Plummer was equally adept at designing physical structures. He designed and implemented a system of lifts, chutes, and conveyors to transport the medical records to the desks of physicians prior to the patient arriving. These innovations set the standard that Mayo Clinic facilities continue to follow: well-coordinated, efficient services in patient care, education, and research, coupled with pleasing design and aesthetics (Berry & Seltman, 2008).

ThedaCare

In 2002, ThedaCare of Appleton, Wisconsin, aimed to create a structured improvement program that enabled sustained change for their health system, as opposed to temporary improvements (Toussaint & Gerard, 2010). Without an existing model for improvement strategies in healthcare, they looked outside and found innovative strategies for permanent change at an unlikely place: the snow blower manufacturer, Ariens Company. At the manufacturing company, ThedaCare doctors, nurses, and managers learned about the TPS quality management approach (Toussaint & Gerard, 2010). After implementing this approach, they reduced inpatient total cost of care by 25% while improving patient satisfaction to nearly 100%, among other outstanding achievements (Toussaint & Berry, 2013).

Seattle Children's Hospital

When Seattle Children's Hospital in Washington vowed to become the best children's hospital in the country, they looked to their Seattle neighbor: the airplane manufacturing corporation, The Boeing Company (Weed, 2010). A Lean-trained sensei at Boeing guided Seattle Children's executives in learning manufacturers' best practices and in adopting process improvements across their hospital—from physical layouts, to medication flow, to patient forms. One example was Seattle Children's inpatient psychiatric unit where they learned to organize outpatient resources at the time of admission, instead of waiting until discharge. These kinds of changes reduced the average length of stay on the unit from 20 to 10 days.

Virginia Mason Medical Center

Another group of visionary leaders is Seattle's Virginia Mason Medical Center whose Lean thinking was such a success that, in 2008, it created the Virginia Mason Institute to train other healthcare systems and their patients to achieve similar improvements (Black, Miller, &

Sensel, 2016). The Virginia Mason Institute shares best practices such as their "Virginia Mason Production System" that examines the nursing-related workplace processes to eliminate waste and increase time for nurses to care for their patients (Nelson-Peterson & Leppa, 2007).

Geisinger Health System

Geisinger Health System is a physician-led, not-for-profit health system operating in Pennsylvania and New Jersey. Beginning in 2005, Geisinger's leadership responded to the low value of U.S. healthcare—poor quality at a high cost—by developing a model for value-based payments (Paulus, 2009). Starting with elective coronary artery bypass graft, Geisinger reengineered the clinical processes, applied evidence-based protocols, and reduced unnecessary variation to deliver better healthcare outcomes for patients at a predictable cost (Berry, Doll, McKinley, Casale, & Bothe, 2009). The program, called "ProvenCare," charged a single, global payment that was all-inclusive of professional services and hospital services. If the amount of spending exceeded the global payment from the preoperative period through 90 days postoperative, then Geisinger absorbed the extra expenses, an approach they dubbed a "warranty." This approach differs significantly from the predominant fee-for-service payment method that encourages volume over value (more care, not better care).

The success of ProvenCare required Geisinger to develop a scalable medical and management infrastructure to translate best practices into reliable care (Paulus, 2009). The challenge was to convince medical and administrative staff to adopt a single standard of evidence-based practices as the ProvenCare model. In addition, the associated delivery system had to be flexible enough to evolve to accommodate new discoveries or technologies (Paulus, 2009). Eventually, Geisinger applied ProvenCare global payment approach to a portfolio of health conditions, including perinatal care (Berry et al., 2011), lung cancer (Katlic et al., 2011), and chronic diseases, such as diabetes (Stock et al., 2014) and psoriasis (Gionfriddo et al., 2018).

Haven, the Health Venture from Amazon, Berkshire Hathaway, and JPMorgan Chase

In the summer of 2018, **Atul Gawande**, MD, surgeon and author, was selected as CEO of Haven, the healthcare company started by Amazon, Berkshire Hathaway, and JPMorgan Chase. Gawande has written healthcare articles for *The New Yorker* and influential books including *Checklist Manifesto*, *Being Mortal*, *Better*, and *Complications*. Gawande supports team-oriented, systems approach solutions for many of the problems in healthcare (Hensley, 2018). In the press release announcing his hire for the partnership, Gawande wrote that the company will seek to "incubate better models of care for all. This work will take time but must be done. The system is broken, and better is possible" (Amazon.com, 2018, para. 3).

SUPPORTING YOUR HEALTHCARE QUALITY MANAGEMENT EFFORTS

Some innovative healthcare organizations adopted quality management methods from industry. However, the U.S. healthcare system still needs significant improvement. Key organizations provide information, tools, and training to support the implementation of quality management.

Institute for Healthcare Improvement

In 1986, a group of visionary leaders formed the National Demonstration Project on Quality Improvement in Healthcare, the precursor of the **Institute for Healthcare Improvement (IHI)**. During his early career as a physician, IHI founder Don Berwick discovered that the United States suffered from grim problems with the quality of healthcare (Laffel & Berwick, 1992). At that time, experts were not convinced that the methods of industrial quality management could help improve healthcare. Early testing at the National Demonstration Project, nevertheless, led to promising results in improving flow, safety, clinical effectiveness, and financial performance (Berwick, Godfrey, & Roessner, 1990). Built on these successes, the IHI Open School for Health Professions was established in 2008 to teach quality improvement and safety knowledge and skills to healthcare quality professionals via online modules (Patel et al., 2012).

In 2007, the IHI published their **Triple Aim** framework (Figure 2.1) that calls for the U.S. healthcare system to continually improve the experience of care and population health while reducing per capita costs—all at the same time (Berwick, Nolan, & Whittington, 2008). The Triple Aim framework acts as an ambitious statement of purpose for healthcare system transformation that encourages organizational learning built on small-scale projects that expand incrementally to achieve eventual system-wide change (Whittington, Nolan, Lewis, & Torres, 2015). In the years since its introduction, healthcare organizations addressing all three components—population health, patient experience, and reducing costs—have found substantial improved performance in measures aligning to the Triple Aim (Whittington et al., 2015).

National Committee for Quality Assurance

Systematic improvement of the U.S. healthcare system requires sound quality measurement (Burstin, Leatherman, & Goldmann, 2016). The **National Committee for Quality Assurance (NCQA)**—also a nonprofit, nongovernmental agency that accredits healthcare organizations— is most famous for its **Health Effectiveness Data Information Set**, known as **"HEDIS."** Since 1993, HEDIS has standardized quality measurement for health plans throughout the United

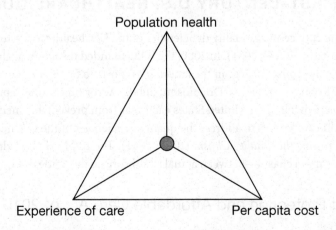

FIGURE 2.1 The Institute of Healthcare Improvement Triple Aim.

Source: Reproduced with permission from the Institute of Healthcare Improvement. (n.d.). *IHI Triple Aim Initiative.* (2019). Retrieved from http://www.ihi.org/Engage/Initiatives/TripleAim/Pages/default.aspx

States (Burstin et al., 2016). Many HEDIS performance measures relate to the process of medical care, each of which are thought to improve health outcomes (Rubin, Pronovost, & Diette, 2001). For example, HEDIS measures the proportion of asthma patients prescribed anti-inflammatories because this medicine prevents asthma attacks. Process-related quality measure sets, such as HEDIS and many others, provide feedback to healthcare providers on their performance and form the basis of all types of quality.

National Quality Forum

The **National Quality Forum (NQF)** was created in 1999 by a coalition of public- and private-sector healthcare leaders to develop systematic information on the quality of healthcare and standards for quality measurement and reporting (Burstin et al., 2016; NQF, 2018). The nonprofit organization runs a consensus-based measurement endorsement practice that aims to develop, test, and disseminate best-practice quality measures. For example, the NQF guides the U.S. Department of Health and Human Services in its selection and implementation of quality measures for Medicare and Medicaid. In its two-decade history, the NQF stakeholders have endorsed over 300 quality measures that are used in more than 20 public reporting and pay-for-performance programs across public and private sectors (NQF, 2018).

Agency for Healthcare Research and Quality

The **Agency for Healthcare Research and Quality (AHRQ)** is a federal agency that provides funding opportunities for healthcare quality researchers and publishes research findings, patient safety information, and tools for quality measurement and improvement (AHRQ, 2018a). Substantial continuing education and curriculum tools are available to teach how to run healthcare quality improvement projects. AHRQ also provides measures and data at no cost to public users.

TWENTY-FIRST–CENTURY U.S. HEALTHCARE QUALITY

By the end of the 20th century, quality deficiencies of the U.S. healthcare system were evident (Institute of Medicine [IOM], 2001). In 2000, the IOM sounded the national alarm on medical errors and respective consequences in the landmark report, *To Err is Human: Building a Safer Health System* (Kohn, Corrigan, & Donaldson, 2000). According to the report, as many as 98,000 people were dying in the United States each year from preventable medical errors. The IOM urged healthcare leaders to address the quality deficiencies of the U.S. healthcare system in the report, *Crossing the Quality Chasm* (IOM, 2001). The IOM acknowledged the need to bridge the huge gap—a chasm—between actual healthcare quality and what could be possible.

The Patient Protection and Affordable Care Act of 2010

Like the Medicare and Medicaid legislation, the passage of the Patient Protection and Affordable Care Act (ACA) of 2010 achieved improved access to healthcare mainly through expanded health insurance coverage (Sommers, Gunja, Finegold, & Musco, 2015). That focal

Table 2.2 Healthcare Quality Improvements Associated With ACA Policies

QUALITY MEASURE	IMPACT OF POLICY
Hospital-acquired condition rates	The ACA required the Hospital-Acquired Condition Reduction Program to penalize hospitals if patients are afflicted with certain conditions while admitted to the hospital (U.S. Department of Health and Human Services, 2015). There were 17% fewer reported hospital-acquired conditions, including pressure ulcers, falls, and infections, in the period following the program implementation (AHRQ, 2018b).
Patient–provider communication	Patient–provider communication is a part of CAHPS, the survey used by Medicare to assess patient experience. CAHPS results are used in Medicare's value-based payment formula (Giordano, Elliott, Goldstein, Lehrman, & Spencer, 2010). Following the ACA, the percentage of adults who reported poor communication with health providers decreased (AHRQ, 2015) and the percentage reporting a highly positive experience increased (Levine, Linder, & Landon, 2016).
Hospital readmissions within 30 days of discharge	Medicare's Hospital Readmission Reduction Program penalizes hospitals for high rates of readmissions (Kocher & Adashi, 2011). After the ACA, readmission rates declined (Zuckerman, Sheingold, Orav, Ruhter, & Epstein, 2016), most prominently in the period immediately following the ACA policy announcement (Ibrahim, Nathan, Thumma, & Dimick, 2017).

ACA, Affordable Care Act; CAHPS, Consumer Assessment of Healthcare Providers and Systems.

achievement notwithstanding, the law also contained provisions intended to improve the performance of the U.S. healthcare system. First, the ACA required that the U.S. government develop the National Strategy for Quality Improvement in Healthcare to reinforce the move toward value-based purchasing systems that reward healthcare providers for improving quality and reducing costs (Rosenbaum, 2011). Medicare led this transition to value-based purchasing, significantly impacting payments to hospitals (Kahn et al., 2015).

The evidence from the ACA's value-based purchasing policies suggests that healthcare quality improvement is possible if the incentives align organizational resources. These value-based policies have shown modest improvements in healthcare quality (Table 2.2).

However, as you have learned, our healthcare system continues to fall behind comparable countries in overall performance. So far, too few in healthcare have followed the lead of the quality management innovators to develop the right mindset, skills, and organizational support for quality management. As policies like these shift the U.S. healthcare system toward value-based purchasing initiatives, healthcare organizations may be compelled to invest in quality management practices.

SUMMARY

Early innovators from manufacturing developed the quality management mindset and skill set that, if emulated, could improve the U.S. healthcare system. High-performing healthcare organizations have adopted these approaches to develop healthcare quality management expertise. Nonprofit organizations with extensive quality management expertise can support implementation of best practices in process improvement, patient safety, patient experience, and performance improvement. Healthcare policy makers, aware of the gap between the U.S. healthcare system's performance and its potential, have developed incentives to compel healthcare organizations to improve the value of health services delivery.

DISCUSSION QUESTIONS

1. Why do you think Ignaz Semmelweis failed where Florence Nightingale succeeded in healthcare quality management?

2. Describe the management innovations employed by quality pioneers, such as Deming and Shewhart, to create reliable processes for delivering quality.

3. What innovation did Avedis Donabedian contribute to the field of healthcare quality? How does this innovation impact the practice of healthcare quality management?

4. What does the term "Lean" mean in the context of Womack and Jones's original research on the Japanese automobile industry? How can Lean be applied to healthcare?

5. Describe the resources available to healthcare quality management practitioners and how these resources could be utilized to improve your healthcare organization.

REFERENCES

Agency for Healthcare Research and Quality. (2015). *2014 National Healthcare Quality & Disparities Report chartbooks.* Retrieved from https://archive.ahrq.gov/research/findings/nhqrdr/2014chartbooks/index.html

Agency for Healthcare Research and Quality. (2018a). *Agency for Healthcare Research and Quality: A profile.* Retrieved from https://www.ahrq.gov/cpi/about/profile/index.html

Agency for Healthcare Research and Quality. (2018b). *Saving lives and saving money: Hospital-acquired conditions update.* Retrieved from https://www.ahrq.gov/professionals/quality-patient-safety/pfp/2014-final.html

Amazon.com. (2018). *Amazon, Berkshire Hathaway and JPMorgan Chase appoint Dr. Atul Gawande as Chief Executive Officer of their newly-formed company to address U.S. employee healthcare* [Press release]. Retrieved from https://www.businesswire.com/news/home/20180620005747/en/Amazon-Berkshire-Hathaway-JPMorgan-Chase-appoint-Dr

Ayanian, J. Z., & Markel, H. (2016). Donabedian's lasting framework for health care quality. *New England Journal of Medicine, 375*(3), 205–207. doi:10.1056/NEJMp1605101

Barritt, E. (1975). *Florence Nightingale and the nursing legacy.* London, UK: Croom Helm.

Baumgart, A., & Neuhauser, D. (2009). Frank and Lillian Gilbreth: Scientific management in the operating room. *Quality & Safety in Health Care, 18*(5), 413–415. doi:10.1136/qshc.2009.032409

Berry, L. L., & Seltman, K. D. (2008). *Management lessons from Mayo Clinic: Inside one of the world's most admired service organizations.* New York, NY: McGraw-Hill.

Berry, S. A., Doll, M. C., McKinley, K. E., Casale, A. S., & Bothe, A. (2009). ProvenCare: Quality improvement model for designing highly reliable care in cardiac surgery. *Quality & Safety in Health Care, 18*(5), 360–368. doi:10.1136/qshc.2007.025056

Berry, S. A., Laam, L. A., Wary, A. A., Mateer, H. O., Cassagnol, H. P., McKinley, K. E., & Nolan, R. A. (2011). ProvenCare perinatal: A model for delivering evidence/guideline-based care for perinatal populations. *Joint Commission Journal on Quality and Patient Safety, 37*(5), 229–239. doi:10.1016/s1553-7250(11)37030-4

Berwick, D. M., Godfrey, A. B., & Roessner, J. (1990). *Curing health care.* San Francisco, CA: Jossey-Bass.

Berwick, D. M., Nolan, T. W., & Whittington, J. (2008). The Triple Aim: Care, health, and cost. *Health Affairs, 27*(3), 759–769. doi:10.1377/hlthaff.27.3.759

Best, M., & Neuhauser, D. (2004). Ignaz Semmelweis and the birth of infection control. *Quality & Safety in Health Care, 13*(3), 233–234. doi:10.1136/qshc.2004.010918

Best, M., & Neuhauser, D. (2006). Walter A Shewhart, 1924, and the Hawthorne factory. *Quality & Safety in Health Care, 15*(2), 142–143. doi:10.1136/qshc.2006.018093

Black, J. R., Miller, D., & Sensel, J. (2016). *The Toyota way to healthcare excellence: Increase efficiency and improve quality with lean* (2nd ed.). Chicago, IL: Health Administration Press.

Burstin, H., Leatherman, S., & Goldmann, D. (2016). The evolution of healthcare quality measurement in the United States. *Journal of Internal Medicine, 279*(2), 154–159. doi:10.1111/joim.12471

Centers for Disease Control and Prevention. (2010). *Life expectancy at birth, at 65 years of age, and at 75 years of age, by race and sex: United States, selected years 1900–2007.* Atlanta, GA: Author. Retrieved from https://www.cdc.gov/nchs/data/hus/2010/022.pdf

Chassin, M. R., & Loeb, J. M. (2011). The ongoing quality improvement journey: Next stop, high reliability. *Health affairs (Project Hope), 30*(4), 559–568. doi:10.1377/hlthaff.2011.0076

Crosby, P. B. (1990). *Quality is free.* New York, NY: Penguin Putnam.

Cutler, D., & Miller, G. (2005). The role of public health improvements in health advances: The twentieth-century United States. *Demography, 42*(1), 1–22. doi:10.1353/dem.2005.0002

The Deming Institute. (2018). *Deming the man.* Retrieved from https://deming.org/deming/deming-the-man

Deming, W. E. (1982). *Out of the crisis.* Cambridge, MA: MIT Press.

Donabedian, A. (1966). Evaluating the quality of medical care. *The Milbank Quarterly, 44*(3), 166–203.

Duffy, T. P. (2011). The Flexner Report—100 years later. *The Yale Journal of Biology and Medicine, 84*(3), 269–276. Retrieved from https://www.ncbi.nlm.nih.gov/pmc/articles/PMC3178858

Flexner, A. (1910). *Medical education in the United States and Canada: a report to the Carnegie Foundation for the Advancement of Teaching* (No. 4). Carnegie Foundation for the Advancement of Teaching.

Gabor, A. (1990). *The man who discovered quality: How W. Edwards Deming brought the quality revolution to America: The stories of Ford, Xerox, and GM.* New York, NY: Times Books/Random House.

Gilbreth, F. B. (1914). Scientific management in the hospital. *Modern Hospital, 3*, 321–324.

Gilbreth, F. B. (1916). Motion study in surgery. *Canadian Journal of Medicine and Surgery, 40*, 22–31.

Gionfriddo, M. R., Pulk, R. A., Sahni, D. R., Vijayanagar, S. G., Chronowski, J. J., Jones, L. K., . . . Pride, H. (2018). ProvenCare-Psoriasis: A disease management model to optimize care. *Dermatology Online Journal, 24*(3). Retrieved from https://escholarship.org/uc/item/5xt2s05b

Giordano, L. A., Elliott, M. N., Goldstein, E., Lehrman, W. G., & Spencer, P. A. (2010). Development, implementation, and public reporting of the HCAHPS survey. *Medical Care Research and Review, 67*(1), 27–37. doi:10.1177/1077558709341065

Hensley, S. (2018). Atul Gawande named CEO of Health Venture by Amazon, Berkshire Hathaway and JPMorgan. *Shots: Health News from National Public Radio.* Retrieved from https://www.npr.org/sections/health-shots/2018/06/20/621808003/atul-gawande-named-ceo-of-health-venture-by-amazon-berkshire-hathaway-and-jpmorg

Ibrahim, A. M., Nathan, H., Thumma, J. R., & Dimick, J. B. (2017). Impact of the Hospital Readmission Reduction Program on surgical readmissions among Medicare beneficiaries. *Annals of Surgery, 266*(4), 617–624. doi:10.1097/sla.0000000000002368

Imai, M. (1986). *Kaizen: The key to Japan's competitive success.* New York, NY: McGraw-Hill.

Institute of Healthcare Improvement. (n.d.). *IHI Triple Aim Initiative.* (2019). Retrieved from http://www.ihi.org/Engage/Initiatives/TripleAim/Pages/default.aspx

Institute of Medicine. (2001). *Crossing the quality chasm: A new health system for the 21st century.* Washington, DC: National Academies of Sciences, Engineering, and Medicine. Retrieved from http://www.nationalacademies.org/hmd/Reports/2001/Crossing-the-Quality-Chasm-A-New-Health-System-for-the-21st-Century.aspx

Jarvis, W. (1994). Handwashing—the Semmelweis lesson forgotten? *The Lancet, 344*(8933), 1311–1312.

The Joint Commission. (2016). *Facts about The Joint Commission.* Retrieved from https://www.jointcommission.org/facts_about_the_joint_commission/

The Joint Commission. (2017). *The Joint Commission: Over a century of quality and safety*. Retrieved from https://www.jointcommission.org/assets/1/6/TJC_history_timeline_through_2017.pdf

Juran, J. M. (1951). *Quality control handbook*. New York, NY: McGraw-Hill.

Kadar, N. (2019). Rediscovering Ignaz Philipp Semmelweis (1818–1865). *American Journal of Obstetrics and Gynecology, 220*(1), 26–39. doi:10.1016/j.ajog.2018.11.1084

Kahn, C. N., Ault, T., Potetz, L., Walke, T., Chambers, J. H., & Burch, S. (2015). Assessing Medicare's hospital pay-for-performance programs and whether they are achieving their goals. *Health Affairs, 34*(8), 1281–1288. doi:10.1377/hlthaff.2015.0158

Kanigel, R. (2005). *The one best way: Frederick Winslow Taylor and the enigma of efficiency*. Boston, MA: MIT Press.

Katlic, M. R., Facktor, M. A., Berry, S. A., McKinley, K. E., Bothe, A., & Steele, G. D. (2011). ProvenCare lung cancer: A multi-institutional improvement collaborative. *CA: A Cancer Journal for Clinicians, 61*(6), 382–396. doi:10.3322/caac.20119

Kocher, R. P., & Adashi, E. Y. (2011). Hospital readmissions and the Affordable Care Act: Paying for coordinated quality care. *Journal of the American Medical Association, 306*(16), 1794–1795. doi:10.1001/jama.2011.1561

Kohn, L. T., Corrigan, J. M., & Donaldson, M. S. (Eds.). (2000). *To err is human: Building a safer health system*. Washington DC: Author. doi:10.17226/9728

Laffel, G., & Berwick, D. M. (1992). Quality in health care. *Journal of the American Medical Association, 268*(3), 407–409. doi:10.1001/jama.268.3.407

Laffel, G., & Blumenthal, D. (1989). The case for using industrial quality management science in health care organizations. *Journal of the American Medical Association, 262*(20), 2869–2873. doi:10.1001/jama.1989.03430200113036

Levine, D. M., Linder, J. A., & Landon, B. E. (2016). The quality of outpatient care delivered to adults in the United States, 2002 to 2013. *Journal of the American Medical Association Internal Medicine, 176*(12), 1778–1790. doi:10.1001/jamainternmed.2016.6217

Mackenbach, J. P. (1996). The contribution of medical care to mortality decline: McKeown revisited. *Journal of Clinical Epidemiology, 49*(11), 1207–1213. doi:10.1016/s0895-4356(96)00200-4

Magnier, M. (1999). Rebuilding Japan with the help of 2 Americans. *The LA Times*. Retrieved from http://articles.latimes.com/1999/oct/25/news/ss-26184

Marjoua, Y., & Bozic, K. J. (2012). Brief history of quality movement in US healthcare. *Current Reviews in Musculoskeletal Medicine, 5*(4), 265–273. doi:10.1007/s12178-012-9137-8

Meyer, B. C., & Bishop, D. S. (2007). Florence Nightingale: Nineteenth century apostle of quality. *Journal of Management History, 13*(3), 240–254. doi:10.1108/17511340710754699

National Quality Forum. (2018). NQF's work in quality measurement. Retrieved from http://www.qualityforum.org/about_nqf/work_in_quality_measurement

Nelson-Peterson, D. L., & Leppa, C. J. (2007). Creating an environment for caring using lean principles of the Virginia Mason Production System. *Journal of Nursing Administration, 37*(6), 287–294. doi:10.1097/01.NNA.0000277717.34134.a9

Patel, E., Nutt, S. L., Qureshi, I., Lister, S., Panesar, S. S., & Carson-Stevens, A. (2012). Leading change in health-care quality with the Institute for Healthcare Improvement Open School. *British Journal of Hospital Medicine, 73*(7), 397–400. doi:10.12968/hmed.2012.73.7.397

Paulus, R. A. (2009). ProvenCare: Geisinger's model for care transformation through innovative clinical initiatives and value creation. *American Health and Drug Benefits, 2*(3), 122–127. Retrieved from https://www.ncbi.nlm.nih.gov/pmc/articles/PMC4106555

Quality Control International. (1997). *An interview with Masaaki Imai*. Retrieved from https://www.qualitydigest.com/june97/html/imai.html

Roberts, J. S., Coale, J. G., & Redman, R. R. (1987). A history of the Joint Commission on accreditation of hospitals. *Journal of the American Medical Association, 258*(7), 936–940. doi:10.1001/jama.258.7.936

Rosenbaum, S. (2011). The Patient Protection and Affordable Care Act: Implications for public health policy and practice. *Public Health Reports, 126*(1), 130–135. doi:10.1177/003335491112600118

Rubin, H. R., Pronovost, P., & Diette, G. B. (2001). The advantages and disadvantages of process-based measures of health care quality. *International Journal for Quality in Health Care, 13*(6), 469–474. doi:10.1093/intqhc/13.6.469

Sommers, B. D., Gunja, M. Z., Finegold, K., & Musco, T. (2015). Changes in self-reported insurance coverage, access to care, and health under the Affordable Care Act. *Journal of the American Medical Association, 314*(4), 366–374. doi:10.1001/jama.2015.8421

Starr, P. (1982). *The social transformation of American medicine: The rise of a sovereign profession and the making of a vast industry.* New York, NY: Basic Books.

Steele, N. M. (2017). A time to celebrate: Florence Nightingale. *Urologic Nursing, 37*(2), 57–60. Retrieved from https://go.gale.com/ps/anonymous?id=GALE%7CA494889956&sid=googleScholar&v=2.1&it=r&linkaccess=abs&issn=1053816X&p=AONE&sw=w

Stock, S., Pitcavage, J. M., Simic, D., Altin, S., Graf, C., Feng, W., & Graf, T. R. (2014). Chronic care model strategies in the United States and Germany deliver patient-centered, high-quality diabetes care. *Health affairs (Project Hope), 33*(9), 1540–1548. doi:10.1377/hlthaff.2014.0428

Toussaint, J., & Gerard, R. (2010). *On the mend: Revolutionizing healthcare to save lives and transform the industry.* Cambridge, MA: Lean Enterprise Institute.

Toussaint, J. S., & Berry, L. L. (2013). The promise of Lean in health care. *Mayo Clinic Proceedings, 88*(1), 74–82. doi:10.1016/j.mayocp.2012.07.025

Ulrich, B. T. (1992). *Leadership and management according to Florence Nightingale.* New York, NY: Appleton & Lange.

U.S. Department of Health and Human Services. (2015). *2013 Annual hospital-acquired condition rate and estimates of cost savings and deaths averted from 2010 to 2013. (AHRQ Publication No. 16-0006-EF).* Rockville, MD: Agency for Healthcare Research and Quality. Retrieved from http://www.ahrq.gov/professionals/quality-patient-safety/pfp/interimhacrate2013.pdf

U.S. News and World Report. (2018). 2018-19 Best hospitals: Mayo Clinic. *U.S. News Best Hospitals Rankings and Ratings.* Retrieved from https://health.usnews.com/best-hospitals/area/mn/mayo-clinic-6610451

Weed, J. (2010, July 9, 2010). Factory efficiency comes to the hospital. *The New York Times.*

Whittington, J. W., Nolan, K., Lewis, N., & Torres, T. (2015). Pursuing the Triple Aim: The first 7 years. *The Milbank Quarterly, 93*(2), 263–300. doi:10.1111/1468-0009.12122

Wilson, J. M. (1995). Henry Ford's just-in-time system. *International Journal of Operations & Production Management, 15*(12), 59–75. doi:10.1108/01443579510104501

Womack, J. P., & Jones, D. T. (1996). *Lean thinking: Banish waste and create wealth in your corporation.* New York, NY: Simon & Schuster.

Womack, J. P., Jones, D. T., & Roos, D. (1990). *The machine that changed the world.* New York, NY: Free Press.

Zuckerman, R. B., Sheingold, S. H., Orav, E. J., Ruhter, J., & Epstein, A. M. (2016). Readmissions, Observation, and the Hospital Readmissions Reduction Program. *The New England Journal of Medicine, 374*(16), 1543–1551. doi:10.1056/NEJMsa1513024

CHAPTER 3

The Mindset

OBJECTIVES

1. Explain the quality management mindset.
2. Evaluate the Lean approach to quality management, including the Plan-Do-Study-Act (PDSA) continuous improvement cycle.
3. Assess the Six Sigma approach to quality management, including the Define-Measure-Analyze-Improve-Control (DMAIC) continuous improvement cycle.
4. Distinguish Lean and Six Sigma quality improvement methodologies.
5. Describe the role of the evidence-based management process in healthcare quality management.

QUALITY MANAGEMENT MINDSET

To overcome the quality challenges of the U.S. healthcare system, you must adopt the mindset championed by the innovators of quality management. "Mindset" refers to your thinking style, motivation, or attitude that leads you to take certain courses of action (Armor & Taylor, 2003). With practice, you will adopt this new mindset (Gollwitzer, Heckhausen, & Steller, 1990).

The quality management mindset requires a driving need to fix problems for the benefit of your customer, which, in healthcare, are the patients, their families, and their caregivers. With this mindset, you will be compelled to observe people where they are doing their work. To satisfy your need to identify root causes of problems, you will constantly ask clarifying questions. Always seeking to simplify and streamline, you will analyze the best available evidence, set concrete goals, and display your targets visually. With your quality management mindset, you will create meaningful change to meet your customer's expectations through small, quick experiments that are continuously applied and evaluated. When your small tests work, you will expand the interventions. Then, you will measure your progress over time and celebrate your success as a team. Never satisfied, your quality management mindset will lead you to find the next problem to fix, sending you on a continuous cycle of improvement.

The quality management mindset is based on hundreds of years of scientific thinking. The scientific method is essentially a practice by which hypotheses are proposed and tested through experimentation, data are collected and analyzed, and, finally, the hypotheses are either proven, discarded, or modified. For many, the scientific method means research. However, the quality management innovators held a more pragmatic view of the scientific method, one concerned with changing processes based on the results of their experimentation.

The innovators of quality management revealed their genius by applying the scientific method to manufacturing processes. Noted quality management expert, Joseph M. Juran, explained that learning is a function of adherence to the scientific method, a way to speed the learning process. The scientific method continues repeatedly until we acquire and confirm our knowledge (Juran & Godfrey, 1999). Later, pioneers in healthcare quality adopted this scientific mindset to improve healthcare services.

To help you and your team follow the rigorous scientific method to improve quality, this chapter describes two quality management approaches commonly adopted by healthcare organizations worldwide (Antony, Palsuk, Gupta, Mishra, & Barach, 2018). In addition, this chapter explains a concept known as **evidence-based management**, which is defined as a science-informed, step-by-step process that relies on evidence to empower better decisions and enable improved outcomes (Kovner & Rundall, 2006).

LEAN

Lean is a mindset, a way of thinking, a set of ideas, or a philosophical approach to quality improvement. The term "Lean" was coined in *The Machine that Changed the World*, the book that described the innovative Toyota Production System® of manufacturing developed in Japan in the 1950s and 1960s (Womack, Jones, & Roos, 1990). Lean is a continuous effort driven by frontline employees to increase the **value** for the customer by reducing **waste** and improving **flow** (Rotter et al., 2018). Value represents the needs of the customer, which, in healthcare, are the patient, family, or caregivers. "Flow" is defined as how items or people in a process move from the first step to the last. Waste, called **muda** in Japanese, is an inefficiency that consumes resources, such as people, time, equipment, space, and money, but does not create value for your customer (Womack & Jones, 1996).

Lean has proven an effective healthcare quality management approach since the early 2000s when organizations recognized the value of eliminating inefficiencies in healthcare delivery, such as wait time, repeated diagnostic tests, and medical errors (Toussaint & Berry, 2013; Young & McClean, 2009). Lean aims to transform the culture of healthcare to eliminate waste, ensure that all processes add value to the patient and caregivers, and improve the flow of patients, providers, and supplies (Rotter et al., 2018). Following the Lean philosophy, healthcare problems are identified and addressed by frontline staff members, such as nurses, pharmacists, and doctors.

Eight Types of Waste

The Lean philosophy will teach you to recognize waste in healthcare. This knowledge will give you "waste goggles" (Fillingham, 2007). Akin to wearing 3-D glasses to get all the benefits of an action-packed 3-D movie, once you wear your waste goggles, waste will spring forward in what you see in your daily work. The Toyota Production System identified seven types of waste (Womack & Jones, 1996):

1. *Transportation* waste occurs when there is an unnecessary movement of parts or people through the different steps in a process. For example, a form being routed to three different departments across four different floors and two buildings to get signatures represents a transportation waste. Another example is a patient checking-in on the first floor, then sent to the third floor for his or her appointment, then across the building and to the second floor for radiology, and finally back to the first floor pharmacy.

2. *Inventory* waste is easily observed when there are stockpiles of raw materials, work-in-progress, or finished goods lying around without getting any value added to them. For example, notice medical supplies tossed on an unused patient bed.

3. *Motion* waste is excessive movement of people or excessive actions during a process. If you observe a person reaching for something every 30 seconds, that might be an indication of wasteful motion. It can be person movement in the sterile processing area or clicks of a mouse or key punches on a keyboard.

4. *Waiting* waste occurs when people, equipment, or supplies are idle. They may be waiting for another step to be completed. Waiting is the most prevalent waste in healthcare. The waiting is so bad in healthcare that we have rooms dedicated to this waste: WAITING ROOMS! Consider the patient's point of view. The patient waits to make an appointment; then, the day of the appointment, waits in the waiting room; then has to wait in the examination room; then waits to get the results back; and even has to wait to pay the bill. Waits exist at every step of every process in healthcare, and they should be eliminated or minimized.

5. *Overprocessing* is doing more than is required by the customer or processing beyond the acceptable standard. If a process calls for only one copy of a form, but the clerk made five copies, that is overprocessing (regardless of his or her reasons for doing so).

6. *Overproduction* is to produce more than needed or to do it sooner than needed. Suppose there was a nurse who was putting packets of lines, bags, and other supplies together for the surgeries for the next day, while there was a backlog of surgeries that day that were not being completed on time. This backlog should have triggered everybody to do everything they could to unclog the unit so that surgeries could be performed. This is analogous to the kid at the sandwich shop continuing to chop peppers and onions for sandwiches for that evening when the line of people waiting for sandwiches during lunch goes around the block. We would never accept that!

7. *Defects* are products or services that do not meet the requirements. In an administrative process, forms that need to be re-routed or orders sent to the wrong address are examples of defects. In healthcare, defects can range from sending inaccurate billing statements to mislabeling lab samples to harming patients (wrong medication, wrong dose, wrong surgery, etc.).

In addition to these seven types, healthcare quality management should consider another important category of waste—underutilizing people's talents or intellect. This is called "not operating at the top of their license" (Russell-Babin & Wurmser, 2016). For example, entering a prescription order into the computer and sending to the pharmacy might take a physician 1 minute. However, communicating the prescription order to a credentialed medical assistant would take the assistant 3 seconds. Multiplied over thousands of prescriptions per year, this process represents hours and hours of waste. Alternatively, the physician could allocate the 57 seconds to medical tasks that only a physician can perform, and the medical assistant can enter prescription orders into the computer. Another way in which we may underutilize people's talents is by not involving them in the improvement process. When staff struggle with inefficient processes, they know what is wrong. Failure to incorporate staff ideas to solve the issues and streamline those processes is wasting people's talents. We should encourage staff to share their input on how to improve the processes.

Five Steps to Implement Lean

In *Lean Thinking*, Womack and Jones (1996) identify five steps to implementation, which have come to be named the "Five Principles of Lean."

1. *Specify value.* You and your team are not the standard-bearer of value. To define value, ask the patients, their families, or their caregivers.

2. *Identify the value stream.* The **value stream** is the set of all the specific actions required to bring a specific product or service to the customer. This step, also known as **value stream analysis**, reveals the large amounts of *muda* in the process. This analysis will allow you to classify each step or action in your value stream as **value-added**, **non–value-added**, but necessary, or pure waste.

3. *Create flow* for the remaining value-added steps. Perform the value-added activities exactly when they are required. Do not produce products or services in **batches**. Through many life experiences, you have come to believe that processing things in batches is a more efficient way of utilizing your resources, when in fact the opposite is true. In essence, flow means that each product or service should be processed individually. Instead of processing a lot of patient bills at a time, you need to process one bill at a time, at the appropriate time, to produce one accurate bill for one patient.

4. *Implement pull.* Provide what the patient wants, when he or she wants it. This is called **pull**. Departments traditionally work on their part of the process and **push** the work down to the next step in the process without any regard for whether or not that next step is ready for the work. In a pull system, all steps are joined and move together, with each following step pulling work from the previous step. It behaves like this all the way down to the end customer, meaning that the whole value stream moves at the pace determined by the customer. Instead of having a patient stop by registration, push him or her to the physician's office, then to the procedure room, then to the recovery room, and finally back to billing and discharge, how about having the patient stay in one room and bring all these people and services

to them when they need them? This has been done successfully in several health-care settings. You just need to think about what the customer defines as value.

5. *Pursue perfection.* The final principle consists of the realization that perfection is created through a continuous cycle. **Perfection** means you should never be satisfied with your current state. There will always be opportunities to improve. Celebrate successes, yes, but always strive for more improvement.

PDSA: Plan-Do-Study-Act

Rather than creating single interventions, Lean enables you to continuously apply the Plan-Do-Study-Act (PDSA) cycle (Taylor et al., 2014). This four-stage iterative process consists simply of developing a plan to test the proposed change (Plan), carrying out the test (Do), observing and learning from the consequences (Study), and determining what modifications should be made to the test or deploying the new process as the standard (Act). See Figure 3.1 for the PDSA cycle of continuous improvement.

The PDSA cycle is Shewhart and Deming's application of the scientific method to industrial quality management. The PDSA cycle provides you with a structured approach to quality management by engaging in objective measurement and goal setting, rapidly testing small-scale projects, and learning from them until the full potential of improvement is achieved. Once you find that improvement occurs, you go about making the improved process as the *standard work* (Staats & Upton, 2011). Then, you set new improvement goals using the PDSA as a continuous quality improvement tool (Toussaint & Berry, 2013).

The best way to learn is through a quick experimentation (Taylor et al., 2014), known, in Lean, as a **rapid improvement cycle** (Toussaint & Berry, 2013). Normally, a PDSA cycle should take in the order of days (1 or 2 days), perhaps a week or 2, depending on the change. If it is longer than that, it is not rapid. Teams sometimes ask which of these phases should take the longest or require the most effort. The Plan stage deserves extra attention, since too

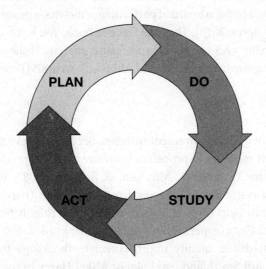

FIGURE 3.1 Plan-Do-Study-Act (PDSA) cycle of continuous improvement.

many times failure to achieve results occurs because of a lack of communication, because a critical stakeholder was not notified, or because the measures of success were not identified.

1. *Plan*—Describe the proposed change and what you want to learn from it. You must also have an idea of expected benefit. In this phase, you also define the measures that will be used to determine the impact and/or success of the change. Often times, organizations embark on a quality improvement project without a clear understanding of how they are going to evaluate change. You must also define the "who," "when," "where," and "how" of the intervention you are planning.

2. *Do*—Carry out the intervention, collect data on your measures, and note your observations. The "Do" phase is where other tools and approaches, such as the A3 problem-solving template, standardized work, and value stream mapping, can bring big benefits to healthcare organizations. Some of the tools and approaches, such as 5S, are continuous cycles in and of themselves.

3. *Study*—What do the data say? Did you impact the measures as expected? Was the impact on the level you predicted? If yes, great! If no, ask why. What did you learn or conclude?

4. *Act*—Do you need to tweak something for the next cycle? If it was successful as you expected, you should expand to a larger scale test or perhaps fully implement the change as the new standard.

Visual Management

Lean methodology creates a fully visual workplace. Understanding a problem or a process is easier when it can be visualized. **Visual management** consists of the various visual tools to monitor operations and support teams in their quality improvement efforts (Bateman & Lethbridge, 2014). Visual management transforms metrics, charts, and labels to convey information graphically and makes it easy to evaluate the current state of performance and compare it to your goals (Shah & Hoeffner, 2002). You will commonly encounter a healthcare team meeting in front of a bulletin board of performance metrics, a practice known as "working the wall" (Toussaint & Berry, 2013). Through this casebook, you learn and practice the visual tools for problem-solving (A3 template), root cause analysis (fishbone diagram), process mapping (spaghetti diagram), management (dashboard), analysis (Pareto chart), and more.

SIX SIGMA

Six Sigma is another quality improvement mindset. Six Sigma seeks to reduce defects (i.e., errors or mistakes) and variation in processes to ensure a reliable product or service reaches the customer every time (Proudlove, Moxham, & Boaden, 2008). You can be trained in a system of Six Sigma certifications, ranging from Yellow Belt (part of your regular work responsibilities) to Green Belts (project leader) to Black Belt (highly technical statistical tool expert) to Master Black Belts (expert trainer of Six Sigma; Pyzdek, 2003).

Six Sigma is a data-driven quality improvement methodology that was developed at Motorola by engineer **Bill Smith** and psychologist **Mikel Harry** in the 1980s (Antony, Snee, & Hoerl, 2017). The emphasis of the Six Sigma methodology has evolved over the decades

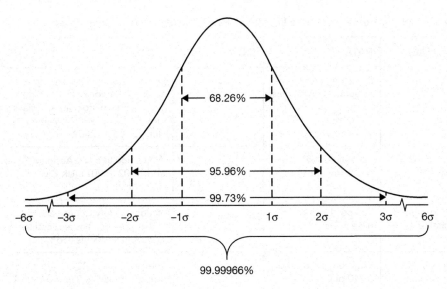

FIGURE 3.2 Normal distribution and standard deviations up to 6σ.

(Harry, 2006). Since its inception at Motorola in the 1980s, defect reduction was the focus; then as companies like General Electric adopted the methodology, the emphasis became cost reduction. In the 2000s, led by DuPont, the attention turned to value creation (Antony et al., 2017).

Six Sigma is named for the Greek letter for the statistical measure of variation: sigma (σ; Chassin, 1998). Under the Six Sigma philosophy, organizations learn to reduce variation, measured as the standard deviation of a normal distribution. When you have a normally distributed process (Figure 3.2), the tiny area under the bell curve beyond six standard deviations (6σ) represents 0.00034% of all your output for the process. If you manage your process such that your customer requirements fall six standard deviations away from your mean, you achieve a Six Sigma process. That is why it is said that a Six Sigma approach intends to achieve only 3.4 defects per million opportunities (DPMO). In other words, Six Sigma tries to produce a quality product or service 99.99966% of the time. Six Sigma empowers organizations to reduce defects in quality to near 0 or "virtually error free business performance" (Pyzdek, 2003).

Six Sigma requires organizations to identify variation in production processes that lead to errors, omissions, and defects (Proudlove et al., 2008). From the customer's standpoint, variation means they can never be sure what to expect. To understand variation at the customer level, think about any experience you have had purchasing a product or service more than once from the same vendor. What was your reaction when you had vastly different experiences in each encounter? Probably not good. Generally, variation leads to customer dissatisfaction.

Variation in the delivery of healthcare represents our greatest challenge. Variation in healthcare is common, often predictable, and frequently preventable (Chassin & Loeb, 2011). The Six Sigma approach to quality improvement was conceived to reduce this variation, making it just as appropriate for the healthcare industry as it is for manufacturing (Harry, 2006). Six Sigma projects in healthcare address both medical issues, such as medical errors and patient throughput, and administrative problems, such as billing inaccuracies, operating room turnaround time, and inpatient discharge processes. Table 3.1 provides a closer examination

Table 3.1 Six Sigma Performance Levels for Healthcare and Other Examples

EXAMPLE	RATE	SIGMA LEVEL	NOTE
Anesthesia mortality	8.2 per million hospital surgical discharges	Near 6σ	Due to improved monitoring and widespread adoption of practice guidelines, mortality from anesthesia is now rare (Chassin, 1998; Li, Warner, Lang, Huang, & Sun, 2009).
Global airplane fatalities	22 fatalities per 1 million flights flown	5σ–6σ	Worldwide airplane Accident Review from 2002 to 2011 (UK Civil Aviation Authority, 2013)
U.S. motor vehicle fatalities	125 per 1 million vehicle miles	5σ–6σ	National Safety Council analysis, including pedestrians and cyclists killed in vehicle accidents (Gorzelany, 2017)
Defects in manufacturing for most U.S. companies	Between 66,807 and 6,210 per million	3σ–4σ	The average DPMO for most manufacturing companies (Thawani, 2004)
Misdiagnosis of cerebrovascular events (stroke)	90,000 per million strokes	3σ–4σ	At initial emergency department presentation, roughly 9% of patients are misdiagnosed (Tarnutzer et al., 2017). Approximately 795,000 people experience a stroke in the United States each year (Benjamin et al., 2019).
Preventable adverse drug events (medication errors)	112,000 per million inpatient admissions	2σ–3σ	Preventable adverse drug events found in 11.2 per 100 admissions in a multisite study (Hug et al., 2010)
Misdiagnosis of myocardial infarction (heart attack)	182,000 per million heart attacks	2σ–3σ	The use of a certain high-sensitivity cardiac lab test in emergency departments associated with misdiagnoses 18.2% of the time (Wildi et al., 2015)
Inappropriate antibiotic prescription	182,700 per million cold-related office visits	2σ–3σ	Of the 29,352,300 office-based visits for cold-related diagnoses, 18.27% were prescribed antibiotics (Imanpour, Nwaiwu, McMaughan, DeSalvo, & Bashir, 2017).

DPMO, defects per million opportunities.

of variation in medical care, as compared to other real-world examples, to illuminate the need for providers to reduce variation.

Types of Variation

Realistically, every process contains variation. The Six Sigma approach seeks to reduce common-cause variation to the level acceptable by the customer. It is your job, however, to understand how much of that variation is acceptable by the customer and ensure your process never goes beyond that. Six Sigma teaches you to distinguish between two types of variation:

1. **Common-cause variation**—This is the variation you can expect when a system is operating under control. This variation is inherent in the process itself.

2. **Special-cause variation**—This is the variation caused by a special circumstance or one-time events, which are not a normal or expected part of the process.

Distinguishing between these types of variation is critical, since you react to each of them in a different way. When a process has only common-cause variation, the ups and downs of the outcomes are part of the process. When you do not understand these boundaries of common-cause variation, you will unnecessarily react to events. Let us say, for example, that a particular nursing unit's boundaries of common-cause variation for readmissions are between 0 and 3 per month. Now, the unit will start counting the readmissions data when the unit had one readmission per month for 2 months in a row. For someone who does not understand the boundaries of common-cause variation, the way they react to this variation can be detrimental to quality management efforts, as illustrated in the following two scenarios.

- Scenario A: The third month's readmission number comes at 0 for the nursing unit in question. The ill-informed manager celebrates the achievement, giving praise to his team for a job well done.

- Scenario B: The third month's readmission number comes at 3 for the nursing unit in question. The manager, who does not understand the difference between common-cause and special-cause variation, goes berserk on the team, telling everyone that they all need to do a better job and be more watchful, contributing to heightened stress and lower morale in the nursing unit.

These two scenarios repeatedly occur in our healthcare organizations, when, in fact, neither of them is an appropriate response. A manager who understands variation knows that for this particular unit, any number between 0 and 3 is within the range of expected values and, therefore, should not react when the result falls within this range. The only time when there should be a reaction is if the unit has 4 or more readmissions in a particular month, as that would indicate an out-of-control condition and would deserve further investigation.

DMAIC: Define, Measure, Analyze, Improve, and Control

Six Sigma's biggest contribution to continuous quality improvement is the structure it provides to identify and solve problems. Six Sigma is deployed by carrying out quality improvement projects using the **DMAIC** framework (Figure 3.3), which stands for Define, Measure, Analyze, Improve, and Control. DMAIC (pronounced "dee-may-ic") is a widely used five-step framework for quality management in healthcare (Antony et al., 2018).

1. In the *Define* phase, you must answer the question, Why do we need to improve? In this early phase, you are not even sure you have a problem yet. The Define phase is about gaining a common understanding of the problem. Once the problem is well understood, the goals of the improvement initiative must be defined as well. You must find out what your customer thinks about the quality of your product or

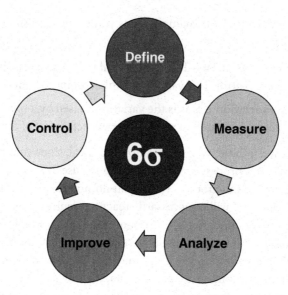

FIGURE 3.3 Define, Measure, Analyze, Improve, and Control cycle of continuous improvement.

service—the **voice of the customer** (VOC). In addition, the Define phase requires that you agree on the scope of the improvement effort. Many well-intended projects have failed because the poorly stated scope created confusion on whether the improvement effort was successful or complete.

2. In the next phase, you need to *Measure* the problem. Measurement is necessary to understand whether your interventions improve quality as you expect (Institute of Medicine, 2005). Measures can be called "metrics," "indicators," "targets," or "key performance indicators" (KPIs). When looking for opportunities for improvement, you will use quality measures to determine how you are currently performing and to set goals. Are you missing your goal by 5% or 95%? This is where you establish what is called your **baseline** to understand where you started so that you can judge whether you are making progress toward your goal.

Sometimes, no credible measures have been developed for your quality improvement project. In other instances, the measures exist, but the accuracy and reliability of the data are suspect. A rigorous approach to establishing a valid measurement system—the **measurement system analysis**—entails determining the accuracy of your data for your measures. If the data are fraught with errors or unreliable in other ways, you must first fix your measurement system before proceeding.

You can monitor your progress with two types of measures: lag and lead. A **lag measure** is something that you ultimately want to improve. A **lead measure** predicts achievement of the lag measure. By tracking a few lead measures every day and adjusting when necessary, you will consequently achieve your lag measure goal. For example, imagine a nursing unit wants to reduce their incidence of pressure ulcers (bedsores). Measuring how many pressure ulcers their patients get every month or every week is a lag measure. At the point when you register the pressure ulcer, there is nothing you can do to prevent that adverse outcome for your patient. The nursing unit instead uses a proactive approach to prevent these ulcers from happening in the first place. They know that turning patients often during their stay is a best practice to reduce the incidence of pressure ulcers. They start measuring "patient turns every 2 hours." If they track how well they are doing in turning patients every 2 hours (their lead measure), they can predict how they will do in reducing their patients' pressure ulcers (lag measure).

3. Next, in the *Analyze* phase, you and your team examine the root causes of the problem. You ask, "What are the possible reasons for the gap in performance?" You must look beyond symptoms and identify those factors that are contributing to your issue. Through relentless curiosity, you and your team seek to understand how much impact the causes have on your problem. This enables you to prioritize fixing the causes that will have the largest impact on your project. This casebook provides you with many opportunities to apply quality management analysis tools and approaches, such as fishbone diagrams, flowcharts, and "five-why's" root cause analysis.

4. Then comes the *Improve* phase where you and your team brainstorm solutions, pilot changes, implement solutions, and collect data to confirm improvement of your measures. Did you notice something? You worked on three of the five phases and did not yet consider any solutions. Many times, teams are so eager to solve the problem that they start formulating solutions too early in the process—often without defining the problem first. It is only after you have defined, measured, and analyzed the problem that you will find yourself in a good position to propose and test the effectiveness of some solutions to eliminate the root cause of the problem.

5. *Control* is the final—and the most difficult—phase. The main purpose during this phase is to ensure the new process continues to deliver quality and value to the customer over time. Communication is a very important element of this phase. You must communicate your successes and lessons learned to others who may not have been directly involved with the project, but who are interested or affected. During the Control phase, you provide a robust documentation for the process owner to ensure the improvements are maintained in the long term.

Combining Lean With Six Sigma

You will often hear the combined phrase "Lean Six Sigma" among healthcare quality management practitioners. Although technically different philosophies, both evolved from the scientific management movement. Six Sigma seeks "uniform process output," whereas Lean aims for "reduced flow time" (Assarlind, Gremyr, & Backman, 2013). However, Nave (2002) has argued that Lean and Six Sigma are basically the same thing, ending at the same place—higher quality. Nevertheless, the result of the integrated Lean and Six Sigma approach may afford some advantages in the form of combining the value-to-customer approach of Lean with the rigorous statistical control of Six Sigma (Arnheiter & Maleyeff, 2005). In our view, these characterizations are overly simplistic, but the combination of a data-driven approach with rapid cycles of quality improvement may be the ideal solution to U.S. healthcare system's problems (de Koning, Verver, van den Heuvel, Bisgaard, & Does, 2006).

EVIDENCE-BASED MANAGEMENT

Evidence to Empower Better Management Decisions

Like quality management philosophies of Lean and Six Sigma, evidence-based management (EBMgt) is a science-informed, step-by-step process that empowers better decisions through evidence (Briner & Walshe, 2014). Scholars cite the success of physicians incorporating evidence into their practice, called "evidence-based medicine" (Rousseau, 2006), and yet, most healthcare managers fail to consider the evidence as a part of their problem-solving process (Pfeffer & Sutton, 2006). As Pfeffer and Sutton (2006, p. 2) write, "If doctors practiced medicine like many companies practice management, there would be more unnecessarily sick or dead patients and many more doctors in jail or suffering other penalties for malpractice."

EBMgt uses evidence to empower better decision-making and enables improved outcomes. Unfortunately, managers have not approached healthcare quality problems systematically. Many healthcare management practitioners lack the skills necessary to assess and utilize evidence for quality improvement projects. Instead, healthcare managers rely on experience, anecdotes, or advice from consultants (Kovner & Rundall, 2006).

You can apply the steps of EBMgt to improve your decision-making (Briner, Denyer, & Rousseau, 2009; Hsu et al., 2009; Kovner, 2014; Kovner & Rundall, 2006). EBMgt begins with an identified management problem, challenge, issue, or concern that you translate into a research question. You then analyze the problem using the best available evidence from a variety of sources. This evidence—assessed for accuracy, applicability, and actionability— provides the necessary insight for developing and implementing interventions. Finally, you monitor and evaluate your interventions to continually improve performance over time. This step-by-step process can be applied to many types of healthcare management challenges, including quality, strategy, finance, and operations (Kovner & Rundall, 2006).

Four Sources of Evidence

There are four sources of evidence for improved management decision-making, according to EBMgt principles (Briner et al., 2009; Briner & Walshe, 2014; Kovner & Rundall, 2006; Reay, Berta, & Kohn, 2009):

1. Perspectives of people affected by the intervention—First, you should ask direct questions of the people who are knowledgeable about the quality management problem, especially the frontline employees and patients. By collaborating with the people who have expertise in and experience with the problem, you improve the likelihood that you will develop the best solution. For example, when choosing among several equally acceptable ideas, the people affected by the intervention may present you with a small piece of practical information that would push the decision away from one particular suggestion, even when other types of evidence suggest that it may be effective (Briner & Rousseau, 2011).

2. Personal experience, stakeholder judgment, and expert opinion—Your past profes-
    sional experiences with similar problems and solutions will be a common source of
    evidence (Kovner & Rundall, 2006). Colleagues who are not personally involved,
    consultants with experience in other organizations, and known subject matter ex-
    perts can also provide you with evidence to support your problem-solving (Kovner
    & Rundall, 2006). Keep in mind, however, that managers tend to seek out advice
    from their peers with similar circumstances, which, in times of poor performance,
    can create a type of inertia. Especially when organizational performance is poor,
    relying on colleagues within your social network can intensify a downward spiral
    of results (McDonald & Westphal, 2003). Furthermore, evidence from consultants
    may be misleading, as their financial incentives involve winning more consulting
    projects, not necessarily evaluating their interventions or solving your problems
    (Pfeffer & Sutton, 2006).

3. Evidence from data and experimentation in the local context—You should always
    examine trends and patterns from data collected from your internal organizational
    sources (Kovner & Rundall, 2006; Pfeffer & Sutton, 2006). In addition, the best
    available evidence can sometimes arise from internal experiments and small-scale
    pilots that test possible solutions (Pfeffer & Sutton, 2006). Another source of evi-
    dence is benchmarking, which is the comparison of your organization's data with
    studies of other organizations (Kovner & Rundall, 2006).

4. Critical evaluation of the best available management literature—Of these four
    sources of evidence used in EBMgt, research found in academic publications pres-
    ents the most accessible to students who may have fewer professional experiences
    or social networks upon which to draw evidence (Briner & Walshe, 2014). The pre-
    viously discussed sources of inward-looking evidence—the organization specific,
    fact based, directly observed—are what Rousseau (2006) calls "little e evidence."
    In contrast, "Big E Evidence" refers to well-conducted management research in
    peer-reviewed literature conducted outside your organization (Rousseau, 2006).
    "Big E Evidence" does not replace "little e evidence," but rather plays a comple-
    mentary role (Kovner & Rundall, 2006).

When considering external research as a source of evidence, the scale of your selected
solution should correspond to the strength of evidence upon which your intervention is
based. That is, when weaker evidence predominates, you should start with small-scale test
projects (Reay et al., 2009). The most rigorous form of external evidence is the systematic
review of published research (Briner et al., 2009). Systematic reviews draw conclusions about
the evidence through an exhaustive search and analysis of all studies related to a certain
research question (Kovner, 2014). Of the available systematic reviews, nearly three-quarters
address clinical issues of interest to managers, while the remaining focus on management-re-
lated interventions (Jaana, Vartak, & Ward, 2014). However, relatively few systematic reviews
on health services management topics exist (Jaana et al., 2014). With the lack of systematic
reviews available, you may have to build evidence from research evidence gained from single
studies. Still, you should evaluate whether the context of the study is applicable to your organization or problem (Briner et al., 2009; Pfeffer & Sutton, 2006).

SUMMARY

The quality management mindset is based on hundreds of years of scientific thinking on which new approaches to quality improvement in manufacturing were based, called "Lean" and "Six Sigma." Lean seeks to increase the value for the customer by reducing waste and improving flow using the PDSA cycle to solve quality problems. The aim of the Six Sigma methodology is to reduce defects and variation in processes within certain statistical control limits. Six Sigma uses the DMAIC continuous quality improvement cycle. An integrated Lean and Six Sigma approach may afford some advantages in the form of combining the value-to-customer approach of Lean with the rigorous statistical control of Six Sigma. Like Lean Six Sigma, EBMgt is a science-informed, step-by-step process that empowers better decisions through evidence.

DISCUSSION QUESTIONS

1. Describe how the quality management mindset compares with the scientific method.

2. How do Lean and Six Sigma approaches to quality management differ? How are they similar?

3. Name a type of waste identified in the Lean approach to quality management and give an example from healthcare.

4. What advantage does the combination of Lean and Six Sigma offer to practitioners of healthcare quality management?

5. Why do you think that evidence-based management has been infrequently adopted by healthcare managers? How would you recommend overcoming these barriers?

REFERENCES

Antony, J., Palsuk, P., Gupta, S., Mishra, D., & Barach, P. (2018). Six Sigma in healthcare: A systematic review of the literature. *International Journal of Quality & Reliability Management, 35*(5), 1075–1092. doi:10.1108/ijqrm-02-2017-0027

Antony, J., Snee, R., & Hoerl, R. (2017). Lean Six Sigma: Yesterday, today and tomorrow. *International Journal of Quality & Reliability Management, 34*(7), 1073–1093. doi:10.1108/ijqrm-03-2016-0035

Armor, D. A., & Taylor, S. E. (2003). The effects of mindset on behavior: Self-regulation in deliberative and implemental frames of mind. *Personality and Social Psychology Bulletin, 29*(1), 86–95. doi:10.1177/0146167202238374

Arnheiter, E. D., & Maleyeff, J. (2005). The integration of Lean management and Six Sigma. *The TQM Magazine, 17*(1), 5–18. doi:10.1108/09544780510573020

Assarlind, M., Gremyr, I., & Backman, K. (2013). Multi-faceted views on a Lean Six Sigma application. *International Journal of Quality & Reliability Management, 30*(4), 387–402. doi:10.1108/02656711311308385

Bateman, N., & Lethbridge, S. (2014). Managing operations and teams visually. In E. Bell, S. Warren, & J. Schroeder (Eds.), *Routledge companion to visual organization* (pp. 306–321). New York, NY: Routledge.

Benjamin, E. J., Muntner, P., Alonso, A., Bittencourt, M. S., Callaway, C. W., Carson, A. P., … Virani, S. S.; on behalf of the American Heart Association Council on Epidemiology and Prevention Statistics Committee and Stroke Statistics Subcommittee. (2019). Heart disease and stroke statistics—2019 update: A report from the American Heart Association. *Circulation, 139*(10), E56–E528. doi:10.1161/cir.0000000000000659

Briner, R. B., Denyer, D., & Rousseau, D. M. (2009). Evidence-based management: Concept cleanup time? *Academy of Management Perspectives*, *23*(4), 19–32. doi:10.5465/amp.2009.45590138

Briner, R. B., & Rousseau, D. M. (2011). Evidence-based I-O psychology: Not there yet. *Industrial and Organizational Psychology*, *4*(1), 3–22. doi:10.1111/j.1754-9434.2010.01287.x

Briner, R. B., & Walshe, N. D. (2014). From passively received wisdom to actively constructed knowledge: Teaching systematic review skills as a foundation of evidence-based management. *Academy of Management Learning & Education*, *13*(3), 415–432. doi:10.5465/amle.2013.0222

Chassin, M. R. (1998). Is health care ready for Six Sigma quality? *Milbank Quarterly*, *76*(4), 565–591. doi:10.1111/1468-0009.00106

Chassin, M. R., & Loeb, J. M. (2011). The ongoing quality improvement journey: Next stop, high reliability. *Health Affairs*, *30*(4), 559–568. doi:10.1377/hlthaff.2011.0076

de Koning, H., Verver, J. P. S., van den Heuvel, J., Bisgaard, S., & Does, R. J. M. M. (2006). Lean Six Sigma in healthcare. *Journal for Healthcare Quality*, *28*(2), 4–11. doi:10.1111/j.1945-1474.2006.tb00596.x

Fillingham, D. (2007). Can lean save lives? *Leadership in Health Services*, *20*(4), 231–241. doi:10.1108/17511870710829346

Gollwitzer, P. M., Heckhausen, H., & Steller, B. (1990). Deliberative and implemental mind-sets: Cognitive tuning toward congruous thoughts and information. *Journal of Personality and Social Psychology*, *59*(6), 1119–1127. doi:10.1037/0022-3514.59.6.1119

Gorzelany, J. (2017). Death race 2017: Where to find the most dangerous roads in America. Retrieved from https://www.forbes.com/sites/jimgorzelany/2017/02/16/death-race-2017-where-to-find-the-most-dangerous-roads-in-america/#3bc631be1324

Harry, M. (2006). Mikel Harry on Six Sigma in healthcare. *Interview by Carole S. Guinane. Journal for Healthcare Quality*, *28*(4), 29–36. doi:10.1111/j.1945-1474.2006.tb00618.x

Hsu, J., Arroyo, L., Graetz, I., Neuwirth, E. B., Schmittdiel, J., Rundall, T. G., … Curtis, P. (2009). Methods for developing actionable evidence for consumers of health services research. In A. R. Kovner, D. J. Fibe, & R. D'Aquila (Eds.), *Evidence-based management in healthcare* (pp. 83–96). Chicago, IL: Health Administration Press.

Hug, B. L., Witkowski, D. J., Sox, C. M., Keohane, C. A., Seger, D. L., Yoon, C., … Bates, D. W. (2010). Adverse drug event rates in six community hospitals and the potential impact of computerized physician order entry for prevention. *Journal of General Internal Medicine*, *25*(1), 31–38. doi:10.1007/s11606-009-1141-3

Imanpour, S., Nwaiwu, O., McMaughan, D. K., DeSalvo, B., & Bashir, A. (2017). Factors associated with antibiotic prescriptions for the viral origin diseases in office-based practices, 2006-2012. *JRSM Open*, *8*(8), 2054270417717668. doi:10.1177/2054270417717668

Institute of Medicine. (2005). *Performance measurement: Accelerating improvement*. Washington, DC: National Academies Press. Retrieved from https://www.nap.edu/catalog/11517/performance-measurement-accelerating-improvement

Jaana, M., Vartak, S., & Ward, M. M. (2014). Evidence-based health care management: What is the research evidence available for health care managers? *Evaluation & the Health Professions*, *37*(3), 314–334. doi:10.1177/0163278713511325

Juran, J. M., & Godfrey, A. B. (1999). *Juran's quality handbook*. New York, NY: McGraw-Hill.

Kovner, A. R. (2014). Evidence-based management: Implications for nonprofit organizations. *Nonprofit Management & Leadership*, *24*(3), 417–424. doi:10.1002/nml.21097

Kovner, A. R., & Rundall, T. G. (2006). Evidence-based management reconsidered. *Frontiers of Health Services Management*, *22*(3), 3–22. doi:10.1097/01974520-200601000-00002

Li, G., Warner, M., Lang, B. H., Huang, L., & Sun, L. S. (2009). Epidemiology of anesthesia-related mortality in the United States, 1999-2005. *Anesthesiology*, *110*(4), 759–765. doi:10.1097/ALN.0b013e31819b5bdc

McDonald, M. L., & Westphal, J. D. (2003). Getting by with the advice of their friends: CEOs' advice networks and firms' strategic responses to poor performance. *Administrative Science Quarterly*, *48*(1), 1–32. doi:10.2307/3556617

Nave, D. (2002). How to compare Six Sigma, Lean and the theory of constraints: A framework for choosing what's best for your organization. *Quality Progress*, *35*(3), 73–78. Retrieved from https://www.lean.org/Search/Documents/242.pdf

Pfeffer, J., & Sutton, R. I. (2006). Evidence-based management. *Harvard Business Review, 84*(1), 62–74. Retrieved from https://hbr.org/2006/01/evidence-based-management

Proudlove, N., Moxham, C., & Boaden, R. (2008). Lessons for Lean in healthcare from using Six Sigma in the NHS. *Public Money & Management, 28*(1), 27–34. doi:10.1111/j.1467-9302.2008.00615.x

Pyzdek, T. (2003). *The Six Sigma handbook: A complete guide for green belts, black belts and managers at all levels, revised and expanded.* New York, NY: McGraw-Hill.

Reay, T., Berta, W., & Kohn, M. K. (2009). What's the evidence on evidence-based management? *Academy of Management Perspectives, 23*(4), 5–18. doi:10.5465/amp.2009.45590137

Rotter, T., Plishka, C., Lawal, A., Harrison, L., Sari, N., Goodridge, D., … Kinsman, L. (2018). What is Lean management in health care? Development of an operational definition for a Cochrane Systematic Review. *Evaluation & the Health Professions, 42*, 366–390. doi:10.1177/0163278718756992

Rousseau, D. M. (2006). 2005 presidential address: Is there such a thing as "evidence-based management"? *Academy of Management Review, 31*(2), 256–269. doi:10.5465/amr.2006.20208679

Russell-Babin, K., & Wurmser, T. (2016). Transforming care through top-of-license practice. *Nursing Management, 47*(5), 24–28. doi:10.1097/01.NUMA.0000482527.15743.

Shah, P., & Hoeffner, J. (2002). Review of graph comprehension research: Implications for instruction. *Educational Psychology Review, 14*(1), 47–69. doi:10.1023/a:1013180410169

Staats, B. R., & Upton, D. M. (2011). Lean knowledge work. *Harvard Business Review, 89*(10), 100–110. Retrieved from https://hbr.org/2011/10/lean-knowledge-work

Tarnutzer, A. A., Lee, S.-H., Robinson, K. A., Wang, Z., Edlow, J. A., & Newman-Toker, D. E. (2017). ED misdiagnosis of cerebrovascular events in the era of modern neuroimaging: A meta-analysis. *Neurology, 88*(15), 1468–1477. doi:10.1212/wnl.0000000000003814

Taylor, M. J., McNicholas, C., Nicolay, C., Darzi, A., Bell, D., & Reed, J. E. (2014). Systematic review of the application of the plan-do-study-act method to improve quality in healthcare. *BMJ Quality & Safety, 23*(4), 290–298. doi:10.1136/bmjqs-2013-001862

Thawani, S. (2004). Six Sigma—Strategy for organizational excellence. *Total Quality Management & Business Excellence, 15*(5/6), 655–664. doi:10.1080/14783360410001680143

Toussaint, J. S., & Berry, L. L. (2013). The promise of Lean in health care. *Mayo Clinic proceedings, 88*(1), 74–82. doi:10.1016/j.mayocp.2012.07.025

UK Civil Aviation Authority. (2013). *Global fatal accident review 2002 to 2011.* Retrieved from https://publicapps.caa.co.uk/docs/33/CAP%201036%20Global%20Fatal%20Accident%20Review%202002%20to%202011.pdf

Wildi, K., Gimenez, M. R., Twerenbold, R., Reichlin, T., Jaeger, C., Heinzelmann, A., … Mueller, C. (2015). Misdiagnosis of myocardial infarction related to limitations of the current regulatory approach to define clinical decision values for cardiac troponin. *Circulation, 131*(23), 2032–2040. doi:10.1161/circulationaha.114.014129

Womack, J. P., & Jones, D. T. (1996). *Lean thinking: Banish waste and create wealth in your corporation.* New York, NY: Simon & Schuster.

Womack, J. P., Jones, D. T., & Roos, D. (1990). *The machine that changed the world.* New York, NY: Free Press.

Young, T., & McClean, S. (2009). Some challenges facing Lean thinking in healthcare. *International Journal for Quality in Health Care, 21*(5), 309–310. doi:10.1093/intqhc/mzp038

CHAPTER 4

The Culture

OBJECTIVES

1. Describe how organizational culture can empower quality improvement and improve patient health outcomes.
2. Recognize common cultural barriers to healthcare quality management initiatives.
3. Distinguish a just culture from a culture of blame, fear, and punishment.
4. Explain how leaders support healthcare quality management efforts.
5. Evaluate the role of interprofessional teams in healthcare quality management.
6. Examine how change management models can support quality management initiatives.

IMPACT OF ORGANIZATIONAL CULTURE

After W. Edwards Deming advised Ford Motor Company on implementing quality management, one executive said, "We wanted to talk about quality, improvement tools, and which programs work. He wanted to talk to us about management, cultural change, and senior managers' vision for the company" (Swift, Omachonu, & Ross, 1998, p. 59). Deming knew that without creating a culture that supports quality, any new initiatives would be destined to fail. Despite this fact, many healthcare organizations adopt quality improvement methodologies in search for the quick fix to their performance problems without addressing cultural barriers (Young & McClean, 2009). You should follow Deming's advice and build an organizational culture that will be responsive to your healthcare quality management efforts.

The culture of an organization is a social system of human relations with shared norms, values, and assumptions (Schein, 2010). **Organizational culture** is the agreement of a group of people when answering the question: How are things done around here? Unique and inimitable, each organization constructs its culture over time by giving feedback—explicit or implicit—to each other on behaviors that are consistent or inconsistent with norms (Roberts & Perryman, 2007).

Organizational culture can empower a quality improvement environment and improve patient health outcomes. Table 4.1 presents examples from peer-reviewed literature that show how organizational characteristics can improve patient health outcomes. You can seek to emulate these cultural characteristics in your healthcare organization.

Table 4.1 Culture of Quality Positively Associated With Improved Patient Outcomes

OUTCOME	CULTURAL CHARACTERISTIC	IMPROVEMENT
Mortality rates	Clinicians are encouraged to seek creative ways to solve problems.	Piloted problem-solving initiatives significantly improved risk-adjusted mortality rates for acute myocardial infarction (Bradley et al., 2012).
Failure-to-rescue	Nurses' opinion of the high level of quality improvement implementation in their neonatal intensive care units.	Quality improvement culture associated with significantly higher rates of infant survival (Mahl et al., 2015).
Readmission rates	A hospital "safety culture" includes good communication, resource availability, teamwork, and application of nonpunitive principles of management.	A lower hospital safety culture is significantly associated with higher 30-day readmission rates for acute myocardial infarction and heart failure (Hansen, Williams, & Singer, 2011).
Adverse events/Medication errors	Hospital staff freely speak about adverse events, readily report errors, receive safety support from management, and cooperate among and within hospital units.	Hospitals with more positive patient safety culture scores experience lower rates of adverse events (Mardon, Khanna, Sorra, Dyer, & Famolaro, 2010).
Patient satisfaction	Promote "customer service climate" to motivate nurses to provide extra assistance to patients beyond their typical job duties.	When nursing staff are supported and rewarded for performance, they act to increase patient satisfaction (Greenslade & Jimmieson, 2011).
Hospital-acquired infections	Support positive safety culture, teamwork, nonpunitive response to error, and management support.	Various dimensions of safety culture associated with lower rates of surgical site infections (Fan et al., 2016).

BARRIERS TO BUILDING A CULTURE OF QUALITY

Despite their positive impact on health outcomes, many organizations face cultural barriers to quality management initiatives (Agency for Healthcare Research and Quality [AHRQ], 2014; Dixon-Woods, McNicol, & Martin, 2012; Speroff et al., 2010). In this casebook, you will analyze case scenarios that involve common cultural barriers. Organized in four quality management categories—process improvement, patient experience, patient safety, and performance improvement—the case study scenarios exemplify common cultural barriers to quality management. Through case study analysis, you will become familiar with cultural barriers to quality improvement and the actions that can overcome them.

Process Improvement

Healthcare process improvement activities seek to streamline, remove bottlenecks, eliminate nonvalue-adding activities, or reduce variability in business or patient care processes. However, as revealed in the following case studies, common cultural barriers impede successful implementation of process improvement initiatives (Table 4.2).

Table 4.2 Cultural Barriers Included in Process Improvement Case Studies

CASE STUDY	BARRIER	CASE DESCRIPTION
Case 1: A Summer Internship Journal	Lack of quality management expertise	A young, ambitious health administration intern neglects to conduct a root cause analysis leading to mistaken problem definition.
Case 2: Claims Payment Processing	Misguided solutions to problems	State Hospital Association lobbies for imprudent legislation to solve claims payment problem.
Case 3: Return-to-Work at a Home Health Care Agency	Lack of resources and technology support	Complex processes made more onerous by outdated technology and poor coordination of human resource processes.
Case 4: The Ophthalmologist Who Could Not See (The Waste)	Lack of awareness of inefficiencies	Providers who are unaware of the financial impact of inefficiencies in care processes can stress health services business health.
Case 5: Building a New IR Suite	Resistance to change	Some are skeptical of process flow innovations intended to improve the design of an IR suite.
Case 6: Emergency Department Heroes	Lack of time and resources	Staff do not have time for quality management because they are constantly "fighting fires" in the emergency room.

IR, interventional radiology.

Patient Experience

Patient experience, similar to the concept of customer satisfaction, is the assessment of a patient's judgment, attitude, or perception of whether his or her expectations in a healthcare environment were met (AHRQ, 2017). Patient experience is principally measured in the United States through standardized surveys. While these are considered valid and reliable instruments, the medical community remains skeptical of their usefulness (Robbins, 2019). Even in organizations that accept patient experience as an important measure of quality, numerous cultural barriers impede progress, as you will learn in the case studies listed in Table 4.3.

Patient Safety

The case studies in Table 4.4 focus on reducing harm to patients, such as hospital-acquired infections, medication errors, and missed diagnoses. To achieve meaningful progress in patient safety, substantial cultural change can be achieved only through teamwork, training, commitment, and systems redesign (Herndon, 2015).

Performance Improvement

This casebook conceptualizes performance improvement as issues related to demands for quality made by external stakeholders, such as auditors, community, health insurance companies, and government regulators. The following performance improvement cases in Table 4.5 illustrate common barriers to creating a culture amenable to quality improvement.

Table 4.3 Cultural Barriers Included in Patient Experience Case Studies

CASE STUDY	BARRIER	CASE DESCRIPTION
Case 7: Hurricane Mia and the Patient Access Call Center	Too much change, too fast	Leaders may be reluctant to make needed change soon after other changes to allow organization to adjust to the change on a psychological level.
Case 8: The Cowboy Doctor's Patient Experience	Lack of interpersonal communication skills	Sound technical skills cannot overcome poor interpersonal skills when addressing low patient experience scores.
Case 9: Patient Navigation at the Orthopedic Clinic	Lack of training and employee development	Variation in patient communication processes negatively impacts patient experience scores.
Case 10: HCAHPS and the Quiet-at-Night Measure	Lack of provider engagement due to cynicism	Clinical leadership is skeptical of the patient experience surveys.
Case 11: Discharge Phone Calls (En Español)	Lack of focus on the customer	A hospital's customer support organization creates operational processes that lack cultural awareness.
Case 12: Patient Experience in Home Care	Resistance to change	Despite customer complaints, staff are reluctant to evaluate outdated processes in staffing of home care services.

HCAHPS, Hospital Consumer Assessment of Healthcare Providers and Systems.

Table 4.4 Cultural Barriers Included in Patient Safety Case Studies

CASE STUDY	BARRIER	CASE DESCRIPTION
Case 13: Reducing Falls: The Sleuth Resident	Complacency with current performance	Satisfied with many improved patient safety measures, hospital staff reluctantly examine patient falls.
Case 14: Sustaining Hand Hygiene	Lack of organizational commitment to sustaining change	Previously improved hand hygiene compliance declined due to leadership and staff indifference.
Case 15: Warning Letter from the State Regulator	Undefined management roles	Unclear responsibilities cause conflict and lack of accountability for error that may result in harsh regulatory penalties.
Case 16: Failure-to-Rescue	Lack of adequate training	Inexperienced care providers fail to follow escalation protocols, causing dire consequences to a patient.
Case 17: CLIF's Medication Errors	Lack of stakeholder acceptance of problem	Leadership unwilling to accept the possible unintended consequences of adopting new technologies.
Case 18: A Mom's Story of Sepsis	Suspicious of quality management approaches developed outside healthcare	Hospital staff hesitantly visit a manufacturing company, where applications of quality management methods improve processes.

Table 4.5 Cultural Barriers Included in Performance Improvement Case Studies

CASE STUDY	BARRIER	CASE DESCRIPTION
Case 19: Operating Room Recovery	Lack of basic management expertise	A hospital executive potentially faces consequences for negligence in management performance.
Case 20: Opioid Overdoses in the Emergency Department	Hierarchical management culture hindering quality improvement	Navigating the political environment in bureaucratic organizations can slow decision-making, problem definition, and organizational change.
Case 21: The Lunchroom: Physician Engagement at a PCMH	Lack of provider engagement due to burnout	A value-based purchasing initiative needs a physician's support, but a doctor's denial, anger, and depression became a counterproductive force against quality improvement.
Case 22: The Fulfillment Affair	Lack of sense of urgency	Despite high-cost claims, management was slow to address root causes of poor health outcomes.
Case 23: Composite Quality Score	Resistance to more work	People resist quality improvement initiatives when they do not agree whether a problem exists.
Case 24: Both/And Thinking in Readmission Prevention	Fear of loss of control or power	Managers at merging organizations struggle for power to implement processes in the ways consistent with their professional perspectives. Such tribalism can jeopardize quality improvement projects.
Case 25: Community Collaboration for Suicide Prevention	Lack of leadership support for resources	Leaders fail to prioritize suicide prevention as a community performance metric leading to tragic personal consequences.

PCMH, patient-centered medical home.

A CULTURE RESPONSIVE TO QUALITY MANAGEMENT

Through effective leadership and teamwork, you can help your organization overcome the aforementioned cultural barriers. Healthcare organizations that emphasize open dialogue and accountability, encourage leadership at all levels of the organization, and foster teamwork among many health professions create cultures responsive to quality management (Braithwaite, Herkes, Ludlow, Testa, & Lamprell, 2017).

Just Culture

As you have learned, poor performance can rarely be blamed on the people of your organization. Usually, a system-related problem is to blame, so punishing people for system failure will not fix your quality problems. **Lucian Leape**, a member of the Institute of Medicine's Committee on Quality of Health Care in America, told Congress, "People are not bad when they make errors, … [b]ut there may be bad systems, and those systems cause the errors" (Leape, 1999, p. 72). The organizations that seek out and identify, blame, and punish the person(s) responsible for errors create cultures of fear (Boysen, 2013). Lack of psychological safety prevents learning and change, which makes quality improvement unmanageable (Edmondson, 2004).

To substitute accountability for blame in your organization, you should develop something called a **just culture**. A just culture fosters a "speak up" environment—open dialogue, elimination of fear, and the ability to escalate problems or concerns (Roberts & Perryman, 2007). A just culture promotes shared responsibility for meeting the standards of quality for performance established by professional societies (i.e., medicine, nursing), the organization (Boysen, 2013; Roberts & Perryman, 2007), and the patient (Berwick, 2009). Of course, actions associated with ineptitude, impairment, or intransigence should be penalized, but in a just culture, individual practitioners are not held accountable for system-related problems.

Leadership in a Culture of Quality

Effective leaders throughout the healthcare organization—from the boardroom to the bedside—prioritize the implementation of quality management (Toussaint & Berry, 2013). Boards of directors of high-performing organizations consider quality metrics when setting the strategy for the organization (Tsai et al., 2015). Successful mid-level and frontline managers provide the necessary personnel, such as quality improvement facilitators and data analysts, and financial resources, such as training and information systems (Alexander, Weiner, Shortell, Baker, & Becker, 2006; Tsai et al., 2015). Leaders working at the bedside in the best performing healthcare organizations communicate quality standards to staff, safely manage workload, support training needs, and collaborate with other organizational leaders (Shaffer & Tuttas, 2009).

Successful leaders ask questions more frequently than unsuccessful ones (Marquardt, 2014). To create a culture that embraces quality management, you should ask the right questions. You do not have to know all the answers; just encourage your team to collaborate to find the answers. As a healthcare quality management leader, you should be prepared to ask the questions listed in Table 4.6.

Interprofessional Teamwork

Effective healthcare quality management encourages teamwork among many professions (Poksinska, 2010). **Interprofessional** practice includes both clinical (e.g., treatment, health communications) and nonclinical health-related work (e.g., patient registration, workforce planning) among all types of team members, including service line managers, administrative staff, physicians, nurses, pharmacists, therapists, allied health disciplines, health information technologists, and quality improvement professionals (Afsar-Manesh, Lonowski, & Namavar, 2017; World Health Organization, 2010).

Healthcare quality management teams vary in size, although the optimal size of the team is between five and eight individuals (AHRQ, 2013). Healthcare quality management teams include members representing at least three different kinds of professional expertise within the organization: system leadership, technical expertise, and day-to-day leadership

Table 4.6 Questions Leaders Ask in a Culture of Quality

QUESTION	NOTE
What do we want to accomplish?	Specific quality improvement goals must be set, and the intention for improvement must be known by the team (Berwick, 1996).
How will we know when we are successful?	Without quality measurement, we will not learn whether our improvement efforts work (Berwick, 1996).
What changes will result in improvement?	Identify promising interventions; avoid dubious ones (Berwick, 1996).
What do patients and their families really want and need?	Leaders continuously ask patients, "What matters to you?" This concept is called patient-centeredness (Berwick, 2009; Institute for Healthcare Improvement [IHI], 2013).
How do patients and their families view the quality of our services?	Patients and their families are the standard-bearers of quality (Berwick, 2009), especially as it relates to their experiences with care (Cleary, 2016).
Do the frontline staff understand the measures of quality?	Those people doing the work must understand the standard of quality and how their work impacts quality (Dempsey, Reilly, & Buhlman, 2014).
What types of relationships exist in the organization among and between professions and departments?	Weak ties or negative relations among operational units will create challenges for building a culture receptive to quality management (Schein, 2010).
How would you describe the current reality?	Without reflection on how things are, quality improvement teams will be unable to explain how things should be (Marquardt, 2014).
What is the current state of problem-solving in the organization?	Your organization should seek out problems and speak up when they are identified. Cultural change is needed if problems get ignored (or worse, covered up; Carney, 2011).
Do people have an understanding of the quality management methods?	Assess the quality management knowledge of your organization. Competent healthcare quality management requires training on related skills (AHRQ, 2013; Institute of Medicine Committee on the Health Professions Education Summit, 2003).
Do interprofessional teams openly discuss problems, issues, or challenges?	Leaders establish collaborative activities that will stimulate new thinking about a problem (Carney, 2011).
Are there better ways of working that we can adopt at our organization?	Cultures with an ethic of constant learning are more likely to adopt quality management practices (IHI, 2013).
What did we learn? How can we build on it?	Leaders continuously reflect on quality management actions to produce cumulative improvements over time (Berwick, 1996).

(Langley et al., 2009). The clinical leader holds the organizational authority to implement the quality management interventions. Technical expertise, sometimes called the "subject matter expert" (SME), can come from both frontline staff and quality management facilitators (Godfrey, Andersson-Gare, Nelson, Nilsson, & Ahlstrom, 2014). Frontline staff understand the problem thoroughly from firsthand experience. A quality management facilitator or leader trained in quality management methodology organizes the problem-solving process and provides guidance on measurement, data collection, analysis, and presentation.

The different types of healthcare professionals, combined with the complexity of healthcare delivery, require regular communication to avoid fragmentation, delays, and errors (Scotten, Manos, Malicoat, & Paolo, 2015). One approach for ensuring effective communication among the team is called **the huddle** (IHI, 2018). These team-driven, stand-up meetings facilitate interprofessional collaboration and improved quality management communication. Usually lasting no longer than 10 minutes, the huddle should occur at a consistent time of day, such as at the beginning of a shift. However, a huddle can be called at any time of day if an issue arises that needs to be resolved. The huddle should take place in front of a bulletin board where an agenda and all relevant key performance indicators (i.e., quality measures) are posted (Toussaint & Berry, 2013). The standard agenda includes a review of the ongoing issues, recognition of the successes in the past day, and identification of safety concerns (IHI, 2018). Covering this agenda permits teams to review performance achievement and proactively address concerns.

Many healthcare organizations hold daily management huddles led by the chief executive officer or chief nursing officer in which leaders of all departments participate. Usually held in the early morning or midday, topics include patient census, announcements of safety concerns, quality improvement successes from the previous day, key updates from each department leader, and appreciation and gratitude for staff performance. The huddle ends with a summary of tasks needed for follow-up by the next day.

During a huddle, you and your interprofessional team can use a standard communication format called **SBAR** (Scotten et al., 2015). SBAR stands for Situation, Background, Assessment, and Recommendations and was originally developed by the U.S. Navy as a situational briefing tool for members of different ranks on a nuclear submarine. Easy to remember and implement, SBAR is a clear, concise, and organized way to communicate (Figure 4.1). Since a team member can logically explain his or her recommendation, the approach makes communicating "up the ranks" more comfortable for frontline staff (Bonacum, 2008). Because SBAR sets expectations for how the message will be presented, there should be no misunderstandings among the interprofessional team about how the recommendation will be received (Woodhall, Vertacnik, & McLaughlin, 2008). According to inventor Doug Bonacum, SBAR "flattens the hierarchy" (Woodhall et al., 2008).

Even with the right team communicating regularly, certain barriers to interprofessional collaboration will create difficulties for your healthcare quality management efforts. The various professions approach problem-solving in different ways. For example, nurses typically address the immediate problems directly, then return to patient care (Tucker & Edmondson, 2002). On the other hand, physicians are trained to efficiently gather information on the history and symptoms, generate hypotheses from a set of most likely causes, test their speculations through diagnostic tools, and then recommend a solution—a problem-solving process

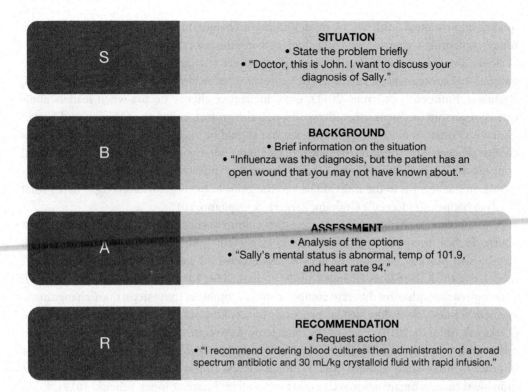

FIGURE 4.1 Situation, Background, Assessment, and Recommendations (SBAR) standard for interprofessional communication.

known as the "differential diagnosis" (Feightner, Barrows, Neufeld, & Norman, 1977). Consequently, nurses may develop solutions for a single problem that may not solve the root cause, and physicians may address the symptoms, but not the underlying causes of the quality management problem. Both problem-solving approaches may be efficient from the perspective of their jobs, but the overall efforts are ineffective for quality management in collaborative settings (Institute of Medicine, 2001).

Interprofessional collaboration can create conflict, but teamwork without conflict may not be possible (Pfeffer, 1997). Interpersonal conflict may actually provide opportunities for quality management teams to learn about each other's professions, build mutual respect, and harness the discipline-specific knowledge of each profession to solve problems (Institute of Medicine Committee on the Health Professions Education Summit, 2003; Manojlovich et al., 2014). It is expected that leaders should encourage the quality management team to evolve the conflict into collaboration that produces sustainable solutions (Kalishman, Stoddard, & O'Sullivan, 2012).

CHANGE MANAGEMENT

Your organization may not be ready to make the changes necessary to support your quality management initiatives. **Change management** is any action or process taken to move from how things currently are to how you want them to be (Varkey & Antonio, 2010). Every quality improvement initiative is, by definition, a change initiative. Nothing can improve unless something changes. Managing change, therefore, is a critical skill for you to master.

There are common mistakes for managing culture change that can lead to serious organizational consequences, such as high turnover or cynical attitudes among staff (Bordia, Restubog, Jimmieson, & Irmer, 2011). First, ineffective change occurs when leaders abdicate sponsorship or disengage midway through the project, called the "Launch and Leave" (Adams, O'Brien, & Scruth, 2015). Instead, you should be visible and active throughout the change process. Also, negative language (e.g., "here's what you're doing wrong") can derail your organization's culture. Instead, frame the quality improvement issues positively by focusing on the benefits to the individuals and the gains to the organization (e.g., "here's what needs to happen to succeed"; Graham, Ziegert, & Capitano, 2015).

You can learn to change your organizational culture to support your quality management efforts. In fact, there are popular change management frameworks that follow a distinct, step-by-step process, including Kotter's 8-Step Process for Leading Change, the ADKAR® model, and the Kübler-Ross Change Curve™ (Hiatt, 2006; Kotter, 1996; Kübler-Ross, 1969). Although each emphasizes different components and combines some steps, these change management frameworks follow similar processes for creating successful organizational change (Varkey & Antonio, 2010). Each of the change models requires you to focus on people and relationships in order to change the organization and to encourage people to adopt change in order to successfully achieve organizational success (Varkey & Antonio, 2010). Without individual change, organizational change is impossible (Bleich & Jones-Schenk, 2019).

ADKAR Model

One well-known change model is the ADKAR model (Figure 4.2). Developed by Jeffrey Hiatt, ADKAR stands for Awareness, Desire, Knowledge, Ability, and Reinforcement (Hiatt, 2006). These five words describe the five phases that people go through as they undergo a change.

Awareness focuses on making team members understand the need for the change. Success in this step requires that you understand others' perceptions of the current state (Bleich & Jones-Schenk, 2019). If an individual agrees that a quality problem exists, then that person may welcome change. However, change will be resisted if the person is satisfied with the status quo.

Desire refers to the readiness of a person to support the change. This phase focuses on identifying intrinsic motivators of team members and how to elicit the desire to support the change, if they do not already have it. During this phase, you should listen to the concerns of your team about the change. In response to someone's fear of change, you should focus on the benefits to the individual and the organization and instill optimism in your team (Hiatt, 2006).

The *Knowledge* phase focuses on providing the appropriate education and training to ensure people have the skills to work in their new reality. It also details any expected behavioral changes that are part of the change effort. Your team should understand their new roles and responsibilities associated with the change.

Ability is about turning that knowledge into change and ensuring the team can implement the new process at the required performance level. You and your team will gain the quality management ability through completing the Case Application Exercise for the case studies

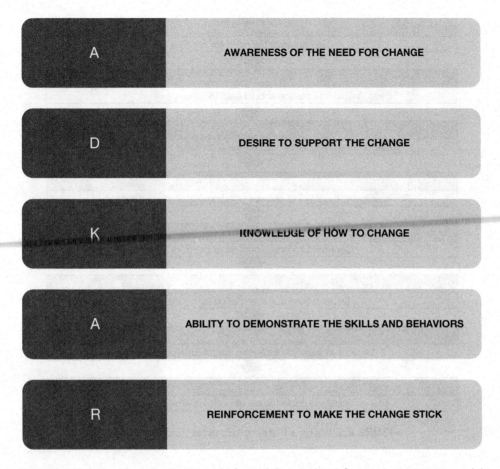

FIGURE 4.2 Awareness, Desire, Knowledge, Ability, and Reinforcement (ADKAR) model.

in Part Two of this casebook, developing your ability to solve real-world healthcare quality problems.

The *Reinforcement* phase focuses on putting processes and systems in place, because the hardest part of any change effort is to sustain the new process and behaviors. In this phase, celebration and recognition will reinforce your team's behaviors. Metrics and audits are also part of the reinforcement phase. If performance is not up to the standard, one or more of the ADKAR phases should be repeated.

Kotter's 8-Step Process for Leading Change

The best-selling book, *Leading Change* by John P. Kotter, describes **Kotter's 8-Step Process for Leading Change** that promotes organizational transformation by engaging individuals through an urgent and compelling vision for change (Figure 4.3; Kotter, 1996). Written for a broad business-oriented audience, the change framework has been successfully applied to healthcare quality management initiatives (Noble, Lemer, & Stanton, 2011; Small et al., 2016).

Step 1: Create a Sense of Urgency—Only when your team accepts the view that a need for change does in fact exist can you establish a sense of urgency for change

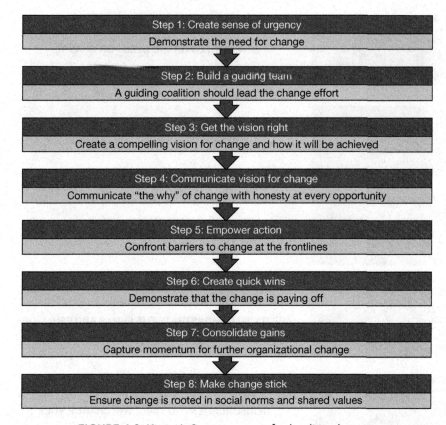

FIGURE 4.3 Kotter's 8-step process for leading change.

(Armenakis & Harris, 2009). You need to create a "burning platform" that vividly describes the discrepancy between how things are and how you want them to be (Kotter, 1996; Kotter & Cohen, 2002). For example, you can show the clinical staff how the medication administration process is broken and describe dire consequences to the patients when adverse events occur. Then you should explain how a new process will protect patients from harm. Establishing an emotional connection to the need for change is critical to generating a sense of urgency (Kotter & Cohen, 2002).

Step 2: Build a Guiding Team—You should choose an enthusiastic team of people to guide the organization through the change. The coalition must have the relevant knowledge, skills, and authority to effect change. In healthcare, the team should include members from all appropriate professions, such as physicians, nurses, allied health personnel, and health administrators, who are representative of the organization (Varkey & Antonio, 2010). Whenever possible, the guiding team should include patient representatives.

Step 3: Get the Vision Right—Leaders of quality management express an intention for improvement (Black, Miller, & Sensel, 2016). You should devise a clear, consistent, and motivating vision that explains "the why" of change. Your vision for change should explain how the patients will be impacted and how the performance of your organization will improve. This is called "unity of purpose."

Step 4: Communicate Vision for Change—Inform people of the need for change and describe your vision for the future at every opportunity (Appelbaum, Habashy, Malo, & Shafiq, 2012). You should make clear and compelling statements about quality improvement—and repeat them often—so your organization mobilizes its energies toward the same goals (Gill, 2002). You should be able to describe—in a couple of sentences—why your change is important and how the future will be different. Speak honestly and speak often. Do not forget to listen, because "two-way communication is always more powerful than one-way communication" (Kotter, 1996, p. 90).

Step 5: Empower Action—Because healthcare delivery is so complex, frontline staff may find it difficult to know what tasks are most important. It will be your job as a leader of healthcare quality management to clarify priorities (Toussaint & Berry, 2013). Frontline staff should be given the independence and authority to identify and solve healthcare quality problems (Small et al., 2016). You should support your quality management teams with resources, such as quality improvement facilitators, and remove obstacles, such as unnecessary workload. Reward quality improvement initiatives, especially those initiated independently by the frontline staff (Kotter & Cohen, 2002).

Step 6: Create Quick Wins—Short-term wins demonstrate that your change effort is paying off, which will create momentum for continuous change (Kotter, 1996). For example, a short-term success of a process improvement may enable nurses to complete their tasks more efficiently and allow them to leave work on time (Small et al., 2016).

Step 7: Consolidate Gains—The quick win does not mean the job is finished (Kotter & Cohen, 2002). Instead, use the positive momentum to continue the quality improvement cycle. Just like continuous quality improvement cycles, change management is an iterative process of planning, implementation, and learning and then sharing that learning throughout your organization (Kerber & Buono, 2005).

Step 8: Make Change Stick—When you have made your changes the norm, you have succeeded. To sustain the success, you should relentlessly communicate to your team how the changes—especially those associated with improved patient outcomes—have impacted your organizational performance (Noble et al., 2011).

The Kübler-Ross Change Curve™

The **Kübler-Ross Change Curve**™ evolved from Elisabeth Kübler-Ross's 1969 book, *On Death and Dying*, that presented the five stages of grief (Figure 4.4; Kübler-Ross, 1969). These are the typical emotions people experience while dealing with loss associated with a terminal illness or the death of a loved one. The stages have been adapted into the Kübler-Ross Change Curve to describe how people react to significant change at work. The five famous psychological stages—Denial, Anger, Bargaining, Depression, Acceptance (DABDA)—cause fluctuations in confidence and morale over time. The stages were not intended as a step-by-step process, but rather as common responses to change that you can expect from your team. Individual team members may go through the change curve at different times or even skip steps (Goodman & Loh, 2011). If you understand the typical reactions to change, you can help to ease the potential negativity that may derail your quality management initiatives (Mind Tools, 2019).

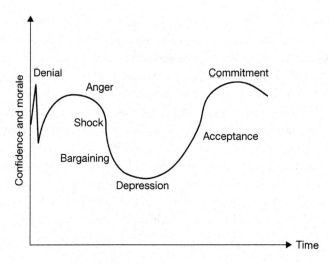

FIGURE 4.4 Kübler-Ross Change Curve.

Denial and Shock—Your team's initial response to change may be shock or denial. They may erect a temporary defense to give them time to absorb news of the change. Give your team as much information about the change as possible.

Anger—Then, as reality of the change sinks in, people tend to react with anger, criticism, or frustration. They will blame you or the system. Listen to their concerns and prepare for the objections that people may have. Take action to minimize the stress people will likely experience.

Bargaining—In the next stage, people will bargain to postpone the expected change. They may say, "What if we do this other thing instead of the change you're recommending?" Show them respect by blending their suggestions with your intended change and answer the question, What's in it for me? (Maurer, 1996).

Depression—Once the inevitability of the change sinks in, the curve bottoms out in depression or low morale. Many quality management initiatives end at this point. Eventually, though, if you insist on change, your team's attitude will rebound.

Acceptance—While not fully engaged, the team members may accept the change and bravely explore the new possibilities associated with change. Make sure to support their experimentation with training and other resources.

Commitment—Finally, if you persist, your team will embrace the change with full commitment. Celebrate and reward the change.

SUMMARY

Organizational culture is a social system of human relations with shared norms, values, and assumptions that organizations manage over time. You can create an organizational culture responsive to healthcare quality management. However, you will face many cultural barriers, such as complacency with current performance, lack of organizational commitment, and resistance to change. To overcome these cultural barriers, you should learn from the successes of healthcare organizations that emphasize a just culture, encourage leadership at all levels of the organization, and foster teamwork among the interprofessional team.

To create change, you must identify what needs to change, assess your team's readiness for change, communicate with urgency why the current system should change, offer clear ideas on better ways to operate, explain how changes will lead to improvement, and empower an interprofessional team to plan, test, implement, disseminate, and sustain the change within the organization through celebration. There are popular change management models, such as the ADKAR model, Kotter's 8-Step Process for Leading Change, and the Kübler-Ross Change Curve™, that can improve your likelihood of creating a culture receptive to healthcare quality management.

DISCUSSION QUESTIONS

1. Identify what you think is the most important cultural characteristic for a healthcare organization to adopt to achieve improved patient outcomes. Why?

2. Which cultural barrier would be the most harmful to healthcare quality management efforts? Why?

3. Describe how an organization can penalize actions associated with ineptitude, impairment, or intransigence, but still maintain a just culture (open dialogue, elimination of fear, and the ability to escalate problems). Give at least one example.

4. Of the questions leaders should ask in a culture of quality, which do you think is most important to improving healthcare quality? Why?

5. Which of the change management models presented in this chapter (Kotter's 8-Step Process for Leading Change, the ADKAR® model, and the Kübler-Ross Change Curve™) would you prefer to employ for quality management initiatives? Why?

REFERENCES

Adams, C., O'Brien, R., & Scruth, E. (2015). Transformational quality in Kaiser Permanente Northern California. *Quality Management in Health Care, 24*(1), 4–8. doi:10.1097/qmh.0000000000000015

Afsar-Manesh, N., Lonowski, S., & Namavar, A. A. (2017). Leveraging Lean principles in creating a comprehensive quality program: The UCLA health readmission reduction initiative. *Healthcare (Amsterdam, Netherlands), 5*(4), 194–198. doi:10.1016/j.hjdsi.2016.12.002

Agency for Healthcare Research and Quality. (2013). Module 14: Creating quality improvement teams and QI plans. In *Practice facilitation handbook*. Rockville, MD: Author. Retrieved from https://www.ahrq.gov/professionals/prevention-chronic-care/improve/system/pfhandbook/mod14.html

Agency for Healthcare Research and Quality. (2014). Toolkit for implementing the chronic care model in an academic environment. Retrieved from https://www.ahrq.gov/prevention/curriculum/chroniccaremodel/index.html

Agency for Healthcare Research and Quality. (2017). What is patient experience? Retrieved from https://www.ahrq.gov/cahps/about-cahps/patient-experience/index.html

Alexander, J. A., Weiner, B. J., Shortell, S. M., Baker, L. C., & Becker, M. P. (2006). The role of organizational infrastructure in implementation of hospitals' quality improvement. *Hospital Topics, 84*(1), 11–20. doi:10.3200/htps.84.1.11-21

Appelbaum, S. H., Habashy, S., Malo, J. L., & Shafiq, H. (2012). Back to the future: Revisiting Kotter's 1996 change model. *Journal of Management Development, 31*(8), 764–782. doi:10.1108/02621711211253231

Armenakis, A., & Harris, S. (2009). Reflections: Our journey in organizational change research and practice. *Journal of Change Management, 9*(2), 127–142. doi:10.1080/14697010902879079

Berwick, D. M. (1996). A primer on leading the improvement of systems. *BMJ, 312*(7031), 619–622. doi:10.1136/bmj.312.7031.619

Berwick, D. M. (2009). What 'patient-centered' should mean: Confessions of an extremist. *Health Affairs (Project Hope), 28*(4), w555–w565. doi:10.1377/hlthaff.28.4.w555

Black, J., Miller, D., & Sensel, J. (2016). *The Toyota way to healthcare excellence: Increase efficiency and improve quality with Lean* (2nd ed.). Chicago, IL: Health Administration Press.

Bleich, M. R., & Jones-Schenk, J. (2019). 70% Failure rate: An imperative for better change management. *Journal of Continuing Education in Nursing, 50*(4), 148–149. doi:10.3928/00220124-20190319-03

Bonacum, D. (2008). Profiles in improvement: Doug Bonacum of Kaiser Permanente. Retrieved from http://www.ihi.org/resources/Pages/AudioandVideo/ProfilesinImprovementDougBonacumofKaiserPermanente.aspx

Bordia, P., Restubog, S. L. D., Jimmieson, N. L., & Irmer, B. E. (2011). Haunted by the past: Effects of poor change management history on employee attitudes and turnover. *Group & Organization Management, 36*(2), 191–222. doi:10.1177/1059601110392990

Boysen, P. G., II. (2013). Just culture: A foundation for balanced accountability and patient safety. *The Ochsner Journal, 13*(3), 400–406. Retrieved from https://www.ncbi.nlm.nih.gov/pmc/articles/PMC3776518

Bradley, E. H., Curry, L. A., Spatz, E. S., Herrin, J., Cherlin, E. J., Curtis, J. P., ... Krumholz, H. M. (2012). Hospital strategies for reducing risk-standardized mortality rates in acute myocardial infarction. *Annals of Internal Medicine, 156*(9), 618–626. doi:10.7326/0003-4819-156-9-201205010-00003

Braithwaite, J., Herkes, J., Ludlow, K., Testa, L., & Lamprell, G. (2017). Association between organisational and workplace cultures, and patient outcomes: Systematic review. *BMJ Open, 7*(11), e013758. doi:10.1136/bmjopen-2017-017708

Carney, M. (2011). Influence of organizational culture on quality healthcare delivery. *International Journal of Health Care Quality Assurance, 24*(7), 523–539.

Cleary, P. D. (2016). Evolving concepts of patient-centered care and the assessment of patient care experiences: Optimism and opposition. *Journal of Health Politics Policy and Law, 41*(4), 675–696. doi:10.1215/03616878-3620881

Dempsey, C., Reilly, B., & Buhlman, N. (2014). Improving the patient experience: Real-world strategies for engaging nurses. *Journal of Nursing Administration, 44*(3), 142–151. doi:10.1097/nna.0000000000000042

Dixon-Woods, M., McNicol, S., & Martin, G. (2012). Ten challenges in improving quality in healthcare: Lessons from the Health Foundation's programme evaluations and relevant literature. *BMJ Quality & Safety, 21*(10), 876–884. doi:10.1136/bmjqs-2011-000760

Edmondson, A. C. (2004). Learning from failure in health care: Frequent opportunities, pervasive barriers. *Quality & Safety in Health Care, 13*, 3–9. doi:10.1136/qshc.2003.009597

Fan, C. J., Pawlik, T. M., Daniels, T., Vernon, N., Banks, K., Westby, P., ... Makary, M. A. (2016). Association of safety culture with surgical site infection outcomes. *Journal of the American College of Surgeons, 222*(2), 122–128. doi:10.1016/j.jamcollsurg.2015.11.008

Feightner, J. W., Barrows, H. S., Neufeld, V. R., & Norman, G. R. (1977). Solving problems—How does family physician do it? *Canadian Family Physician, 23*, 67–71. Retrieved from https://www.ncbi.nlm.nih.gov/pmc/articles/PMC2378939

Gill, R. (2002). Change management--or change leadership? *Journal of Change Management, 3*, 307–318. doi:10.1080/714023845

Godfrey, M. M., Andersson-Gare, B., Nelson, E. C., Nilsson, M., & Ahlstrom, G. (2014). Coaching interprofessional health care improvement teams: The coachee, the coach and the leader perspectives. *Journal of Nursing Management, 22*(4), 452–464. doi:10.1111/jonm.12068

Goodman, E., & Loh, L. (2011). Organizational change: A critical challenge for team effectiveness. *Business Information Review, 28*(4), 242–250. doi:10.1177/0266382111427087

Graham, K. A., Ziegert, J. C., & Capitano, J. (2015). The effect of leadership style, framing, and promotion regulatory focus on unethical pro-organizational behavior. *Journal of Business Ethics, 126*(3), 423–436. doi:10.1007/s10551-013-1952-3

Greenslade, J. H., & Jimmieson, N. L. (2011). Organizational factors impacting on patient satisfaction: A cross sectional examination of service climate and linkages to nurses' effort and performance. *International Journal of Nursing Studies, 48*(10), 1188–1198. doi:10.1016/j.ijnurstu.2011.04.004

Hansen, L. O., Williams, M. V., & Singer, S. J. (2011). Perceptions of hospital safety climate and incidence of readmission. *Health Services Research, 46*(2), 596–616. doi:10.1111/j.1475-6773.2010.01204.x

Herndon, J. H. (2015). Editorial comment—Symposium: Patient safety: Collaboration, communication, and physician leadership. *Clinical Orthopaedics and Related Research, 473*(5), 1566–1567. doi:10.1007/s11999-014-4122-8

Hiatt, J. M. (2006). *ADKAR: A model for change in business, government, and our community.* Loveland, CO: Prosci Learning Center Publications.

Institute for Healthcare Improvement. (2013). A promise to learn—A commitment to act: Improving the safety of patients in England. London, UK: National Advisory Group. Retrieved from https://assets.publishing.service.gov.uk/government/uploads/system/uploads/attachment_data/file/226703/Berwick_Report.pdf

Institute for Healthcare Improvement. (2018). Daily huddles. Retrieved from http://www.ihi.org/resources/Pages/Tools/Huddles.aspx

Institute of Medicine. (2001). *Crossing the quality chasm: A new health system for the 21st century.* Washington, DC: National Academies Press. Retrieved from http://www.nationalacademies.org/hmd/Global/News%20Announcements/Crossing-the-Quality-Chasm-The-IOM-Health-Care-Quality-Initiative.aspx

Institute of Medicine Committee on the Health Professions Education Summit. (2003). *Health professions education: A bridge to quality.* Washington, DC: National Academies Press. Retrieved from https://www.nap.edu/catalog/10681/health-professions-education-a-bridge-to-quality

Kalishman, S., Stoddard, H., & O'Sullivan, P. (2012). Don't manage the conflict: Transform it through collaboration. *Medical Education, 46*(10), 930–932. doi:10.1111/j.1365-2923.2012.04342.x

Kerber, K., & Buono, A. F. (2005). Rethinking organizational change: Reframing the challenge of change management. *Organization Development Journal, 23*(3), 23.

Kotter, J. P. (1996). *Leading change: An action plan from the world's foremost expert on business leadership.* Cambridge, MA: Harvard Business Review Press.

Kotter, J. P., & Cohen, D. S. (2002). *The heart of change: Real-life stories of how people change their organizations.* Cambridge, MA: Harvard Business Review Press.

Kübler-Ross, E. (1969). *On death and dying: What the dying have to teach doctors, nurses, clergy, and their own families.* New York, NY: Scribner.

Langley, G. L., Moen, R. D., Nolan, K. M., Nolan, T. W., Norman, C. L., & Provost, L. P. (2009). *The improvement guide: A practical approach to enhancing organizational performance* (2nd ed.). San Francisco, CA: Jossey-Bass Publishers.

Leape, L. (1999). Medical Mistakes, U.S. Senate, One Hundred and Sixth Congress Session.

Mahl, S., Lee, S. K., Baker, G. R., Cronin, C. M. G., Stevens, B., Ye, X. Y., & Canadian Institutes of Health Research Team in Maternal-Infant Care. (2015). The association of organizational culture and quality improvement implementation with neonatal outcomes in the NICU. *Journal of Pediatric Health Care, 29*(5), 435–441. doi:10.1016/j.pedhc.2015.01.011

Manojlovich, M., Kerr, M., Davies, B., Squires, J., Mallick, R., & Rodger, G. L. (2014). Achieving a climate for patient safety by focusing on relationships. *International Journal for Quality in Health Care, 26*(6), 579–584. doi:10.1093/intqhc/mzu068

Mardon, R. E., Khanna, K., Sorra, J., Dyer, N., & Famolaro, T. (2010). Exploring relationships between hospital patient safety culture and adverse events. *Journal of Patient Safety, 6*(4), 226–232. doi:10.1097/PTS.0b013e3181fd1a00

Marquardt, M. (2014). *Leading with questions: How leaders find the right solutions by knowing what to ask.* San Francisco, CA: Jossey-Bass.

Maurer, R. (1996). Using resistance to build support for change. *The Journal for Quality and Participation, 19*(3), 56.

Mind Tools. (2019). The change curve: Accelerating change, and increasing its likelihood of success. Retrieved from https://www.mindtools.com/pages/article/newPPM_96.htm

Noble, D. J., Lemer, C., & Stanton, E. (2011). What has change management in industry got to do with improving patient safety? *Postgraduate Medical Journal, 87*(1027), 345–348. doi:10.1136/pgmj.2010.097923

Pfeffer, J. (1997). *New directions in organizational theory* (pp. 98–100). New York, NY: Oxford University Press.

Poksinska, B. (2010). The current state of Lean implementation in health care: Literature review. *Quality Management in Health Care, 19*(4), 319–329. doi: 10.1097/QMH.0b013e3181fa07bb

Robbins, A. (2019). The problem with satisfied patients. Retrieved from https://www.theatlantic.com/health/archive/2015/04/the-problem-with-satisfied-patients/390684

Roberts, V., & Perryman, M. M. (2007). Creating a culture for health care quality and safety. *The Health Care Manager, 26*(2), 155–158. doi: 10.1097/01.HCM.0000268620.79233.8a

Schein, E. H. (2010). *Organizational culture and leadership*. Hoboken, NJ: John Wiley & Sons.

Scotten, M., Manos, E. L., Malicoat, A., & Paolo, A. M. (2015). Minding the gap: Interprofessional communication during inpatient and post discharge chasm care. *Patient Education and Counseling, 98*(7), 895–900. doi:10.1016/j.pec.2015.03.009

Shaffer, F. A., & Tuttas, C. A. (2009). Nursing leadership's responsibility for patient quality, safety, and satisfaction: Current review and analysis. *Nurse Leader, 7*(3), 34–38. doi:10.1016/j.mnl/2009.03.011

Small, A., Gist, D., Souza, D., Dalton, J., Magny-Normilus, C., & David, D. (2016). Using Kotter's change model for implementing bedside handoff: A quality improvement project. *Journal of Nursing Care Quality, 31*(4), 304–309. doi:10.1097/ncq.0000000000000212

Speroff, T., Nwosu, S., Greevy, R., Weinger, M. B., Talbot, T. R., Wall, R. J., ... Dittus, R. S. (2010). Organisational culture: Variation across hospitals and connection to patient safety climate. *Quality & Safety in Health Care, 19*(6), 592–596. doi:10.1136/qshc.2009.039511

Swift, J. A., Omachonu, V. K., & Ross, J. E. (1998). Strategic quality planning. In V. K. Omachonu & J. E. Ross (Eds.), *Principles of total quality* (pp. 59–79). Boca Raton, FL: St. Lucie Press.

Toussaint, J. S., & Berry, L. L. (2013). The promise of Lean in health care. *Mayo Clinic Proceedings, 88*(1), 74-82. doi:10.1016/j.mayocp.2012.07.025

Tsai, T. C., Jha, A. K., Gawande, A. A., Huckman, R. S., Bloom, N., & Sadun, R. (2015). Hospital board and management practices are strongly related to hospital performance on clinical quality metrics. *Health Affairs, 34*(8), 1304–1311. doi:10.1377/hlthaff.2014.1282

Tucker, A. L., & Edmondson, A. C. (2002). Managing routine exceptions: A model of nurse problem solving behaviour. In A. L. Tucker & A. C. Edmondson (Eds.), *Advances in health care management* (*Vol. 3*, pp. 87–113). Bingley, UK: Emerald Group Publishing Limited.

Varkey, P., & Antonio, K. (2010). Change management for effective quality improvement: A primer. *American Journal of Medical Quality, 25*(4), 268–273. doi:10.1177/1062860610361625

Woodhall, L. J., Vertacnik, L., & McLaughlin, M. (2008). Implementation of the SBAR communication technique in a tertiary center. *Journal of Emergency Nursing, 34*(4), 314–317. doi:10.1016/j.jen.2007.07.007

World Health Organization. (2010). *Framework for action on interprofessional education and collaborative practice (WHO/HRH/HPN/10.3)*. Geneva, Switzerland: Author. Retrieved from http://www.who.int/hrh/resources/framework_action/en

Young, T., & McClean, S. (2009). Some challenges facing Lean thinking in healthcare. *International Journal for Quality in Health Care, 21*(5), 309–310. doi:10.1093/intqhc/mzp038

CHAPTER 5

The Casebook

OBJECTIVES

1. Distinguish an active problem-based learning approach from a more passive style of learning.
2. Describe how the case method supports learning of healthcare quality management.
3. Examine the problem-based learning cycle in the context of the exercises and discussion questions provided in this casebook.
4. Assess the motivation for healthcare quality management courses evolving to the case method.
5. Identify the case studies that support healthcare professional competency development for health administrators, nurses, physicians, and the interprofessional team.

HOW TO USE THIS CASEBOOK

Problem-Based Learning and the Case Method

You face enormous challenges to improve the U.S. healthcare system and serious cultural barriers at your organization. Fortunately, you do not have to fix it on your own. The quality management innovators developed proven problem-solving approaches. Now, it is up to you to adopt the mindset, master the skills, and build organizational culture responsive to your healthcare quality management efforts. This casebook will help. The case method strips away passive teaching in favor of active, team-based learning through realistic and challenging case studies. If you commit to the problem-based learning approach and the practical application of quality management, you will achieve the standard of quality that patients and their caregivers deserve.

The **case method** is a prominent form of problem-based learning (Hmelo-Silver, 2004). The history of the case method dates back hundreds of years to the days of craftsmen apprentices (Allchin, 2013). More recently, schools of business, medicine, nursing, law, education, and engineering have adopted the case method to train their students (Kim et al., 2006). Harvard Business School instituted the case method as early as 1912 (Mesny, 2013), and over a century later, they still view the case method as "the best way to prepare students for the challenges of leadership" (Harvard Business School, n.d., para. 3).

Ideally, case studies involve realistic and complex situations in which problems are solved, decisions made, or policies reconsidered. When utilized for problem-based learning purposes, case studies should not act merely as "teasers" (Allchin, 2013). Instead, effective case studies feature messy scenarios, all the better to prepare you to solve real-world problems (Allchin, 2013). Well-constructed case studies place you in the role of problem solver, requiring you to define the problem, assess the facts, uncover false assumptions, and discard distractions (Savery, 2015). When analyzing the case studies in Part Two of this casebook, you will apply your new skills to articulate the problem statement, analyze the problem, and seek evidence outside the case study to recommend potential solutions (Gamble & Jelley, 2014).

In Part Two of this casebook, case studies are separated into four major sections: (a) process improvement, (b) patient safety, (c) patient experience, and (d) performance improvement. The diverse collection of case studies describes management problems from a variety of healthcare settings, including hospitals (large and small, urban and rural, academic and community), postacute care facilities (skilled nursing facilities, rehabilitation), managed care organizations, outpatient clinics, and home care. Each case study tells a unique healthcare story with conflict, emotion, humor, and true-to-life characters.

Case Application Exercises

You and your team will complete the **Case Application Exercise** for each case in Part Two using the A3 problem-solving template (see Chapter 6, The Template). Each Case Application Exercise will follow the steps based on the problem-based learning cycle described by Hmelo-Silver and Eberbach (2012).

1. Explore the scenario—Each case study presents you with an authentic, complex quality management scenario containing at least one ill-structured problem (Barrows, 1986; Hmelo-Silver, 2004). Although your instructor may prefer certain problem statements or countermeasures, there is no single correct answer. Problem-based learning encourages varying perspectives, especially when correctly reasoned and effectively supported with evidence. Alternative problem definitions, analyses, or creative solutions can—and should—be discussed with your team and instructor.

2. Engage in self-directed learning—The problem-based learning method makes you responsible for your independent learning (Savery, 2015). Although your instructor will be your guide, you must identify the relevant facts in the case study scenario, formulate the problem statement, generate the research question, analyze the problem, and develop potential solutions. You will acquire evidence to support your problem-solving through the four sources of evidence-based management, as presented in Chapter 3, The Mindset, especially peer-reviewed literature. Make note of the references following each case study, as these sources may be a good place to start your research. Furthermore, each case study will feature data files—some quite extensive—that will require your analysis. This casebook provides data files in the Microsoft® Excel® spreadsheet format.

3. Apply new knowledge to the problem—A new quality management tool or approach will be introduced for each case study in this casebook. You are encouraged to apply each tool or approach to previous or subsequent cases, as necessary. For

example, a fishbone diagram is a type of root cause analysis that will be introduced in Part Two and can be used to analyze case studies throughout the casebook. At first, you may feel uncertain about applying new quality management tools without explicit instruction (Dahlgren & Dahlgren, 2002), but research shows that when learning is self-directed, you are more likely to transfer your knowledge to new situations (Hmelo-Silver, Chernobilsky, & DaCosta, 2004).

4. Collaborate in learning groups—The problem-based learning approach encourages collaborative learning (Savery, 2015). You will work with a small group of empowered learners to solve professionally relevant problems. Teamwork can take place in face-to-face or online learning environments. To maximize the power of collaborative engagement, you and your team should assure individual contribution and accountability (Allchin, 2013). In other words, following your independent analysis, you should present your perspective regarding the case study to your group. Again, there is no single right answer to case study analysis. It is very likely that you and your team will have different views on the problem definition, root cause analysis, or potential countermeasures. This is okay. You should work as a team to refine your case study analysis and agree on the most appropriate problem statement and best set of solutions. Assuming adequate individual preparation, teamwork among many unique contributors will actually enhance your creative problem-solving (Greeno, Collins, & Resnick, 1996).

5. Obtain instructor guidance—In the problem-based learning approach, your instructor becomes the facilitator—no longer the bearer of knowledge—who will steer you to a collection of facts, application of tools, and development of solutions (Hmelo-Silver, 2004), and who will guide you through the learning process through facilitation, modeling, and questioning (Hmelo-Silver & Eberbach, 2012). Early in the quality management learning process, the instructor will facilitate the completion of the Case Application Exercise, and may ask, "Have you tried this quality management tool?" After you gain more problem-solving experience, the instructor will model the role of the "expert learner," rather than the provider of content knowledge. He or she may suggest, "It seems to me that those problems are related" or "Maybe that problem is really a symptom of another root cause." After you hone your problem-solving skills and master the Case Application Exercise process, your instructor will adopt a more questioning role, encouraging you to justify your thinking, and may ask, "What evidence makes you think that solution will solve this problem?"

6. Reflect on new knowledge—You should answer the discussion questions provided at the end of each Case Application Exercise. The case study discussion questions encourage reflection on the professional competencies required for effective quality management, such as community collaboration, accountability, interpersonal understanding, and leadership. Case study scenarios and character behaviors were created to present you with successful (and unsuccessful) expressions of professional competencies. You should reflect how your newly acquired knowledge relates to your prior understanding of quality management. The reflection process will help you transfer the problem-solving approaches to new situations (Hmelo-Silver & Eberbach, 2012).

COMPETENCIES OF A HEALTHCARE QUALITY MANAGEMENT WORKFORCE

The shift from the traditional lecture-and-examination instruction to problem-based learning using the case method has been partly motivated by higher education accrediting bodies, such as the Commission on Accreditation of Healthcare Management Education (CAHME, 2018) and the Accreditation Council on Graduate Medical Education (LaMantia, 2002). Accrediting bodies mandate that academic programs adopt a competency-based curriculum, informed by models such as the National Center Healthcare Leadership model (NCHL, 2018). Competencies create a common language about performance standards regarding professional knowledge, skills, abilities, and judgment that would be valuable in the workplace (Garman, 2018).

Academic programs must assess competency attainment at a range of cognitive skill levels—from lower level understanding to higher level analyzing, evaluating, or creating (Bloom, Engelhart, Furst, Hill, & Krathwohl, 1956). In response to the need to assess attainment of higher levels of competency, healthcare quality management courses have evolved to require group collaboration and case study analysis. This casebook supports your instructor's teaching evolution and your competency development.

Healthcare Administrators

Healthcare administrators manage and lead healthcare systems. Healthcare administrators include executive leaders, middle management, and frontline administrative staff, who may have achieved advanced graduate education and professional certification (Garman, Leach, & Spector, 2006). In healthcare quality management, administrators identify and resolve opportunities for improvement (White & Griffith, 2015). Healthcare administrators add value through coordination, team building, and conflict mediation (Begun, White, & Mosser, 2011). Healthcare administrators champion the quality management culture, hold quality improvement teams accountable for outcomes of projects, and support quality projects with resources, such as allocating administrative time for clinicians and creating quality-related organizational governance structures (Begun et al., 2011; Bradley, Webster, Schlesinger, Baker, & Inouye, 2006; Goeschel, Wachter, & Pronovost, 2010). Healthcare administrators even play an important quality management role for clinical processes that they may not fully understand (Begun et al., 2011).

The CAHME (2018) standards require that accredited university programs of health management rigorously assess student competencies. There is no universally accepted health administration competency model (Begun, Butler, & Stefl, 2018), but many programs have embraced the NCHL model. Some programs modify the NCHL model, and others create alternatives to match their educational mission, student developmental needs, and healthcare industry stakeholder requirements (Begun et al., 2018; Broom & Gentry, 2018; Clement et al., 2010). Nevertheless, this casebook was created to enhance your development of essential health administration competencies.

Most obviously, this casebook will develop your competency in "process and quality improvement" (Clement et al., 2010; Mangelsdorff, 2014; NCHL, 2018). According to the

NCHL (2018), healthcare leaders must be able to improve organizational process through skills in process mapping, benchmarking, organizational design, and the principles of high reliability and continuous quality improvement (NCHL, 2018). Completing any of the case studies provided in Part Two of this casebook will support your process and quality improvement competency development.

In addition, you will enhance other essential NCHL health administration competencies by completing the Case Application Exercises in this casebook. First, you will improve your "analytical thinking" competency. Analytical thinking requires that you investigate a problem systematically and make connections between cause and effect, which is a skill fundamental to completing the Case Application Exercises (NCHL, 2018). Analytical thinking can also be viewed as skill with numbers, called "quantitative analysis" in many competency models (Clement et al., 2010; Mangelsdorff, 2014). Most cases provided in this casebook require that you analyze data files in the spreadsheet format. When completing the Case Application Exercises, you will also master the competencies of "performance measurement" (ability to use metrics to track goals for organizational performance against evidence-based criteria), "project management" (ability to create project plans with quality improvement steps, personnel responsibility assignments, and timelines for completion), and "communication skills: writing" (ability to create precise, accurate, complete, and logical written communication that conveys meaning in a manner appropriate for the audience).

Your instructor may find some health administration competencies especially difficult to assess at higher levels of cognitive complexity (Broom, Turner, & Brichto, 2016). For example, higher level competency attainment of collaboration, leadership, and interpersonal relations cannot be effectively assessed through examinations or term papers. However, through Case Application Exercises, your instructor will be able to assess your knowledge, skills, abilities, and judgment related to these domains (Barrows, 1996; Hmelo-Silver, 2004; Savery, 2015). All of the case studies in Part Two will empower you to develop the following NCHL (2018) competencies:

- Collaboration—Solicit input from your team, learn from your peers, and encourage resolution to conflict.

- Initiative—Identify a problem, clarify the situation, encourage innovative ideas, and take action.

- Information Seeking—Conduct investigations into problems by asking questions, conducting root cause analyses, and seeking expert opinions.

- Change Leadership—Define needed change and outline a change strategy.

- Communication Skills: Speaking and Facilitating—Communicate your ideas, engage in group problem-solving, and build team consensus on problem definition, analysis, and recommended solutions.

Moreover, this casebook will enable you to develop other NCHL competencies through team collaboration and application of skills required by select case studies. Table 5.1 demonstrates the competencies addressed by designated case studies provided in Part Two.

Table 5.1 Case Studies Relevant to Select Health Administration Competencies

COMPETENCY	CASES
Community Collaboration—Engage external stakeholders to achieve a community need	Case 18: A Mom's Story of Sepsis Case 20: Opioid Overdoses in the Emergency Department Case 25: Community Collaboration for Suicide Prevention
Organizational Awareness—Recognize formal and informal decision-making structures and power relationships	Case 1: A Summer Internship Journal Case 4: The Ophthalmologist Who Could Not See (The Waste) Case 5: Building a New IR Suite Case 9: Patient Navigation at the Orthopedic Clinic Case 20: Opioid Overdoses in the Emergency Department Case 24: Both/And Thinking in Readmission Prevention
Accountability—Set standards for performance and ensure that results are achieved	Case 12: Patient Experience in Home Care Case 15: A Warning Letter From the State Regulator Case 16: Failure-to-Rescue Case 19: Operating Room Recovery Case 21: The Lunchroom: Physician Engagement at a PCMH Case 23: Composite Quality Score Case 24: Both/And Thinking in Readmission Prevention
Impact and Influence—Persuade, convince, or impress others to move toward a specific position	Case 2: Claims Payment Processing Case 4: The Ophthalmologist Who Could Not See (The Waste) Case 5: Building a New IR Suite Case 6: Emergency Department Heroes Case 10: HCAHPS and the Quiet-at-Night Measure Case 13: Reducing Patient Falls: The Sleuth Resident Case 14: Sustaining Hand Hygiene Case 12: Patient Experience in Home Care Case 17: CLIF's Medication Errors Case 20: Opioid Overdoses in the Emergency Department Case 21: The Lunchroom: Physician Engagement at a PCMH
Interpersonal Understanding—Seek to accurately interpret others' emotions, behaviors, and concerns	Case 1: A Summer Internship Journal Case 2: Claims Payment Processing Case 4: The Ophthalmologist Who Could Not See (The Waste) Case 5: Building a New IR Suite Case 9: Patient Navigation at the Orthopedic Clinic Case 10: HCAHPS and the Quiet-at-Night Measure Case 14: Sustaining Hand Hygiene Case 17: CLIF's Medication Errors Case 20: Opioid Overdoses in the Emergency Department Case 21: The Lunchroom: Physician Engagement at a PCMH Case 22: The Fulfillment Affair
Professional and Social Responsibility—Demonstrate ethics, social accountability, and sound professional behaviors	Case 8: The Cowboy Doctor's Patient Experience Case 9: Patient Navigation at the Orthopedic Clinic Case 11: Discharge Phone Calls (En Español) Case 19: Operating Room Recovery Case 20: Opioid Overdoses in the Emergency Department Case 25: Community Collaboration for Suicide Prevention

HCAHPS, Hospital Consumer Assessment of Healthcare Providers and Systems; IR, intervention radiology; PCMH, patient-centered medical home.

Nursing

Working on the frontline of clinical care, nurses are in the perfect position to identify quality problems and help design changes to improve performance (Sherwood, 2011). However, gaps regarding healthcare quality management in nursing education may exist (Fater, Weatherford, Ready, Finn, & Tangney, 2014; Tella et al., 2014). Recent teaching innovations in quality management nursing education, including the case method approach, have been shown to be an effective way for nurses to learn quality improvement and patient safety competencies in preparation for their work in the clinical setting (Ross & Bruderle, 2016, 2018).

Nurse professional competency includes quality management, performance improvement, and patient safety concepts (Greiner & Knebel, 2003; National Research Council of the National Academies, 2005). Various nursing competency models recognize quality management as essential for professional practice, including the American Association of Colleges of Nursing (AACN, n.d.), Quality and Safety Education for Nurses (Cronenwett et al., 2009), and the American Organization of Nursing Leadership (AONL, n.d.).

As nurses advance through levels of professional training, the requirements for quality management competence increase. As a baccalaureate graduate, nurses must be able to understand quality improvement concepts, processes, and outcome measures and apply them in basic quality and safety investigations (AACN, 2008). At the more advanced level of training, masters-prepared nurses must be able to monitor, analyze, prioritize, and quantify the impact of quality management initiatives designed to improve health outcomes (AACN, 2011). At the Doctor of Nursing Practice (DNP) level, graduates must be proficient in advanced communication skills in order to lead quality improvement and patient safety initiatives. DNP graduates should be able to design, direct, and evaluate quality improvement projects to create sustained changes at both the organizational and policy levels (AACN, 2006).

As nurses become leaders of healthcare organizations, they require greater professional proficiency in quality management. Nurse leaders must be able to collaborate with other organizational stakeholders, such as other executives and boards of governors, to develop strategic initiatives that establish quality performance measures consistent with accreditation and regulatory bodies (AONL, n.d.). Nurse leaders must also communicate these quality standards across the organization, identify gaps in performance, analyze variation from quality standards, recommend evidence-based interventions, control solutions, and sustain success (AONL, n.d.).

You will develop nursing-related quality management competencies through completion of the Case Application Exercises. Nurses play prominent roles in a variety of case studies in Part Two of this casebook, as listed in Table 5.2.

Medicine

Along with the basic and clinical sciences, physicians must attain competence in health systems-based practice (Skochelak et al., 2016). The health systems-based practice competency requires that physicians understand patient care within the broader healthcare system, including quality management and patient safety. Health systems constitute one of the six core competencies of graduate medical education, as defined by the Accreditation Council on Graduate Medical Education (*New England Journal of Medicine* [NEJM] Knowledge+ Team, 2016). Specifically,

Table 5.2 Case Studies for Nurses in Quality Management

CASE STUDY	NURSING ROLE
Case 1: A Summer Internship Journal	A chief nursing officer and an inpatient nursing director help direct a misguided administrative intern though the process of identifying the root causes of patient delays.
Case 6: Emergency Department Heroes	A director of nursing leads the team through a rapid improvement event in order to reduce the emergency department chaos.
Case 8: The Cowboy Doctor's Patient Experience	A patient complains of poor nurse communication. Patient experience scores are terrible, but are the nurses to blame?
Case 9: Patient Navigation at the Orthopedic Clinic	A recent bachelor of science in nursing graduate experiences an ethical dilemma and workflow issues in her new job as a patient navigator.
Case 12: Patient Experience in Home Care	Home care nurses react too late to patient complaints that negatively impact their organization's overall patient experience scores.
Case 14: Sustaining Hand Hygiene	Can the nurse in charge of infection prevention and employee health prevent unsafe hand hygiene practices at an ambulatory surgical center?
Case 15: A Warning Letter From the State Regulator	Multiple patient identification errors at the skilled nursing facility threaten their nursing home license. Blame and conflict among the nurse managers ensue. Will creating a just culture prevent future errors?
Case 16: Failure-to-Rescue	The lawyer of a fatally harmed woman's family deposes a chief nursing officer after a young nurse fails to follow correct escalation procedures. Is the chief nursing officer liable for the death of the patient?
Case 17: CLIF's Medication Errors	A nurse's critical thinking skills and good judgment prevent patient harm. What are the benefits and limitations of safety-enhancing technologies?
Case 18: A Mom's Story of Sepsis	A young boy's life is endangered when a sepsis diagnosis is missed. Without a sepsis protocol in place, can the nurses reduce the variation in sepsis care outcomes?
Case 20: Opioid Over-doses in the Emergency Department	A chief nursing officer must convince the CEO to properly identify root causes of the opioid crisis impacting the hospital's emergency depart-ment and the lives of people in their community.
Case 22: The Fulfillment Affair	Will the brilliant but bad-mannered nurse in charge of the quality de-partment identify the root cause of high-cost medical claims at the na-tion's second largest online retailer?
Case 24: Both/And Thinking in Readmission Prevention	The chief nursing officer must improve team functioning and overcome professional differences to develop best practices in hospital readmis-sion prevention.

physicians should learn to recognize system error, monitor practice, set goals for improvement, and advocate for system change. However, the health systems–based practice may be the most challenging competency domain to incorporate into medical education because of the

Table 5.3 Case Studies for Physicians in Quality Management

CASE STUDY	PHYSICIAN ROLE
Case 4: The Ophthalmologist Who Could Not See (The Waste)	An ophthalmology practice is losing money on every cataract surgery, but one-eye surgeon sees no room for improved efficiency. Can the quality improvement team convince her that waste exists throughout the process?
Case 7: Hurricane Mia Hits the Patient Access Call Center	Each of the various physician specialties of an academic medical center prefers different rules for scheduling patient appointments. Will the hurricane make patient wait times even worse?
Case 8: The Cowboy Doctor's Patient Experience	Patient complaints and low patient experience scores compel the rural hospital's chairman of the board to investigate physician communication survey results.
Case 10: HCAHPS and the Quiet-at-Night Measure	The chief medical officer doubts the validity of patient experience surveys and their value in pay-for-performance systems. Will a night spent in the hospital change his mind about the HCAHPS quiet-at-night scores?
Case 13: Reducing Patient Falls: The Sleuth Resident	A resident physician's relentless questioning and data analysis uncovers the truth about patient falls in the hospital.
Case 14: Sustaining Hand Hygiene	Clinical staff at an outpatient surgery center, including surgeons, are not compliant with the Five Moments for Hand Hygiene, leading to increasing rates of surgical site infections.
Case 18: A Mom's Story of Sepsis	When a young boy presents to the emergency department, the sepsis diagnosis is missed. Mistakes are made throughout the treatment process, leading to serious consequences for the child.
Case 20: Opioid Overdoses in the Emergency Department	A community is in crisis, and the emergency department struggles to manage opioid overdoses. Are the physicians prescribing practices to blame?
Case 21: The Lunchroom: Physician Engagement at a PCMH	A primary care practice implemented a PCMH model, but one doctor fails to meet quality targets. Will he continue to grieve the loss of the "good old days" or adopt the new value-based purchasing model?
Case 22: The Fulfillment Affair	A health plan medical director seeks to solve the mystery of the high-cost patient claims. Will the brilliant but rude quality improvement nurse just make her job more difficult?

HCAHPS, Hospital Consumer Assessment of Healthcare Providers and Systems; PCMH, patient-centered medical home.

intense demands to master other content areas, such as knowledge of disease, diagnostic skills, patient treatment, and physician–patient interactions (Johnson, Miller, & Horowitz, 2008). Nevertheless, addressing health systems–based practice curriculum in medical education using a problem-based learning approach can be successful (Pruitt et al., 2017).

This casebook will enable you to attain physician-related system-based practice competencies, such as quality improvement and patient safety. Table 5.3 features case studies with prominent physician roles in quality management.

Interprofessional Team

Interprofessional teamwork is the means by which a group of people from different professional backgrounds—with diverse knowledge, skills, and talents—collaborate to work together and with patients, their families, caregivers, and communities to deliver the highest quality of care

Table 5.4 Case Studies for the Interprofessional Team

CASE STUDY	INTERPROFESSIONAL COLLABORATION
Case 3: Return-to-Work at a Home Healthcare Agency	After a back injury, a nurse takes leave from the home health agency. The overly complicated return-to-work process vexes the treating physician, nurse manager, human resources administrator, and information technology team.
Case 4: The Ophthalmologist Who Could Not See (The Waste)	Can the interprofessional team collaborate to identify waste in the cataract surgery process?
Case 5: Building a New IR Suite	A healthcare architect takes a risk to design an innovative IR suite configured for improved patient flow.
Case 6: Emergency Department Heroes	The interprofessional team collaborates in a rapid improvement event to redesign the ED process from intake to discharge.
Case 12: Patient Experience in Home Care	Low patient satisfaction requires leaders from nursing, physical therapy, and quality improvement to commit to meeting daily for improvement.
Case 16: Failure-to-Rescue	The escalation process breaks down with errors by the cardiac monitor telemetry technician, certified nurse assistant, and nurse. The lawyers inevitably get involved.
Case 17: CLIF's Medication Errors	One nurse catches a "near miss," but a physician, pharmacists, and nurse make an error on a medication reconciliation that kills a patient. A pharmacist warns against the potential dangers of artificial intelligence.
Case 18: A Mom's Story of Sepsis	A misdiagnosis of a young boy's sepsis by the nurses and doctors leads to a collaboration among the clinical staff and the mother of the boy—an industrial quality improvement expert.
Case 20: Opioid Overdoses in the Emergency Department	A chief medical officer and chief nursing officer must work together to convince the CEO that his idea to reduce opioid overdoses is foolish.
Case 21: The Lunchroom: Physician Engagement at a PCMH	A team of professionals—quality director, program manager, chief medical officer, chief financial officer, and CEO—each intervene to improve a headstrong physician's quality scores.
Case 22: The Fulfillment Affair	The health plan medical director and director of quality team up to discover the root cause of the high-cost medical bills. Are the managers at the world's second largest online retailer to blame?
Case 24: Both/And Thinking in Readmission Prevention	Conflict between the case management leaders of two recently merged hospitals (one a nurse and one a social worker) leads to a discovery about best practices in hospital readmission prevention.

ED, emergency department; IR, interventional radiology; PCMH, patient-centered medical home.

across settings (Scaria, 2016; World Health Organization, 2010). Interprofessional teams are typically trained in separate disciplines and educational settings, leaving them unprepared to collaborate (Institute of Medicine [IOM], 2001). Each healthcare profession evolved over time to claim certain scopes of practice and perform different roles with patients, and each discipline speaks a particular professional language and holds unique values (Hall, 2005). Without learning to collaborate, performance cannot improve.

To improve interprofessional collaboration skills, this casebook includes a variety of case studies suitable for a variety of healthcare professions, such as medical social workers, pharmacists, nurses, certified nurse aids, physicians, architects, telemetry technicians, information technologists, and health administrators (Table 5.4).

SUMMARY

The case method is a prominent form of problem-based learning. This casebook offers realistic healthcare case studies for the practical application of quality management. In the tradition of the problem-based learning, a Case Application Exercise for each case study requires exploration of the case scenario, self-directed learning, application of new knowledge to the problem, collaboration in learning groups, facilitation from the instructor, and reflection on learning.

Most education accrediting bodies mandate that academic programs adopt competency-based curriculum and assessment. To meet this teaching challenge, healthcare quality management courses encourage active learning with group collaboration. This casebook meets the need for learners, such as health administrators, nurses, physicians, and the interprofessional team, to develop high levels of professional competency in quality management.

DISCUSSION QUESTIONS

1. Why are competencies associated with interpersonal relations, such as collaboration and leadership, difficult to assess at the higher levels of cognitive complexity?

2. Choose a competency relevant to your profession and describe how the problem-based learning approach through the case method enables your learning of that competency.

3. Choose a step of the problem-based learning cycle defined by Hmelo-Silver and Eberbach and explain why that step is the most important in completing the Case Application Exercises in Part Two of this casebook.

4. Describe the role of the health administrator in the quality management efforts. Do you think that nonclinical management personnel belong to clinical quality improvement teams? Why or why not?

5. Identify a quality management competency that you want to develop and explain how attaining this knowledge, skills, abilities, or judgment will improve your professional performance.

REFERENCES

Allchin, D. (2013). Problem- and case based learning in science: An introduction to distinctions, values, and outcomes. *CBE-Life Sciences Education, 12*(3), 364–372. doi:10.1187/cbe.12-11-0190

American Association of Colleges of Nursing. (2008). *The essentials of baccalaureate education for professional nursing practice*. Retrieved from https://www.aacnnursing.org/Portals/42/Publications/BaccEssentials08.pdf

American Association of Colleges of Nursing. (2011). *The essentials of master's education in nursing*. Retrieved from https://www.aacnnursing.org/Portals/42/Publications/MastersEssentials11.pdf

American Association of Colleges of Nursing. (2019). *AACN essentials*. Retrieved from https://www.aacnnursing.org/Education-Resources/AACN-Essentials

American Organization of Nursing Leadership. (n.d.). *Nurse executives competencies*. Retrieved from https://www.aonl.org/resources/nurse-leader-competencies

Barrows, H. S. (1986). A taxonomy of problem-based learning methods. *Medical Education, 20*(6), 481–486. doi:10.1111/j.1365-2923.1986.tb01386.x

Barrows, H. S. (1996). Problem-based learning in medicine and beyond: A brief overview. *New Directions for Teaching and Learning, 1996*(68), 3–12. doi:10.1002/tl.37219966804

Begun, J. W., Butler, P. W., & Stefl, M. E. (2018). Competencies to what end? Affirming the purpose of healthcare management. *Journal of Health Administration Education, 35*(2), 133–155. Retrieved from https://www.ingentaconnect.com/contentone/aupha/jhae/2018/00000035/00000002/art00004?crawler=true

Begun, J. W., White, K. R., & Mosser, G. (2011). Interprofessional care teams: The role of the healthcare administrator. *Journal of Interprofessional Care, 25*(2), 119–123. doi:10.3109/13561820.2010.504135

Bloom, B. S., Engelhart, M. D., Furst, E. J., Hill, W. H., & Krathwohl, D. R. (1956). *Taxonomy of educational objectives: Handbook 1: Cognitive domain*. New York, NY: David McKay.

Bradley, E. H., Webster, T. R., Schlesinger, M., Baker, D., & Inouye, S. K. (2006). The roles of senior management in improving hospital experiences for frail older adults. *Journal of Healthcare Management, 51*(5), 323–336; discussion 336–327. doi:10.1097/00115514-200609000-00009

Broom, K., Turner, J., & Brichto, E. (2016). How well do programs fulfill their role in management development? An analysis of competency assessments using CAHME accreditation outcomes. *Journal of Health Administration Education, 33*(4), 559–579. Retrieved from https://www.ingentaconnect.com/content/aupha/jhae/2016/00000033/00000004/art00005#

Broom, K. D., & Gentry, D. (2018). The past, present and future: Our journey through competency-based education. *Journal of Health Administration Education, 35*(2), 123–132. Retrieved from https://www.ingentaconnect.com/contentone/aupha/jhae/2018/00000035/00000002/art00003

Clement, D. G., Hall, R. S., O'Connor, S. J., Qu, H., Stefl, M. E., & White, A. W. (2010). Competency development and validation: A collaborative approach among four graduate programs. *Journal of Health Administration Education, 27*(3), 151–173. Retrieved from https://www.ingentaconnect.com/content/aupha/jhae/2010/00000027/00000003/art00002

Commission on Accreditation of Healthcare Management Education. (2018). *2017 CAHME eligibility requirements and accreditation criteria*. Retrieved from https://www.cahme.org/files/accreditation/FALL2017_CAHME_CRITERIA_FOR_ACCREDITATION_2018_06_01.pdf

Cronenwett, L., Sherwood, G., Pohl, J., Barnsteiner, J., Moore, S., Sullivan, D. T., ... Warren, J. (2009). Quality and safety education for advanced nursing practice. *Nursing Outlook, 57*(6), 338–348. doi:10.1016/j.outlook.2009.07.009

Dahlgren, M. A., & Dahlgren, L. O. (2002). Portraits of PBL: Students' experiences of the characteristics of problem-based learning in physiotherapy, computer engineering and psychology. *Instructional Science, 30*(2), 111–127. doi:10.1023/a:1014819418051

Fater, K. H., Weatherford, B., Ready, R. W., Finn, K., & Tangney, B. (2014). Expanding nurse of the future nursing core competencies across the academic-practice transition: A pilot study. *Journal of Continuing Education in Nursing, 45*(8), 366–372. doi:10.3928/00220124-20140716-03

Gamble, E. N., & Jelley, R. B. (2014). The case for competition: Learning about evidence-based management through case competition. *Academy of Management Learning & Education, 13*(3), 433–445. doi:10.5465/amle.2013.0187

Garman, A. N. (2018). Competency-based education in healthcare management: Current state & future directions. *The Journal of Health Administration Education, 35*(2), 119–122. Retrieved from https://www.ingentaconnect.com/content/aupha/jhae/2018/00000035/00000002/art00002

Garman, A. N., Leach, D. C., & Spector, N. (2006). Worldviews in collision: Conflict and collaboration across professional lines. *Journal of Organizational Behavior, 27*(7), 829–849. doi:10.1002/job.394

Goeschel, C. A., Wachter, R. M., & Pronovost, P. J. (2010). Responsibility for quality improvement and patient safety: Hospital board and medical staff leadership challenges. *Chest, 138*(1), 171–178. doi:10.1378/chest.09-2051

Greeno, J. G., Collins, A. M., & Resnick, L. B. (1996). Cognition and learning. In D. C. Berliner & R. C. Calfee (Eds.), *Handbook of educational psychology* (pp. 15–46). New York, NY: Macmillan Library Reference.

Greiner, A. C., & Knebel, E. (Eds.). (2003). *Health professions education: A bridge to quality.* Washington, DC: National Academies Press.

Hall, P. (2005). Interprofessional teamwork: Professional cultures as barriers. *Journal of Interprofessional Care, 19*(Suppl. 1), 188–196. doi:10.1080/13561820500081745

Harvard Business School. (n.d.). *The HBS case method.* Retrieved from https://www.hbs.edu/mba/academic-experience/Pages/the-hbs-case-method.aspx

Hmelo-Silver, C. E. (2004). Problem-based learning: What and how do students learn? *Educational Psychology Review, 16*(3), 235–266. doi:10.1023/B:EDPR.0000034022.16470.f3

Hmelo-Silver, C. E., Chernobilsky, E., & DaCosta, M. C. (2004). Psychological tools in problem-based learning. In O. Tan (Ed.), *Enhancing thinking through problem-based learning approaches: International perspectives* (pp. 17–37). Singapore, Singapore: Cengage.

Hmelo-Silver, C. E., & Eberbach, C. (2012). Learning theories and problem-based learning. In S. Bridges, C. McGrath, & T. Whitehill (Eds.), *Researching problem-based learning in clinical education: The next generation* (pp. 3–17). New York, NY: Springer.

Institute of Medicine. (2001). *Crossing the quality chasm: A new health system for the 21st century.* Washington, DC: National Academies Press. Retrieved from http://www.nationalacademies.org/hmd/Global/News%20Announcements/Crossing-the-Quality-Chasm-The-IOM-Health-Care-Quality-Initiative.aspx

Johnson, J., Miller, S., & Horowitz, S. (2008). Systems-based practice: Improving the safety and quality of patient care by recognizing and improving the systems in which we work. In K. Henriksen, J. Battles, M. Keyes, & M. Grady (Eds.), *Advances in patient safety: New directions and alternative approaches* (Vol. 2: Culture and Redesign). Rockville, MD: Agency for Healthcare Research and Quality. Retrieved from https://www.ncbi.nlm.nih.gov/books/NBK43731/

Kim, S., Phillips, W. R., Pinsky, L., Brock, D., Phillips, K., & Keary, J. (2006). A conceptual framework for developing teaching cases: A review and synthesis of the literature across disciplines. *Medical Education, 40*(9), 867–876. doi:10.1111/j.1365-2929.2006.02544.x

LaMantia, J. (2002). The ACGME core competencies: Getting ahead of the curve. *Academic Emergency Medicine, 9*(11), 1216–1217. doi:10.1197/aemj.9.11.1216

Mangelsdorff, A. D. (2014). Competency-based curriculum, outcomes, and leader development: Applications to a graduate program in health administration. *Journal of Health Administration Education, 31*(2), 111–133. Retrieved from https://www.ingentaconnect.com/content/aupha/jhae/2014/00000031/00000002/art00003

Mesny, A. (2013). Taking stock of the century-long utilization of the case method in management education. *Canadian Journal of Administrative Sciences—Revue Canadienne Des Sciences De L Administration, 30*(1), 56–66. doi:10.1002/cjas.1239

National Center Healthcare Leadership. (2018). *Healthcare leadership competency model 3.0.* Retrieved from https://www.nchl.org/page?page=272

National Research Council of the National Academies. (2005). *Advancing the nation's health needs: NIH research training programs.* Washington, DC: National Academies Press.

New England Journal of Medicine Knowledge+ Team. (2016). *Exploring the ACGME core competencies.* Retrieved from https://knowledgeplus.nejm.org/blog/exploring-acgme-core-competencies

Pruitt, Z., Mhaskar, R., Kane, B. G., Barraco, R. D., DeWaay, D. J., Rosenau, A. M., ... Greenberg, M. R. (2017). Development of a health care systems curriculum. *Advances in Medical Education and Practice, 8*, 745–753. doi:10.2147/amep.s146670

Ross, J. G., & Bruderle, E. (2016). Student-centered teaching strategies to integrate the quality and safety education for nurses competency, safety, into a nursing course. *Nurse Educator, 41*(6), 278–281. doi:10.1097/nne.0000000000000273

Ross, J. G., & Bruderle, E. (2018). Effects of active, student-centered teaching strategies on nursing students' knowledge, skills, attitudes, and comfort related to patient safety. *Nurse Educator, 43*(1), 2–3. doi:10.1097/nne.0000000000000400

Savery, J. R. (2015). Overview of problem-based learning: Definitions and distinctions. In A. Walker, H. Leary, C. E. Hmelo-Silver, & P. A. Ertmer (Eds.), *Essential readings in problem-based learning: Exploring and extending the legacy of Howard S. Barrows* (pp. 5–15). West Lafayette, IN: Purdue University Press.

Scaria, M. K. (2016). Role of care pathways in interprofessional teamwork. *Nursing Standard, 30*(52), 42–47. doi:10.7748/ns.2016.e10402

Sherwood, G. (2011). Integrating quality and safety science in nursing education and practice. *Journal of Research in Nursing, 16*(3), 226–240. doi:10.1177/1744987111400960

Skochelak, S., Kawkins, RE, Lawson, L., Starr, S., Borkan, J., & Gonzalo, J. (2016). *Health systems science*. St. Louis, MO: Elsevier Health Sciences.

Tella, S., Liukka, M., Jamookeeah, D., Smith, N. J., Partanen, P., & Turunen, H. (2014). What do nursing students learn about patient safety? An integrative literature review. *Journal of Nursing Education, 53*(1), 7–13. doi:10.3928/01484834-20131209-04

White, K. R., & Griffith, J. R. (2015). *The well-managed healthcare organization* (8th ed.). Chicago, IL: Health Administration Press.

World Health Organization. (2010). *Framework for action on interprofessional education and collaborative practice* (WHO/HRH/HPN/10.3). Geneva, Switzerland: Author. Retrieved from http://www.who.int/hrh/resources/framework_action/en

CHAPTER 6

The Template

1. Describe the components of the A3 problem-solving template.
2. Connect the A3 problem-solving template to the Plan-Do-Study-Act (PDSA) and Define, Measure, Analyze, Improve, and Control (DMAIC) continuous quality improvement cycles.
3. Identify four common mistakes made in the problem identification and definition stage of completing an A3 problem-solving template.
4. Recognize well-written examples of background statements and problem statements.
5. Describe various ways to illustrate current and future states in an A3 template.
6. Summarize the purpose of root cause analysis in healthcare quality management.

A3 PROBLEM-SOLVING TEMPLATE

Powerfully simple, the A3 problem-solving template encourages a collaborative, systematic approach to healthcare quality management. The template, borrowed from Lean thinking and the Toyota Production System® described in Chapter 3, The Mindset, arranges eight sections on a single page to provide the structure for a practical, step-by-step problem-solving process. The name, "A3," comes from the size of the paper used to document your problem-solving activities. In countries where the metric system is used, A3 is the 297 × 420 mm size, which is very close to the 11 × 17 inches format used in countries with the English system. An electronic A3 template form has been provided for you to practice the problem-solving process, called the "Case Application Exercise," in this casebook.

The A3 template fosters the teamwork described in Chapter 5, The Casebook. Completing the template compels professionals to interact and share decision-making to work as a team. As your team deliberates the A3 template, you will strengthen the commitment to the project, a requirement for sustaining healthcare quality improvements (Morrow, Robert, Maben, & Griffiths, 2012).

The A3 template approach requires an iterative analysis of the problems and scientific experimentation of the solutions (Table 6.1). Exhibits 6.1 and 6.2 refer to the left and right sides of the A3 problem-solving template, respectively. Appendix E illustrates the A3 problem-solving template in the full 1-page format. In the problem definition and analysis phase,

Table 6.1 A3 Template and Continuous Quality Improvement Cycles

A3 TEMPLATE	PDSA CYCLE	DMAIC CYCLE
Problem Statement	Plan	Define
Background	Plan	Define
Current State	Plan	Measure
Problem Analysis	Plan	Analyze
Future State	Plan	Analyze
Identify, Test and Implement Countermeasures With Implementation Plan	Do	Improve
Control and Sustain Results	Study	Control
Follow-up & Lessons Learned	Act	Control

DMAIC, Define, Measure, Analyze, Improve, and Control; PDSA, Plan-Do-Study-Act.

Exhibit 6.1 Left Side of A3 Problem-Solving Template

DEFINE AND ANALYZE THE PROBLEM
Background What is the context of the issue? Who are the key players, and what are their view points? Are there conflicts to be resolved? Briefly explain the history. How does the problem fit within the organization's goals? Why is this problem important to the patient/organization? What are the consequences of the problem? Why is a change needed? What are the symptoms of the problem?
Problem Statement Be specific. Is the focus of improvement appropriately scoped to be described to sufficient detail within this A3? Avoid defining a problem as its consequence, symptom, or solution. A sentence or two describing Where, When, What, How Much, How Do You Know, and What is "The Pain"?
Current State What is going on? Use facts. Be visual—use Pareto charts, pie charts, or sketches. Draw a diagram of what happens now. Identify problems explicitly in the diagram. What are the key measures or metrics that can describe the Current State?
Problem Analysis Use the simplest problem analysis tool that will suffice to find the root cause of the problem: Five why's, fishbone diagram, failure mode and effects analysis, and so on. Does the problem above contain multiple root causes? Do causes align to explicitly illustrate problems in the Current State section? Prioritize problems.

you will learn to effectively identify, analyze, and revise the problem statement. In the solution phase, you will become comfortable with quick experimentation cycles. The process described in this chapter matches the scientific approach advocated by PDSA and DMAIC continuous quality improvement cycles, as outlined in Chapter 3, The Mindset.

You should apply the A3 problem-solving template to each case study provided to you in Part Two of this textbook. An electronic file of the A3 template is available by accessing the following url: https://www.springerpub.com/hqm. Recommended solutions to each Case Application Exercise can be provided to you by your instructor.

Exhibit 6.2 Right Side of A3 Problem-Solving Template

DEVELOP, IMPLEMENT, AND CONTROL SOLUTION(S)
Future State Draw a diagram of a new way to work. Create measureable targets for new way to work. What are the success factors? Define requirements of Future State.
Identify, Test, and Implement Countermeasures What will be done to test and validate those countermeasures? (Think quality improvement cycles.) Countermeasure #1: Countermeasure #2: Countermeasure #3:

IMPLEMENTATION PLAN: MUST INCLUDE CONSULTATION OF ALL IMPACTED			
Item	What	Who	When

Measure and Control Improvements:			
Primary Metric	Baseline	Target	Current

Define operational effectiveness. Chart, as appropriate. These data become the new Current State in the Continuous Quality Improvement cycle. Define verification plan. Define plan to sustain and control changes. Develop Control Plan.
Follow-Up and Lessons Learned What issues remain that need to be closed? What worked? What could be improved?

BACKGROUND

Begin the A3 template by asking the following questions to describe the **background** of your quality management problem:

1. What is the context of the issue?
2. Who are the key stakeholders in the organization who have direct influence on the issue?
3. How does the issue fit within the organization's goals? Why is this problem important to the patient or customer?
4. Why is a change needed? You should create a sense of urgency.
5. Does this issue influence organization-wide priorities?
6. What are the symptoms of the problem? What indicates that the problem exists?
7. What are the consequences of the problem? What is the earliest known cause?
8. Are there conflicts to be resolved? Briefly explain the history.

Table 6.2 includes examples of a background description appropriate for an A3.

Table 6.2 Examples of Background Statements

EXAMPLE BACKGROUND STATEMENT	EXPLANATION
Guidelines recommend that a patient with myocardial infarction with ST-segment elevation receive a PCI within 90 minutes of arriving to hospital. Reducing "door-to-balloon time" significantly reduces mortality and morbidity. Hospital's quality scores are below accepted benchmarks. Evaluation of best practices not yet conducted. Cardiology and ED staff disagree on best strategies for reducing door-to-balloon time.	Good. Describes the context, the symptom of the problem, the consequence to patients, and the conflict within the organization.
Government regulators require the managed care company's provider directory to be updated on a monthly basis, but there is no process for communicating changes in the provider network to the team that publishes the directory online.	Could be improved. The background does not explain the "so what?" of the issue. Are there fines involved for not complying? How does it impact patients' access to care or satisfaction?
A new partnership between hospital and large physician groups wants to better coordinate care for patients admitted to the inpatient setting. The organizations operate two separate EHRs systems, making the transfer of medical and medication information between the organizations difficult. Inefficient or inaccurate information makes the goal of improved patient care coordination more challenging. Poor coordination of care can lead to mistakes in care (e.g., medication reconciliation) and worse health outcomes for patients. Neither the hospital nor the physician group leadership seems willing to adopt each other's EHR system.	Good. Background adequately explains the context, how the issue relates to the organization's goals, the consequences of the issue, and conflict between stakeholders.

(continued)

Table 6.2 Examples of Background Statements (*continued*)

EXAMPLE BACKGROUND STATEMENT	EXPLANATION
A new law will mandate certain nurse-to-patient ratio minimums, which may require additional nurses to be hired. Given the current nursing supply shortage, the hospital's vice president of human resources, CFO, and chief nursing officer are concerned about the law's impact on budgeting, hiring, and staffing.	Good. Describes key stakeholders, urgency of the issue, and the relationship of the issue to organization-wide priorities.
Due to Hurricane Pablo, the supply of small saline IV bags manufactured in Puerto Rico has been disrupted. The small IV bags are used to dilute drugs before administering intravenously.	Could be improved. It is not clear that this will impact care. Are there other suppliers? Why is change needed? You should create a sense of urgency.
The CHC has a high appointment on show rate. The CHC currently has patient navigators employed to help patients overcome barriers to making their appointments on time. Unfilled appointment slots mean inefficient use of provider time. Patients who do not come to their appointments are more likely to require more expensive emergency care.	Good. Explains symptoms, consequences, and stakeholders.

CHC, community health clinic; EHRs, electronic health records; IV, intravenous; PCI, percutaneous coronary intervention.

PROBLEM STATEMENT

Before moving on to the analysis of the problem, you need to write the **problem statement**, a formalized expression of the concern requiring improvement. You should devote sufficient time with your team to discuss the problem statement. You will be tempted to skip ahead to brainstorming and solving. Do not do this. Successful quality management projects dedicate enough time to problem identification and definition (Choo, 2014).

Discuss the problem. Careful definition of the problem assures that all members of the team understand the problem the same way. If you allow the team members to ask questions and voice concerns in the problem identification and definition stage, you will prevent disagreement later in the problem-solving process.

You should ask fact-finding questions concerning the problem. What is "the pain" felt by the organization? What is preventing the organization from achieving the organizational objectives? Why should anyone care "the so what?" How do you know that it is a problem? Who is impacted? What is the perspective of the customer or patient? Where and when does the problem occur? How much or how often?

Quality management teams make four common mistakes when identifying and defining the problem. With practice, you will learn to avoid these mistakes.

1. Solution—The **solution** should never be included in your problem statement. Even the most experienced professionals can sometimes unwittingly fall into this trap. Some may incorrectly write the problem statement as, "Medication errors should be reduced by implementing a physician order entry system." Perhaps the physician order entry system would be the correct solution, but without first defining the problem, you cannot be sure. What if the problem was not related

to misunderstanding physician orders, but instead associated with timing of the medication administration? In this case, the implied solution would not solve the problem.

2. Symptom—A **symptom** is the indication that the problem exists. Solving the symptoms will not solve the problem. For example, patients waiting in the emergency department hallways may be a symptom of a delay in hospital patient discharges, not an inefficient inpatient admission process. In other words, the symptom is not a direct result of something, but rather an indication that the root cause may be several steps back in a chain of events.

3. Consequence—A **consequence** is something caused by something else; it is the direct result of an earlier event. Instead, start with the earliest known cause. Again, you may eventually identify another cause of your identified problem later in the problem-solving process. This is okay, but you should begin with the problem statement with the earliest known cause you can define with the information available to you. If you can eliminate the consequence as the potential problem statement with the information available to you, then you should do so.

4. Scope—The **scope** is the size of the problem to be solved. Used correctly, the A3 will prevent you from making the problem statement too big or too small. The entire problem-solving process should fit on the one-page form. For example, "patients are dissatisfied" may certainly be true, but analyzing the many ways patients could be unhappy would not fit succinctly within the single-page A3 template. A more narrowly defined problem statement will improve the chances of timely and effective resolution to your quality management problem.

Table 6.3 includes examples of good problem statements and those that could be improved.

Table 6.3 Examples of Problem Statements

EXAMPLE PROBLEM STATEMENT	EXPLANATION
The problem to be addressed is that patient boarding in the emergency department creates a safety risk due to ineffective communication between emergency department staff and hospitalists.	Good. The problem statement clarifies "the pain" felt by the organization and why the problem is important.
The Department of Family Medicine can increase staff productivity by improving employee engagement.	Could be improved. The problem statement includes a solution. Never mistake a solution for a problem statement.
Nursing staff morale is low in the obstetric unit.	Could be improved. Low morale is a symptom of a problem that cannot be resolved by itself. The underlying problem might be poor management or disruptive behavior by coworkers.
The problem is that the payment receipts for submitted medical claims from managed care organizations have declined over the past 6 months.	Could be improved. Declining payments from managed care organizations is very likely a consequence of something else, such as lower patient volume, ineffective billing, miscoding, or another root cause.

(continued)

Table 6.3 Examples of Problem Statements (*continued*)

EXAMPLE PROBLEM STATEMENT	EXPLANATION
Patient experience scores for patients admitted through the emergency department are low, which risks decreasing Medicare payments.	Could be improved. The scope of the problem is too large. Since these surveys measure multiple domains of patient experience, it is likely that multiple root causes could be identified. Consider creating multiple A3 problem-solving worksheets.
Increasing infection rates from peripherally inserted intravenous lines increase patient mortality.	Good. The problem statement identifies the "so what" of the problem.

CURRENT STATE

Once you have defined the problem, describe the **Current State**. Illustrate how things exist right now. Be explicit. Collect the facts related to the problem through staff interviews, extensive observation, or data analysis. Organize the facts to demonstrate the extent of the problem. Be visual. Use sketches, charts, diagrams, maps, and symbols (Jimmerson, Weber, & Sobek, 2005). Draw in pencil—create, erase, refine, and perfect.

For process-related problems, illustrate the steps of the Current State with symbols. Flowcharts and value stream maps are useful styles for demonstrating a step-by-step sequence of the Current State.

For patient experience challenges, such as barriers to effective escalation of patient complaints by staff, qualitative data collection (e.g., interviews) may identify descriptive themes. Be creative with your depiction of qualitative data in the Current State section of the A3 template (Jimmerson, 2007). Use symbols, such as fluffy clouds, lightning bursts, stick figures, thought bubbles, and even emoji.

For performance issues, start with measures, metrics, or key performance indicators associated with the problem. Existing measures may be available from department leaders, quality department, risk management, and finance department, among many others. If no measures currently exist, find available data that will clearly define the magnitude of the problem. For example, if you are studying the problem of staff turnover, then quantitative data collection, such as average length of employment, may be the right approach.

Figures 6.1 to 6.3 illustrate examples of potential descriptions of the Current State.

PROBLEM ANALYSIS

The Problem Analysis section of the A3 usually entails some sort of **root cause analysis**, the systematic process for uncovering the underlying reasons for a given problem. In your root cause analysis, it is important to avoid making assumptions, since the root cause of the problem is usually not obvious. Your goal is to "analyze deep." Ask: what sequence of events leads to the problem? What conditions allow the problem to occur?

Many quality management tools exist to help you conduct root cause analysis. You should use the simplest tool sufficient to identify the root cause of the problem. Part Two of this casebook will present root cause analysis tools, such as five Why's, fishbone diagrams, and

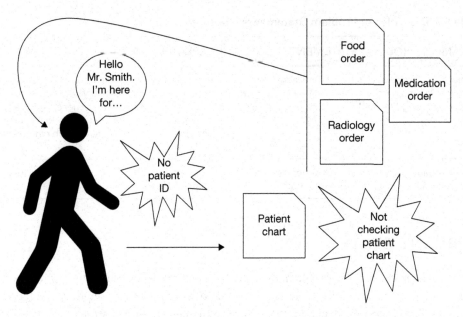

FIGURE 6.1 Current State for a problem with patient identification.

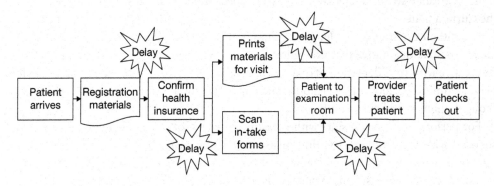

FIGURE 6.2 Current State for a problem with primary care wait times.

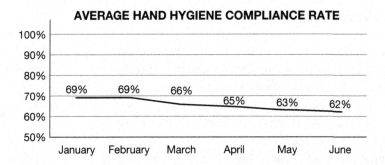

FIGURE 6.3 Current State for a problem with hand hygiene compliance.

failure mode and effects analysis (FMEA), within the context of realistic healthcare quality management scenarios.

When analyzing the root causes, you may discover that another cause relates to your central problem, but does not align closely to the problem, as defined in the Current State section. In this instance, you may need to address these causes separately as problems in other A3 templates. Alternatively, you may also find that there are multiple closely related causes of your defined problem. In this case, you should prioritize the development of solutions for these root causes later in the A3 problem-solving process (see following section "Identify, Test, and Implement Countermeasures").

As stated throughout, the quality management process is a cycle. Many times, the A3 Problem Analysis gives you feedback on your defined problem statement that leads you to revise your problem statement. That is, through additional analysis, you may learn that your problem is actually a symptom or a consequence of another problem. Therefore, you may determine that addressing a different problem would solve your previous problem more effectively. The A3 problem-solving process may involve creating numerous iterations with your team before finalizing your problem statement. Again, create, erase, refine, and perfect.

FUTURE STATE

Once you have defined and analyzed the problem, you are ready to visualize the Future State, or the ideal conditions in the A3 template. Illustrate how things should be in the future (Figures 6.4 and 6.5). Like the Current State step of the A3 problem-solving process, you should communicate visually with sketches, charts, diagrams, maps, and symbols (Jimmerson, 2007). Exemplify what you want to achieve.

The Future State section of the A3 template should also include clear and measurable objectives. How will you know if the project is successful? What are the success factors? When you define, measure, and track performance, you show your team which solution(s) provide the desirable results. For example, if the problem is the high percentage of organization staff turnover, the objectives will be described as reduce turnover to below 15% consistent with national benchmark. Be careful not to attempt to "boil an ocean" and develop objectives that are too extensive for the defined problem. Also, consider how the data will be collected, because the best measures should be readily available.

Future State: Below national benchmark of 3.56 falls per 1,000 patient days

Provide safety companions

FIGURE 6.4 Future State for patient fall reduction.

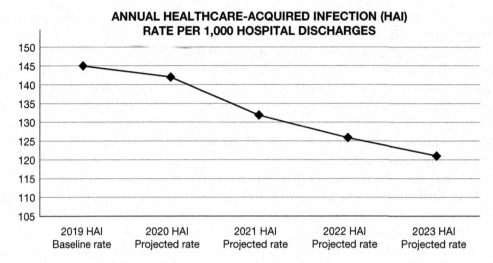

FIGURE 6.5 Future State for annual healthcare-acquired infections.

IDENTIFY, TEST, AND IMPLEMENT COUNTERMEASURES

The next step in the A3 problem-solving process is composed of identifying, testing, and implementing **countermeasures**. Countermeasures are the various short-, medium-, or long-term interventions that you think will solve your defined problem. This is usually where most people mistakenly start the quality improvement process, implementing presumed solutions without rigorous analysis. Following the A3 template sequence, it is not until the problem has been defined and analyzed and the Future State has been visualized that solutions are explored.

To identify potential countermeasures, you and your team should brainstorm. Brain-storming includes collecting all the ideas that could close the gap between the Current State and the Future State. At first, no idea is discarded.

Next, apply the evidence-based management (EBMgt) process described in Chapter 3, The Mindset, to select the most promising countermeasures. Evidence for your potential countermeasures may come from a variety of sources. Chapter 3, The Mindset, describes four sources of evidence in EBMgt: (a) perspectives of people affected by the intervention; (b) personal experience, stakeholder judgment, and expert opinion; (c) evidence from data and experimentation in the local context; and (d) critical evaluation of the best available management literature. When completing the A3 for these case studies, you may search the Internet for sources of evidence to identify potential countermeasures. You should use cred-ible healthcare management sources, such as peer-reviewed literature, industry whitepapers (e.g., Advisory Board, McKinsey & Company), or nonprofit quality management support organizations (e.g., Institute for Healthcare Improvement, National Quality Forum), or gov-ernment reports (e.g., Medicare Advisory Commission or Agency for Healthcare Research and Quality), to discover potential solutions to the problems provided in the case studies.

Your selected countermeasures should then be tested with small, quick experiments (i.e., pilots) to test whether they address the previously identified root causes of the problem. Quick experimentation—the essence of continuous quality improvement cycles—will help

Table 6.4 Implementation Plan: Fall Prevention

ITEM	WHAT	WHO	WHEN	STATUS	COMMENTS
1.	Change workflow when patient is flagged as "very high fall risk" to require that patient wear yellow hospital gown	Linda	8/18	0%	Linen services to stock yellow hospital gowns

your team arrive at a robust final solution that addresses the problem. The quicker your team can perform the experiments, the quicker you can learn from them.

Once the countermeasures prove effective at addressing the root cause of your identified problem, you implement. Every quality management implementation project contains actions that need to be completed. Whether those actions are for the experimentation, implementation, or sustainment phase, they need to be documented and tracked in an Implementation Plan to assure completion (Table 6.4). A very simple Action Plan ("What," "Who," "When") could be used to this effect.

- What—Describe the action so that everybody understands the meaning, even if they were not present when the action was developed.

- Who—List the person responsible for the action. It is important to note that the person responsible for the action and the person carrying out the action could be two different people. The person responsible for the action and whose name goes on the Action Plan must be part of the team currently participating in the A3 problem-solving exercise. When conducting the Case Application Exercises, you may speculate about the Implementation Plan using characters from the case studies.

- When—Establish an estimated deadline for completion. If that date is not clear, you could document the date when you expect to have an update on the action, although it may not mean the action will be completed by then. When conducting the Case Application Exercises, you may speculate about the implementation dates.

- Status—A column could be added to show progress toward completion (i.e., open/closed; ongoing/complete; or 25%, 50%, 75%, 100%).

- Comments—This column could be added to the A3 template to record notes regarding the implementation action, such as "tentative deadline" or "approval needed."

MEASURE AND CONTROL IMPROVEMENTS

After the solution or solutions have been fully implemented, the team needs to define how you will ensure that the improvements are tracked and sustained going forward. If you want to be successful with your A3 problem-solving process, defining the process for measure and control is necessary.

Once permanent solutions are identified and implemented, measurement must continue to show how implementation is progressing and to alert the team of any issues. Use the A3 template to track where you started (baseline), where you are going (target), and where you are in the journey (current). Data measuring your current achievement become the new Current State for future quality management projects, following the continuous quality improvement cycle.

PRIMARY METRIC	BASELINE	TARGET	CURRENT
Outpatient appointment scheduling delay	13 days	3 days	6 days

A **Control Plan** details what measures to monitor, at what frequency, and how to react when the countermeasures fail to work as planned. A Control Plan is a simple and visual way to improve the "stickiness" of your quality management project. How will the improvements be communicated? Who is responsible for monitoring the changes? What happens if your countermeasures (i.e., interventions, changes, behaviors, or processes) do not continue after sharing your solution throughout the organization? For example, suppose one action item in a patient falls prevention program fails to occur. What is the process for turning around this outcome? Who is responsible? When will this occur? Keep these tips in mind completing the A3 template for each case study in this text.

PROCESS STEP	CHARACTERISTIC	SPECIFIED LIMIT/ REQUIREMENT	SAMPLE SIZE	FREQUENCY	ACTION
Arrival-to-Triage	Time	5 minutes	100%	Weekly	Refer to RN director for resolution
Arrival-to-DC	Time	160 minutes	100%	Weekly	Refer to RN director for resolution

DC = discharge; RN = registered nurse.

Finally, sustaining your quality improvement results usually requires the development of a plan to share the solution throughout the organization. Of course, you should not introduce too much change all at once. If several successful solutions were identified for deployment, you may want to prioritize the solutions in the Action Plan for a phased implementation. For example, a successful pilot project conducted with a small team of one nurse and one case manager could be applied to the whole unit, then the whole floor, then the whole hospital, and, potentially, the whole healthcare system.

FOLLOW-UP AND LESSONS LEARNED

In the final section of the A3 template, you should reflect on the problem-solving process. If there are issues that still need to be addressed, document them in the **Follow-Up and Lessons Learned** section of the A3. What did we learn that can help us address a similar problem in the future? What worked? Be sure to cite your major successes. What could be improved for the next time? Lessons learned should be captured throughout the project. Subsequent healthcare quality management projects can use this documentation to start a new A3. For your Case Application Exercises, use the case study scenarios to create your "lessons learned."

SUMMARY

The A3 problem-solving template guides you through the continuous quality improvement cycle using a sequence of eight sections arranged on a single page. You begin the A3 template by describing the background of your quality management problem. Then, you write the problem statement, a formalized expression of the concern requiring improvement. The next step is to collect the facts related to the problem and describe the Current State. Next, you conduct the Problem Analysis, a systematic process for uncovering the underlying reasons for the problem. Once you have defined and analyzed the problem, you visualize the Future State, which should include objectives for your quality management project. Only after all these previous steps are complete will you identify and test countermeasures. If proven effective at addressing the root cause of your identified problem, you begin implementation. Finally, you should define how you will assure any improvements are tracked and sustained, a process called "measure and control."

DISCUSSION QUESTIONS

1. How do the PDSA and DMAIC cycles of healthcare quality management compare to the A3 template approach?
2. What are common mistakes made in the problem definition stage of problem-solving?
3. Which is the most important element of the A3 template on which to gain consensus with your quality improvement team?
4. What is the difference between the Current State and the Future State?
5. What approach does the Problem Analysis section of the A3 usually entail?
6. What evidence source would you use to identify the most promising countermeasures for your healthcare quality management problem?

REFERENCES

Choo, A. S. (2014). Defining problems fast and slow: The U-shaped effect of problem definition time on project duration. *Production and Operations Management, 23*(8), 1462–1479. doi:10.1111/poms.12219

Jimmerson, C. (2007). *A3 problem solving for healthcare.* New York, NY: Healthcare Performance Press.

Jimmerson, C., Weber, D., & Sobek, D. K. (2005). Reducing waste and errors: Piloting Lean principles at intermountain healthcare. *Joint Commission Journal on Quality and Patient Safety, 31*(5), 249–257. doi:10.1016/s1553-7250(05)31032-4

Morrow, E., Robert, G., Maben, J., & Griffiths, P. (2012). Implementing large-scale quality improvement: lessons from the productive ward: releasing time to care™. *International Journal of Health Care Quality Assurance, 25*(4), 237–253.

## PART TWO

Cases in Healthcare Quality Management

Process Improvement

Everything that happens is a process. A process is a collection of steps that, when carried out in a specific order, produces results. A collection of processes constitutes a system. Therefore, the healthcare system is really just a huge collection of processes. Process improvement is the proactive, ongoing practice of observing, identifying, describing, analyzing, diagnosing, and correcting suboptimal processes. Questions to ask during process improvement projects include:

- Are staff and equipment utilized efficiently? Are they at capacity? Is there idle time?
- What are the patient throughput times? Do patients wait?
- What is the cycle time or turnover time per patient?
- Are patients tardy? Are there cancellations or other scheduling problems?
- Are there duplications in the processes? Can we eliminate unnecessary steps?
- Can the process be made more consistent from one situation to the next?
- Can the process be standardized, introducing a set of sequencing rules?

The goals of healthcare process improvement are often to streamline, remove bottlenecks, eliminate non–value-adding activities, or reduce variability in patient care or business processes. When successful, the process improvement results enhance healthcare quality, patient satisfaction, productivity, efficiency, and profits.

The following are descriptions of the process improvement case studies included in this casebook.

Case 1: A Summer Internship Journal

A 250-bed academic medical center expanded the size of its ED, increasing its patient volume. Unfortunately, since the hospital did not expand the number of inpatient beds, patients often waited in the ED hallways to be admitted. Long wait times caused numerous bad outcomes, such as poor patient satisfaction scores, employee burnout, and even financial loss. The new health administration intern decided to address ED boarding in his Master of Health Administration summer internship report. To the administrative intern's surprise, long wait times were not unique to the ED. Under the leadership of the CEO and several department heads, the intern carefully examined the patient throughput process from admission to discharge.

Case 2: Claims Payment Processing

Managed care organizations (MCOs) pay healthcare service providers for services provided to patients, a function called "claims payment." In one state, the three Medicaid MCOs frequently change their claims submission rules, but share the new rules with hospitals only twice a year. If the claims do not meet the submission rules, then the MCOs can refuse to pay the claims. Hospitals had to alter claims submissions to meet new guidelines, a delay in payment that financially stressed the hospitals. The state's Hospital Association lobbied to create a new law mandating MCOs to pay hospitals more quickly. At a Senate Committee hearing, the regulator faces a series of tough questions about how he can ensure that MCOs comply with laws and regulations related to claims processing. The Senators want to know: Is there a way to improve the claims payment process?

Case 3: Return-to-Work at a Home Healthcare Agency

After a back injury, a home health nurse took a leave of absence from work allowed under the Family and Medical Leave Act (FMLA). When she wanted to return to work, the overly complicated process exasperated the treating physician, nurse manager, Human Resources administrator, and information technology team. The dysfunctional return-to-work process hampered the home care company's ability to schedule nurses and care for patients. Can a new work flow be designed to reduce delays in the return-to-work process?

Case 4: The Ophthalmologist Who Could Not See (The Waste)

According to financial analysis, an ophthalmology practice is losing approximately $1,000 per cataract case, a fact that troubled the Vice President of Operations. However, the head physician of the medical practice could not see where their processes could be streamlined to achieve cost savings. Can the quality improvement team convince her that waste exists throughout the process?

Case 5: Building a New IR Suite

A hospital finally approved the budget to update the interventional radiology (IR) suite to meet The Joint Commission requirements for accreditation as a Thrombectomy-Capable and Comprehensive Stroke Center. This new IR suite design represented an opportunity for improved work flow, but the most senior member of the architectural team resisted the innovative ergonomics approach to design. "If it ain't broke, don't fix it!" he said. The other architects risk their careers to configure the IR suite for improved patient flow.

Case 6: Emergency Department Heroes

The daily chaos in the hospital's ED caused unnecessary delays, unhappy patients, and stressed-out staff. So, the nursing director decided to take action. "I do not think it is fair that our patients depend on us being heroes every day," she said. After consulting with the new Process Excellence team, she proposed her innovative idea—conduct a kaizen event. This rapid improvement event would require key representatives of the department to collaborate over 4 consecutive days. Is kaizen really worth the time and energy?

CASE 1: A Summer Internship Journal

1. Describe the major components of patient throughput/patient flow, including various access points for inpatient admissions, boarding, discharge turnaround time, and patient discharge.

2. Analyze multiple root causes of patient wait times in the patient flow.

3. Identify area for needed change in patient throughput process.

4. Describe the importance of seeking input from others to identify problems and develop solutions.

5. Understand how to communicate quality management problem-solving in order to impact decision-making and influence change.

INTRODUCTION

The University of Montana Medical Center (UMMC) is a 250-bed academic medical center in Missoula, Montana. Based on its first 6 months, the newly remodeled emergency department (ED) predicts over 35,000 visits in its first year, a 15% volume increase. The ED admits approximately 20% of its patients. UMMC did not add any additional inpatient beds with the recent ED expansion.

John Laidlaw, UMMC's Chief Executive Officer, graduated from the Montana State University's Master of Health Administration (MHA) program 25 years ago. For his last 5 years as CEO, he has acted as a preceptor for the MHA student summer internship at UMMC. The goals of the 3-month supervised work experience are to prepare students for careers in health management and for UMMC to attract top talent to their hospital after they graduate. The preceptor provides mentorship and evaluates the students' performance.

During the summer internship, MHA students shadow the preceptor and work on various tasks, as assigned. MHA students must write an internship report that requires them to identify a management problem, analyze the issue, and make recommendations to their preceptor. Throughout the summer, students must write about their internship experiences in order to

DATA FILE FOR CASE 1

Data files for students are available by accessing the following url: https://www.springerpub.com/hqm

The data file for Case 1 provides Patient-level inpatient discharge data, including data dictionary, 344 lines of time stamp data, and calculated discharge turnaround times (TAT).

evaluate their own performance, a process called "journaling" or "reflective learning." The journal is assessed by the student's professor, and not anyone at the internship site. The following are selections from the reflective journaling from the UMMC summer intern, Ben Barrett.

CASE SCENARIO

Day 3

This may be the easiest internship report ever written. After only my third day at UMMC, I found what is probably the biggest quality management problem at the hospital. So obvious. The new, expanded ED—while beautiful—has caused patients to be boarded in the hallways. I went there about dinnertime, and the ED was overflowing with patients waiting for inpatient beds. I talked to one poor old woman waiting in the hall; she asked me to go get her nurse for her. When I went to the nurse station, it seemed that they had forgotten about the woman. There's no way that ED boarding can be very safe. These patients have been admitted to the hospital, but don't yet have an inpatient room. Also, it must be super frustrating for patients to wait for a room. I'll bet this impacts their patient experience quality scores. I definitely could fix this problem this summer.

I asked the ED administrator, Kent Jones, about the issue. He said that the larger, more efficient ED has increased the number of patient visits. However, there's nowhere to put the admitted patients because they did not expand the number of inpatient beds at UMMC. Apparently, there is no easy way to increase the number of inpatient beds. They can't expand the number of beds without getting permission from the state regulators, a process called Certificate of Need (CON).

Kent told me (in confidence) that he is frustrated with both Mr. Laidlaw and Chief Nursing Officer, Morgan Fein, because neither seems to have a handle on the safety and service issues with patients holding in the ED. According to Kent, if the ED boarding problem is not rectified, then patient care will suffer and the ED staff will burn out. These symptoms will lead to reduced patient volumes, declines in revenue, and significant staff turnover. Kent seems stressed, so I told him that I would help.

Day 4

Kent sent me ED encounter data from the last 6 months with timestamp information associated with each visit's disposition (either discharged from the ED or admitted). Using the data, I created a chart (Figure C1.1) that shows there is a steady increase of patients in the ED throughout each hour of the day, starting at about 8 a.m. and peaking at about 7 p.m., then slowly declining throughout the night and into the early morning.

Day 5

Today, I asked Kent if they tracked the ED boarding length of stay. This question really got Kent fired up. Apparently, he shares similar data every week with the nurse managers of each unit, but nobody seems to do anything about it. He told me that ED boarding problem would be a perfect internship project, and that he would help me any way he could. I agree, and I look forward to running some solutions by Mr. Laidlaw. I am going to research some best practices starting tomorrow.

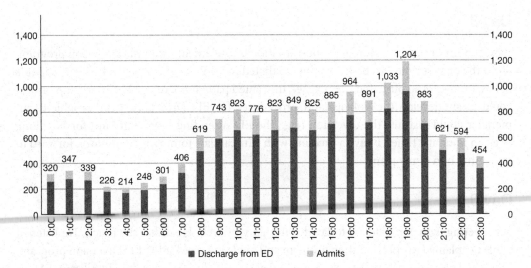

FIGURE C1.1 University of Montana Medical Center emergency department (ED) visits over last 6 months.

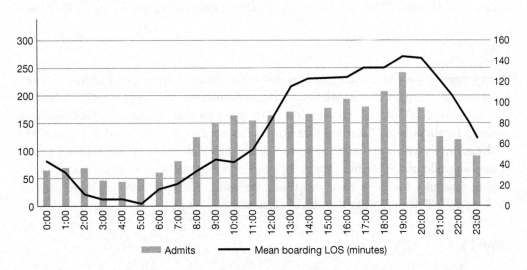

FIGURE C1.2 University of Montana Medical Center emergency department admissions and boarding length of stay (LOS) over last 6 months.

Day 6

Kent sent me the data on ED admission boarding times (Figure C1.2). Just as I figured, the boarding times relate to the number of admits from the ED. There's a bit of delay from the start of the admissions increase to the increase in ED boarding, but then the boarding falls off soon after the admissions from the ED decline.

Day 8

Based on my literature research, the best solution is implementing an ED Diversion program. Since the busiest times in the ED can be predicted, UMMC could proactively divert patients before things got so busy that they caused unwanted patient boarding. My internship project could easily develop the policies and procedures for ED Diversion, such as which staff member could institute the diversion (e.g., the ED Attending Physician) and for how long (e.g., an hour at a time). I have a meeting with Mr. Laidlaw tomorrow, and I look forward to informing him of my plans.

Day 9

My meeting with Mr. Laidlaw today did not go very well. He didn't say much. He listened while I explained the ED boarding problem and made my case for the ED Diversion program. Then, he made sort of a half-smile at me and asked slowly, "So, we just built a larger ED for $4 million, and you want me to close it down when we get busy?" I think his question was rhetorical. I didn't bring up Kent's frustrations with the ED boarding and potential safety issues. No wonder Kent is so frustrated; these executives don't seem to listen to solid analysis. I guess I need to strengthen the case before broaching Kent's complaints with Mr. Laidlaw.

Day 10

Okay, I figure if the ED boarding is a quality of care issue, then we could address it with a program that ensured that the patients waiting in the hallways received care. One solution is to develop a special hospitalist team in the ED that can provide ongoing care for the patients awaiting inpatient beds. I learned that hospitalists are hospital-employed physicians who work exclusively with hospitalized patients. Since we have data on the patient volumes by time of day, we could match the busy times with the extra hospitalist staff. By creating different staffing schedules for these days and times, we could efficiently care for these patients. Mr. Laidlaw will definitely like the idea of efficiency.

Day 11

Another terrible meeting with Mr. Laidlaw today. Again, he asked only one question, "So, you want me to hire more staff?" I don't think he likes me very much. He wants me to look into whether patients are just waiting in the ED or if they are also waiting in other inpatient entry points. Good idea. I didn't think to look at other areas of the hospital where patients could be waiting.

Day 13

Today, I started visiting the other areas of the hospital that admit patients. I met with the Post-Anesthesia Care Unit (PACU) administrator, Jerry Dalton. The PACU is the area where surgical patients get care as they recover from anesthesia. According to Jerry, patients definitely wait in the PACU, but he wasn't sure how long. I guess it can't be too bad, if he doesn't know.

Day 14

Today, I went over to the Cardiac Catheterization Lab. The Cath Lab is where the providers perform heart procedures, mostly diagnostic catheterizations, but also things like coronary angiographies and percutaneous coronary interventions (PCIs). The Cath Lab administrator, Sandy Madden, told me that patient waits were a *huge* problem for them, although she didn't know the actual mean wait time. (How can she not know??) She says that wait time impacts patient revenues, because they can only handle so many patients in the Cath Lab recovery area. She said that patients get upset about having to wait for an available time for the Cath Lab, and the physicians cancel their scheduled patients in frustration because the lab did not have enough staff to manage the postprocedure care. I guess Kent's problems in the ED are not unique. This internship report may take longer than I thought.

Day 15

Today, I talked to the Senior Inpatient Nursing Director, Christine Martinez, about the direct admissions. I learned that the direct admit patients are both planned and unplanned. Planned direct admits are when a patient is scheduled for a routine procedure, and unplanned direct admits happen when a physician decides to admit a sick patient directly to the hospital, rather than through the ED. Christine said that the waits for direct admits are not that bad, because they developed an improved process last year. They worked on the communication processes between the hospital and the community-based admitting providers. They also created a list of diagnoses that were ineligible for direct admission, such as respiratory distress. They apparently decreased the average wait time for both types of direct admits from 66 to 31 minutes.

Day 16

Christine Martinez told me that Milton Adams, the Information Technology Analyst, helped her pull reports on wait times. Milton was nice, but he kept asking me questions about how to measure wait times, which I thought were self-evident. Turns out … not so much. First, I had to tell him what the beginning of the process was, which was easy: when the discharge order was placed by the provider in the system (a field called DISCH_ORD_DT_TM, apparently). Then, things got messier. Milton asked me, "When do we stop the clock?" For that, I did not have a good answer.

Day 17

Today, I think I figured out how we could determine the end point of the patient discharge. I talked to the unit director of the fourth floor of the Patient Tower, Mark Conway. After some back and forth, I learned that the financial system in the electronic medical record requires that nurses end the patient encounter. As I knew from yesterday, there is a timestamp for the discharge order time in the financial records system that we can pull (DISCH_ORD_DT_TM). According to Mark, there is also a timestamp for when the patient is ultimately discharged from the hospital (DISCH_DT_TM). Unfortunately, the nursing staff enter the data in slightly different ways. Some close the patient encounter when the patient leaves the unit area; others wait until the Patient Care Technicians (PCTs) come back to the unit to say that the patient had left the hospital. We can worry about standardization later. So, the time between when the provider enters the discharge orders in the system (DISCH_ORD_DT_TM) to when the patient encounter is closed (DISCH_DT_TM) is called "turnaround time" (TAT).

Day 20

Over the past few days, I've been helping Mr. Laidlaw prepare for the UMMC board meeting. This was fine with me, because I was told by Information Technology (IT) that it would take some time to work my request for timestamp data related to the waiting periods. Today, I got the raw data, and Table C1.1 are the results. What I did not expect to be in the data are the timestamp data for all the inpatient discharges. Discharges are when a patient is sent home or to another care facility from an inpatient bed. Clearly, the ED has a boarding problem, just like Kent has been saying. Still, to Mr. Laidlaw's credit, the ED is not the only place where patients are waiting. I am eager to share these findings with Mr. Laidlaw. I hope he approves of my analysis.

Day 22

Mr. Laidlaw looked at the table of wait times for a long time without saying anything. I wasn't sure what he thought. Then he looked at me with his poker face for a long time. Then he spoke his typically few words. "So, admissions are not the only time patients wait?" That's right, I told him. The patients wait for an average of 153 minutes to be discharged, nearly as bad as the ED. He didn't exactly say "good job," but he did seem kind of happy. He told me that the hospital often operates at 95% daily average occupancy. "Keep looking into this," he told me, "and look up the phrase 'patient throughput.'"

Day 25

Today I met with the CNO, Morgan Fein. She was super nice and interested in my MHA program. She asked me a bunch of questions about the type of work I want to do when I

Table C1.1 UMMC Waiting Periods

LOCATION	WAIT TIME (MINUTES)
Direct Admission	31
Emergency Department	170
Post-Anesthesia Care Unit (PACU)	38
Cardiac Catheterization Lab	132
Inpatient Discharge	153

graduate. She listened to my perspective on things so that I almost forgot that I was supposed to be listening to her opinion on the potential causes of discharge waits. When I stopped talking and listened to her, I learned that there are major components of patient throughput (she called it "patient flow") to consider. According to Morgan, delays in the patient discharge process are critical to understand. She said that a performance metric related to patient discharge is TAT. There are many potential causes of TAT delays.

Here's what I learned. The nurses have a lot to do to discharge a patient from their unit. There are lengthy duty lists and checklists to follow. Nurses need to print discharge papers that include a summary of diagnoses, procedures, discharge instructions, medication list, current functional status, care follow-up plan, and treatment goals. Once all their paperwork is complete, they also have to educate the patients and their families on these care instructions. Patient discharge education is very important because hospitals get penalized by Medicare for readmissions within 30 days.

Unfortunately, lots of things can go wrong in the discharge process. Patients must have arranged transportation home and their prescriptions must be filled. Also, the nurse-to-patient ratio may be too high. Another reason is that less experienced nurses are usually less efficient in care delivery. Another big deal is whether the night staff completes diagnostic testing so that the discharge orders can be completed by the provider, who usually rounds on patients early in the morning. Once ready to go, the PCTs are called to transport them out of the hospital in a wheelchair, and this is often overlooked. There are a limited number of PCTs, so nurses need to think ahead to allow for prep time which is included in the discharge wait time calculation. According to Morgan, safe and efficient routine-to-home discharges should be planned. There should be no surprises; this is called "bed ahead thinking." Nurses should use a discharge checklist to document a standardized quality-driven process, but they usually don't.

Unreliable discharge processes pose a problem, because the "recency effect" applies to patient experience. That is, the last memorable thought of an organization is the discharge process, and if patients are told they are going home today or tomorrow, they expect this to be early and efficient. Patients discharged before 11 a.m. indicate the patients are usually highly satisfied with care. When later than expected, patient experience scores suffer. Mostly, nurses get busy with admissions that come in throughout the day, and aren't able to discharge patients in a timely manner.

Finally, once the patient is transported out of the hospital by the PCT, the Environmental Services (EVS) staff has to clean the room for it to be ready for another patient, but technically this is not included in the TAT.

Day 26

Today I ran into Kent in the ED. He was not happy that I was looking into the inpatient discharges, not ED boarding. He wanted to know how he was going to fix the patient boarding, if he could not get additional resources. Kent told me, "You're not doing me any favors." I'm not sure what he thought I could do, but I don't think Kent likes me anymore. I wish my problem definition for my project were as easy as he thought, because I might be farther along completing the report.

Day 27

I gave Mr. Laidlaw my root cause analysis for the inpatient discharge issue. He did not respond to the analysis, but asked, "Same discharge delays for all units?" I probably should have anticipated that question. I told him I would find out.

Day 28

I learned that not all hospital units have the same discharge TAT. Of course, I realized that some units have sicker patients (higher acuity). So, I separated data for the last week with the Discharge Disposition field equal to "Routine to Home." (See Case 1 Data file provided in the Instructor's and Student ancillary materials.) This was a quick and dirty way to standardize the patient data to make comparisons across units. Morgan Fein told me that the goal of TAT for "Routine-to-Home" discharges was 90 minutes. Clearly some units (3 North, 3 South) are better than others (Table C1.2).

Day 30

Today, I showed the Discharge TAT by Unit to Mr. Laidlaw. He told me to examine the root causes and TAT for each unit to isolate patterns. I need to answer why some units have better TAT than others.

Day 35

I thought the issue might be that some units had more experienced nurses, and thus made them more efficient. I just got the report from Human Resources with each nurse's National Council Licensure Examination (NCLEX®) pass date and his or her principal unit (Table C1.3). I don't think average experience has anything to do with discharge delays.

Day 36

I also thought that nurse-to-patient ratio might cause patient discharge delays (Table C1.4). Again, I don't think this factor accounts for the differences in TAT by unit.

Table C1.2 Discharge TAT by Unit

UNIT	PATIENT DISCHARGE TAT (MINUTES)
2 North	142
2 South	163
2 Tower	133
3 North	71
3 South	64
4 Tower	240

TAT, turnaround time.

Table C1.3 Average Years of Licensure by Unit

UNIT	PATIENT DISCHARGE TAT (MINUTES)	AVERAGE YEARS OF LICENSURE
2 North	142	22.3
2 South	163	25.5
2 Tower	133	21.8
3 North	71	14.1
3 South	64	18.1
4 Tower	240	15.2

TAT, turnaround time.

Table C1.4 Average Nurse-to-Patient Ratio by Unit

UNIT	PATIENT DISCHARGE TAT (MINUTES)	AVERAGE PATIENT-TO-NURSE RATIO
2 North	142	6:1
2 South	163	5:1
2 Tower	133	4:1–5:1
3 North	71	5:1
3 South	64	3:1
4 Tower	240	5:1

TAT, turnaround time.

Day 37

I think I've figured out the root cause of patient delays. I cannot believe it took me a month to define and analyze the problem. I did some manipulation in the spreadsheet of the TAT data I had for "Routine-to-Home" discharges. (See Case 1 Data file provided in the Instructor's and Student ancillary materials.) When nurses discharge before 11 a.m., the process is more efficient because they don't get too busy to discharge patients in a timely manner. Of course, the nurses need to get the orders from the physicians ahead of time. I am very excited to share my findings with Mr. Laidlaw. I hope he signs off on this for my internship report.

DISCUSSION QUESTIONS

1. Were Ben Barrett's original expectations for problem definition and analysis realistic? Why or why not?
2. What mistakes in the problem-solving process did Ben make?
3. How could Ben have improved his interpersonal skills?
4. If you were the ED administrator, Kent Jones, how would you have addressed the ED boarding problem? Do you think Kent's leadership would energize stakeholders to change hospital processes?
5. What aspect of Mr. Laidlaw's leadership style do you admire? How could Mr. Laidlaw's leadership improve? What about the Chief Nursing Officer, Morgan Fein?

 ## PODCAST FOR CASE 1

Listen to how experts approach the topic (you can access the podcast by following this url to Springer Publishing Company Connect[TM]: https://connect.springerpub.com/content/book/978-0-8261-4514-7/front-matter/fmatter2)

FURTHER READING

Broom, K., & Hilsenrath, P. (2015). ACHE member survey: Perspectives on graduate health management education. *Journal of Health Administration Education, 32*(3), 341–358.

Destino, L., Bennett, D., Wood, M., Acuna, C., Goodman, S., Asch, S. M., & Platchek, T. (2019). Improving patient flow: Analysis of an initiative to improve early discharge. *Journal of Hospital Medicine, 14*(1), 22–27. doi:10.12788/jhm.3133

Khanna, S., Sier, D., Boyle, J., & Zeitz, K. (2016). Discharge timeliness and its impact on hospital crowding and emergency department flow performance. *Emergency Medicine Australasia, 28*(2), 164–170. doi:10.1111/1742-6723.12543

TOOLS AND APPROACHES

CHECKLIST

A checklist is a list of actions that must be performed to carry out a given process safely and effectively. Checklists protect us against skipping steps, since we tend to forget mundane, routine tasks when we are bored or under stress. Checklists make the minimum necessary steps explicit. While checklists alone do not guarantee processes will be followed, they act as a reminder system for disciplined, meticulous performance (Gawande, 2010). See Exhibit C1.1 for a sample checklist.

Checklists have been successfully adopted in many types of healthcare quality management scenarios, such as:

- Inpatient discharge processes

- Operating room surgical safety

- Hospital emergency operations plan activation

- Patient communication for improved patient experience

- Peer-to-peer performance observations for central line-associated bloodstream infection (CLABSI) reduction

REFERENCES

Gawande, A. (2010). *The checklist manifesto: How to get things right*. New York, NY: Metropolitan Books.
World Health Organization. (2009). *WHO surgical safety checklist*. Retrieved from https://www.who.int/patientsafety/safesurgery/checklist/en

Exhibit C1.1 Sample Checklist Used in Healthcare (Surgical Safety Checklist)

Surgical Safety Checklist

World Health Organization | Patient Safety
A World Alliance for Safer Health Care

Before induction of anesthesia

(with at least nurse and anesthetist)

Has the patient confirmed his/her identity, site, procedure, and consent?
☐ Yes

Is the site marked?
☐ Yes
☐ Not applicable

Is the anesthesia machine and medication check complete?
☐ Yes

Is the pulse oximeter on the patient and functioning?
☐ Yes

Does the patient have a:

Known allergy?
☐ No
☐ Yes

Difficult airway or aspiration risk?
☐ No
☐ Yes, and equipment/assistance available

Risk of >500 ml blood loss (7 ml/kg in children)?
☐ No
☐ Yes, and two IVs/central access and fluids planned

Before skin incision

(with nurse, anesthetist, and surgeon)

Confirm all team members have introduced themselves by name and role.

Confirm the patient's name, procedure, and where the incision will be made.

Has antibiotic prophylaxis been given within the last 60 minutes?
☐ Yes
☐ Not applicable

Anticipated Critical Events

To Surgeon:
☐ What are the critical or nonroutine steps?
☐ How long will the case take?
☐ What is the anticipated blood loss?

To Anesthetist:
☐ Are there any patient-specific concerns?

To Nursing Team:
☐ Has sterility (including indicator results) been confirmed?
☐ Are there equipment issues or any concerns?

Is essential imaging displayed?
☐ Yes
☐ Not applicable

Before patient leaves operating room

(with nurse, anesthetist, and surgeon)

Nurse Verbally Confirms:
☐ The name of the procedure
☐ Completion of instrument, sponge and needle counts
☐ Specimen labeling (read specimen labels aloud, including patient name)
☐ Whether there are any equipment problems to be addressed

To Surgeon, Anesthetist, and Nurse:
☐ What are the key concerns for recovery and management of this patient?

This checklist is not intended to be comprehensive. Additions and modifications to fit local practice are encouraged.

Revised 1 / 2009

© WHO, 2009

Source: World Health Organization. (2009). *WHO surgical safety checklist.* Retrieved from https://www.who.in/patientsafety/safesurgery/checklist/en

CASE 2: Claims Payment Processing

1. Describe healthcare claims submission and payment processes.
2. Identify regulation and payment issues that affect healthcare organizations' finances.
3. Describe importance of healthcare industry's collaboration with regulators and legislators.
4. Evaluate performance assessment approaches used by policy makers, including regulatory agencies and legislative oversight committees.

INTRODUCTION

Beginning a year ago, the State Medicaid Managed Care Program required 95% of the 240,000 individuals eligible for Medicaid health insurance to enroll into one of three private health insurance plans. These managed care organizations (MCOs) are responsible for paying healthcare service providers, such as hospitals and doctors, based on the claims submitted for the services they provide to beneficiaries. Claims are the bills for healthcare services submitted to insurance companies by hospitals, doctors, and other clinical providers. Certain laws and regulations govern the accuracy and timeliness of claims payment to the providers by MCOs. For example, MCOs must pay accurately submitted claims within 30 days.

To support this new program, the governor of the state created the Office of Medicaid Managed Care (OMMC) within the existing Agency for Health and Human Services to regulate MCO performance, including claims payment accuracy and timeliness. The Director of OMMC, Vivek Bhattacherjee, DHA, previously worked for a large hospital system in the state, and is respected for his collaborative approach to managing the relationships between the providers and MCOs.

The State Senate Committee on Health and Human Services oversees the State Agency for Health and Human Services, including the OMMC. Periodic public oversight committee hearings permit the senators to hold the OMMC accountable for ensuring MCO compliance with state Medicaid laws and regulations. State Senator Gina Stevens is the chairwoman of the oversight committee.

CASE SCENARIO

"Come in," Senator Gina Stevens said at the knock on her State Capitol office door. Brent Stevens, her husband of 10 years, walked in carrying her skirt in a dry cleaning bag.

"Sorry, I didn't realize you were in a meeting," Brent said.

"No, it's okay. Mr. Stockwell was just leaving," she said. "Shawn, this is my husband, Brent. Brent, this is Shawn Stockwell, the head lobbyist of the State Hospital Association."

"Great to meet you," Stockwell said as he left Senator Stevens's office.

"Nice to meet you, too," said Brent.

"Ugh!" Senator Stevens whispered to her husband. "Close the door."

"Who was that character?" Brent said locking the door. "Are all lobbyists such flashy dressers?" Brent asked.

"No, he's special," Senator Stevens said as she took the skirt from her husband and removed it from the hanger. "Never mind him. Thank you so much for bringing me this. I can't believe I split my suit skirt. Today of all days."

"It's my pleasure. Besides, my meetings are not until later this afternoon," Brent said. "What's happening today?"

"We're holding the oversight committee for the Office of Medicaid Managed Care. That's why Mr. Stockwell was in here to see me," Senator Stevens said.

"Presiding over a contentious oversight committee from your wood-paneled committee room is what I imagine you doing all day at work," Brent said. "Do you pepper some poor bureaucrat sitting at a table with nothing but a microphone, a large pitcher of water, and a glass?"

"Funny. No, not exactly, but the Senate committee room has a gallery in the back where the lobbyists sit. So I imagine it'll be a tense scene. According to Stockwell, hospitals throughout the state—especially the powerful members of the State Hospital Association—are concerned that they are not getting paid correctly by the Medicaid managed care organizations. As you can imagine, the hospitals get very frustrated when large bills go unpaid for administrative issues. They are saying that financial stresses may reduce their ability to provide high quality medical care to patients. Some are threatening to leave the Medicaid program."

"No margin, no mission," Brent said.

"That's what Stockwell said. He bent my ear about a bill that Senator McWilliams may bring to committee. Stockwell basically threatened to withdraw support for my re-election if I opposed McWilliams's effort to hold the managed care companies accountable," Senator Stevens told her husband.

"Why would you oppose holding insurance companies accountable?" Brent asked.

"In principle, I wouldn't, but McWilliams is really just posturing to oppose the governor's statewide Medicaid Managed Care plan. He's taken a hardline on the State Hospital Association's position for political purposes. He sometimes lets his antagonism interfere with his good sense." Senator Stevens slipped off the torn skirt and pulled on the new one.

"How do you mean?" Brent asked.

"McWilliams's bill would limit the proportion of healthcare claims, or bills, the managed care organizations could reject. It's a bit complicated, but my understanding is that the MCOs reject claims only when the provider has not supplied all the information they need to pay the claim. An example of a rejected claim might be if a hospital forgot to include the diagnosis related to the healthcare service."

"Why would they forget that?" Brent asked.

"Stuff happens, I guess. A better example of a billing error that gets rejected that Stockwell gave me is when the combination of each individual service dollar amount doesn't equal the total claim amount. You're really stretching my knowledge of the issue now, Brent."

"Impressive," her husband said.

"Thanks. Anyway, the lobbyist for the State Association of Medicaid Health Plans visited me yesterday," Senator Stevens said. "She told me that the MCOs shouldn't be held accountable for things they can't control. According to her, providers need to submit clean claims; otherwise they have to reject them."

"That sounds reasonable to me," Brent said.

"Sure does. So, when the managed care companies got word of potential legislation limiting the number of claim rejections, they were very concerned. 'Bad policy,' they say. The Medicaid health plans lobbyist also made it clear to me that support for my re-election is tenuous."

"Ouch. Getting it from both sides, huh? Don't worry, you'll figure something out. You always do," Brent reassured her with a kiss on her cheek. "Have a good day!"

Transcript: Senate Health and Human Services Committee

The Senate Committee on Health and Human Services convened at 9 a.m. on Tuesday, August 20, in Room 802 of the State Capitol for the purpose of conducting a public hearing on a Medicaid Managed Care quarterly briefing. This transcript of the Senate Health and Human Services Committee public hearing was prepared by the clerk of the Legislature Transcriber's Office. Senators present: Chairwoman Gina Stevens and members Barry McWilliams, Gene Ryerson, Sue Howard, and Blake Halverson.

SENATOR STEVENS: I want to thank the people joining us this morning. The fact that so many folks joined us here just shows the critical importance of this oversight committee, and the commitment to the almost 240,000 Medicaid beneficiaries served by the State Health Insurance Program. By means of opening, this is the Medicaid Oversight Sub-committee which is a part of the Health and Human Services Committee. My name is Gina Stevens, and I am the Ranking Member of the committee, and I represent the 10th District. Now, my colleagues will introduce themselves starting with my friend to my right, Senator Ryerson.

SENATOR RYERSON: I am Gene Ryerson, and I represent the 16th District.

CHRISTY O'SHEA: Christy O'Shea, legal counsel.

SENATOR HOWARD: Sue Howard, 3rd District.

SENATOR MCWILLIAMS: I'm Barry McWilliams, representing the 22nd District, and I would also like to thank those in attendance today. We've made some major moves in the last year to radically change our Medicaid program by engrafting (sic: integrating) the physical, behavioral, and pharmacy care into contracts with private Medicaid Managed Care Programs. In our past oversight hearings, we have heard of operational missteps. The healthcare service providers that serve our most vulnerable fellow citizens should be commended for their patience throughout the past year. We have a fidentiary (sic: fiduciary) duty to promote good experiences for the Medicaid beneficiaries, providers, and taxpayers. Anecdotal stories from the healthcare services providers tell me we are not serving these medical heroes who provide the lifesaving care to patients. They should have every expectation that they will be paid. We must continue to improve our systems and our processes.

SENATOR HALVERSON: Blake Halverson, 15th District.

SENATOR STEVENS: Thank you. With introductions of this sub-committee complete, I would like to invite Director Dr. Vivek Bhattacherjee to the proceedings.

VIVEK BHATTACHERJEE: Thank you very much, Senator Stevens. My name is Vivek Bhattacherjee; that is spelled V-i-v-e-k space B-h-a-t-t-a-c-h-e-r-j-e-e. I am with the Agency for Health and Human Service's Office of Medicaid Managed Care. Today we, the team at

Office of Medicaid Managed Care, are pleased to submit for your review, the FY19 second quarter report on the Medicaid Managed Care Program. The quarterly performance report enhances our capabilities to evaluate the program and provides a mechanism for improved collaboration and coordination with stakeholders. I would like to thank the three MCOs and their leadership teams for their spirit of collaboration and responsiveness shown to our Office. The three MCO CEOs here today are Gilbert Huff of InsuraCare Health, Leonard Wilcox of VitaNational Health, and Maggie England of CommunityCare. Lastly, I want to thank the staff of Office of Medicaid Managed Care for their hard work over the last month in compiling this report.

SENATOR STEVENS: Thank you, Dr. Bhattacherjee. Shall we begin the review?

VIVEK BHATTACHERJEE: Yes, let's begin on page 3, in the section labeled "Operational Performance." We closely monitor the MCOs through the review of performance metrics. In Table C2.1, we report the number of claims received by each MCO on a monthly basis.

Table C2.2 shows the number of claims adjudicated. Adjudicated claims are those that were successfully processed by the MCO's billing systems. After a claim is entered into the system, the health plans either pay or deny the claim. It is not unusual for the MCOs to adjudicate more claims than they received in a given month because the adjudication number includes reprocessed claims. Claims can be reprocessed for a number of reasons. Anyway, the point of this figure is to understand the number of claims that MCOs pay or deny on a monthly basis. Claims can be adjudicated only when a claim does not contain any errors. Healthcare bills submitted without errors are called "clean claims." Healthcare bills submitted with any type of error that prevents automatic processes are called "uncleaned claims."

On the same page, Table C2.3 reports the percentage of claims rejected for each month of the second quarter. Rejected claims are claims that do not meet basic legibility, format, or completion requirements and, therefore, are not processed into the MCO's system for adjudication. Common reasons for rejected claims include clerical errors and missing information.

Table C2.1 Number of Claims Received

	APRIL	MAY	JUNE
CommunityCare	359,264	362,317	383,762
InsuraCare Health	212,278	193,145	208,823
VitaNational Health	317,759	322,182	331,672

Table C2.2 Number of Claims Adjudicated

	APRIL	MAY	JUNE
CommunityCare	365,662	313,910	385,670
InsuraCare Health	192,279	191,674	215,389
VitaNational Health	321,468	311,055	339,071

Table C2.3 Percentage of Claims Rejected

	APRIL (%)	MAY (%)	JUNE (%)
CommunityCare	1.13	0.93	0.87
InsuraCare Health	3.55	3.72	3.63
VitaNational Health	0.65	0.52	0.33

SENATOR STEVENS: Thank you, Dr. Bhattacherjee. If I may ask you to pause there for a moment. Senator McWilliams, did you have a question?

SENATOR MCWILLIAMS: I certainly did (laughter). Thank you, Director Bhattacherjee, for your thorough reporting thus far. Before you move on to other operational measures, I want to ask you a question regarding claims rejections, if I may. We've talked about the rejected claims in the past, and I wonder, is there a relationship between the number of rejections and the profitability of the health plan? I see that InsuraCare Health has higher rejections than the other health plans. I know that InsuraCare Health is doing exceptionally well financially. Is that because they've had success at not paying the healthcare providers?

VIVEK BHATTACHERJEE: Um, well, gosh, uh, it could be for a variety reasons, sir, but I don't have any analysis on this particular association. I can get back to you with that.

SENATOR MCWILLIAMS: Okay. Well, I have some other questions, but I want to give some of my colleagues a chance to ask some questions before I come back to this.

SENATOR STEVENS: Okay, Senator McWilliams, we'll come back to you. Anyone else? Okay, then. If no one else has a question, I would like to understand this process a little better, Dr. Bhattacherjee.

VIVEK BHATTACHERJEE: Yes, well, it is a very interesting process. It would be my pleasure to explain.

SENATOR STEVENS: Thank you, sir. So, tell me if I have this right. Provider delivers the healthcare service then creates a bill, known as a "claim," for that service, right?

VIVEK BHATTACHERJEE: Yes, ma'am.

SENATOR STEVENS: Then the provider submits that claim to the MCO?

VIVEK BHATTACHERJEE: Um hum.

SENATOR STEVENS: And if the claim is clean, meaning the claims contain all the right information, such as patient, identification numbers, provider, and appropriate procedure code, then the claim is paid or denied. Am I right again?

VIVEK BHATTACHERJEE: Yes. All health plans have a claims check process. If the claim includes all the required data, such as name and ID, then the claim is considered clean. A clean claim can be paid or denied.

SENATOR STEVENS: What happens if the claim cannot be processed by the health plans' systems?

VIVEK BHATTACHERJEE: Then it is rejected.

SENATOR STEVENS: So, a claim that can be processed is either paid or denied?

VIVEK BHATTACHERJEE: Well, no.

SENATOR STEVENS: I'm confused!

VIVEK BHATTACHERJEE: I'm sorry, Senator. Let me explain. When the claim cannot be processed automatically, for whatever reason, then the claim is pended. When the claim is pended, it means that the MCO needs more information.

SENATOR STEVENS: So what happens when the claim is pended?

VIVEK BHATTACHERJEE: Sometimes the MCO needs to conduct a medical record review, also called a "chart review," to examine medical necessity of the particular medical service.

SENATOR STEVENS: And other times?

VIVEK BHATTACHERJEE: Well, um, it is my understanding that sometimes the MCO needs more information that does not require a chart review. In those instances, the claims are rejected. The MCO will send rejected claims back to the healthcare provider for more information.

SENATOR STEVENS: Claims that make it into the billing systems can still be rejected?

VIVEK BHATTACHERJEE: Um hum. Yes.

SENATOR STEVENS: I see. Let's go back to chart reviews type of pended claim. Why do MCOs conduct chart reviews?

VIVEK BHATTACHERJEE: Chart reviews are a part of the process that allows MCOs to have oversight into the providers' billing practices. In effect, the MCOs need to make sure the providers are providing the right kind of care at the right place of service for the right patient. Also, there are instances where some providers try to game the system. The medical review is part of the MCOs' claims integrity function. For instance, the U.S. health system notoriously conducts too many diagnostic tests. Some say this is a consequence of practicing quote, defensive medicine, unquote. That is, some doctors order what is called the quote, million-dollar work-up, unquote for patients to avoid any legal liability associated with missing a diagnosis. What I'm saying is that the MCOs' medical record review seeks to pay for only procedures that are clinically appropriate. MCO's call this "medical necessity."

SENATOR STEVENS: I understand. So what causes the pended claims to be eventually rejected?

VIVEK BHATTACHERJEE: Uh, well, this is usually due to a logic change in the MCO's system. That is, the rules that allow the claim to be automatically processed are changed, and the health providers need to provide additional information. For example, the claim could be missing an associated diagnostic test that is needed to make a decision. This type of requirement may be unique to that MCO, and the rule may be instituted without the providers knowing about it.

SENATOR STEVENS: So, the changed rule causes a rejection?

VIVEK BHATTACHERJEE: That's right.

SENATOR STEVENS: Thank you, Dr. Bhattacherjee. I do have some follow-up questions regarding the rejected claims that are not under medical review, but I will let my colleagues jump in here, if they wish.

SENATOR MCWILLIAMS: Senator Stevens, if I may? Are you telling me that MCOs can change the rules on the healthcare providers without telling them.

VIVEK BHATTACHERJEE: Um, well, um, each plan has control over the type of processing logic they employ. As I said, one plan may want to program their billing system logic to look for certain services associated with the claim, such as an x-ray. The reason for this change is that they may have discovered some abuse associated with the service, so they may want to apply more stringent criteria for automatically processing the claim. All MCOs have unique systems in this regard, so all have different rules.

SENATOR MCWILLIAMS: So the MCOs are gaming the system?

VIVEK BHATTACHERJEE: Oh! Ah, I would not say that. I would say that there is a quote, cat and mouse situation, unquote (laughter). The providers and MCOs keep each other accountable.

SENATOR MCWILLIAMS: Thank you, Director Bhattacherjee. That's all for now.

SENATOR STEVENS: Do others have anything to ask? Anyone?

VIVEK BHATTACHERJEE: I will use this opportunity to recover and drink some water (laughter).

SENATOR STEVENS: So, if you have recovered some, I would like to ask you some more questions about rejected claims, just so I can be sure to understand the issue.

VIVEK BHATTACHERJEE: That sounds like a good idea.

SENATOR STEVENS: Can you tell me again why claims are rejected?

VIVEK BHATTACHERJEE: They get rejected because the claims do not contain the needed information. The claims can be rejected before entering the billing system or after entering the system.

SENATOR STEVENS: Why are there two types of rejected claims?

VIVEK BHATTACHERJEE: Well, sometimes claims are rejected because they do not meet basic eligibility, format, or completion requirements and, therefore, are not received into the health plan's system for automatic adjudication. These are called "unclean claims." Examples include clerical errors or missing demographic information. Other times they get accepted into the system, but then the health plan needs additional information. These claims are called "pended claims."

SENATOR STEVENS: Why are claims pended then rejected?

VIVEK BHATTACHERJEE: Pended claims may require additional review of the medical records. That is, the health plan may need more clinical information. Once the health plan gets the information they need, the MCO either pays or denies the claim. In other instances, the health plan needs more details. When they need more detail, but are not reviewing the charts, then these pended claims are rejected.

SENATOR STEVENS: Can you look at *Table C2.3: Percentage of Claims Rejected?* Why are the proportions of rejected claims different for each health plan? Are the processing rules not the same?

VIVEK BHATTACHERJEE: Um, well, the initial processing rules, known as the "SNIP edits," are the same for all three health plans. However, claims can be pended according to each of the health plan's differing rules. Since beginning the program last year, each of the MCOs have regularly modified their claims-processing logic.

SENATOR STEVENS: So why does InsuraCare Health pend then reject significantly more claims than other health plans?

VIVEK BHATTACHERJEE: I think that is because the providers have adapted to the rules of the other health plans but not InsuraCare Health.

SENATOR STEVENS: Why have the providers not adapted to the rules of InsuraCare Health?

VIVEK BHATTACHERJEE: They probably have adapted, but new and different rules have been created without the knowledge of the providers. InsuraCare Health and the other managed care organizations are required to publish their claims payment rules twice per year. This has been the regulation as long as I can remember, years probably.

SENATOR STEVENS: Earlier, you mentioned the collaboration between MCOs and you and your staff. Could you develop a requirement for health plans to share their processing rules so that providers don't have to learn of them after the claims have already been rejected?

VIVEK BHATTACHERJEE: We could certainly try that. Our office convenes regular bi-weekly meetings between payers and providers to resolve these pended claims. Perhaps a better process could be discussed on this call?

SENATOR STEVENS: Thank you, Dr. Bhattacherjee. While these challenges are certainly not unique to any large program, we must seek continuous improvement. This Senate sub-committee provides a legislative branch oversight function and is not—I repeat, not—operationally responsible for the administration of Medicaid, which, as all of you know, is a function of the executive branch. That said, we must be working diligently going forward.

SENATOR MCWILLIAMS: Senator Stevens, if I may? I think it is outrageous that health plans can just change their rules willy-nilly. Let me be clear, Director Bhattacherjee, you need to hold the health plans accountable.

VIVEK BHATTACHERJEE: Well, um, I see that uh, well, as Senator Stevens suggested, there may be a way to improve communication surrounding pended claims that are rejected. I, uh, understand that it can be frustrating. But again, I want to express my appreciation to the MCO leadership here today. Their collaboration on this issue, of, um, rejection of pended claims, will be helpful going forward. And, um, if I may request that we take a short break? It seems that this water has finally processed through my system (laughter).

DISCUSSION QUESTIONS

1. What was the central conflict for Senator Gina Stevens? Describe her approach to resolving her dilemma.

2. Describe how the quality management approach can be implemented in the regulatory oversight of healthcare programs, such as Medicaid Managed Care.

3. Why was Senator McWilliams's solution to create a law that limits the number of claims rejected by the MCOs the wrong solution?

4. Do you think Dr. Vivek Bhattacherjee's reputation for collaboration is justified?

5. To what extent do you think that laws and regulations impact healthcare organizations' finances and the delivery of patient care?

 ## PODCAST FOR CASE 2

Listen to how experts approach the topic (you can access the podcast by following this url to Springer Publishing Company Connect[TM]: https://connect.springerpub.com/content/book/978-0-8261-4514-7/frontmatter/fmatter2)

FURTHER READING

Harris, M. T., & Kaplan, D. (2015). The revenue cycle. In N. Baum, R. G. Bonds, T. Crawford, K. J., Kreder, K. Shaw, T. Stringer, & R. Thomas (Eds.), *The complete business guide for a successful medical practice* (pp. 107–119). Cham, Switzerland: Springer.

Hodges, J. (2002). Effective claims denial management enhances revenue: Claims denial management has become a critical component of a hospital's strategic effort to offset the adverse impact of Balanced Budget Act payment reductions. *Healthcare Financial Management, 56*(8), 40–50. Retrieved from https://go.gale.com/ps/anonymous?id=GALE%7CA90317285&sid=googleScholar&v=2.1&it =r&linkaccess=fulltext&issn=07350732&p=AONE&sw=w

Rauscher, S., & Wheeler, J. R. (2008). Effective hospital revenue cycle management: Is there a trade-off between the amount of patient revenue and the speed of revenue collection? *Journal of Healthcare Management, 53*(6), 392–404. Retrieved from https://journals.lww.com/jhmonline/ Citation/2008/11000/Effective_Hospital_Revenue_Cycle_Management__Is.8.aspx

TOOLS AND APPROACHES

PROCESS MAP

A Process Map is a graphical representation of the sequence of steps in a process. Also called a "flowchart," a Process Map is the simplest representation of a process. The basic Process Map does not need to show more than two components of a process:

1. Steps

2. Decisions

While more details can be incorporated, the vast majority of processes can be represented well with just these two components, as seen in Figure C2.1.

To build a Process Map or a flowchart, there is no better way than to gather a team of people who really know the process in a room. The facilitator can hang a piece of paper on the wall to serve as the backdrop of the Process Map. Team members are instructed to write down their steps on Post-It® notes and affix them to the paper. The advantage of using Post-It notes is that it allows to move steps around quickly and still produces a clean version of the process. People typically forget steps and using Post-It notes allows for quick modifications once someone realizes a step has been missed or that steps are not in the right order.

A facilitator could also choose to meet with team members one-on-one to understand their portion of the process and draw each piece individually. If this approach is employed, the entire team must be brought together once the entire Process Map is completed to review it.

Once the Process Map is completed in this fashion, the facilitator may choose to produce a final version of the Process Map, either drawing it on paper or using software tools such as Microsoft® Visio® or PowerPoint®.

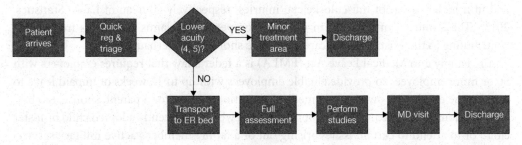

FIGURE C2.1 Example of Process Map (emergency department patient flow).

CASE 3: Return-to-Work at a Home Healthcare Agency

OBJECTIVES

1. Analyze patient care service implications of delays in Human Resources-related administrative work flows.

2. Understand how the administration of employment laws and processes can affect workforce management in a healthcare setting.

3. Differentiate the nonclinical functions of various healthcare professions that support direct patient care, such as Human Resources, Information Technology, and Risk Management.

4. Demonstrate how best practices research and benchmarking can be used to improve nonclinical organizational practices.

5. Identify how information technology can be leveraged to improve healthcare administration processes.

INTRODUCTION

Employees in healthcare occupations miss work due to occupational injury or illness more than twice as much as other occupations (Bureau of Labor Statistics, 2013). Among nurses and nursing aides in the United States, musculoskeletal injuries, such as low back, shoulder, knee, neck, and hand/wrist, cost an estimated $2 billion annually (Waehrer, Dong, Miller, Haile, & Men, 2007). Among all U.S. workers, nurses and nursing aides have the sixth and fifth highest rates of musculoskeletal injuries, respectively (Bureau of Labor Statistics, 2013). These injuries often result in workers' compensation claims and leaves from work, contributing to the existing healthcare workforce shortages (Buerhaus, 2008).

The Family and Medical Leave Act (FMLA) is a federal law that requires employers with 50 or more employees to provide eligible employees with up to 12 weeks of unpaid leave to care for the employee's own serious medical condition; to care for a parent, spouse, or child with a serious medical condition; to bond with a newborn or recently adopted child or foster child; or to attend to certain issues arising out of a family member's active military service. Employee absence, leave, and disability management are the top employment issues for the healthcare industry where 91% healthcare risk managers identified "improving FMLA administration" as one of their three top priorities (Mercer, 2010).

Return-to-work (RTW) processes represent a major challenge associated with FMLA. When an employee is ready to RTW from FMLA leave, the employer must reinstate him or her to the same position the employee held prior to the leave or an equivalent position, in terms of pay, benefits, and other working conditions. Even if the employee fails to give notice, the employer must still return the employee to work within 2 business days.

CASE SCENARIO

Advantage Home Care Center is a subsidiary of The Golden Life Corporation, a for-profit long-term healthcare company founded in 1992 that employs over 4,000 people nationwide. In addition to operating 15 freestanding skilled nursing facilities, the corporation recently expanded to include home healthcare. Home healthcare is an alternative to hospitalization that provides medical, paramedical, and social services to patients in their homes.

The following interviews were conducted by Steve Doering, Director of Quality Management, for the RTW project at Advantage Home Care Center in Springfield. The timeline was estimated based on the information provided in the interviews.

Two Years Ago

LINDA OKAFOR, HOME HEALTH NURSE

I am a licensed vocational nurse (LVN) at Advantage Home Care. As an LVN in home care, I work under my nurse manager, a registered nurse who schedules all of our patient visits. I go to patients' homes to take vital signs, insert catheters, change bandages, administer medications, and help patients with mobility. I don't usually help patients with personal hygiene and stuff like that, because Advantage hires home health aides to help with the tasks considered activities of daily living or ADLs.

Before I started working at Advantage, I hurt my back assisting a 100-pound, 80-year-old man get out of bed. I used proper body mechanics, just like I'm supposed to, but I depended on him to assist me, like he had earlier in the evening. He was just too weak to help me. Neither of us realized it until I went to help him move. That's when I felt the pain. I was diagnosed with a herniated disc at L4-5. I had pain in my legs and feet usually, but the pain went away after physical therapy, massage, and doing flexibility and strength exercises.

Last year, while working at Advantage, the pain in my legs and feet came back, so I started physical therapy again. I told my boss, Eunice Black, about it at the time. I kept on taking shifts because Eunice is a good woman, and I didn't want to let her down when she was short staffed.

EUNICE BLACK, NURSE MANAGER

Oh, yeah, we're always short staffed. Because of the overall nursing shortage, it's hard for me to find dependable LVNs. I do hire a few RNs to conduct the assessments to determine the nature and level of services required per patient, but the LVNs handle the majority of nursing care in our home healthcare agency.

It's my job to schedule the visits. I begin with the allocation procedure where I need to figure out which patient services are assigned among the LVNs and home health aides that need to be scheduled. We've got software that helps, but still, it's a big time suck. Then the routing software figures all patients' and nurses' time windows, nurses' meal breaks, continuity of care, maximum distance between two consecutive visits by the same nurse, and each nurse's route beginning and ending at the main office. I need to track all employees' skills and preferred territory. To get this scheduling done, the software helps me calculate the historical patient demand, but still there are always challenges with allocation and routing because of the high variability with new patient referrals.

What I'm saying to you is that scheduling is a real nightmare. I need to keep the staff happy and working. If I lose a nurse or aide for some reason, I have to scramble to fix the schedule which can cause big problems with patient care, really big. And I mean really big. It impacts patient quality of care and health outcomes since we have fewer staff to care for the same number of patients.

So, I treat the good employees like family. Linda Okafor is family. I feel really bad for her. Home healthcare exposes nurses to all kinds of ergonomic risks, and every patient's house is unique—totally different from the traditional skilled nursing facility or hospital setting.

August 18

LINDA OKAFOR, HOME HEALTH NURSE

After over a year of on-and-off physical therapy, my pain didn't go away. I notified my manager that I needed to take a leave of absence.

EUNICE BLACK, NURSE MANAGER

Yep, she told me. So I said to her, you need to get workers' comp. Linda, that's a work-related injury. You can get paid while you're healing your back.

August 19

LINDA OKAFOR, HOME HEALTH NURSE

So, I did as Eunice told me. I notified her and Human Resources, and submitted all the necessary information.

August 20

ORSON CARTE, MANAGER OF RISK MANAGEMENT AND LOSS CONTROL

According to my files, we received Linda Okafor's workers' compensation claim on August 20th. Sorry, by "we," I mean Golden Life's Corporate Department of Risk Management and Loss Control. We handle claims against the company and administer the risk management program on a day-to-day basis. This means analyzing risk management data, conducting risk management educational programs, and interfacing with corporate lawyers. We keep up with the ever-changing state and federal regulatory requirements and the resulting compliance concerns. We also promote patient safety, quality care, and the minimization of loss to protect the company's assets. We seek to reduce the possibility that losses will occur and, if they do occur, we seek to reduce their severity.

So, I evaluated Linda Okafor's workers' compensation case on August 20th. Based on my review, I denied her initial claim, because, according to our state law, the employee must file a claim within 1 year after the date of injury. In the case of an occupational disease or cumulative injury, the injury date is when the employee first experienced disability (often when they missed work or had to get medical treatment), and they knew or should've known it was caused by work. She began treatment for her back pain over 1 year ago. I sent the denial to Human Resources and Mrs. Okafor.

August 22

LINDA OKAFOR, HOME HEALTH NURSE

I guess I should have submitted the workers' comp claim earlier, but I just didn't know. I didn't want to appeal the decision, but still wanted to take some time off to get my back right. Instead, I notified my manager and HR that I intended to take a leave of absence under FMLA.

ORSON CARTE, MANAGER OF RISK MANAGEMENT AND LOSS CONTROL

Then I evaluated Mrs. Okafor's FMLA claim. A workers' compensation claim is entirely different from the FMLA. Under the FMLA, the employee is entitled to continued health insurance benefits during an employee's absence from work, but he or she will not be paid during the same time period. I approved her application for the FMLA leave, and then I sent the approval to Human Resources (HR), Information Technology (IT), and Mrs. Okafor.

August 23

TROY DIXON, DIRECTOR OF IT

The FMLA process involves temporary suspension of access to the various information systems, such as scheduling and patient medical records. When our team gets a FMLA ticket from Human Resources, we work the tickets to remove access to the electronic medical records system, the medication management system, the scheduling system, and the mobile applications system.

August 24

GLORIA WONG, HUMAN RESOURCES BENEFITS MANAGER

Oh, yes, Linda Okafor, bless her heart. We processed her FMLA benefits. Poor thing. I remember thinking at the time that I hoped she would be able to start seeing patients again as soon as possible. She is such a sweet, caring woman, and I know she wanted to help her patients. I tried to stay in touch with her, dropping her a couple of emails within the first few weeks of her FMLA. It is the philosophy of our HR Benefits Department to focus on retaining experienced employees. They care for patients; we care for them.

One of our core values is that healthcare workers must be 100% healthy before they return to work. Nurse managers worry about the safety of patients and what could happen in an emergency; we worry about getting employees back to work and back to earning their paycheck.

I've done some research on best practice processes and benchmarks through my membership in the American Society for Healthcare Human Resources Administration. Most healthcare organizations have Leave Specialists positions to manage the leave-of-absence and RTW processes. That's probably why the benchmark for the percent of staff that can work on their first day back is 85%. Do you know what our first-day-back metric is; it's 25%, which is pretty yucky. I just feel so terrible for our clinical staff and the nurse managers trying to schedule them.

ORSON CARTE, MANAGER OF RISK MANAGEMENT AND LOSS CONTROL

I'm not sure what the Human Resources policy is, quite frankly. I know HR wants the Risk Management and Loss Control department to develop an internal disability case management program. My take is that we just can't afford to hire case managers specifically for the oversight of FMLA and workers' compensation leave.

While RTW interventions may shorten the disability duration associated with FMLA, I don't think people are all that eager to come back to work. Trust me … I see it all the time. People just want to milk the system.

September 21

LINDA OKAFOR, HOME HEALTH NURSE

After a few weeks on FMLA, on September 21st I was ready to come back to work. I missed the patients! Also, my mother in Nigeria had been very ill, and I needed the extra money to go visit her. Luckily, my physical therapy had gone really well, and my back felt better. My physical therapist recommended that I see the physician in her office to fill out the paperwork that I needed to release me from my FMLA. I saw Dr. Margarita Hernández later that day.

DR. MARGARITA HERNÁNDEZ, TREATING PHYSICIAN

Because I work closely with physical therapists in our practices, I often fill out these fitness-for-duty certifications that allow injured workers to return to their jobs. Based on the particular health condition that caused the need for FMLA leave, I just identify physical limitations and work restrictions. Then, I sign off on the WH-380 certification form allowing an employee to return to work, just as I did for Linda Okafor.

Some companies, especially the local hospital systems, have online portals that allow me to check the history of the patient, the expected leave time, physical requirements for the duties of their work, and any transitional work plans. This gives me a "one-stop shop" to get whatever information I need on the RTW program. They also provide employees with documentation to bring to their first doctor visit, such as work restriction sheets, to be filled out if the employee can return to work with restrictions, and pamphlets on the RTW program.

However, I had not worked with Advantage Home Care Center or The Golden Life Corporation before, so I was not sure of their processes. When I don't have a relationship with the specific employer, I just wait until I get a bunch of RTW forms to sign. In my view, batch-processing paperwork of this type improves my efficiency. At the end of each day, sometimes the day after, my administrative staff scans and emails the completed approval to RTW to the respective HR department contacts for the employee. This is what we did for Linda Okafor.

By the way, I never got any information on Linda's work restrictions or any description of the tasks she would be expected to perform. So, I just assumed that she could return to her job when her back fully recovered. To tell you the truth, our care teams are typically more focused on treating the employees' symptoms than on returning the employee to work. We cannot always spend the time needed to create these plans or to communicate with HR departments because we are busy tending to patients.

EUNICE BLACK, NURSE MANAGER

Look, it seems to me that healthcare organizations have better access to physicians than most other types of organizations. Why can't we readily interact with physicians to help recovering employees return to work? Why the delay? Shouldn't this process be queued up in advance?

September 22

GLORIA WONG, HUMAN RESOURCES BENEFITS MANAGER

Once we get the forms from the physician, we request certain information from the employee, usually in the form of an email. We ask when they plan to come back and whether there are any work modifications needed.

LINDA OKAFOR, HOME HEALTH NURSE

Yes, I got the email from HR the next day. I was told to fill out an RTW form. I had to print it, scan it, and email it back. I could also fax it back, but, come on, who has a fax machine anymore?! Honestly, it wasn't exactly clear what information to submit. I remember thinking: Is there a checklist or something?

EUNICE BLACK, NURSE MANAGER

Once I heard from Linda that she was coming back, I was already looking to slot her back into the schedule. I had some major needs in her territory, so I thought it would work perfectly. Little did I know it would actually be a week until I could get her on the schedule.

September 23

GLORIA WONG, HUMAN RESOURCES BENEFITS MANAGER

Unfortunately, Linda Okafor did not fill out the required forms needed to reinstate her IT system access. I felt really bad for her, but we were missing information for her RTW form packet. We followed up by requesting additional information from her via email.

September 24

LINDA OKAFOR, HOME HEALTH NURSE

The next day, I got an email from HR telling me that I had not provided all the correct IT system access information. There were three separate forms for four different systems, including the electronic medical records system, the medication management system, the scheduling system, and the mobile applications system. So, I had to print, fill out, scan, and email the forms to HR. HR also notified me that I had to recertify my Basic Life Support or Advanced Care Life Support, which I could complete online. I couldn't get this done until the next day.

EUNICE BLACK, NURSE MANAGER

So Linda told me that day that she had missed some of the RTW paperwork. Why does she need to tell me and not HR? Why don't I have access to some centralized HR system? What notifications should be in place to manage the process? Shouldn't I get a status report on all potentially returning employees? Most big hospitals have an employee intranet on which RTW programs place all their forms and documents, along with information on company policy, and answers to frequently asked questions. The employee should know exactly what is needed to return them with all accesses needed for successful shift work. We've got none of this. Seriously!? What a total cluster!

September 26

GLORIA WONG, HUMAN RESOURCES BENEFITS MANAGER

Two days later we received all the completed RTW forms from Linda. Once we verified the information supplied by the physician and the employee, we submitted the RTW forms to IT.

TROY DIXON, DIRECTOR OF INFORMATION TECHNOLOGY

It's my vision to leverage IT systems to allow for optimal communication among all Golden Life employees. This includes FMLA-related processes. I want the communication to be seamless and transparent for HR, IT, treating physicians, the employee, and the managers. The lack of effective organizational communication and an absence of a tracking system is an organizational need, for sure. I understand that employees need immediate access to all these things to return to work, but we're not there yet. It's true that we have separate processes to reactivate an employee in our electronic medical records system, medication management system, scheduling system, and the mobile apps system that allows access to things like on-site appointment schedules and GPS-enabled electronic visit verification. Once these systems are reactivated, we let Human Resources know that the employee is ready to return to work.

September 27

GLORIA WONG, HUMAN RESOURCES BENEFITS MANAGER

Once we hear from IT that the systems have been reactivated for the employee, we let the nurse manager know that the employee is ready to be scheduled to see patients.

EUNICE BLACK, NURSE MANAGER

Finally, I got a notification from IT that Linda could be scheduled. Of course, there's a lag time to get her on the schedule. I wish I had a way of anticipating my employees' return to work.

September 28

LINDA OKAFOR, HOME HEALTH NURSE

I finally was able to return to work with full access to all IT systems, a week after I told my boss I was ready to come back. My back has been really good since then. I was able to save enough money to visit my mother in Nigeria. She is also doing much better now.

DISCUSSION QUESTIONS

1. What methods are effective in helping doctors, employees, and managers understand the RTW process?

2. How long did the FMLA RTW process officially take in Linda Okafor's case? What is the optimal duration?

3. Dr. Margarita Hernández prefers batch processing of FMLA paperwork to one-piece flow. What consequence does this approach have on the FMLA RTW process?

4. What would happen if Linda Okafor had returned to work 2 days after her physician's approval?

5. How could the use of technology improve healthcare processes at Advantage Home Care?

 ## PODCAST FOR CASE 3

Listen to how experts approach the topic (you can access the podcast by following this url to Springer Publishing Company Connect™: https://connect.springerpub.com/content/book/978-0-8261-4514-7/front-matter/fmatter2)

REFERENCES

Buerhaus, P. I. (2008). Current and future state of the US nursing workforce. *Journal of the American Medical Association, 300*(20), 2422–2424. doi:10.1001/jama.2008.729

Bureau of Labor Statistics. (2013). *Nonfatal occupational injuries and illnesses requiring days away from work, 2012*. Retrieved from https://www.bls.gov/news.release/archives/osh2_11262013.pdf

Mercer. (2010). *US Survey on absence and disability management*. Retrieved from https://www.imercer.com/products/absence-disability-management.aspx

Waehrer, G. M., Dong, X. S., Miller, T., Haile, E., & Men, Y. (2007). Costs of occupational injuries in construction in the United States. *Accident Analysis & Prevention, 39*(6), 1258–1266. doi:10.1016/j.aap.2007.03.012

FURTHER READING

Denne, J., Kettner, G., & Ben-Shalom, Y. (2015). Return to work in the health care sector: Promising practices and success stories. *Mathematica Policy Research*. Retrieved from https://ideas.repec.org/p/mpr/mprres/8f6a0bc8267942a5bd2b0a336f8ef5d3.html

Lanzarone, E., Matta, A., & Sahin, E. (2012). Operations management applied to home care services: The problem of assigning human resources to patients. *IEEE Transactions on Systems, Man, and Cybernetics-Part A: Systems and Humans, 42*(6), 1346–1363. doi:10.1109/TSMCA.2012.2210207

SWIM LANE DIAGRAM

A swim lane diagram is a special type of flowchart (Figure C3.1). On a swim lane diagram, different functions or roles are assigned "lanes," and their steps are drawn within their respective lane. In this way, one can get an idea not only of the sequence of steps involved in the process but also who performs each of those steps. A swim lane diagram is particularly useful when looking at multidisciplinary processes. It is not uncommon, after creating a swim lane diagram, to find redundancies in a process (similar steps performed by different people).

To build a swim lane diagram, there is no better way than to gather the multidisciplinary team in a room. The practitioner hangs a piece of "butcher" paper on the wall and identifies the "lanes" (roles involved in the process) with Post-It notes along the left-hand side of the paper. Each team member is instructed to write down his or her steps on additional Post-It notes and affix them to the paper aligned with his or her lane.

Once every team member has completed their lane, the entire flowchart is reviewed by the team to ensure it is an accurate representation of the actual process. This exercise inevitably uncovers previously unknown details of the process and provides the team a thorough comprehension and appreciation for the process and each other.

If the practitioner wishes, he or she can use the completed flowchart to create a cleaner version of the swim lane diagram, using software tools such as Microsoft Visio or PowerPoint.

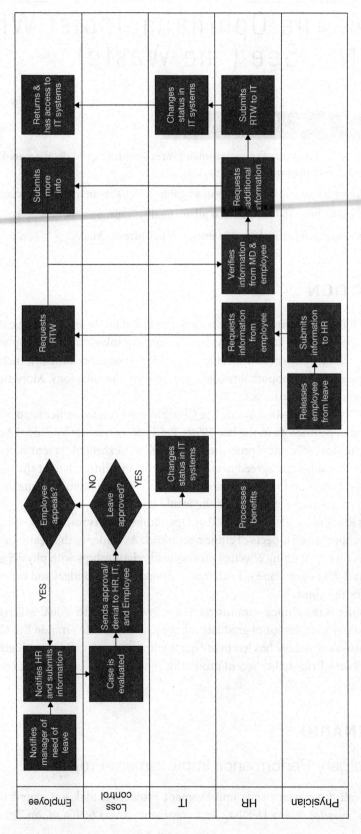

FIGURE C3.1 Example of swim lane diagram for family medical leave act request and return-to-work.

CASE 4: The Ophthalmologist Who Could Not See (The Waste)

OBJECTIVES

1. Evaluate the awareness of organizational power structures and decision-making processes of quality improvement managers.
2. Apply change leadership strategies to a healthcare quality management scenario.
3. Describe how financial analysis can justify quality improvement efforts.
4. Analyze an organizational process using a Value Stream Map.

INTRODUCTION

Rio Grande Eye Clinic is a stand-alone outpatient clinic that has been serving the Rio Grande Valley community for more than 30 years. The six ophthalmologists and two optometrists at Rio Grande Eye Clinic perform about 1,300 outpatient procedures annually, including very complex oculoplastics, neuroophthalmology, and even ocular oncology. More than 50% of the procedures are simple cataracts.

Dr. Elena DeSilva came to Rio Grande Eye Clinic in 2001 following her residency at Mayo Clinic in Rochester, Minnesota in the late 1990s. Dr. DeSilva quickly became the clinic's star because of her surgical efficiency, procedural volume, and excellent patient outcomes. Last year, Dr. DeSilva begrudgingly agreed to assume the role of Clinic Chair at the behest of the clinic management team and several of her peers. She is unaccustomed to making business and operational decisions, but vowed that she would try her best.

Jane Lucas is Rio Grande Eye Clinic's VP of Operations. Jane is responsible for leadership, direction, and support to all aspects of clinic operations. As leader of the health management staff, she focuses on maintaining effective professional relationships with physicians, clinical staff, patients, and the public. Jane is in charge of developing the budget and expense reduction strategies for the clinic.

Ashley Schaeffer is the clinic's administrator. She graduated with a dual MBA/MHA, and Jane Lucas hired her straight out of graduate school to come to Rio Grande Eye Clinic as an assistant administrator. Ashley has led many quality improvement efforts with great success over the last 10 years. Prior to her recent promotion, she earned a Lean Expert certification.

CASE SCENARIO

Cataract Surgery Performance Improvement Project

"Why did you call it a performance improvement project? It makes it sound like we are low performers," was Dr. Elena DeSilva's first comment. It was 6:30 a.m. on Thursday, and

Dr. DeSilva and Ashley Schaeffer were in Jane Lucas's office to discuss the Cataract Surgery Performance Improvement Project.

"Well," replied Jane, "we need to improve your financial performance. Cataracts are our biggest money-loser, Dr. DeSilva," said Jane. "I know you don't concern yourself with money as much as I do, but, as I advised you when you took the role of Clinic Chair, now you have to be mindful of the financial, as well as the clinical performance, of the clinic."

Dr. DeSilva broke eye contact with Jane. Staring at her shoes, she asked, "Okay, how much money are we really losing?"

"Dr. DeSilva," Ashley said while opening her black Mont Blanc® padfolio, "I have studied your financial reports for the last year and confirmed that cataracts are, in fact, costing approximately $1,000 more than what Medicare pays us. That's $650,000 each year in losses. The trend, as you can see here (see Figure C4.1), is not looking good. A year ago, we were about $800 over Medicare reimbursement, but the losses have been steadily increasing. I believe that there are some opportunities for improvement."

"Please, tell me what they are," Dr. DeSilva said, in a half-sarcastic, half-serious tone.

"Actually," replied Ashley, "we are going to ask the staff."

Dr. DeSilva looked befuddled. She looked at Jane and back at Ashley twice. She reclined back on her chair and all she could mutter while resting her elbows on the armrests and joining her hands, just by her fingertips in front of her chest was, "okay."

Ashley continued, "We are going to bring your team together in a room for a day. We are going to involve representatives from all parts of the process, all the way from scheduling to Pre-Op, intra-op and PACU…"

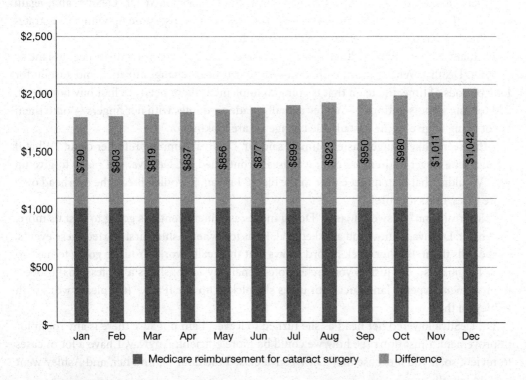

FIGURE C4.1 Total cost of cataract surgery versus Medicare reimbursement.

"I'm sorry," interrupted Dr. DeSilva, snapping to attention, "did you say 'for a day'?"

"Yes," continued Ashley. "That should be enough to understand the current state and identify some opportunities."

"I'm sorry," interrupted Dr. DeSilva again, this time looking at Jane. "Jane, are you hearing what I am hearing? Did she just say we are going to spend a full day just to identify some opportunities? Or, did I misunderstand?"

Jane kept Dr. DeSilva's stare, then Ashley continued, "Yes, Dr. DeSilva, that is what I said. Our method includes bringing the team together, since they are the ones who understand the process and probably have some good ideas on where the opportunities are, and in our experience, investing a day in this early part of the performance improvement process pays dividends in the end."

"Well, then, I am hoping you are planning to do this on a weekend!" replied Dr. DeSilva.

"Well, not unless we are going to pay the team overtime for working over the weekend," replied Ashley nonchalantly.

Dr. DeSilva's eyes got even bigger as she muttered something unintelligible. She then continued, "So, let me get this straight. You are coming in to help me improve my financial performance, and your first idea is to close the clinic for a day while we identify some opportunities? How is that going to help me improve my financial performance? It seems to me that would be even more detrimental to my finances!"

"No, we are not going to close the clinic," replied Ashley as she had done many times before to skeptics of process improvement. "I mentioned that we are going to bring in representatives of each of the areas of the process. We will not bring in everybody, but just a selection of team members who can speak to the whole process."

"Okay, and what do we expect to gain from that?" questioned Dr. DeSilva and, again turned to Jane Lucas. "Jane, wouldn't it be easier if you and I just came up with some strategies that I can implement over the next few months?"

"Actually," replied Ashley, "that very rarely works. I do not mean any disrespect to Jane or you, Dr. DeSilva. What I mean is that, in order for process changes to stick and sustain for long periods of time, the team that is going to implement them needs to first buy into them. Just forcing some 'solutions'"—Ashley actually made air quotes with her fingers—"onto them is not going to give us the sustainable change we are looking for."

"This seems like a huge waste of time!" said Dr. DeSilva slumping into her chair. "What if we just set a target to do more cataract cases?" continued Dr. DeSilva, not ready to give up yet. "Wouldn't that help us get closer to the black? I mean, it would spread the overhead over more cases, that's for sure!"

"Not, really, no," answered Jane. "Doing more cases inefficiently is going to cost us more. Listen, Dr. DeSilva, I know you are skeptical, I was too when Ashley first started these events, as she calls them. But her track record shows that this really works. You are going to have to trust her, just as I do. Just as you are a professional physician, she is a professional process improvement expert." Jane Lucas got up as she picked up her iPad®. "Just please work with Ashley on this."

Dr. DeSilva lowered her head as she turned to leave. "I am not sure there is any room for improvement. I just don't see how we could be more efficient. Anyway, I have a lot of cases to review, so, if you'll excuse me," Dr. DeSilva closed the door behind her, and Ashley went back to her office.

Change of Mind

Ashley woke up the next morning and immediately grabbed her phone and checked her email while still in bed as she does every morning. She saw she had an email from Dr. DeSilva from 9:37 p.m. the night before. Ashley was not sure what to expect, but she opened it anyways.

"Team," the email started. "This month's staff meeting will be different than what we have done in the past. We are going to use this time, and in fact, the entire day for a Current State Mapping Session to try to identify some opportunities for improvement in our operations, specifically around cataract surgery procedures. Not everyone will participate in this session. We will select a few team members that represent all the different steps in the process from scheduling all the way to discharge from PACU to help us understand our current challenges better and hopefully to help us come up with ideas on how to improve. Ashley Schaeffer, our clinic's administrator, will lead us through this effort. Look for more information coming from her over the next few days. Thank you very much and have a great Friday! Respectfully, Elena DeSilva, MD."

Ashley almost fell off her bed! She jumped out of bed and started getting ready for work. When Ashley stopped by Dr. DeSilva's office first thing, she was already in the OR, so Ashley caught up with Dr. DeSilva as she came out of the OR from her first case. "Thank you for sending that email out and for changing your mind!"

"Well, I am not fully convinced yet, but I really am stumped about what opportunities we have or how to uncover them, so, I figured, 'What the heck!'"

Ashley smiled and said, "I'll take it! I need some time with you and Jane to identify the team members we want to bring to the session." As she walked back to her office, Ashley could not help feeling dumbfounded. "What happened last night? It's like a switch went off inside her head!" she thought.

Value Stream Mapping Session

Eleven days later, Jane, Dr. DeSilva, and Ashley along with the seven team members selected gathered for the mapping session. The seven team members were:

- Alicia Sherburne from scheduling and registration
- Jake Ackerman from Pre-Admission Testing (PAT)
- Olga Sebring, Director of Nursing for Rio Grande Eye Clinic
- Kelley Glenn, Pre-Op Nurse
- Carlos García, Circulator Nurse
- Veronica Nader, Surgical Tech
- Layla Domínguez, PACU Nurse

Jane welcomed everyone, thanked them for their time, and set the stage for what she expected from them. Dr. DeSilva followed and made a compelling call for help even though "she could not see how they can be more efficient." Ashley Schaeffer then took the reins and started guiding the team through the exercise. She explained that they would be creating a Value Stream Map (VSM) of their current process. Ashley highlighted that they were going to focus only on cataract cases during this exercise. Jane and Dr. DeSilva let the team know that they were going to leave them with Ashley, and that they were looking forward to coming back at the end of the day to hear the results of the exercise.

"The first thing we need to do to create our Value Stream Map is to identify some high-level steps of the cataract surgery process. I have taken the liberty of adding those high-level steps to get us started, as you can see here," Ashley said, pointing to the piece of butcher paper with Post-it notes on the wall. "Those high-level steps are Scheduling, Pre-Admission Testing (PAT), Registration, Pre-Op, Intra-Op/Procedure, and PACU. Now, what we need from you is to add some detail below each of those high-level steps. We want to know five or six subprocesses or tasks that you do in those areas. You are also going to estimate how long each of those tasks takes you, on average." While she was explaining this, Ashley showed them a slide with a picture of what she meant (Figure C4.2).

She added, "Document what happens the majority of the time. Do not replicate the procedure manual; we want to know what is really happening. Finally, do not guess."

As the day progressed, Ashley introduced the concepts of value and waste and taught them The Eight Wastes (Transportation, Inventory, Motion, Waiting, Over-processing, Over-production, Defects, and Underutilizing People's Talents).

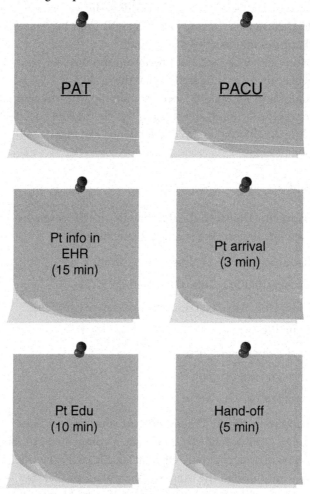

FIGURE C4.2 Adding detail to Value Stream Map.
Edu, education; EHR, electronic health record; PACU, post-anesthesia care unit; PAT, pre-admission testing; Pt, patient.

"Now that you know what waste is," Ashley continued, "you will now use these other color sticky notes to identify our opportunities for improvement and place the sticky close to where that opportunity is on the map. I do not want you to write only what kind of waste it is (transportation, waiting). I want a more detailed explanation of what you feel the opportunity is. Let's walk through an example. Who has an idea?"

"What about the fact that patients wait different amounts of time for their scheduled surgeries?" Sherburne asked.

"Good idea!" Ashley said. "So, in this case, I'll write, 'Variance in timing to schedule surgeries' on the Post-it and place it right around here close to the 'Scheduling' step," she said as she stuck the yellow sticky on that portion of the Value Stream Map. "By the way," Ashley noted, "in a VSM these are called 'kaizen bursts.' Kaizen bursts are graphical stars on the Value Stream Map indicating opportunities for improvement in the process."

"Okay," added Olga Sebring. "I got one! Every physician communicates to us the need for surgery in a different way. Some use email, some use texts, some phone calls, and others apparently expect Alicia and her team to get that information from hallway conversations!"

Alicia Sherburne nodded, while she added, "Also, do you know that we have to schedule the surgery in three different places?"

Ashley's eyes were wide open.

"That's right! We have to schedule it in the EHR, on the OR schedule, and in the surgeon's Outlook® calendar!" Sherburne finished.

"I have a question for the team," said Kelley Glenn. "Do we need to undress the patient for these very simple cataracts cases? I mean, to me that seems like waste and patients have told me as much."

"That's a good question, Kelley," Ashley affirmed.

"Oh, and while we are on the Pre-Op subject," Kelley continued, "can we do something to standardize the eye drops that each surgeon uses? I mean, is that in-play here or are we not touching what the physicians do?"

"Tell me a little more," Ashley wanted to understand better.

"Each surgeon uses different eye drops that we have to give to patients in Pre-Op. Not only do we have to store all these different kinds of drops, but I think it adds opportunity to make mistakes and since we are talking about reducing costs, I am assuming some of these drops will be more expensive than others."

"Well, Kelley, that definitively belongs here. Please, add a sticky about that around Pre-Op," Ashley instructed her.

"And on a related subject, or maybe part of the same one, Pharmacy has to verify those drops every time, so, we have to wait for their phone call. Okay, I'm done!" added Kelley.

Veronica Nader, now feeling empowered, jumped in, "There is something that's been bothering me for quite some time. Do we have to mop the floor between eye cases every time? I mean, obviously, if there is blood or any spills, I can understand it, but it seems excessive to me that we have to mop every time in between these very simple cases. I mean, it takes longer to mop the floor than it takes the surgeon to do the whole case sometimes. And while we are waiting to finish mopping, I cannot open the sterile field, so, I have to wait for that to finish in order to start setting up for the next case."

"Write it down and stick it on the map!" Ashley said, encouraging Veronica.

"Well, since we are questioning all these things, let me ask you something," added Carlos, addressing the team. "Do we need anesthesiologists or even nurse anesthetists for cataracts cases? Some of us are trained on conscious sedation and it seems to me that that is a huge, what did you call it?" he said as he tried to remember. "Underutilization of talent!"

"Good one, Carlos!" said Olga Sebring.

"Again, I am not sure how much we are supposed to question or suggest how the surgeons spend their time," continued Alice Sherburne, "but it seems to me there may be opportunities in the post-op appointments we schedule. They normally want to see the patients all the way through, but some of those appointments could be handled by the optometrists, in my opinion."

Ashley nodded.

"Oh, and sometimes," Alice Sherburne added, "I am not sure who is supposed to schedule the appointments because we have two different resources doing it and we kind of go by whoever gets to it first."

"I think we can improve our room turnover process," interjected Veronica Nader. "During turnover, everybody kind of does everything and I am sure we are duplicating work. We should all have assignments that everyone knows what everyone is supposed to do."

The team identified all these opportunities on the Value Stream Map.

"Great work everybody!" continued Ashley. "The next part of the mapping is usually quick, but it is an important one. We are now going to document flow interruptions. Remember we talked about continuous flow as I discussed the Lean principles? Well, what I need now is for you to document how much wait there is in between each of these high-level steps," she said as she was pointing at the sticky notes across the top of the map with the headings 'Scheduling', 'PAT', etc. (Figure C4.3). She showed them a slide explaining what she wanted them to do.

"Let me ask you," Ashley continued, "how long is it usually after booking the case until the patient goes through the pre-admission testing?"

Jake Ackerman answered, "There is variation, but I would say, normally it is about a week."

"And I think the fastest I have seen it is 2 days," added Alicia Sherburne.

"Great information, thank you! So, I am writing 2 to 7 days in this Post-it note and sticking it between 'Scheduling' and 'PAT', you see?" said Ashley.

"Yes," added Jake Ackerman. "And to continue down the map, I would say PAT is around 5 days before the day of surgery". As he said this, he wrote 5 days on a sticky and placed it between PAT and Registration.

"Registration usually takes no more than 15 minutes," added Sherburne, as a true expert of Value Stream Mapping by this point.

FIGURE C4.3 Adding flow interruptions to a Value Stream Map.
PAT, pre-admission testing.

"Pre-Op varies a lot," said Kelley Glenn, feeling it was her turn.

"True," Ashley replied immediately. "However, we are focusing on cataracts cases for this exercise, so, what is it for those procedures?"

"Oh, I would say, about 30 minutes?" Kelley Glenn answered.

"From the OR to PACU is really nothing," added Carlos García. "It is however long it takes us to transport the patient."

"Right, I would say about 2 minutes," added Layla Domínguez.

"This is great, Team!" Ashley said contemplating all the detail in the Value Stream Map. "The last thing we need to do to complete this Value Stream Map is to identify all the information sources and flows. Here in this top area of the map, we are going to identify all the sources of information you use to make this process work. For example, the EHR is one of them, so, we write EHR in one green sticky, put it up here and then draw links from there to all the steps that interact with this information source."

The team, following Ashley's guidance, identified several sources of information with which they interacted, including the financial system and the Outlook calendar.

Ashley explained that now that they had completed the current state map and identified all these opportunities, they were going to suggest a few potential solutions for some, or all of them.

The last hour of the day was dedicated to the debrief. Jane Lucas and Dr. DeSilva showed up a few minutes before 3:00 p.m. The team had been quickly coached by Ashley on how to present the fruits of their hard day's work to their leaders. When Jane and Dr. DeSilva walked into the room, they immediately fixed their eyes on all the flipcharts, butcher paper, and Post-it notes on the walls around the room.

"Wow! You've been busy!" noted Jane.

"Yes, you have!" agreed Dr. DeSilva smiling as she kept looking around the room and honing in on the flipcharts with the titles of "Opportunities" and "Potential Solutions."

Both Jane and Dr. DeSilva could not help but feel the energy from the team as they summarized how their day went.

Jake Ackerman introduced the "why," the concept of the Value Stream and the Value Stream Mapping method. Veronica Nader followed him explaining The Eight Wastes and pointing out some of the examples of waste they identified in their processes. Carlos García and Layla Domínguez took turns highlighting the potential solutions the team came up with and Kelley Glenn led the lessons learned and reflections of the day.

When the team finished their presentation, Jane and Dr. DeSilva could not hide their excitement and pride. Jane Lucas congratulated the team on a great effort and reminded them that "This is just the beginning. We now have to make all this work for everybody: our patients, our surgeons and our staff." All those in the Value Stream Map team nodded their agreement.

Dr. DeSilva said, "I cannot thank you enough! For weeks, I have been observing my own cases and racking my brain on where we can find some efficiencies. I have asked Jane and Ashley for some suggestions and when Ashley said we were going to ask you for some suggestions, I was not 100% convinced. I could not imagine how we could have been more efficient. Well, you have achieved what I asked you to do. You have opened my eyes to the waste and the opportunities we have. It is our job now, as leaders," she said as she briefly turned to look at Jane and Ashley, "to make sure we get all this going. Some of these ideas will take longer than others, and I definitely have to have some conversations with my peers about some of them."

When there was a moment of silence, Olga Sebring said, looking at Dr. DeSilva and Jane, "Dr. DeSilva and Jane, I really want to commend you and thank you for including our team in this effort! For so long, this team has had all these ideas and they have been frustrated by so much of this waste and we have felt powerless against it. Today that has changed. By involving us in this effort, you have shown us that you value our opinions and our ideas and for that, I am very grateful," she finished, as her voice broke a little.

"Of course! We value your, and your team's, ideas," replied Jane.

"Yes, we do, very much," added Dr. DeSilva, "and I apologize for not doing this earlier. I want you all to know and I want you to let all your peers know that I value your ideas and input very much and that I will try to be more deliberate about soliciting it going forward."

The Change

As the team carried out the project plan, testing and implementing the solutions they came up with over the next several months, they achieved great success, including:

- 31.5% time savings between cataract cases
- 30% cost reduction per cataract case
- 33% improvement in surgeon utilization
- Turnover time reductions

As the project was coming to a close, Dr. DeSilva stopped by Ashley Schaeffer's office one day. "Hey Ashley," Dr. DeSilva called, "I am seeing some issues with OR room and block utilization. I want to jump in front of this thing before it becomes worse. You ready for our next challenge?"

With a big smile on her face, Ashley replied, "Absolutely!"

DISCUSSION QUESTIONS

1. Discuss the importance of balancing clinical and financial performance in healthcare delivery.

2. Why was it so difficult for Dr. DeSilva to see the waste in their processes?

3. Was organizational change successful? Identify each of the steps of a change leadership approach that Jane Lucas and Ashley Schaeffer applied at Rio Grande Eye Clinic in the case scenario.

4. Discuss the pitfalls of not including frontline team members in the improvement process.

5. Identify the type of waste of each of the opportunities for improvement, or "kaizen bursts," identified in the cataract surgery process.

PODCAST FOR CASE 4

Listen to how experts approach the topic (you can access the podcast by following this url to Springer Publishing Company Connect™: https://connect.springerpub.com/content/book/978-0-8261-4514-7/front-matter/fmatter2)

FURTHER READING

Gong, D., Jun, L., & Tsai, J. C. (2017). Trends in Medicare service volume for cataract surgery and the impact of the Medicare physician fee schedule. *Health Services Research, 52*(4), 1409–1426. doi:10.1111/1475-6773.12535

Henrique, D. B., Rentes, A. F., Godinho Filho, M., & Esposto, K. F. (2016). A new value stream mapping approach for healthcare environments. *Production Planning & Control, 27*(1), 24–48. doi:10.1080/09537287.2015.1051159

Jimmerson, C. (2017). *Value stream mapping for healthcare made easy*. London, UK: Productivity Press.

VALUE STREAM MAP

The Value Stream is the path in which value flows from the point where it gets generated to the customer who receives it. Mapping this path in a way that allows us to see all the flows of customers, staff, services, supplies, equipment. and information enables us to uncover opportunities for improvement by focusing on those issues that hinder the flow (Figure C4.4). This is how Lean thinking differs from conventional thinking: It is all about flow.

A Value Stream Map (VSM) is the preferred method for uncovering opportunities for improvement in a process, especially when you need to identify bottlenecks and disconnections between processes and/or functions.

Just as with other types of process maps, to build a VSM, there is no better way than to gather the team members who know the process in a room. You should map the high-level steps that occur from the moment a customer need is identified to the point that need is satisfied and payment is received for providing that service or product.

There are two key pieces of information depicted in a VSM that differentiate it from other process maps:

- The flow of information
- A timeline showing value-added and non–value-added time

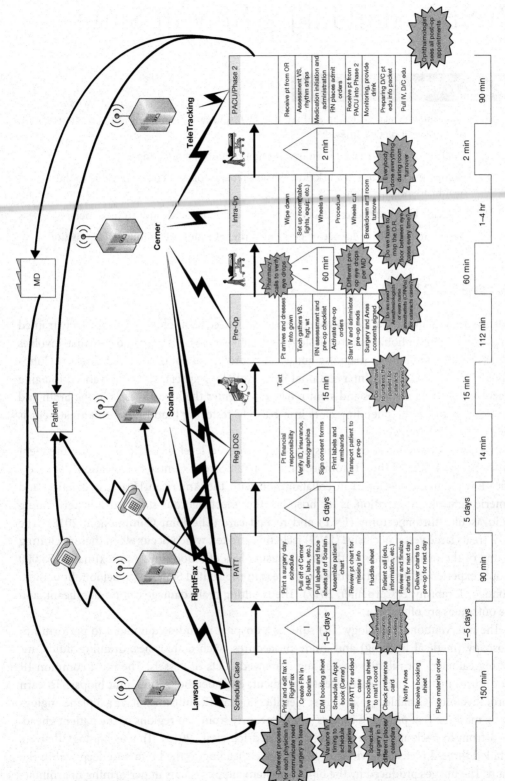

FIGURE C4.4 Value Stream Map example.

CASE 5: Building a New IR Suite

OBJECTIVES

1. Describe how accreditation and regulatory requirements influence the development of new hospital service lines.
2. Analyze processes related to interventional radiology suite design.
3. Compare approaches to work flow design in terms of efficiency and value to the healthcare organization.
4. Describe how healthcare quality managers relate to outside industry partners.
5. Assess methods to influence or persuade others to support an innovative position.

INTRODUCTION

Not all stroke centers are alike. Some have more advanced technologies with specially trained physicians. Interventional neuroradiology is a subspecialty within radiology that involves catheters and radiology to diagnose and treat neurological conditions and diseases (Johns Hopkins Medicine, 2019). Interventional neuroradiology specialists use advanced imaging machinery with guide wires and stent retrievers to enter the blood vessels of the brain and physically remove the offending clots immediately restoring blood flow. This treatment is called "thrombectomy."

The Joint Commission offers hospitals an advanced level of certification for inpatient stroke programs called the "Thrombectomy-Capable Stroke Center Certification." This certification program, developed in collaboration with the American Heart Association and American Stroke Association, is for hospitals that meet rigorous standards for performing endovascular thrombectomy (EVT) and related care (The Joint Commission, 2018). The EVT treats large vessel occlusive (LVO) ischemic strokes, which occur when there is clotting in one of the major arteries of the brain causing loss of blood flow. Approximately 78,000 people experience this kind of stroke each year in the United States (Rai, Seldon, Boo, Link, Domico, Tarabishy, & Carpenter, 2017). The resulting brain damage can be significant, and the outcomes are often poor.

The interventional radiology (IR) suite of a hospital includes equipment to perform fluoroscopy (medical imaging) and guide procedures, such as biopsies, draining fluids, inserting catheters, or dilating or stenting narrowed ducts or vessels. The most common IR procedures include angioplasty, stent placement, chemoembolization, and biopsy. To earn Thrombectomy-Capable Stroke Center Certification, an IR suite must have a biplane angiography machine that produces images simultaneously from two regions of the patient's head, from front to back and from side to side (Friedrich et al., 2019). This technology delivers detailed three-dimensional views of blood vessels leading to the brain and deep within the brain. The images produced by the biplane system aid physicians in performing neurointerventional procedures, such as thrombectomies.

CASE SCENARIO

"OK, approved," said the head of the hospital capital committee.

"It only took 8 months," said Donna Jones, VP of Operations and COO of Madeira Health, a system with four hospitals in the Greater Madeira Valley metro area, as she came out of the meeting. "Now, the real work can start."

At the behest of Dr. Ito Manituro, chief of IR, Jones has been requesting capital expenditures in the budget to build or upgrade Madeira Health's St. Francis's IR Suite to comply with The Joint Commission's requirements to become a Thrombectomy-Capable Stroke Center and subsequently a Comprehensive Stroke Center. It was not until the National Stroke Act required that, as of July 1, 2018, any facility without an IR Biplane Neurointerventional Suite would be bypassed for victims suffering a stroke, that they were finally able to secure the needed capital. The addition of a new IR suite with biplane capabilities will allow St. Francis Hospital to do advanced thrombectomy work, coiling, and aneurysm repairs.

"Dr. Manny, we finally got it! The capital committee approved the budget for the new IR suite!"

"Finally! That's great news, Donna!" replied Dr. Manituro over the phone, as he removed his reading glasses and placed them on the pile of medical records on his desk. He sounded excited and smiling, although there was no one else in his office. "When can we get with CZE and get the work started? What do you need from me?"

Jones and Dr. Manny (as everybody called Dr. Manituro) had already selected an architectural firm, CZE and Associates, to design and build the new IR suite. "I'm emailing Laura as soon as we hang up, and I will follow up with a call tomorrow morning." They hung up, and as he got up from his desk, Dr. Manituro did a small fist pump while quietly saying, "cha-ching!" as if to allow himself a short moment of levity. He then went to the IR suite to observe the work and start envisioning what will become of the area and his practice. While he could not let the staff know just yet, they noticed him "lighter," as if a load had been taken off his shoulders.

"Finally! I was not sure it was going to happen for you this year!" said Laura Randall, lead architect, owner, and cofounder of CZE and Associates. In her early forties, Ms. Randall was very accomplished for her years, having started as a drafter at a small architectural firm less than two decades before and worked her way through her MS in Advanced Architectural Design from the famed Graduate School of Architecture, Planning and Preservation (GSAPP) at Columbia University. She found her niche designing healthcare spaces, and launched CZE 10 years ago to focus solely on healthcare.

She put her green tea down on her humongous, all-glass desktop and walked over to her 30th-floor glass window. She looked down the Hudson and at Lady Liberty in the distance as she did every morning as if to savor the fruits of her success. Folding her arms across her chest, she continued on her Bluetooth headset, "We are pretty booked over the next 2 weeks, Donna. We can come meet with you guys by early November. It will be a good time to get away from the New York weather!"

Laura assembled a team to handle Madeira St. Francis's IR Suite. At the team's first meeting, she announced, "This is a no-brainer! We can use the same approach that we used with the last two IR suites Frank and Ray did." Frank puts his hand in front of his large belly showing four fingers. "Oh, four?" Frank nodded. "Pardon me. The last four IR suites Frank and Ray did. Take Sarah, it will be good exposure for her."

Frank Deshevsky had been with Laura pretty much her whole career. He was her informal mentor at her first firm, and she took him with her when she opened CZE. Frank knew his stuff cold.

Ray Figueroa was a mid-career architect trying to make a name for himself. He only knew CZE (he was one of Laura's first hires), but he showed a lot of promise, and Ms. Randall has taken notice. Ray's usual high energy was even higher today since he just attended A'18 (The American Institute of Architects Conference on Architecture) right in his hometown in NYC, where he just learned the latest techniques and trends. He was eager to try some of them.

Sarah Crofton was the latest addition to CZE. Months ago, when CZE searched for someone to fill the junior position at CZE, Sarah interviewed as a long shot. To make an impression, Sarah assertively pitched the value an Industrial and Systems Engineer (ISE) could bring creating highly efficient healthcare spaces. Laura had not been fully convinced of the value an ISE could bring to her already successful firm, but Sarah's accomplishments impressed her, especially the ISE Magazine's Early Careerist of the Year Award she won in 2016. Sarah knew she could make a difference for CZE.

CZE's team visit to Madeira Health consisted mostly of interviewing leaders, physicians, and IR staff, in addition to Donna Jones and Dr. Manny, to discuss requirements and constraints. "Well, that wraps it up for today. Should we go to early happy hour?" said Frank, as he reached for his briefcase after finishing the last interview they had planned for the day.

Ray looked at his watch. *It's only 2 p.m., man*, he thought.

"I would like to go to the floor and understand the flow a little bit better," said Sarah. "Experience shows that traditional IR suites and procedural areas in general are poorly designed from a human factors standpoint."

The International Ergonomics Association (n.d.) defines human factors, also known as "ergonomics," as "the scientific discipline concerned with the understanding of interactions among humans and other elements of a system, and the profession that applies theory, principles, data and methods to design in order to optimize human well-being and overall system performance" (para. 1).

Sarah continued: "We need to take into account that there are many people and machines interacting in this space and, if we can make it more efficient for them, why wouldn't we?"

"Poorly designed?" Frank fidgeted in his seat, playing with the car keys and, feeling almost chastised, he looked at Ray.

"I did not mean it in a disrespectful way, Frank. I just think that if we infuse your already winning design concepts with some human factors concepts, we could build something special here: the IR Suite of the Future!" Sarah said trying to paint the picture of a futuristic place.

Ray looked at Frank and back at Sarah as if he were watching a tennis match. When there was an awkward silence, he said, looking at Sarah, "Actually, I think finishing early has presented us with this great opportunity, and I'd like to take advantage of it as well. I'll go with you."

"OK. Well, I have everything I need here. You kids have fun!" said Frank in a patronizing tone. "It's not like we have built dozens of these suites or anything," he mumbled as he put his notepad in his briefcase. As Ray and Sarah stood up, Frank added, "You see this briefcase?

The very smart people at Samsonite® have not changed this design in probably 30 years!" Ray and Sarah paid special notice to Frank's briefcase for the first time, and they both wondered if it was actually 30 years old. "And do you kids know why? Because, it works! If it ain't broke, don't fix it!" Frank closed the latches of his briefcase loudly, grabbed it, and walked out.

Ray and Sarah grabbed their notepads and headed for the procedural areas. As they wandered around for a little bit, trying to get their bearings, Ray, in a lower voice (almost as if he did not want anyone else to hear), said to Sarah, "Honestly, I have no idea how we are going to 'understand the flow' when we get there, but I would love for you to show me how to do that, if you don't mind."

Sarah looked at him, her eyes gleaming. "Of course! It's really not that difficult, once you know what to look for. Hopefully you won't be disappointed."

"Dr. Manituro, hi! I am Sarah and this is Ray from CZE. We met briefly this morning."

"Yes, of course. What brings you to our neck of the woods?" said Dr. Manny as he came out of the lounge.

"Well, we finished the interviews and meetings early, and we thought we could take a look at the flow in your IR area. It would definitely give us a better understanding of your team's needs."

Dr. Manny looked at Sarah over his glasses and held her gaze for a few seconds. He then turned around and said, "Come with me!"

I think he just smiled at me, Sarah thought to herself, working hard to hide her smile.

As they walked through the area, Dr. Manny was talking and introducing them to his staff and pointing at a few undesirable design features with the current design of his 30-year-old IR area. Sarah saw a nurse bending over a cart to get some forms from the printer. Ray noticed a technician almost run into a radiologist coming out of a room.

At one point Dr. Manituro said, "Hey, do you guys want to see a procedure?"

Sarah and Ray looked at each other bewildered and Sarah seized the opportunity. "Sure! That would be great! Do we need to change into scrubs?"

"Nah! We'll just get you some bunny suits, and you can watch from the control room behind radiation shielding," said Dr. Manituro.

As they donned their bunny suits, Sarah, almost whispering, started explaining to Ray, "Okay, when we get in there, we are going to look for how the information and the work flow. Look at how people communicate important information, how they move around the procedure room or how many times they come in and out of the room, how many times they do not have the materials and supplies they need… things of that nature."

Ray could only manage nodding as this was all happening really fast, but he felt like a kid in a candy store.

Sarah and Ray watched the team in the IR suite perform an angioplasty on a 67-year-old male patient. Sarah drew a simple diagram of the procedure room on her notepad while Ray looked over her shoulder (Figure C5.1).

"Who is that who keeps moving all over the place?" asked Sarah.

"That is Jay, our IR Tech" replied Dr. Manny. "He is gathering all the supplies and instruments for the interventionalist, when she needs them. I know!" he said, as he noticed Sarah's wide-open eyes. "And this is not even a complex case! I mean, we do the best we can within the space we have. And it's not necessarily that this is a 30-year-old room. In my last institution, they had newer suites, and they all have the same issues. Even the new ones! They have not changed this design in probably 50 years!"

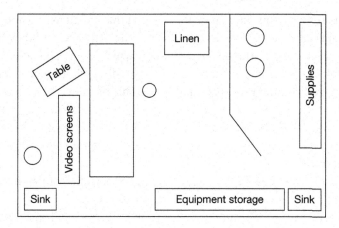

FIGURE C5.1 Sample diagram of a procedure room.

Ray was counting ceiling tiles. "So, this room is approximately 30 by 20, or about 600 square feet. It seems big in numbers, but with all that equipment and people in there, it sure looks cramped!" he added, and Dr. Manny turned toward him.

"Ray, what would you say is the distance between the table where the patient is and that supply cabinet back there?" asked Sarah.

"At least 20 ft." replied Ray after counting ceiling tiles again.

"In the 15 minutes we have been here, Jay has gone back-and-forth five, oh wait, six times! And where is he going now? He just left the room!"

"That's our core area back there," said Dr. Manituro, easing into his teaching physician mode. "It's where we keep the guide wires and other supplies. The interventionalist just asked for a different guide wire."

Sarah updated her sketch showing where the door to the core area was.

As Jay was coming back in the room with a new guide wire, he almost bumped into the nurse who was moving to the other side of the patient table to adjust the video screens. He talked with the interventionalist for a brief moment then hurried back toward the core.

"Jay is on the move again!" noted Ray.

Jay came back a few minutes later empty-handed and shaking his head. "I couldn't find it," said Jay.

"Did you check the back behind the cabinet with the expired wires?" asked the tech in the control room, startling Sarah.

"What is he looking for? Another wire?" asked Sarah.

"No, the SonoSite," answered the tech in the room. "That's the ultrasound machine they use after every angio to make sure everything is okay with the stent's location and position," she continued, noticing Sarah and Ray's puzzled looks.

Jay came back a few minutes later with the SonoSite rolling alongside him. "I swear it is in a different place every time I go looking for it!" he said.

When the procedure was completed, Dr. Manny accompanied Ray and Sarah while they removed their bunny suits. "Time well spent, I think!" Dr. Manny said. "You guys made me think: I have to talk to the interventionalists and Donna to make sure we don't forget to identify what else can be done in this new IR suite. We are cramped in the Cath Lab holding area and this new area may give us an opportunity to decompress it."

As they wrapped up their visit to the IR area, Ray and Sarah realized, almost at the same time, that they did not have a ride back to the hotel.

"Let's just take Uber," Sarah said. "I'll pay for it. I'm sure Laura will reimburse me."

"I'm glad to see you made it back in one piece!" Frank said to Ray and Sarah the next morning, while loading a full stack of pancakes on his plate. "I figured you would get a cab back to the hotel when you were done with your little field trip. So, how did your trip to Dr. Manny's area go? Did he run you all out of there?"

"No, actually, it went really well. Totally the opposite! He was very welcoming and eager to show us around and have us talk to more of his people," replied Ray.

"We really did not need to talk to any more people. We already had everything we needed. Plus, the staff does not know one thing about designing and building IR suites. We do!" Frank continued, while dousing his pancakes with maple syrup, visibly annoyed.

"They may not, but they know a few things about using and working in IR suites," said Sarah, conversationally. "We actually got some really good insights and some leads on more people we may want to talk to," Sarah said as she flipped through what seemed like a dozen pages of notes from her observations.

Back in New York, Frank looked for an opportunity to catch Laura alone in her office. "How did it go?" asked Laura.

"How does it always go?" Frank replied pointing his fingers at himself. "Although I'm not so sure this is the right project for the new girl."

"Why do you say that?" asked Laura.

Frank moved his chair closer to Laura's desk, looked around, lowered his voice, and continued, "Well, I don't think she has a good idea of what we do or how we do it. I mean, hey, I understand she's young and she's still learning, but I do feel she will slow us down. She keeps insisting on talking to more people and asking more and more questions. I mean, the other day, she practically forced Ray into taking her to go observe an IR procedure! Can you believe that?" he said, shaking his head and feigning a laugh.

Laura moved her chair closer to her desk and placed her forearms on her desk, with her hands clasped, looking intensely at Frank.

"I felt sorry for poor Ray. You know he can't say 'no' to people. And, I'm going to level with you, Laura, she keeps criticizing our designs and our design process and babbling about human factors and flow and things of that sort. I don't want to get anybody in trouble. I am just letting you know now before you hear it from someone else."

"Well, thank you for letting me know, Frank. Is that all?" Laura got up.

"Yes, that was it. Just wanted to let you know that it went great at Madeira and we should be ready to finish the quote and sign the contract within 2 weeks!" said Frank, straining as he stood up.

"Thank you very much", said Laura as she turned around and moved closer to her favorite window.

Frank understood he was being dismissed and left her office.

The next day, the team met with Laura Randall to debrief the visit to Madeira Health and finalize the project plan for the IR suite.

Frank had large architectural prints showing the current space and future plans for the IR Suite at Madeira's St. Francis Hospital. He had done all the talking so far.

Laura noticed Ray and Sarah look at each other several times during Frank's presentation.

Frank said, "So, there you have it! Nothing more, nothing less. Pretty much what you are used to seeing from us," pointing at Ray and himself as if to say *"We are the dream team!"*

Laura found this pause appropriate and she turned to Ray while allowing her eyes to find Sarah's for a brief moment and asked, "Ray, you've been kind of quiet. This is so unlike you. Is anything on your mind?"

Ray propped himself up, fixed his tie, glanced in Sarah's direction and then back at Laura. "Well, actually, yes", he said. *I'm going for it!* he said to himself. "Laura, while this is great work, and we know it works…"

"And it's profitable," interrupted Laura.

"Right! We," he said pointing at Sarah and himself, "found a few inefficiencies with this design … from the standpoint of the physician and the staff in the room doing the procedure."

"Inefficiencies?" asked Laura, while assuming her go-to pose closer to the table, her forearms on the desk, hands clasped. She looked at both Sarah and Ray.

Frank shook his head. *Oh, my poor Ray. You are going down! It was nice knowing you, kid,* he thought.

Ray felt the knot of his tie get tighter around his neck. *Am I sweating?* he thought, while looking at Sarah.

That's my cue, thought Sarah. *It's only my career that's at stake here.* "Yes, Laura, when you look at the flow of people, instruments, meds, information, all of them, they are not streamlined. When we observed the procedure, we saw people going back-and-forth, in and out of the room, looking for items, supplies, equipment, and moving things around. It is, really, not good. And this design," she said pointing at Frank's design plans on the wall, "while it incorporates the new biplane capabilities and newer equipment and fixtures, it does nothing to improve the flow."

Frank rolled his eyes.

Laura was silent, looking intently at Sarah.

Ray was looking at everyone, Sarah, then Laura, then Frank, wondering whose head was going to explode first.

Never losing eye contact with Laura, Sarah continued, "The cookie-cutter approach of just modifying floor plans to fit in the space provided does not work for the current needs of the team. We could do so much better by the team! We have the opportunity here to go into uncharted territory and give Dr. Manny's and St. Francis's team a really functional, efficient procedural area where it will be a delight to work. All we have to do is observe and listen to what the team thinks."

"Pfft!" exclaimed Frank.

"And, how do you propose we do that?" asked Laura, finally breaking her silence.

"We do a more in-depth analysis. I mean, this," Sarah said, while holding her notepad and thumbing through the pages quickly, "was just from one procedure! If we observe more procedures, perhaps over a week or so, we will have much more information about the different configurations needed. While we are there, observing, we solicit staff's input. Dr. Manny introduced us to a few members of his team, and they were very eager to share their thoughts! Once we have that … have you heard of a 3P Lean Design Event?" she asked, now unable to control her excitement and interrupting herself. The 3P Lean Design Event, which stands for "Production Preparation Process," encourages the design team to start from scratch to create and test potential processes that require the least time, material, money, and effort.

Laura shook her head. Ray nodded emphatically. He had just seen some presentations about 3P Events at the A'18 conference.

"That's fine," Sarah continued. "I'm not saying we do a full 3P Event, but we can take a page from it and mock-up the area in real life-size, using cardboard boxes, etc., and we can allow the team to experiment with various configurations. They will tell us what the right configuration is and what options they need."

"Wow! That sounds like it will take a lot of time, Sarah! Have you thought about that?" asked Laura, with a hint of incredulity.

"Not to mention expensive!" added Frank, seizing the opportunity to shoot this nonsense down.

"Well, that is true. It will take longer, in fact, several months longer," replied Sarah. "However, the product will be much better! I am sure Madeira would like the best product we can give them. Doing things right usually takes longer and is harder. I am sure you know that; otherwise you would not be where you are," added Sarah, now appealing to Laura's ego.

"And about cost, Ray and I ran some quick numbers…"

"Oh, you have, have you?" asked Laura.

"Yes, they would have to be verified by Frank and you, of course. We think we are probably looking at adding another $75K, maybe $100K, to the budget, tops. I understand we have not sent them an official quote yet, have we?"

Laura reclined back in her chair while crossing her legs and crossing her arms across her chest. "Well, that may be true, but they have already obtained budget approval for a specific amount, based on their research and conversations with us, and some of our competitors! And it took them 8 months to get it approved!"

"I understand, and I thought, what's another $100K in a budget of $1.5 million? Right? I am guessing that is close to what they asked for." Sarah now leaned onto the table and lower her voice, "Laura, could we just present them with this option as we progress with negotiations? I think Dr. Manny understands what we are trying to accomplish, and he would be on board."

"Well, Sarah, of course he is!" Frank said. "Physicians always want more! However, Donna knows that money does not grow on trees. Have you thought about that? How do we convince her?"

"Well, if we have Dr. Manny on our side, that is a big help," Sarah said. "Then, if we show her, and I mean, physically show her what the staff goes through and how inefficient this design is, she could be convinced. If we show her that due to these inefficiencies they are wasting resources—time, expired supplies—perhaps she will see that with a more efficient design they will actually come out ahead. Maybe they can do more cases than anticipated!"

"You are not going to let this go, are you?" Laura said with a hint of a smile and a sparkle in her eyes that neither Sarah nor Ray had seen before.

"OK, here is what I want," Laura said pointing at Sarah. "I want you to come up with a full plan on how this would go, including visits to observe and mock and do that P3 design thing you mentioned."

Frank's jaw dropped to the floor.

It is 3P, but whatever! I can't believe she's going for it! Sarah thought while nodding emphatically.

"I also want you and Ray," she continued, still pointing at Sarah, "to give me a full report on those notes you have about your observations. I want to have the whole picture before I talk to Donna. And Frank," she added while turning to face him, "we cannot do this without your expertise. Please, support them incorporating their ideas into the design. Hey, looks like we are in for a learning journey on this one, huh, pal!"

Frank's bewildered look said it all.

Frank's head just exploded, thought Ray.

"Alright!" added Laura, closing her Gucci® binder. "It looks like we have our work cut out for us! We will meet again next week. In the meantime, please let me know if there are any further concerns," she said looking at all three. She got up and left the conference room through the large all-glass door.

As the team was wrapping up and collecting their things, Frank was removing his design plans from the wall. Still facing the wall, he said, "Well, looks like you won."

Ray and Sarah stopped putting their notepads into their bags and looked at each other. Ray did not know what to say.

Sarah replied, "It is not about winning or losing, Frank. I think this is a big win for everybody: Dr. Manny and his staff, their patients, even for us! I hope you can see that soon. And, hey, we could never build *The IR Suite of the Future* without you, my friend. You have so much knowledge and expertise to bring to the table. We are counting on you, aren't we, Ray?"

"Absolutely!" It was Ray's first word in the last 45 minutes. "We are still the dream team, man! Only now we are a team of three! Hey, how about happy hour today, after work?" said Ray, with a big smile.

Frank turned around, still rolling up his design plans and putting them inside cardboard tubes. "You buying?" he asked, cracking a smile.

DISCUSSION QUESTIONS

1. Why is going to the Gemba important when attempting to design and build new spaces and install new equipment?

2. How would you approach Donna Jones to get her buy-in on the new way to design and build the new IR suite? What are her concerns?

3. What are the shortcomings of the "cookie-cutter" approach to designing and building spaces in healthcare?

4. Discuss the benefits and challenges of the Lean 3P design approach.

5. How would Donna measure the success of the new IR suite?

6. Describe the key stakeholders for a project this big and the needs and expectations of each stakeholder.

PODCAST FOR CASE 5

Listen to how experts approach the topic (you can access the podcast by following this url to Springer Publishing Company Connect™: https://connect.springerpub.com/content/book/978-0-8261-4514-7/front-matter/fmatter2)

REFERENCES

Friedrich, B., Maegerlein, C., Lobsien, D., Mönch, S., Berndt, M., Hedderich, D., … & Zimmer, C. (2019). Endovascular stroke treatment on single-plane vs. bi-plane angiography suites. *Clinical Neuroradiology, 29*(2), 303–309. doi:10.1007/s00062-017-0655-z

International Ergonomics Association. (n.d.). *Definition and domains of ergonomics.* Retrieved from https://www.iea.cc/whats/index.html

Johns Hopkins Medicine. (2019). *Endovascular neurosurgery and interventional neuroradiology.* Retrieved from https://www.hopkinsmedicine.org/health/treatment-tests-and-therapies/endovascular-neuro-surgery-and-interventional-neuroradiology

The Joint Commission. (2018). *Certification for thrombectomy-capable stroke centers.* Retrieved from https://www.jointcommission.org/certification/certification_for_thrombectomycapable_stroke_centers.aspx

Rai, A. T., Seldon, A. E., Boo, S., Link, P. S., Domico, J. R., Tarabishy, A. R., … & Carpenter, J. S. (2017). A population-based incidence of acute large vessel occlusions and thrombectomy eligible patients indicates significant potential for growth of endovascular stroke therapy in the USA. *Journal of Neurointerventional Surgery, 9*(8), 722–726.

SPAGHETTI DIAGRAM

A spaghetti diagram is a graphical representation of how people (or things) move within a process (Figure C5.2). Spaghetti diagrams are relatively easy to create, yet they provide a very powerful visual complement during process analysis.

To draw a spaghetti diagram, you start with a sketch or a drawing of the layout of the area where the process occurs. This area is also known as the "Gemba." Armed with this sketch, you go to the Gemba and observe the movements of people or things, depending on the focus of the improvement. The movements are traced onto the drawing of the area as they happen in real time. The duration of the observation is subjective, as it should provide the observer with enough detail to represent the whole process being observed.

For example, if a nurse travels from the PACU to the PreOp area to obtain medications stored in PreOp three times for one patient, the spaghetti diagram should represent that. One way to do this is to write "x3" next to the line representing the travel, to avoid overcrowding the diagram. You may choose to draw this motion three times to show the repetition to draw attention to the inefficiency. A comparison of these approaches is presented in Figure C5.3.

You can use the completed sketch to create a cleaner version of the spaghetti diagram, using software tools such as Microsoft Visio or PowerPoint, although many practitioners opt to use the original sketch to show the chaos more dramatically. After all, it is called a "spaghetti diagram" because it resembles a bowl of spaghetti with squiggly lines going all over the place and crossing over each other.

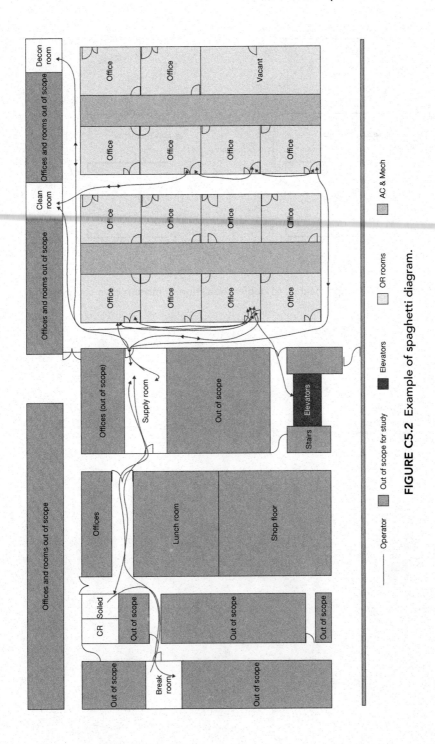

FIGURE C5.2 Example of spaghetti diagram.

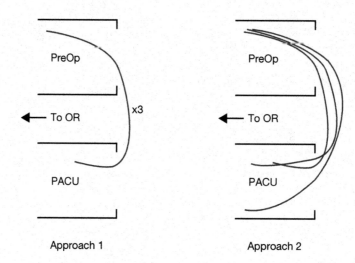

FIGURE C5.3 Two approaches to depict repetition of motion on a spaghetti diagram.

CASE 6: Emergency Department Heroes

OBJECTIVES

1. Analyze opportunities for improved emergency department workflow to ensure patient quality and safety in the future.

2. Evaluate the ability of a quality management expert to influence others in an effort to improve healthcare processes.

3. Describe the role of collaboration in healthcare quality management.

4. Identify the value of leadership commitment to healthcare quality management initiatives.

5. Differentiate between priority in solving emergency workflow and minor initiatives.

INTRODUCTION

Lakefront Regional Medical Center (LRMC), a 72-bed, rural hospital in Hachettas County recently experienced heavy changes in leadership—most of them positive—after the merger with a large health system. One of the latest management additions included Amy Haskell, the nursing director, who was hired to supervise all nursing departments, including the emergency department (ED), the operating room (OR), the inpatient units, as well as the ICU. As a result of the merger, LRMC was required to achieve certain targets in their key performance indicators (KPIs). One of these KPIs is the length of stay (LOS) of patients in the ED. The LOS target is 113 minutes, but the ED LOS at LRMC is currently 213 minutes. Haskell had only been the nursing director for 4 months, yet she frequently observed delays in the ED.

 DATA FILE FOR CASE 6

Data files for students are available by accessing the following url: https://www.springerpub.com/hqm

The data file for Case 6 provides over 8,500 lines of emergency department patient encounters with length of stay (LOS) and Emergency Severity Index (ESI) acuity level designations for each patient discharge.

CASE SCENARIO

"We are losing him! Grandpa … stay with me. Somebody?! HELP!" As the frightened man tried to keep his grandfather's body upright, the old man's body slumped motionless toward his left side. Out of nowhere, three nurses came running through the doors, placed the older man on a miraculously appearing stretcher, and took him to the back through a very crowded waiting room.

It was 9:15 a.m. on a Thursday. There were people standing along the walls, children crying, patients and family members all trying to get updates on when they were going to be seen. "Mom, let's go home," said a girl in her teens. "I am sure it's not broken. I'll just rest my finger for a day or two," she said as she got up and started walking toward the door, her mother by her side. "Anything is better than waiting here."

That was the familiar scene in the ED at LRMC. No special circumstances caused higher-than-normal delays, it was just a typical Thursday morning, and it was like this pretty much every day. "Well, at least nobody died today," said the staff nurse.

At the daily LRMC leadership huddle on Friday, Haskell brought up the story about the gentleman who experienced the episode the day before, and how, through heroic efforts from the staff, they were able to save his life. Everybody congratulated her and her staff for their heroic efforts. The cheerful bubble fizzled out when Haskell continued, "This is no reason for celebration." People nodded their heads, but most of all, their faces showed bewilderment and shock.

Haskell continued, "I do not think it is fair to our staff to ask them be heroes every day. And *most of all*, I do not think it is fair that our patients depend on us being heroes every day. There has to be a way that our staff can treat all those patients who come to our ED without feeling rushed or overwhelmed. In fact, I know there is a way, and I am going to find it … with your help." The room was silent.

Haskell trained in quality management, having completed formal Lean training and **kaizen** facilitator certification. She had been spending a good amount of time on the ED floor and observed firsthand that there were multiple redundant steps in the process of triaging, treating, and discharging patients. Haskell also pulled detailed daily reports on the LOS of all ED patients for 2 months. She tracked their acuity level, or Emergency Severity Index (ESI), whether they were leaving without treatment (LWOT), being admitted to an inpatient bed, or discharged directly from the ED. She also tracked patients' registration times, to identify any potential trends based on the time of the day.

Haskell developed a spreadsheet (Table C6.1) into which all the data could be dumped (see Case 6 Data file provided in the Instructor's and Student ancillary materials). She analyzed the data every week and built a chart to track the LOS visually. One thing that jumped out at her during her analysis was the long LOS for patients categorized with ESI levels (acuity level) 4 and 5 compared to ESI levels 1 and 2 (the lowest levels). Low-acuity patients are those suffering from things such as minor sports injuries (e.g., ankle twist), minor infections (e.g., urinary tract), stomach flu, and lacerations and bruises from accidents or falls. These patients do not need a lot of attention and are therefore not expected to spend a lot of time in the ED. With this discovery, Haskell did a deeper dive and found that about 35% of patients who were identified as ESI level 4 or 5 had a lot of diagnostic procedures performed on them. She did not expect this as these patients typically do not need many procedures performed

Table C6.1 Sample Data Collection Table

ED ENCOUNTER #	DATE	REG TIME	ESI LEVEL	ED LOS (MINUTES)	ED DISPOSITION (ADMIT/DISCHARGE/LWOT)

on them and wondered if there would be an issue with correctly assigning ESI levels. She kept collecting and analyzing the data until, at the end of the 2 months, she felt she had a solid handle on the current state.

At LRMC, improvement projects normally consisted of gathering a team of leaders (not frontline staff) that met for a 1-hour meeting every week for a long period of time until mild improvement was achieved or until the team was disbanded. Haskell wanted to try a different approach. The merger to the larger health system gave LRMC access to the Process Excellence team. To Haskell, the expertise of these process improvement professionals proves invaluable to engaging teams in problem-solving activities and facilitates change. This is not something LRMC has done in the past so Haskell knew what she wanted to do would ruffle some feathers.

Her training in quality management had taught Haskell that involving the frontline staff in the improvement effort is essential to its success. She wanted to do a kaizen event, sometimes called a "Rapid Improvement Event" or "Rapid Process Improvement Workshop." The health system's Process Excellence coach informed her that their current standard work for kaizen events was based on a 4-day engagement. Now that she found the information she was seeking, she wondered how she could persuade the leadership team at LRMC that this was the right approach. She knew they would question if spending 4 consecutive days in an improvement event would yield the results they needed.

Haskell ran into Frank Seda, LRMC's president, during their safety rounds. "Frank, I need 20 minutes in the agenda at the next Executive Leadership Team (ELT) meeting. I have been collecting data, observing processes, and talking with staff in the ED, and I have an idea of where I want to go next, but I need everyone on board." Seda, intrigued, granted her the slot on the agenda.

At the ELT meeting, Haskell was pleased to see everyone gathered around the table including the president, Mr. Seda. When her time came, Haskell presented her case finishing with her suggestion to run a kaizen event with the ED staff to work on their issues and come out with some tangible results. "I have seen the power of kaizen events firsthand in my previous organization. If we get the right people in the room, they really work!" She allowed the team to process her presentation and let her suggestion sink in.

As Haskell may have expected, the first one to talk was her ED nurse manager, Vanessa García. "Wait! You want to take our ED staff off the floor for a 4-day meeting?" she asked as her brow frowned. "What are we going to do? Close the ED for 4 days?" she added with a little bit of sarcasm for good measure.

"We do not need 4 days to solve this issue. All we need to do is hold people accountable," added Rebecca Pellitteri, Director of Operations for LRMC. "Do they even know our target? We just need to make sure the staff are all working all-hands-on-deck toward that goal. It's that simple!" There were a few head nods around the table. As people kept looking back at Seda, he kept his hands clasped on the table in front of him, listening and observing everyone's reaction.

"Well, that may be true for nursing, but, in the lab, we are understaffed," replied Martin Schneider, manager of the laboratory. "Frank, you know I have two positions I have not been allowed to backfill in almost a year. If I had those two people back on staff, we would be able to meet the demand put on us by the ED." Frank Seda remained silent.

When she saw an opportunity, Haskell addressed their concerns. "First of all, this is *not* a 4-day meeting. This is a hands-on, very dynamic, very productive workshop that engages everyone in the problem-solving effort. Second, no, we are *not* going to take all our staff off the floor for the duration of the event, so we will not need to close the ED. We will take a representative sample of our staff into the event," she said while looking directly at García. "And Martin," Haskell said to the lab manager, "while being understaffed certainly sounds like a challenge, do we even know what our real capacity is with our current resources?"

As a young executive, Frank Seda was open to the idea of trying radically different ways to solve their challenges. He had read about the experiences of organizations like Virginia Mason in Seattle, WA and ThedaCare in Appleton, WI, and he was intrigued enough by these methodologies to bring breakthrough improvement to his hospital. "OK," he said. "If we were to do this kaizen event, my one requirement is that any solution the team comes up with should not hinge on adding more staff." Haskell's eyes brightened and shoulders relaxed.

Seda then turned to everyone else at the table, "Listen, guys, I know this is a big change for us, but, I think we all can agree that we need to try something different, because what we are doing clearly is not working." There were some head nods. "I say, let's give it a shot. Amy, work with Lynda to get this planning meeting scheduled in the next week or two. Please, let's make every effort to get this on everyone's calendar promptly," he said as he looked around the table.

A week later, the kaizen event steering committee gathered in a large conference room with the Process Excellence coach for a pre-event planning meeting. Haskell, Vanessa García, Meredith St. John (a staff nurse from the ED), Rebecca Pellitteri, Martin Schneider, Frank Seda, Joy Christensen (the registration manager), and Laura Walton (imaging manager) were all in attendance. Haskell brought the data she had been collecting and shared it with the team. Haskell introduced her peers to the A3 template and problem-solving mindset. The meeting followed the A3 template, going from identifying the background and environment in which the issues had transpired, to clearly verbalizing the problem and defining what was considered the *current state*. All this information was collected on flip charts along the walls of the conference room. She also presented them with the summary (Table C6.2). She added that, on average, more than 3% of patients were LWOT every month.

Toward the end of the planning meeting, they were identifying team members to bring into the kaizen event. Seda said, "Aren't we going to need some providers as well?" They all agreed.

Table C6.2 ED Length of Stay (LOS) Summary

WEEK	ED DISPOSITION	AVG ED LOS (MINUTES)	VOLUME
Overall	Discharge	188	7,237
Overall	Admit	391	921
Overall	LWOT	213	272
Overall	All	213	8,513

"We are never going to get a physician attend a 4-day event!" said Pellitteri.

"Well, I don't know about that. Besides, does it have to be a physician?"

"Actually, no, it doesn't," said St. John. "Most of our patients do not need to be seen by a physician. A physician assistant (PA) usually sees them. What about Sean?" She was referring to Sean McCall, a PA with about 18 years of experience at LRMC. He was well-liked, established with the provider body, and he had shown interest in trying new things.

"Sean would be great!" answered Haskell. "I will talk to him."

Over the next 4 weeks, Haskell and her kaizen-event steering committee continued to collect and analyze data. They made sure they communicated with the rest of the ED staff, who had rarely been asked their opinion about their work or their issues. In fact, as the date for the kaizen event neared, there were a few running jokes about the "celebrities" among the staff who were going to participate in this 4-day engagement.

The day finally came and a team of eight people assembled for the first kaizen event at LRMC:

- Amy Haskell—Director of Nursing
- Vanessa García—ED Nurse Manager
- Meredith St. John—ED Staff Nurse (day shift: 7 a.m.–7 p.m.)
- Julianna Oppenheimer—ED Staff Nurse (night shift: 7 p.m.–7 a.m.)
- Martin Schneider—Lab Manager
- Luis Matías—Registrar
- Jill Dawson—X-ray tech
- Sean McCall—ED Physician Assistant

Frank Seda kicked off the event, encouraging everyone to have an open mind and to speak freely. He started with the "Why." He highlighted the challenges they continue to have in the ED. He complimented them and their peers on the heroic efforts, and then echoed Haskell's earlier advice, "But, we cannot depend on you being heroes every day." He explained that he would be "popping-in" toward the end of every day throughout the event to hear about their progress.

With the assistance of the Process Excellence coach, Haskell proceeded to review the A3 with the team. They discussed the background, problem statement, and current state. The team observed the different processes (registration, triage, diagnosis, treatment, discharge) for a few hours. After returning to the conference room, the team was able to map their current state process and highlight some of the issues they observed and others they encountered frequently.

The team found that they disagreed on the acuity (ESI) level assigned to patients. "Well, I think the issue is mostly with the lower-acuity levels, 3, 4, and 5," said Julianna Oppenheimer, a night shift staff nurse. "For levels 1 and 2, I think we are all on the same page. But, for the lower-acuity patients, I saw some classifications this morning that I disagreed with. On night shift, we go strictly by how many resources are needed to take care of the patient: 2 or more, it's a '3,' 1 resource is a '4' and if no resources are needed, then it is a '5.'"

"I agree that we are on the same page for the higher-acuity levels, the 1s and 2s. For the lower-acuities, we take a more holistic approach during day shift, and we allow the triage nurse to make the determination, based on her expertise and assessment of the patient," added St. John.

"Hmm!" added Haskell, feigning surprise in an amicable way. "Did we just find a discrepancy in process between day and night shift?" There were giggles.

"I agree," replied Oppenheimer. "I think we should all be doing it the same way. We probably need to do some quick refresher training on ESI levels."

While the Process Excellence coach and Haskell knew it was early in the process to be coming up with solutions, they allowed the team to have this and further conversations because they were gaining momentum toward an improved future state.

At the end of Day 1, as promised, Frank Seda stopped by, he looked around the room at all the information posted on the walls in process maps and flipcharts, and he was fascinated. He asked, "So, did you solve all our issues?"

"Well, we found out we have a lot of opportunities for improvement!" said Martin Schneider, the lab manager. The team shared a laugh; then everyone started talking at once.

"Like what? Give me some examples of what you learned today," replied Seda.

Vanessa García, the nurse manager who was not convinced that "a 4-day meeting" was the solution, added, "For example, we found out that we have inconsistency among the staff in how we assign acuity levels."

Sean McCall, the physician assistant, continued, "Yes, and, the fact that the provider sees all acuity levels with no prioritization regardless of what level they are, I think is an opportunity. I know we are not supposed to be thinking of solutions yet," he said as he smiled at the Process Excellence coach, then he shared some best practices he'd learned at the Exploring Emergency Department Intake Strategies Summit. "However, these countermeasures would have minimal to no impact if the ESI levels are not assigned correctly", he concluded.

"Wow!" Seda finally said. "Sounds like you guys found a lot of issues! Great work! I can't wait to stop by tomorrow to hear how you are going to fix all of this!"

As the second day of the event started, the team reviewed the long list of opportunities from Day 1. The Process Excellence coach offered some guidance. "While you found a lot of issues yesterday, in order for you to be successful today, we need to narrow that list down to three to five issues that we are going to work on. You each have three votes and you are going to place your votes next to the issues that matter the most to you. You can give all your three votes to one issue, or you can spread them among several issues. We will then count the votes and determine which our top issues are. This technique is called 'multi-voting.'"

After they voted, they narrowed down their list of issues to the following:

■ Inconsistency in ESI level assignment

■ Provider sees all acuity levels with no prioritization

■ Waiting for provider to see patient

The Process Excellence coach kept guiding the team. "OK. Now that you have narrowed down the list of issues to work on, you need to find the root cause of these issues, so we can then work on how to solve them. You will use this table I have created for you on these flipcharts" (Table C6.3).

Table C6.3 Root Cause Analysis and Development of Countermeasures

OPPORTUNITY	ROOT CAUSE	COUNTERMEASURE	EXPECTED RESULT

"In order to complete the second column, you need to ask why this is happening. For example, Why are we waiting for the providers to see the patients? Because they are busy with other patients who are taking longer than they expected."

"Once you are satisfied that you have found the root cause," the Process Excellence coach continued, "then you will be ready to suggest some potential solutions, otherwise known as "countermeasures," and what you expect to see when you implement those."

Sean McCall suggested they start with the issue of "Waiting for provider to see the patient." After the team was adjourned the day before, he had done some more research about what he had seen at the conference he mentioned. He searched the health management literature database for terms such as "emergency department triage," "emergency department intake," and "emergency department door-to-physician time." As the team learned about these solutions, they wanted to use them to build a great new process that worked for LRMC.

Meredith St. John shared a few ideas she had read about on the latest issue (May, 2017) of the Emergency Nurses Association topic brief on "ED Throughput."

When they tackled the issue about "Inconsistency in ESI Level Assignment," Oppenheimer, the night shift staff nurse, jumped up (she had been waiting all morning for a chance) and said, "Last night, after we were done here, I took a closer look at the data Amy has been collecting and I found some trends I think you will find interesting." She then passed around some charts showing different "slices" of the data. Most team members' eyes got big, and some even had some smiles on their faces.

"Wow!" muttered St. John.

Once they had several countermeasures they wanted to try, their Process Excellence coach guided them through the design of the experiments to test them. "For each countermeasure that we want to try tomorrow, we need to define who is going to be involved in it, what the process is going to be for them to follow, who else needs to be informed, and what is going to be our sample. Is it going to be one patient? 10 patients? An hour? Three hours? And the most important thing we must define for each experiment is *how we are going to measure success*. It would not be good if we run these experiments tomorrow and come back here without clearly understanding if they worked in the way we expected them to work or not. So, we need some kind of metric that we are going to track for each of them."

As expected at the end of the second day, Frank Seda stopped in and again, he was taken aback by all the work the team was doing. "How did it go today?" he asked. The team explained that they had narrowed down the list to three main issues and had developed some potential solutions they were going to try the next day. Seda's eyes got big again. "You have potential solutions already?" he asked.

Haskell explained how they were going to run some experiments, and she would be on the floor during the experiments to offer support. The team told Seda that the kaizen gave them the courage to continue experimentation and learning. Seda left the room impressed.

DISCUSSION QUESTIONS

1. What was wrong about the approach the leaders wanted to take to "solve" the issue during the Executive Committee meeting? Why is it important to seek a deeper understanding of department functions to affect change?

2. Which other quality management tools would be appropriate for the team to utilize through their kaizen event? How would you use them?

3. What is the best response to Martin Schneider, manager of the laboratory, when he suggested hiring additional staff to meet demand?

4. Describe the approach Amy Haskell used to get the buy-in from her president and leadership team.

5. What would have happened if they had not involved a medical care provider in this improvement effort?

 ## PODCAST FOR CASE 6

Listen to how experts approach the topic (you can access the podcast by following this url to Springer Publishing Company Connect™: https://connect.springerpub.com/content/book/978-0-8261-4514-7/front-matter/fmatter2)

REFERENCE

Arbune, A., Wackerbarth, S., Allison, P., & Conigliaro, J. (2017). Improvement through Small Cycles of Change: Lessons from an Academic Medical Center Emergency Department. *Journal for Healthcare Quality, 39*(5), 259–269. doi:10.1111/jhq.12078

FURTHER READING

Schwarz, U. V., Hasson, H., & Athlin, A. M. (2016). Efficiency in the emergency department—A complex relationship between throughput rates and staff perceptions. *International Emergency Nursing, 29,* 15–20. doi:10.1016/j.ienj.2016.07.003

KAIZEN EVENT

"Kaizen" means continuous, incremental improvement of an activity to create more value with less waste (Imai, 1986). A kaizen event is an intense workshop focused solely on analyzing current processes and implementing changes to redesign care delivery. A typical kaizen event runs for 4 or 5 days.

Figure C6.1 shows an example of a high-level agenda of a kaizen event.

REFERENCE

Imai, M. (1986). *Kaizen: The key to Japan's competitive success*. New York, NY: McGraw-Hill.

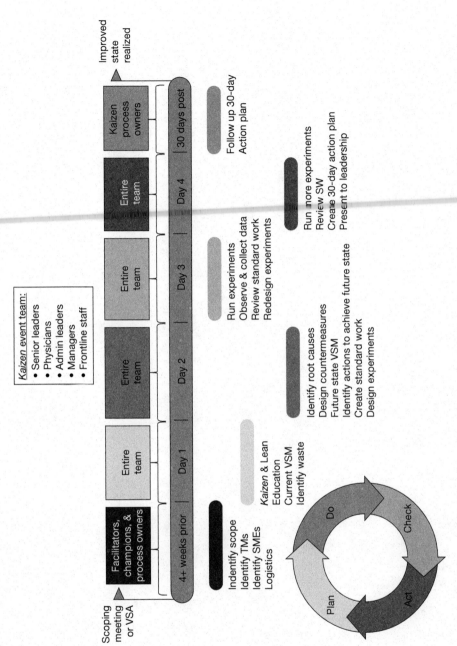

FIGURE C6.1 Kaizen event high-level agenda.

Source: Reproduced with permission from Imai, M. (1986). *Kaizen: The key to Japan's competitive success.* New York, NY: McGraw-Hill.

Patient Experience

Patient experience is the judgment, attitude, or perception of all interactions in a healthcare environment. Patient experience is a concept related to patient satisfaction that encompasses whether a patient's expectations about their care environment were met (Agency for Healthcare Research and Quality [AHRQ], 2017b).

Patient experience is measured in the United States principally through a set of standardized survey instruments known as the Consumer Assessment of Healthcare Providers and Systems (CAHPS®; AHRQ, 2017a). CAHPS assesses various aspects of patient experiences, such as communication with doctors and nurses, getting timely appointments, easy access to information, responsiveness of office or hospital staff, communication about medicines, hospital cleanliness and quietness, discharge information, overall experience ratings, and more (AHRQ, 2017a). The surveys do not ask patients how satisfied they were with their care (AHRQ, 2017b). The results of the survey are available through the Medicare Hospital Compare website. This publicity motivates healthcare organizations to improve patient experience through quality management approaches.

The following are descriptions of the patient experience case studies included in this casebook.

Case 7: Hurricane Mia Hits the Patient Access Call Center

The patient experience scores of a multispecialty physician practice for patient access–related survey items were below the national average, likely because of the unreasonable high patient wait times for appointments. The executive responsible for the patient appointment scheduling call center pointed out that different scheduling rules across the 14 clinical departments led to scheduling mistakes and increased wait times. After Hurricane Mia hit Apollo Bay area, the chief executive officer (CEO) ordered a disaster recovery plan for scheduling patient appointments. Will the hurricane make patient wait times even worse? Or is this an opportunity to implement a better patient appointment scheduling process?

Case 8: The Cowboy Doctor's Patient Experience

Decades ago, the considerable charm of the rural Texas hospital's first medical director earned him the nickname, "The Cowboy Doctor." Now long-retired, aged, and in poor health, the Cowboy Doctor was discharged from the hospital he started. Unfortunately, he experienced an unpleasant communication exchange with a member of his care team. Hot-tempered as ever, he complained to the chairman of the board about a rude nurse. When investigating the complaint, the chairman learned that the hospital's Hospital Consumer Assessment of

Healthcare Providers and Systems (HCAHPS) patient experience scores on the provider communication items were well below the state average. The chairman decided to visit the disgruntled Cowboy Doctor to learn the truth about his patient experience.

Case 9: Patient Navigation at the Orthopedic Clinic

The CEO asked his niece, the newly hired nurse navigator, to investigate the low patient experience scores at his hospital's outpatient orthopedic and spine clinic. However, she was unaware that her Uncle Dave plans to use her to spy on the medical practice's managers. She succeeded in exposing the variation in healthcare quality, but failed to foresee the consequences of the ethical dilemma.

Case 10: HCAHPS and the Quiet-at-Night Measure

To improve the hospital's patient experience survey scores, the CEO needed to gain the cooperation of his chief medical officer (CMO). However, the CMO was skeptical of patient experience surveys, especially the question about whether the patient's room was "quiet at night." The CMO said, "Hospitals are just noisy places." Viewing this perspective as unacceptable, the CEO concocted a secret shopper experience to show the importance of patient-centered care and a good night's rest. Once the CMO spent the night in the hospital, would he change his mind?

Case 11: Discharge Phone Calls (En Español)

A hospital served a largely Hispanic population, but the hospital's call center staff did not speak Spanish. Unsurprisingly, numerous phone calls from irate Spanish-speaking patients caused confusion among the call center staff. The hospital director in charge of improving patient experience was determined to find the root causes of declining survey scores. Will the team's analysis of the survey data reveal the root cause of rapidly deteriorating patient experience scores?

Case 12: Patient Experience in Home Care

In the competitive field of home healthcare, patient referrals are critical to success. However, a home healthcare agency's patient experience scores, as measured by the Net Promoter Score and Patient Experience Percentile, exposed serious operational inefficiencies. Even though the CEO read two letters from patients—one good, one bad—at the weekly leadership meetings, performance failed to improve. Perhaps the staff reacted too late to patient complaints? Is there a better way to monitor and improve patient experience?

REFERENCES

Agency for Healthcare Research and Quality. (2017a). CAHPS patient experience surveys and guidance. Retrieved from https://www.ahrq.gov/cahps/surveys-guidance/index.html

Agency for Healthcare Research and Quality. (2017b). What is patient experience? Retrieved from https://www.ahrq.gov/cahps/about-cahps/patient-experience/index.html

CASE 7: Hurricane Mia Hits the Patient Access Call Center

INTRODUCTION

Apollo Bay is the regional area known for its beautiful beaches and 250 days of sunshine each year. Of the over 2 million people who populate the area, over 600,000 live in Bay City, the metropolitan home of one of the best public universities in the state. Operating within the university, Bay City University Health System (BCUHS) is a nationally prominent academic medical center with an annual operating budget of more than $2 billion (Pruitt, 2017). The BCUHS faculty practice group is called Bay City University Medical Group (BCUMG) whose 1,400 physicians practicing in 30 different medical specialties are organized into 14 different clinical departments.

A centralized call center, called the "Patient Access and Capacity Management (PACM) Department," manages patient scheduling, registration, and referral management for all BCUMG clinical departments. The primary method for patients to schedule an appointment with a physician is to contact the call center. Over 100 agents support the physician practice with inbound appointment scheduling and outbound appointment reminder calls. The call center uses a comprehensive, cloud-based physician-scheduling system that is integrated with the health system's electronic medical records (EMR) system to schedule patient appointments.

The CEO, Gary Anderson, MD, MHA, practiced as an emergency medicine physician for 20 years, but transitioned into health administration to give himself more time for high-adrenaline sports, such as heli-skiing, windsurfing, and bungee jumping. Or so he told people. In actuality, Anderson soon discovered his talent for turning around struggling healthcare organizations, so now he worked more hours than ever. Anderson viewed himself as a professional problem solver with fighting spirit. Others saw him as mean. Nevertheless, he agreed that his aggressive decision-making and autocratic leadership style could make him somewhat intimidating. Maybe it was all those years working in the emergency department.

Danny Eno, MHA, was recently recruited to BCUMG from a successful academic medical center in upstate to "fix the poor patient experience scores" (Anderson's words). In fact, the CAHPS Clinician & Group Survey (CG-CAHPS) scores that relate to patients' timely access to patient care were so unacceptably low that BCUMG elevated the top position of the PACM Department to the compensation level commensurate with an assistant vice president. This was a significant investment for the faculty practice group, so the interview process was comprehensive and competitive. Eno secured the job at BCUMG because Anderson respected his ability to stand up for himself during his grueling interviews. Eno was not at all intimidated by Anderson's prickly nature. To Eno, Anderson was a softy. Prior to excelling in his health administration career, Eno was a professional dancer in several ballet companies whose artistic directors immunized him against all kinds of verbal abuse. Eno negotiated the title of "chief access officer," which he thought communicated the importance of the Patient Access function.

CASE SCENARIO

Aftermath of Hurricane Mia

Hurricane Mia slammed into Apollo Bay as a Category 3 on the Saffir-Simpson Hurricane Wind Scale with winds of 127 mph (NOAA, n.d.). The hurricane path entered the mouth of Apollo Bay and traveled straight over downtown Bay City. While there was minimal wind damage to buildings and infrastructure, Mia caused a 12-foot storm surge that flooded many areas of Bay City, especially along the low-lying downtown area. The university area, built on higher land north of the city, was mostly spared.

BCUMG closed operations for 2 days prior to Hurricane Mia's landfall. All scheduled patient appointments were canceled. On the morning following Mia, Gary Anderson, the CEO of BCUMG, met with his team of direct reports in the large conference room. His team included Cindy Jacobs (assistant vice president of human resources [HR]), Alicia Thomas (assistant vice president and chief administrative officer), and Danny Eno (assistant vice president and chief access officer). Sabrina Whitley, the assistant vice president and chief financial officer for the practice plan, called into the meeting because the streets around her home were still flooded.

Anderson opened the meeting with a simple statement. "It's time for triage, folks," he said. He told his team that his experience as an emergency medicine physician made him uniquely prepared to lead BCUMG operations during the disaster recovery period. "This is a scarce resource situation," he said. "We need to take a different approach from our daily practices and to make decisions how best to handle our resources efficiently, fairly, and consistently." In rapid succession, he asked his team to evaluate the constraints, such as What is the availability of each of our clinicians? What is the space availability for the clinics and administrative offices? He wanted to resume delivering healthcare services as soon as possible.

The executive team knew the answers, based on their disaster preparedness plan. A list of available providers was being updated three times daily by PACM analyst, Jenny Roberts. Almost all facilities for BCUMG, located high above the Apollo Bay shoreline, appeared to be operational. They were awaiting the "all clear" from the university disaster response team. Operations would most likely open the next day. Once authorized, they would communicate the status to the agents who would come to the call center based on their availability. Some call center agents, like many clinicians, would not be able to come to work because of physical impediments to travel or family obligations.

Anderson said, "I need all of you to develop a plan for operational recovery. For example, Danny," Anderson pointed aggressively, "I need you to figure out how we are going to schedule all our patients as soon as possible so that our offices are not idle."

Danny responded with a hint of a smirk, "Remember that discussion we had 3 weeks ago?" Eno already had a plan in mind for patient appointment scheduling, and now that all existing patient scheduling rules had been suspended, the time was now.

Anderson cut off any discussion. "Danny, this is not a time for talk, just action. All of you, get your plans to me by noon."

Eno and two key members of his team, Jenny Roberts (analyst) and Anna Nguyen (director of HR), began to break down the disaster response efforts into individual tasks, starting with simple step-by-step rules for patient scheduling.

Three Weeks Prior to Hurricane Mia

Anderson was not happy. He and Eno sat at a small table in the CEO's office. Anderson passed over a laminated list of CG-CAHPS survey questions to Eno as a way to make his disappointment clear. CG-CAHPS evaluates patients' satisfaction with their outpatient experience, including five questions regarding patient access:

1. When you phoned this provider's office to get an appointment for care you needed right away, how often did you get an appointment as soon as you needed?

2. When you made an appointment for a checkup/routine care, how often did you get an appointment as soon as you needed?

3. When you phoned this provider's office during regular office hours, how often did you get an answer to your medical question that same day?

4. After regular office hours, how often did you get an answer to your medical question that same day?

5. Wait time includes time spent in the waiting room and examination room. During your most recent visit, did you see this provider within 15 minutes of your appointment time?

Eno read over the list of CG-CAHPS survey questions with a pensive look on his face even though he knew all the items by heart.

"As the executive in charge of Patient Access and Capacity Management, these scores are your responsibility," Anderson finally said. "Unfortunately, the top-box scores for composite Patient Access questions are abysmal." Anderson was referring to the percentage of respondents who answered "always" to all of the five patient access–related questions. Anderson passed the results of the most recent Top-Box CG-CAHPS scores for timely appointments, care, and information divided by patient health insurance type (Table C7.1).

"Not good, no," Eno conceded. "However, Dr. Anderson, we have made progress in our first initiative. As you understand, we are systematically addressing each of the patient access issues. When I first started, BCUMG had a no-show rate of 39% for new patients and 56% for established patients. Patients were simply failing to show up for their appointments. I'm pleased to say that our no-show rates have decreased substantially to around 8%, close to other top academic medical groups in the U.S."

Table C7.1 Top-Box CG-CAHPS Scores for Timely Appointments, Care, and Information

	ADULT MEDICAID	CHILD MEDICAID	CHIP	MEDICARE	PRIVATE INSURANCE
National average	59%	74%	75%	68%	78%
Bay City University Medical Group	52%	62%	61%	59%	66%

CG-CAHPS, Consumer Assessment of Healthcare Providers and Systems' Clinician & Group Survey; CHIP, Children's Health Insurance Plan.

Anderson gave Eno an unpleasantly inquisitive look.

Eno continued, "Why is this important to patient experience scores? Well, patient no-shows impact appointment scheduling. To account for no-shows, many of our clinical departments were double- and triple-booking patients, which caused substantial wait times and dissatisfied patients. We accomplished significant improvement first through implementing the concept of 'the return recall.' Instead of scheduling appointments 6 to 8 months out, our outbound call teams now call patients 2 weeks before their follow-up visit is due to schedule appointments. Second, we convinced as many clinical departments as possible to sign up their patients for text message reminders. Our new notification system uses SMS messaging that is integrated with our patient scheduling component of our EMR. Texts are sent automatically to patients 2 days prior to their appointment," Eno explained.

"But the CG-CAHPS scores?" Anderson asked.

"Right. Reduction in no-shows was the good news. Now the bad news," Eno said. "The measure for outpatient appointment wait times recommended by the Institute for Healthcare Improvement is called the 'third next available appointment.' Our EMR creates this statistic by counting the number of days between a dummy request for an appointment and the third next available appointment. The third appointment is used because the first and second available appointments are created mostly by patients cancelling appointments, which makes them not good measures for accessibility."

Eno gave the report to Anderson and said, "Here is the report of Third Next Available Appointments (TNAAs) by clinical department (Table C7.2). The weighted average for TNAAs for all departments is 37.7 days. This is probably the most important cause of my department's poor patient experience scores."

"What's a good TNAA average?" Anderson asked.

Eno sighed. "Well, if the supply of physicians matches the demand for services from patients, then the TNAA performance is close to zero days for primary care and 2 days for specialty care. As you can see, though, there is large variability in wait times by our clinical department."

"I see that. Why are some much worse than others?" Anderson asked.

"Well, I think there are several reasons. First, as I mentioned, some of it has to do with patient demand outstripping clinician supply. That is, there are more patients needing appointments than there are physician appointment slots."

"Of course. We are aware of these issues, and I am working with our health system Human Resources and Graduate Medical Education departments to recruit physicians to our practice," Anderson said.

Table C7.2 Third Next Available Appointment (Days) by Clinical Department

BCUMG DEPARTMENT	THIRD NEXT AVAILABLE APPOINTMENT (DAYS)
Family Medicine	6
Oncology	17
Internal Medicine	22
Urology	25
OB/GYN	27
Pediatrics	29
Otolaryngology	32
Psychiatry	36
Dermatology	51
Surgery	62
Neurology	64
Ophthalmology	72
Plastic Surgery	79

BCUMG, Bay City University Medical Group.

"But that's only part of it. I think there are two main drivers of wait times and patient access from the perspective of my department. Here, I created a 2-by-2 matrix to illustrate my point (Figure C7.1). The first dimension is the use of technology, and the second is complexity of their scheduling methods. I placed each of the 14 clinical departments within the four boxes," Eno said as he presented his matrix to Anderson.

"Nice work. Did you create this?" Anderson asked.

"Yes," Eno said, satisfied at gaining Anderson's approval. "First, let me explain the use of technology on the vertical axis. As I mentioned, some of the clinical departments adopted our new texting platform for their patients—Family Medicine and Surgery departments are good examples. Other departments were less enthusiastic, and their outbound teams still make outbound reminder calls. Psychiatry, urology, oncology, ophthalmology, and neurology are examples of low adopters of our technology platforms."

"You've included online portal as a component of technology use?" Anderson asked.

"Yes," Eno said. "Some departments really encourage patients to book their own appointments through the web-based patient portal. Adoption of the web-portal is really a generational thing. Millennials and Gen-Xers prefer online booking features, but Baby Boomers seem to be indifferent about online booking."

"Yeah, but I don't get it. How is technology related to patient wait times?" Anderson asked.

"Well, I hate to admit it, but the more the clinical departments rely on the call center to schedule appointments, the greater likelihood there is for mistakes. Which brings me to the horizontal axis of my 2-by-2 matrix," Eno said.

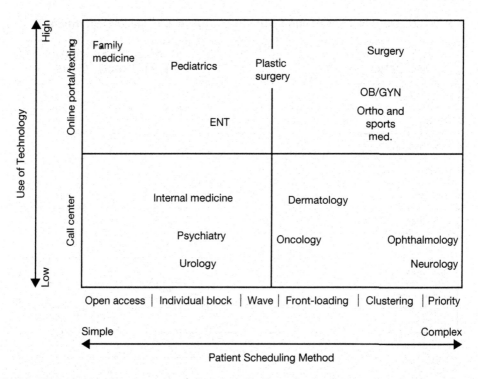

FIGURE C7.1 Matrix of patient-scheduling complexity and use of technology by department.
ENT, ear, nose, and throat; OB/GYN, obstetrics and gynecology.

"Patient Scheduling Method," Anderson read the axis title on the bottom of the matrix.

"Yes. This continuum is not as complicated as it seems," Eno said. "These are just types of patient appointment scheduling from simple on the left to complex on the right. Some clinical departments' method of scheduling fits nicely within the categories, but most have some sort of hybrid of these types."

"Why are there so many different patient appointment scheduling methods?" Anderson asked.

"That's the key question. Over time, the department leaders have developed different ways for handling patient scheduling. Basically, all of the clinical departments have developed special preferences for how they want to schedule patients. We accommodate all of them. None have really been tested for efficiency of reducing wait times or improving patient experience. This is my point. Balancing these preferences for patient appointment scheduling among our departments makes our scheduling processes exceedingly complex and often frustrating for patients." With this, Eno explained the various patient appointment scheduling types, starting with the most complex on the right.

- Priority means that patients are scheduled based on illness acuity. Urgent patients were scheduled first, while pushing routine visits and less acute conditions to a later time, or even date. This is the most complex method for PACM because it requires call center agents to correctly identify the clinical condition, which may be inaccurate. Priority-based scheduling leads to back-and-forth communication with the clinical staff, creating something called the "triage and double booking hassle."

- Clustering is the scheduling method in which similar cases and procedures are booked on specific days, for example, all assessments one day and all surgeries the next. The challenge is identifying the patient's condition and correctly scheduling them on the right day.

■ Front-loading means overbooking patients in the early part of the day in order to ensure there is a sufficient number of waiting patients throughout the day.

■ Wave scheduling, also known as the "two-at-a-time rule," means that patients are booked only during the first half-an-hour of each hour. Whichever patient arrives first is the first to be seen while the other waits.

■ The individual block rule scheduling practices tend to have several different appointment types, so each appointment type gets its own block of time, which varies. For example, pediatrics can schedule blocks of appointments based on the average time for typical visits, such as new patients, return patients, well-visits, sick-visits, attention deficit disorder assessments, or vaccinations.

■ The open access or advance access model is known for same-day appointments. The practice leaves about half of the day open, and each clinician manages patients' demands for office care on a daily basis without regard to urgency. The central question is simply, Is your personal clinician here today? If yes, the patient is scheduled that day. If no, the patient can be scheduled to see another clinician the same day or their personal clinician on a future date. For specialist clinicians, a day is usually added to allow for the call center agents to capture referrals and authorizations.

"So, when we centralized patient access into one call center, we allowed the departments to keep their preferred scheduling type," said Eno. "This meant that we organize our call center agents into six teams, each trained to handle patient scheduling according to similar rules. Six teams meant six training programs because each has to learn the specific scheduling rules for the assigned clinical departments. The more complex rules, the more mistakes we make, which causes higher wait times and lower patient experience scores. Here is a simplified organizational chart for our PACM team" (Figure C7.2).

"I get it. Complicated and inefficient. Tell me, why do we offer so many scheduling options to the clinical departments?" Anderson asked.

"I was going to ask you the same question. Why not standardize the work? This would simplify patient appointment scheduling and organizational design."

Anderson thought for a moment. "Because the previous administrative leadership was focused on keeping the physicians satisfied," he finally said. "However, since I became CEO, we moved to performance-based compensation which includes productivity, including number of patients seen, and patient experience scores, as measured by CG-CAHPS."

"So, I propose we simplify the patient scheduling processes," Eno said as confidently as possible. "The open access model applies the principles of queuing theory in an effort to match the demand for appointment visits with the supply. This scheduling approach adopts Lean thinking, which is the standard in modern manufacturing and service industries, to maximize patient flow."

"Maybe," responded Anderson. "Many of our clinicians are recovering from the change to performance-based compensation. I made some people angry, so I am still rebuilding their trust. I am not sure the docs would be ready for another change so soon. Plus, there may not be a one-size-fits-all scheduling method. Part of the value of academic medicine is the specialized nature of the care provided by especially particular physicians."

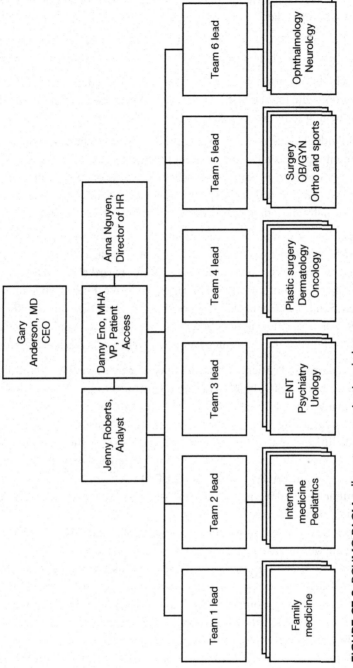

FIGURE C7.2 BCUMG PACM call center organizational chart.
BCUMG, Bay City University Medical Group; ENT, ear, nose, and throat; PACM, patient access and capacity managment.

"Fair enough," Eno said. "There are other initiatives to improve patient experience, but none will be as impactful."

"Again, I said 'maybe.' Still, I'm interested. What did you have in mind?" Anderson asked.

"I think we could use Family Medicine as the ideal and try out a pilot with other clinical departments. As the matrix shows, Family Medicine uses a simple and effective scheduling method—the open access model. This was first implemented before my time here, at the insistence of their chair, Dr. Rotzek. Here's how it works, at a high level. Again, add a day for specialist clinicians to allow for ability to capture referrals & authorizations." Eno showed Anderson the open access patient-scheduling flowchart (Figure C7.3).

"That does seem simple, but I am not sure all the departments would go for it," Anderson said.

Eno agreed. "Probably right. Anyway, many of the practices have a substantial backlog, and it would take a while to work it down. In a world where the schedule was wiped clean and the supply matched the demand, we could adopt the open access approach across all practices. It is hard for me to imagine clearing the slate of all scheduled patient appointments in one fell swoop, though."

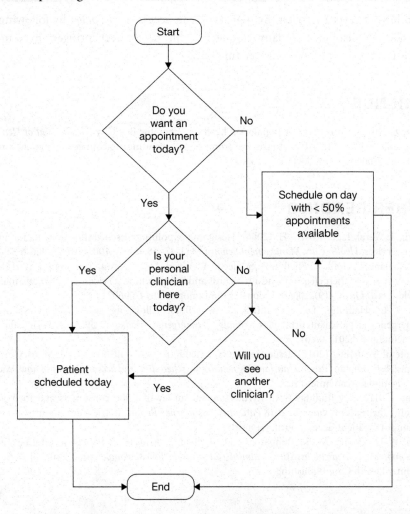

FIGURE C7.3 Family medicine open access patient-scheduling standard work process.

DISCUSSION QUESTIONS

1. What is the organizational impact for BCUMG of high patient wait times and low patient experience scores?

2. Discuss your opinion of Dr. Gary Anderson's leadership style. Do you think his approach to holding his team accountable is effective during regular operations? What about during emergency situations? Why or why not?

3. Describe the reasons that an academic medical center physician practice would have so many patient appointment-scheduling methods (open access, individual block rule, clustering, priority-based, etc.).

4. Discuss the quality management principles that apply to emergency management situations. How are these approaches similar or different from normal healthcare operations?

PODCAST FOR CASE 7

Listen to how experts approach the topic (you can access the podcast by following this url to Springer Publishing Company Connect™: https://connect.springerpub.com/content/book/978-0-8261-4514-7/front-matter/fmatter2)

REFERENCE

Pruitt, Z. (2017). Case study: A population health strategy for Bay City. *The Journal of Health Admin Education*, *34*(4), 133–178. Retrieved from https://www.ingentaconnect.com/contentone/aupha/jhae/2017/00000034/00000001/art00009

FURTHER READING

Cayirli, T., Veral, E., & Rosen, H. (2006). Designing appointment scheduling systems for ambulatory care services. *Health Care Management Science*, *9*(1), 47–58. doi:10.1007/s10729-006-6279-5

De Lusignan, S., Mold, F., Sheikh, A., Majeed, A., Wyatt, J. C., Quinn, T., ... Rafi, I. (2014). Patients' online access to their electronic health records and linked online services: A systematic interpretative review. *BMJ Open*, *4*(9), e006021. doi:10.1136/bmjopen-2014-006021

Hick, J. L., Hanfling, D., & Cantrill, S. V. (2012). Allocating scarce resources in disasters: Emergency department principles. *Annals of Emergency Medicine*, *59*(3), 177–187. doi:10.1016/j.annemergmed.2011.06.012

Institute of Medicine. (2015). Issues in access, scheduling, and wait times. In J. M. McGinnis, M. H. Lopez, & G. Kaplan (Eds.), *Transforming health care scheduling and access: Getting to now*. Washington, DC: National Academies Press.

Kyruus. (2018). Key findings from Kyruus' annual survey of 1,000 consumers and their journey to finding the right provider. In *2018 Patient Access Journey Report*. Retrieved from https://www.kyruus.com/2018-patient-access-journey-report

Lindh, W. Q., Pooler, M. S., Tamparo, C. D., & Dahl, B. M. (2009). Patient scheduling. In *Delmar's comprehensive medical assisting: Administrative and clinical competencies* (4th ed.). Albany, NY: Delmar Health Care Publishing.

Mazaheri, M. H., Abadi, F. M., Tabesh, H., Vakili-Arki, H., Abu-Hanna, A., & Eslami, S. (2018). Evaluation of patient satisfaction of the status of appointment scheduling systems in outpatient clinics: Identifying patients' needs. *Journal of Advanced Pharmaceutical Technology & Research, 9*(2), 51–55. doi:10.4103/japtr.JAPTR_134_18

Muhlestein, D., Saunders, R., & McClellan, M. (2017). Growth of ACOs and alternative payment models in 2017. In *Health Affairs Blog*. Retrieved from https://www.healthaffairs.org/do/10.1377/hblog20170628.060719/full

Murray, M., & Berwick, D. M. (2003). Advanced access: Reducing waiting and delays in primary care. *Journal of the American Medical Association, 289*(8), 1035–1040. doi:10.1001/jama.289.8.1035

Murray, M., Bodenheimer, T., Rittenhouse, D., & Grumbach, K. (2003). Improving timely access to primary care: Case studies of the advanced access model. *Journal of the American Medical Association, 289*(8), 1042–1046. doi:10.1001/jama.289.8.1042

National Oceanic and Atmospheric Administration National Hurricane Center (n.d.). Storm surge overview Retrieved from https://www.nhc.noaa.gov/surge

Rose, K. D., Ross, J. S., & Horwitz, L. I. (2011). Advanced access scheduling outcomes: A systematic review. *Archives of Internal Medicine, 171*(13), 1150–1159. doi:10.1001/archinternmed.2011.168

Vijayan, A. P. (2015). *Effect of appointment schedules on the operational performance of a University Medical Clinic* (LSU Master's Theses, 1871). Louisiana State University, Louisiana.

TOOLS AND APPROACHES

2 × 2 MATRIX

On many occasions in healthcare quality management, you will face an issue with several dimensions or attributes. To investigate, try looking at a pair of those dimensions using a 2 × 2 matrix (Figure C7.4). A benefit of the 2 × 2 matrix is that it creates four quadrants to help you stratify the attributes that you are evaluating. Once you examine the issue along the two dimensions, you can make decisions and prioritize.

A classic example of a 2 × 2 matrix in healthcare quality management is the Impact/Effort matrix, which helps teams evaluate several ideas for improvement based on the impact they may have on achieving the goal and the effort required to take them to fruition.

In the Impact/Effort matrix, a team ranks a number of ideas they are considering for implementation. Ideas in quadrant A should definitely be implemented, since they are high impact but low effort. Ideas in quadrant D should not be considered because they are low impact and high effort.

Another example of the implementation of a 2 × 2 matrix is a complement to the stakeholder analysis. You can place the stakeholders along two dimensions: power and interest. You can then consider how to negotiate with each stakeholder when running your quality management project.

Here are other examples of pairs of dimensions that suit themselves to be used in a 2 × 2 matrix:

- Time versus Cost
- Patient Satisfaction versus Length-of-Stay
- Risk Severity versus Occurrence
- Aspects of patient experience (e.g., use of technology vs. ease of communication)

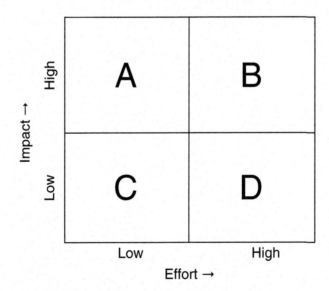

FIGURE C7.4 Example of an Impact/Effort matrix.

CASE 8: The Cowboy Doctor's Patient Experience

1. Describe how clinician-patient communication can impact patient experience.
2. Appraise a problem-solving approach related to patient complaints.
3. Analyze patient experience survey data to identify root causes of low ratings.
4. Identify the behaviors associated with professional and social responsibility.
5. Summarize challenges associated with quality management in rural hospital settings.

INTRODUCTION

Patient experience surveys assess whether a patient's expectations about their care experience were met (Agency for Healthcare Research and Quality, 2017). The Centers for Medicare and Medicaid Services (CMS) requires hospitals to publicly report patient experience scores, as measured by Hospital Consumer Assessment of Healthcare Providers and Systems (HCAHPS; CMS, 2013). Once the surveys are collected and tabulated, the results are available through the Medicare Hospital Compare website. Prospective consumers can make informed decisions about healthcare purchases by comparing the patient experience ratings of hospitals. In addition, the HCAHPS results are a significant part of Medicare's inpatient payment rate calculation, which creates significant incentive for hospitals to improve their patient experience (Dempsey, Reilly, & Buhlman, 2014).

The HCAHPS survey asks patients about their experience at the hospital, including questions related to staff responsiveness, hospital environment, medication instructions, and discharge information. Patients are asked separate questions about their interactions with physicians and nurses, including being treated with courtesy and respect, listening to the patient, and explaining patient care. For example, the HCAHPS asks the following questions about patients' communication with nurses:

1. During this hospital stay, how often did nurses treat you with *courtesy and respect*?
2. During this hospital stay, how often did nurses *listen carefully to you*?
3. During this hospital stay, how often did nurses *explain things* in a way you could understand?

DATA FILE FOR CASE 8

Data files for students are available by accessing the following url: https://www.springerpub.com/hqm

The data file for Case 8 provides HCAHPS patient experience surveys with 29 questions from 80 patients. Includes data dictionary.

Bremen Memorial Hospital is a 40-bed, nonprofit, community hospital in Bremen, Texas. The town of about 7,500 citizens was established in 1854 by German Catholic immigrants who settled in Texas and whose descendants still speak German in their homes today. In 1955, the citizens of Bremen established Bremen Memorial Hospital with funds provided by the Hospital Survey and Construction Act (also known as the "Hill-Burton Act"). The Sisters of Charity of the Incarnate Word agreed to train their nuns to operate the hospital, and Sister Mildred Klaftenegger served as the first hospital administrator. Dr. Marvin Meyer, who worked at Walter Reed Army Medical Center as an Army surgeon at the end of World War II, was the first medical director. Dr. Meyer had a series of articles written about him in the national press over the years, calling him "The Cowboy Doctor." His undeniable charm—and hot temper—made Dr. Meyer something of an iconic figure around Bremen.

Family practice physicians provide the majority of medical care to rural areas in the United States (American Association of Family Physicians [AAFP], 2014). In 1997, Bremen Memorial Hospital affiliated with the University of Houston Medical Center to create a family medicine residency training program. As part of the affiliation agreement, five family medicine residents have spent a 4-week rotation working under two Bremen Memorial attending hospitalist physicians employed by the hospital to supervise the residents. Bremen Memorial leaders believed that training family practice residents would increase the chances that they would stay to practice in their community after completing their residency. However, resident physicians have been reluctant to stay in the Bremen area, citing loan repayment, the rural lifestyle, and spouse preferences as barriers to recruitment (Roseamelia et al., 2014).

Bremen Memorial Hospital has long suffered financial distress, like many rural hospitals in the United States (Kaufman et al., 2016). Many rural hospitals have closed and stopped providing inpatient services (Thomas, Holmes, & Pink, 2016). In the previous month, the Bremen Memorial Hospital board of directors announced their impending closure, stating, "At Bremen, we have weathered low patient volumes, high number of uninsured patients, low reimbursement rates, difficulty in getting payment from private insurance providers, and the state's refusal to expand Medicaid. The trickle of revenue has not been enough to remain financially viable for the long term. As such, we have decided that we will close the hospital at the end of next month."

CASE SCENARIO

Chief Executive Officer

The Bremen Memorial Hospital Wellness Center, a modest fitness facility recently updated to attract paying community members, was empty on this early Tuesday morning. The lone exerciser was the CEO, Mark Holmes, who was sweating away on the elliptical trainer.

The Chairman of the board of directors, Stephen Schafer, knew to visit Bremen Memorial's CEO at the Wellness Center early in the morning, even if he felt out of place in his boots, jeans, and Stetson hat. "Hi, Mark. I got a phone call last night," Schafer said to Holmes in an ominous tone.

"Good morning, Dr. Schafer," Holmes said cheerfully. Whoosh, whoosh, whoosh went the elliptical.

"Mark, I've told you this before. Don't call me 'doctor' at the hospital. I'm a large animal veterinarian, doggonit. It just confuses people," Schafer said. Whoosh, whoosh, whoosh! "Anyway, like I said, I got a call." Whoosh, whoosh, whoosh! "Can you please hop off that thing so we can talk?"

"Sure, Steve, I was cooling down anyway." Holmes climbed down from the machine and pulled three wipes from the nearby dispenser and began to clean the equipment assiduously.

"Larry Meyer called me last night. We discharged his daddy home yesterday, and he is none too happy," Schafer said. "Dr. Marvin Meyer is the 97-year-old founding medical director of this hospital. Larry owns the Ford dealership."

"I know who Larry is, and his father, too. This does not surprise me. Has the crusty, old Cowboy Doctor ever been happy?" asked Holmes,

"Well, Dr. Meyer is crustier than usual, I suppose," Schafer said. "I told Larry that I would look into the problem for his daddy. Apparently, a nurse treated him something awful."

"You see, Steve." Holmes said, finally looking Schafer in the eyes. "This is what you never understood about being the chairman of the board. You were always stuck in the weeds. Always operational, never strategic. If you want to follow a dying man's request, then be my guest. I've got hospital operations to unwind and staff to lay off by the end of next month."

"Mark, you don't gotta be like that. I told the man I would look into it, and I aim to do what I said. Can you tell me who to talk to?" Schafer asked.

"Talk to the chief nursing officer for nurse-related problems. Rita Richter is usually in her office early. You can speak to her there."

Chief Nursing Officer

True enough, Rita Richter was sitting at her desk when Schafer knocked on her door. Schafer knew Richter to be a friendly, detailed-oriented nurse who always presented professionally at Board meetings. She spoke with a thick Texas accent, but in an unexpectedly proper manner. She chose her words carefully in public settings, but always defended the Bremen Memorial nurses when needed. However, on several occasions, she swiftly had addressed performance issues with intransigent nurses. She did not shy away from firing nurses who failed to measure up to her standards. "How you doing, Steve? What brings you by this early?" Richter asked with a tired smile.

"Duty calls," Schafer said. He explained the patient's complaint as plainly as he could. He told her that the patient was Dr. Marvin Meyer, the famed Cowboy Doctor.

Richter listened attentively with concern and then asked, "Are you sure it was a nurse?"

"That's what Larry told me. He didn't get a name of the woman. Apparently, his daddy had some salty language to describe the experience," Schafer said.

"Well, that surprises me, our nurses rarely get complaints like that. But we have struggled with our nursing communication component of our H-caps scores," Richter said with a sigh. "I suppose morale is low, and we have been short staffed lately."

"H-caps?" Schafer asked.

"Sorry, H-C-A-H-P-S. Pronounced 'aich-caps.' It's the survey on patient experience we send to patients that's used at hospitals nationwide. Let me show you our recent annual scores," Richter said as she pulled a binder from her desk (Figure C8.1).

"Our overall top-box patient experience ratings are below the Texas average. This concerns me because rural hospitals usually do quite well. Texas friendly and all," Richter said.

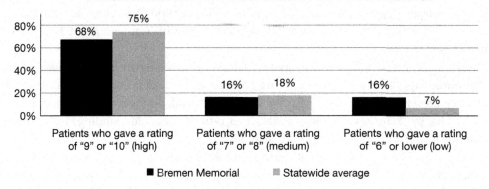

FIGURE C8.1 HCAHPS scores for overall rating of the hospital.
HCAHPS, Hospital Consumer Assessment of Healthcare Providers and Systems.

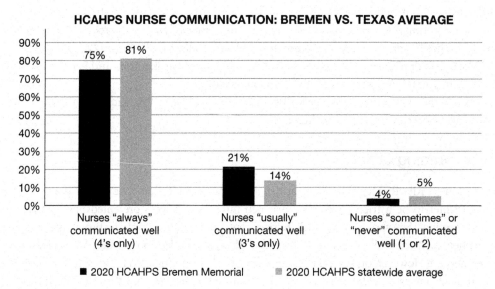

FIGURE C8.2 HCAHPS scores for nursing communication-related items.
HCAHPS, Hospital Consumer Assessment of Healthcare Providers and Systems.

"So this report tells you whether patients were satisfied with nurses?" Schafer asked.

"No, no. This is the overall rating of the hospital. Patients are asked to score the hospital from 1 to 10, with 10 being the highest. On the left, the chart presents the top-box, which are the 9's and 10's. On the right, the bottom-box, which are the scores 6 and lower. The middle group are 7's and 8's," Richter said.

"So what all goes into this score?" Schafer asked.

"Well, it's actually its own question on the survey, something like, 'What number would you use to rate this hospital with 10 being the highest?' Another item on the survey asks, 'Would you recommend this hospital to your friends and family?'" Richter said. "There are maybe two dozen other questions. Nurse communication has three questions. The same three questions are asked about the doctors. I have the Nurse Communication chart, too. See here," Richter said as she flipped through the binder to find the right chart (Figure C8.2).

Richter continued, "As you can see, the composites of the three nurse communication items are on this chart. The top-box is on the left. It is the 'always' category, which are coded 4's. The category in the middle is 'usually' category, coded with 3's. On the right is the bottom-box that includes the 'sometimes' and 'never' categories, which are coded with 1's or 2's."

"Sorry, I don't get it. This chart is three different survey questions rolled into one?" Schafer asked.

"Yes, that's right. This is a composite score for all nurse communication questions. Basically, for the top-box, they count up all the 'always' responses for each of the three survey items—courtesy and respect, listening, and explaining care—then divide by the total number of responses. So we had 80 HCAHPS returned to us by our patients last year. That's 80 surveys times three nurse communication questions. So, of the 240 possible 'always' responses, the patients rated our nurses 'always' 180 times or 75% of the time. The same calculations are made for the other two categories, also. So the three categories—top-box, middle-box, and bottom-box—total 100%," Richter explained.

"Right. So I see that the bottom-box is lower for us than the statewide average, right?" Schafer asked.

"Yes. Like I said, our nurses rarely upset patients," Richter said. "Patients who complain, like Dr. Meyer, usually rank us a 6 or below. I suppose it is possible one of our nurses ticked him off. Naturally, I'm skeptical. I could ask around for you."

"No, that's alright. If it's okay with you, I might ask the charge nurse about his nurse complaints," Schafer said.

"Sure, no problem. I'll get you the name," Richter said as she swiveled to her computer. As she wrote the charge nurse and unit on a piece of paper, Richter said, "Steve, let me ask you something. Why are you looking into this? We're closing this place down soon."

Schafer thought about that question, surprised that this point had not occurred to him yet. "I don't know, Rita. I reckon I just hate to see Dr. Meyer treated this way. He started this place. He would want it to run right all the way to the end."

Charge Nurse

Charlotte Becker was the charge nurse for Unit D, and Schafer had known her since she was a baby. Her family owned a nearby ranch with plenty of horses and cattle, and Schafer was still their family vet. Now that Charlotte was a grown-up, Schafer treated her two horses too, though she kept them just for trail riding.

"Hi, Dr. Schafer!" Becker said as she gave him a hug. "What brings you up this way? Don't you have animals to care for?"

"Hi, Charlotte. Yes, I'm heading over to the Vogel Ranch later, but I got some business here this morning," Schafer said.

"Oh, what I can I help you with, sir?" Becker asked.

Schafer told her about Dr. Meyer's complaint and told her what he learned about the HCAHPS scores.

"Well, first off, Dr. Schafer, I wasn't here when Dr. Meyer went off like a firecracker, but I heard about it. He's kinda cranky anyway, so I didn't think much of it."

"So you think it's true?" Schafer asked.

"I think he got upset, but are you sure it was a nurse?"

"According to his son, he said it was a nurse." Schafer said.

"Okay. About the HCAHPS scores. Trouble is, though, with the financial difficulties, we've had a hard time retaining nurses. We seem to be operating short all the time. Still, I think our nurses can do better," Becker said.

"That's what Rita told me," Schafer said.

"Yeah, well we're trying our best. Rita's always talking about empathy. 'Focus on the patient's needs, not on the needs of Bremen Memorial,' she says. 'Treat patients with respect and courtesy. Listen. Explain things in a way the patient can understand,'" Becker said in Rita's drawl.

"That sounds really nice, Charlotte. I know you all do a good job. Tell me, what does it look like when you treat patients with empathy?" Schafer asked.

"Hmm. Well, the nurses do hourly rounding on patients. We address the three 'P's' of potty, position, and pain. We perform an environmental assessment, such as water, tissue, trash can, and remote controls. We always tell the patient they were 'rounded on' and tell them that we'll be back in an hour. Finally, we ask the patient if there's anything else the nurse can do before leaving."

"That's all good stuff, but isn't that part of the job of a nurse?" Schafer asked.

"Are you asking if empathy is a part of the job or if finding the TV remote under pillows is a part of the job?" Becker asked.

"Uhh," Schafer stammered.

"That's okay, Dr. Schafer. I get it. What I mean is that when nurses are busy, that patient communication stuff can feel like extra. Remember, nurses are responsible for care planning, administering medications and treatments, monitoring changes in condition, and changing medication as indicated. All of this has to be updated on the patients' whiteboards and discussed with the patient and their families. Then there's all the electronic medical record documentation."

"That's a lot," Schafer said.

"Yes, and that's for six to 10 patients per nurse on medical–surgical units, depending on the shift. It's not easy. But back to your question. Yes, empathy is our job that sometimes means getting an extra blanket if they're cold."

"Sounds like our nurses are doing the right things. So, what set the Cowboy Doctor off?" Schafer asked.

"Speaking of empathy." Becker said with a smile. "Rita always tells us to try and use 'us,' not 'them,' when talking about the care team. We try and see things from others' perspectives. Whenever possible, use positive, inclusive language. She says that this encourages interprofessional collaboration."

"What do you mean?" Schafer asked.

"Umm. I don't think it was a nurse who angered Dr. Meyer. I think it was one of the family practices residents. Umm. You see, these young doctors are still learning. And, umm, I guess I'd say that some of them learn faster than others."

Schafer was dumbfounded, so Becker continued. "We get them for month-long stretches. Some are a great fit with our patients, others might be better to stay near Houston, you know."

"I hadn't even thought to ask about the doctors, Charlotte," Schafer said. "I'll look into it."

"You might wanna look at the physician HCAHPS scores for those who score us at a 6 or below, those are the ones that get really mad at us, like Dr. Meyer," Becker suggested.

"I'll do that. First, I'm going to pay the Cowboy Doctor a visit."

"Is a visit really necessary? I know you're the chairman of the board and all, but this place is closing. Shoot, I'll call him and apologize, if that's what's right," Charlotte said.

"Naw. I'll take care of it. Once this place closes, these people will still be my community. I don't want to let him down."

Cowboy Doctor

After performing blood draws for Coggins tests on a dozen of the Vogel Ranch horses, Schafer stopped by Larry Meyer's place off Route 39 where Dr. Marvin Meyer was staying. Larry was in his 70s now and widowed, so it was just Larry and his dad at the old farm house. The home health nurse was just leaving for the evening, and the Meyer men were just sitting down to supper.

"Join us, Steve," Larry Meyer said. "We've got corn bread."

After dinner, Schafer apologized for Dr. Meyer's poor patient experience at Bremen Memorial. Then, he asked the Cowboy Doctor, "Was it something someone said?"

Dr. Meyer, still struggling to breathe from his chronic obstructive pulmonary disease, raised his voice, "She interrupted me! I was uncomfortable, and she was more interested in getting her information and getting out of the room. She wouldn't let me even finish my first darn sentence. You ain't learning nothin' when your mouth's a-jawin'." His son reached over and wiped some cornbread from his father's chin.

"What information?" Schafer asked.

"Medications, symptoms, test results," Dr. Meyer said with a wave of his hand.

"Are you sure it was a nurse?" Schafer asked.

That's when The Cowboy Doctor said, "Yes, I'm sure. It was a woman!"

DISCUSSION QUESTIONS

1. How do you think the Chairman of the board, Stephen Schafer, performed in his root cause analysis? In what way did he succeed? How can he improve?

2. What do you think of the CEO's opinion of Stephen Schafer's performance as Chairman of the board? Do you think his assessment was fair? Why or why not?

3. What is your opinion of Stephen Schafer's effort to address patient complaints despite the hospital closing at the end of the next month? Does he have a professional or social responsibility to address the patient complaints?

4. In what ways is recruitment of primary care physicians challenging for rural communities? How would you recommend increasing the supply of physicians in rural areas?

5. Compare and contrast nurse communication strategies with physician communication strategies using evidence from peer-reviewed research. How do these similarities and differences impact which interventions you would choose to improve patient experience scores?

PODCAST FOR CASE 8

Listen to how experts approach the topic (you can access the podcast by following this url to Springer Publishing Company Connect™: https://connect.springerpub.com/content/book/978-0-8261-4514-7/front-matter/fmatter2)

REFERENCES

Agency for Healthcare Research and Quality. (2017). *What is patient experience?* Retrieved from https://www.ahrq.gov/cahps/about-cahps/patient-experience/index.html

American Association of Family Physicians. (2014). *Rural practice, keeping physicians in* (Position Paper). http://www.aafp.org/about/policies/all/rural-practice-paper.html

Centers for Medicare and Medicaid Services. (2013). *Hospital consumer assessment of healthcare providers and systems.* Baltimore, MD. Retrieved from http://www.hcahpsonline.org

Dempsey, C., Reilly, B., & Buhlman, N. (2014). Improving the patient experience: Real-world strategies for engaging nurses. *Journal of Nursing Administration, 44*(3), 142–151. doi:10.1097/NNA.0000000000000042

Kaufman, B. G., Thomas, S. R., Randolph, R. K., Perry, J. R., Thompson, K. W., Holmes, G. M., & Pink, G. H. (2016). The rising rate of rural hospital closures. *The Journal of Rural Health, 32*(1), 35–43. doi:10.1111/jrh.12128

Roseamelia, C., Greenwald, J. L., Bush, T., Pratte, M., Wilcox, J., & Morley, C. P. (2014). A qualitative study of medical students in a rural track. *Family Medicine, 46*(4), 259–266. Retrieved from https://www.stfm.org/FamilyMedicine/Vol46Issue4/Roseamelia259

Thomas, S. R., Holmes, G. M., &Pink, G. H. (2016). To what extent do community characteristics explain differences in closure among financially distressed rural hospitals? *Journal of Health Care for the Poor and Underserved, 27*(4), 194–203. doi:10.1353/hpu.2016.0176

FURTHER READING

Beckman, H. B., & Frankel, R. M. (1984). The effect of physician behavior on the collection of data. *Annals of Internal Medicine, 101*(5), 692–696. doi:10.7326/0003-4819-101-5-692

Blanchard, J., Petterson, S., Bazemore, A., Watkins, K., & Mullan, F. (2016). Characteristics and distribution of graduate medical education training sites: Are we missing opportunities to meet US health workforce needs? *Academic Medicine, 91*(10), 1416–1422. doi:10.1097/ACM.0000000000001184

Boissy, A., Windover, A. K., Bokar, D., Karafa, M., Neuendorf, K., Frankel, R. M., … & Rothberg, M. B. (2016). Communication skills training for physicians improves patient satisfaction. *Journal of General Internal Medicine, 31*(7), 755–761. doi:10.1007/s11606-016-3597-2

Bumpers, B., Dearmon, V., & Dycus, P. (2019). Impacting the patient's experience in a children's hospital using a communication bundle strategy. *Journal of Nursing Care Quality, 34*(1), 86–90. doi:10.1097/NCQ.0000000000000336

Long, L. (2012), Impressing patients while improving HCAHPS. *Nursing Management, 43*(12), 32–37. doi:10.1097/01.NUMA.0000422891.99334.68

Richter, J. P., & Muhlestein, D. B. (2017). Patient experience and hospital profitability: Is there a link? *Health Care Management Review, 42*(3), 247–257. doi:10.1097/HMR.0000000000000105

Salmond, S. W., & Echevarria, M. (2017). Healthcare transformation and changing roles for nursing. *Orthopedic Nursing, 36*(1), 12. doi:10.1097/NOR.0000000000000308

PARETO CHARTS

The Pareto chart is a tool for establishing priorities based on the Pareto Principle (Figure C8.3). The 19th-century Italian economist, Vilfredo Pareto, developed the famous rule that 20% of the causes result in 80% of the impact. The Pareto Principle is also called the "80/20 rule."

For example, 20% of the causes of defect opportunities tend to cause 80% of the defects. Or 20% of the types of medication errors cause 80% of the patient adverse reactions. Or 20% of surgeons make up 80% of the total revenue for the medical practice.

The Pareto chart's left-side axis measures the count of the occurrences and arranges the categories of data in descending order, with largest number occurrences shown first (on the left), then the next most occurrences, and so on. When presented in a chart, the category with the most number of occurrences on the left becomes the highest bar.

What makes the Pareto chart unique from a simple bar chart is that it also includes a secondary axis (on the right side). This right-side axis measures the cumulative percentage of each category/bar. Cumulative percentage is defined as the addition of successive instances of the proportion of the total. For example, if the first category/bar is 40% of the total and the second category/bar is 20% of the total, then the cumulative percentage for the first two categories equals 60%. The cumulative percentage continues to increase with each successive category/bar until it reaches 100%.

The Pareto chart, then, helps demonstrate the Pareto Principle. Looking at your Pareto chart, you can identify which of the categories/bars add up to a cumulative percentage of 80%. Joseph Juran, one of the innovators of quality management, called these categories on the left the "Vital Few." The purpose of identifying the vital few is to prioritize which problems to solve first (Juran, 1951).

REFERENCES

Juran, J. M. (1951). *Quality control handbook.* New York, NY: McGraw-Hill.

Pronovost, P., & Hill, J. (2015). *10 Most common patient complaints, grievances with hospitals.* Retrieved from https://www.beckershospitalreview.com/quality/10-most-common-patient-complaints-grievances -with-hospitals.html

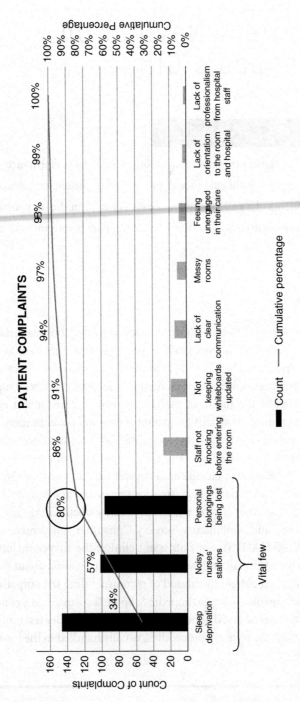

FIGURE C8.3 Pareto chart.

Source: Pronovost, P., & Hill, J. (2015). *10 Most common patient complaints, grievances with hospitals.*
Retrieved from https://www.beckershospitalreview.com/quality/10-most-common-patient-complaints-grievances-with-hospitals.html

CASE 9: Patient Navigation at the Orthopedic Clinic

1. Evaluate how management priorities impact organizational performance.
2. Describe the Nurse Navigator care model and its role in patient experience.
3. Describe components of a patient experience survey used in the outpatient setting.
4. Analyze how variation from standardized quality management practices influences the patient's experience of care.

INTRODUCTION

Godfrey Community Hospital is a 336-bed, not-for-profit community hospital headquartered in the suburban community of Medford Groves. Godfrey provides healthcare to more than 140,000 patients in the area. The hospital is led by CEO David Marshall and a board of directors comprising local community leaders, such as bankers, lawyers, nonprofit leaders, the school superintendent, and others who are invested in the future of the community. The institution employs 3,500 employees and has received numerous awards for quality of care and patient experience.

The Centers for Medicare and Medicaid Services (CMS) calculates star performance ratings for more than 3,600 hospitals in the United States using experience of care data derived from the Hospital Consumer Assessment of Healthcare Providers and Systems (HCAHPS) survey. The CMS publishes the patient experience performance scores for each hospital in an effort to increase transparency and consumer empowerment in making treatment decisions. The CMS also conducts the Outpatient and Ambulatory Surgery Consumer Assessment of Healthcare Providers and Systems (OAS CAHPS). For outpatient clinics, the survey includes questions about patient experience with the staff and facility, staff communication about the procedure, patient rating of the facility, and patient likelihood of recommending the outpatient clinic.

Godfrey's outpatient orthopedic clinic, Orthopedic & Spine Institute (OSI), conducts certain minimally invasive musculoskeletal and diagnostic procedures, laboratory tests, and evaluations performed in association with the primary procedures, usually handled in the inpatient setting.

 ## DATA FILE FOR CASE 9

Data files for students are available by accessing the following url: https://www.springerpub.com/hqm

The data file for Case 9 provides publicly reported Outpatient and Ambulatory Surgery CAHPS facility-level data for over 1,200 ambulatory surgery centers (655 facilities with "linear mean scores"). Includes instructions on how to create Percent Rank in Excel.

CASE SCENARIO

Uncle Dave

"Mr. Marshall, your 9:30 appointment is waiting in your office," David Marshall's executive assistant said as he exited the conference room and headed to his office. The Godfrey Community Hospital CEO was overweight, disheveled, and in a hurry. Marshall was not surprised to be running late already. The weekly executive team meetings often run over time.

"Okay, thank you. Hey Matt, will you walk with me back to my office?" Marshall asked his chief operating officer (COO), Matt George. "I want to introduce you to someone." Marshall did not wait for George's reply as he lumbered away.

As the two men entered the CEO's office, Cindy Barrett rose to greet her uncle. But Marshall spoke first. "Cindy Barrett, how are you? Thank you for coming to the office before you start your job with Godfrey." Cindy was confused by the formality. She stuttered an unintelligible reply.

Cindy Barrett graduated with her bachelor of science in nursing degree the previous year and passed the National Council Licensure Examination (NCLEX-RN) to become a registered nurse after graduation. She was 23 years old, but looked 18, despite her smart, professional dress. She wore the same suit for recent interviews for the nurse navigator position at Godfrey's OSI.

Marshall said, "I want to introduce you to Matt George, the hospital's COO. Matt this is Cindy Barrett, the new nurse navigator at OSI."

"Nice to meet you, Cindy. So, you'll be working for Karen Clayton, the chief nursing officer (CNO)? She's great," George said.

Regaining her composure, Barrett said, "Well, I was told that I will also be reporting to Mary Freehoff, the senior administrator of the OSI. Something called a matrix reporting structure?"

"Oh, that's right. The nurse navigators report to both administration and the CNO. As a senior administrator, Mary Freehoff reports directly to me."

An awkward silence ensued as the CEO and COO exchanged a knowing look that Barrett could not decipher. "Well, nice to meet you, Cindy," George said. "Welcome to the team."

"Thank you," Barrett said as she shook his hand.

After George had left, Marshall gave Barrett a hug with the warmth she expected of her mother's older brother.

"Uncle Dave, why did you not tell Mr. George that I am your niece?" Barrett asked.

"Well, some information is best kept secret. But before we get to that, how is your mom feeling?" Uncle Dave asked.

"She is feeling much better, thank you. Complete remission. She sends her love," Barrett said.

"Great to hear. She told me you helped her navigate the healthcare system, coaching her about questions that needed to be asked and how to ask them," Uncle Dave said.

"Yes, I tried to support her as best as I could," Barrett said. "With my nursing school knowledge, I could help with the medical stuff. I said, 'mom, this is when and where chemotherapy would be done and what it will be like.' I also help with her appointment scheduling and tracking various stuff, like medications."

"That's why I thought you would be perfect for the nurse navigator position. In addition to removing barriers to effective care, which you did for your mom, you will also be coordinating the care team's communication and collaborating with other providers on treatment plan development. I think you'll be perfect for the job," said Marshall.

"Thank you," Barrett said.

"Which is why I did not tell my COO that you were my niece," Marshall said with a dismissive wave.

"What do you mean?" Barrett asked.

"Well, I need you to do me a favor." Marshall patted a manila folder on his desk. "As you probably know, Godfrey has won awards for our high patient experience scores for our inpatient services. The CMS requires all hospitals to conduct HCAHPS surveys—sorry, Hospital Consumer Assessment of Healthcare Providers and Systems—to evaluate hospital patient experiences."

"Yes, I learned about HCAHPS in nursing school," Barrett said.

"Good. Well, there is another survey called the Outpatient and Ambulatory Surgery CAHPS—or OAS CAHPS—that can be used to survey Medicare patients of hospital outpatient departments and ambulatory surgery centers. At this point, the OAS CAHPS is optional, but in the future, I suspect that Medicare will require it."

Marshall pulled a report from a manila folder. "Anyway, I was curious how we scored in our outpatient departments, especially our OSI. We hired a CMS-approved survey vendor, Survey Analytics, Inc., to ask our Medicare patients about their experiences at OSI. Whenever a Medicare patient had a qualified outpatient procedure at OSI, Survey Analytics sent them a survey. They sent out 375 surveys and got 98 completed. Here are the results," Marshall said (see Table C9.1).

"I see," said Barrett. "What do the linear mean scores mean?"

Marshall explained, "There are linear mean scores for each of the four categories of measures in the OAS CAHPS—facilities and staff, communication about your procedure, patients' rating of the facility, and patients recommending the facility. The CMS converts survey responses in each category to a linear scale ranging from 0 to 100. Survey responses such as 'always,' 'definitely yes,' and 'strongly agree,' get more points on the scale than their negative counterparts, such as 'never,' 'no,' or 'strongly disagree.'"

"So, linear mean scores for OSI are mostly A's and B's. Not too bad," Barrett said.

"Ha! Not so fast. These are not scored like school grades. Actually, the CAHPS scores should be thought of as kind of like your SAT score. That is, your raw score is less important than the percentile. You really want to know how your score compares to everyone else's, right? Well, it's the percentile that matters. Say you scored in the 95% percentile on the SAT, this means that you scored better than 95% of the people who took that SAT test."

"I don't think my score was quite that good," said Barrett.

"Right? Well, I'm sure you did very well. However, I'd bet that if you compared our OAS CAHPS scores to other hospitals, you'll find we didn't score very well. I'll have my assistant send you the scores for hundreds of hospital outpatient units across the United States. These scores are also available publicly on the CMS website. You need to calculate our percent rank for each of the four linear mean scores. Do you know how to analyze spreadsheet data?" See Case 9 Data file provided in the Instructor's and Student ancillary materials.

"I think I can figure it out. We learned how to write the spreadsheet formula for percent rank in my quality management course," Barrett said. She knew she could always Google it.

"Impressive," Marshall beamed. "Speaking of quality management, that's what I want you to do for me when you start your job. Please tell me what the senior administrator is doing so wrong. Run the analysis and then ask around."

Table C9.1 Godfrey Community Hospital (GCH) Orthopedic & Spine Institute (OSI) Outpatient and Ambulatory Surgery CAHPS (OAS CAHPS) Results

SURVEY ITEM	PERCENTAGE
Patients who reported that staff definitely gave care in a professional way and the facility was clean	96
Patients who reported that staff somewhat gave care in a professional way or the facility was somewhat clean	3
Patients who reported that staff did not give care in a professional way or the facility was not clean	1
Facilities and staff linear mean score	97
Patients who reported that staff definitely communicated about what to expect during and after the procedure	79
Patients who reported that staff somewhat communicated about what to expect during and after the procedure	15
Patients who reported that staff did not communicate about what to expect during and after the procedure	6
Communication about your procedure linear mean score	87
Patients who gave the facility a rating of 9 or 10 on a scale ranging from 0 (lowest) to 10 (highest)	83
Patients who gave the facility a rating of 7 or 8 on a scale ranging from 0 (lowest) to 10 (highest)	14
Patients who gave the facility a rating of 0 to 6 on a scale ranging from 0 (lowest) to 10 (highest)	3
Patients' rating of the facility linear mean score	93
Patients who reported *yes* they would *definitely* recommend the facility to family or friends	78
Patients who reported *probably yes* they would recommend the facility to family or friends	18
Patients who reported *no*, they would not recommend the facility to family or friends	4
Patients recommending the facility linear mean score	92

"So you want me to spy?" Barrett asked.

Marshall just laughed. "You'll do great at OSI, Cindy. Please let me know if you need anything. Let's meet again in a couple of weeks. Send my love to your parents," Marshall said as he stood to give her a hug.

The Matrix Situation

Cindy Barrett's first day at Godfrey's OSI began inauspiciously. Mary Freehoff, the OSI senior administrator met her directly after Barrett signed her human resources paperwork. "Good to see you again, Cindy. Welcome to Godfrey," Freehoff said.

"Thank you," Cindy replied. "Happy to be here."

Freehoff led Barrett to her clinic office across from the breakroom. Freehoff removed a stack of papers from a chair and asked Barrett to sit down. Freehoff just leaned against the office wall next to a framed motivational poster of a soaring eagle that read, "Achievement: accomplishment through superior ability, special effort, and great courage."

Freehoff crossed her arms. "Let me ask you a question. How do you know the Chief of Orthopedics, Dr. Adam Jensen? He really advocated for you to be hired," Freehoff said as she searched Barrett's face for a reaction.

Without blinking, Barrett replied, "That's nice. I met him for the first time at the interview."

"Uh huh," Freehoff gave her a smile that did not reach her eyes. "Well, he was certainly impressed with you. The competition for your job was very tough, so you should feel thankful to Dr. Jensen."

"I do, thank you," Barret replied with a smile she hoped seemed more genuine than Freehoff's. "I'm grateful to all of you."

"Listen," Freehoff said, "I am thinking of moving you out of the OSI clinic and into a space at the hospital for the first few weeks just so you can become accustomed to the primary orthopedic and spine procedures that OSI provides at Godfrey. Sound good?"

Barrett hoped to keep her mission from Uncle Dave a secret. "Well," Barrett said, "That certainly sounds interesting. Is that what Karen Clayton wants, too?"

"Well, I haven't discussed it with Karen, but I'm sure I can work something out," Freehoff said. "The inpatient success associated with OSI is one reason the ortho and spine unit is one of the most profitable service lines at Godfrey. I'm sure you understand why I prioritize the inpatient procedures and surgeries over things here at the outpatient clinic. I expect this focus to continue."

"I understand," Barrett said, but she did not really understand.

"Any questions for me before I take you to meet with Karen?" Freehoff asked.

"Yes, just one quick question," Barrett said. "I know that Godfrey's HCAHPS scores are excellent. Do you track patient experience scores for the outpatient clinic, also?"

"No, don't worry about that," Freehoff said.

The Mentor

Barrett showed up for her next meeting with the CNO uncertain how to prevent her relocation, albeit temporary, to the hospital. Luckily, Karen Clayton was warm, welcoming, and protective—a contrast to her other boss.

After polite introductions and a speech about patient-centered values of the nursing staff at Godfrey, Clayton explained the philosophy and practice of nurse navigation. The overall goal of the navigation process is to achieve timely and effective care. A nurse navigator is assigned to each patient for the entire course of care, from initial visit to completion of visits after procedure. Nurse navigators educate patients regarding screening, diagnosis, or treatment options via phone or in person. They review charts for proper documentation and track performance improvement data.

After a delightful discussion, Clayton asked, "Do you have any questions or concerns that I can address?"

"In fact, I do. Ms. Freehoff said that she wanted me to observe the inpatient operations for the first few weeks. I was under the impression that I would be located at the clinic. Can you clarify this for me?" Barrett asked.

Clayton paused for a moment, then asked, "Mary told you that you would be at the hospital first?" Barrett nodded. "Honey, I'll take care of that. You just shadow the other nurse navigators as planned. First, shadow with Andrew Eng, then Kate Gordon. In between, you're having lunch with the Chief of Orthopedics, Dr. Adam Jensen, who is in the clinic today. I hope you like Mexican."

Whatever Works

The first nurse navigator, Andrew Eng, was a wishy-washy man in his 40s. He greeted Barrett with a weak handshake and an unenthusiastic, "Hello again." Eng had worked at the OSI for 3 years, but he had the attitude of a weary veteran who had seen it all.

In her shadowing experience, Barrett observed Eng making calls to patients to schedule preprocedural testing, procedure, and postprocedural follow-up. Eng asked patients about barriers to attending their appointments and explored the patients' concerns regarding their procedures. Eng answered patients' questions—both on the phone and in person—about preprocedure and postprocedure and testing.

Communication with the patients seemed especially complicated to Barrett. When she asked about scripts that they use with patients to standardize communication processes, Eng just shrugged and said, "I'm not sure if we are supposed to use any specific verbiage. You'll learn the way that works best for you."

"How do you know what works best for the patient?" Barrett asked, but got no real answer.

Barrett learned that the nurse navigators work closely with clinic coordinators, who receive referrals, set up appointments, and complete preprocedural phone calls to provide education about the inpatient and outpatient procedures. When she asked to see the job descriptions, he was hesitant that job descriptions had been created. Then he said, "They are probably on the shared drive."

Taco Mondays

"Don't you love tacos?" Dr. Andrew Jensen asked. The Chief of Orthopedics smiled broadly before he stuffed a half of a taco into his mouth. He was wearing scrubs and a lab coat, which hung loosely on his lanky frame. He looked younger than a Chief of Orthopedics should, gifted with a fast metabolism and a full head of hair.

"Not just on Tuesdays," Barrett lied as she took the smallest possible bite of her taco. As a former vegan, she still had not come around to enjoying ground beef.

"As I was saying, your uncle and I play golf together. He recommended you in the strongest terms. But, while I love doing favors for David, I wanted to interview you first. You were exactly what we need at the OSI, so I was happy to vouch for you. I am so frustrated with how things are currently run here."

"What's so frustrating?" Barrett asked.

Dr. Jensen explained that their communication problems were varied and complex. By and large, communication processes centered on providers, rather than the patients. There are 18 orthopedic surgeons involved in the clinic, and a majority are not employed by the OSI. Some surgeons use this clinic to see patients and evaluate them prior to surgery, and some do not. According to Dr. Jensen, employed surgeons do a great job of following the standard communication processes, but the community physicians are not held to the same standards. Some community physicians will group text referral information to clinic coordinators. Although texting is a quick and simple way of communicating, information is often lost or confusing. It is also a major Health Insurance Portability and Accountability Act (HIPAA) security issue because text lacks encryption, which means they could be intercepted, a violation of the law meant to protect patients' personal health information.

"Can the OSI require the community physicians to follow the communication policies?" Barrett asked.

"Yes and no. The OSI always wants to promote process standardization, but we also have to respect physician autonomy. The surgeons are highly skilled practitioners and the source of new patient volume, so they cannot be required to adhere to processes they do not embrace," Dr. Jensen said.

"Even when it violates HIPAA regulations?" Barrett asked.

"Well, texting referrals is not the only example. There seems to be a hundred different ways we communicate with patients before and after their procedures," Dr. Jensen said. "For example, some docs thoroughly educate patients, some explain the bare minimum, hoping that the clinical staff will educate the patient. This leaves the nurse navigators unclear about their responsibilities to explain inpatient and outpatient procedures and answer any patient concerns."

"You mean sometimes nurse navigators don't conduct pre- and postprocedural education?" Barrett asked.

"They are supposed to, but some surgeons do such a good job of explaining that the nurse navigators assume that it's been covered. But sometimes, patient education gets skipped. All this leaves patients feeling like the left hand doesn't know what the right hand is doing," Dr. Jensen complained, "which leads to lower patient satisfaction and fewer patients recommending OSI to their friends and family."

Description Dysfunction

Barrett's shadowing of OSI's second nurse navigator, Kate Brewster, followed her lunch with Dr. Adam Jensen. Brewster was an extra-small woman in an extra-large cardigan sweater. At first impression, Brewster seemed to be perpetually flinching from some perceived threat.

However, she was gentle and empathetic with her patients, and they all seemed to connect with her. She was clearly in the right occupation.

In a lull between patient visits and calls, Barrett brought up her confusion regarding clinical staff job responsibilities to Brewster. Barrett explained, "Nurse navigators educated patients about preprocedure and postprocedure and testing, right?"

"Right," Brewster agreed.

"Well, the clinic coordinators also make calls to schedule preprocedural testing, procedure, and postprocedural follow-up. They also answer patient questions. Are both clinic coordinators and nurse navigators responsible for patient education? Are there job descriptions that we can look at?" Barrett asked.

Brewster knew exactly where to look for job descriptions on the Godfrey Intranet. Quickly reading each description, Brewster said, "Yes, I guess both are responsible for patient education. The nurse navigator job description says, 'patient education via phone and face-to-face visits—procedure, diagnostic testing.' And under 'patient check-in/check-out' in the clinic administrator job description, it reads 'educate and instruct patients in regard to procedures and testing.'"

"So who does what?" Barrett asked.

"Some clinic coordinators do a great job of patient education, some not so much. I don't worry about it so much, especially for outpatient procedures. Let's put it this way, the clinic coordinators complete preprocedural phone calls in different ways. I get it, though. We're often overbooked in the clinic, rushing around trying to focus on other administrative tasks related to the primary inpatient procedure."

"So you focus on patient education in the inpatient setting, but not really in the outpatient setting?" Barrett asked.

Brewster looked around to make sure no one was listening. "Mary told us that OSI nurse navigators are supposed to focus on primary procedures conducted at the hospital, not the outpatient procedures. That's one reason we deliver nice education materials after inpatient surgeries, but not for procedures at the outpatient clinic."

The Interim CEO

For 2 weeks, Barrett collected information related to patient experience at the OSI that she felt Uncle Dave would appreciate, but then her plans changed. Freehoff asked the clinical staff to convene to the conference room for an announcement. Freehoff said in an authoritative tone, "I have some news to share. Godfrey's board of directors has made a decision to remove David Marshall as CEO."

"Uncle Dave?" Barrett gasped.

Freehoff continued, "The COO, Matt George, will be the interim CEO until a replacement can be selected. Until then, assume operations will continue as before. Any questions?" The clinical staff just sat in stunned silence.

Soon afterward, Barrett was called to meet with Interim CEO, Matt George, at the Godfrey executive offices. "I want to assure you of how valuable I think the work you've been doing is to the OSI," George told Barrett.

"Thank you. I'm relieved to hear you say that," Barrett replied.

"Oh, I knew that you had been asked to scrutinize Mary Freehoff's outpatient operations on behalf of David. I am fully aware of the struggles at the OSI," George said.

"You did? You are?" Barrett asked.

"Of course. Please tell me what you learned. We always want to improve. Do you have a report for me?" George asked.

Barrett began to pull out the quality management analysis that she developed, including the OSI OAS CAHPS scores compared to the national percentiles and a draft A3 problem-solving worksheet. But then she hesitated, wondering how much she should share.

DISCUSSION QUESTIONS

1. Through what mechanisms do patient experience performance scores, such as the CAHPS, impact organizational success? Consider financial and community relations perspectives.

2. How can quality management practices promote patient-centered values, such as respecting patient choice and ensuring continuity of care?

3. Did Mary Freehoff provide an environment conducive to opinion sharing and investigation of problems? Explain your conclusion with examples from the case study.

4. How should David Marshall have confronted the performance problems at the OSI? What were the consequences of his secretive approach, if any?

5. Uncle Dave placed Cindy Barrett in a difficult situation at her new job. What recommendation would you give to her for successfully navigating the political environment?

PODCAST FOR CASE 9

Listen to how experts approach the topic (you can access the podcast by following this url to Springer Publishing Company Connect™: https://connect.springerpub.com/content/book/978-0-8261-4514-7/front-matter/fmatter2)

FURTHER READING

Giordano, L. A., Elliott, M. N., Goldstein, E., Lehrman, W. G., & Spencer, P. A. (2010). Development, implementation, and public reporting of the HCAHPS survey. *Medical Care Research and Review*, *67*(1), 27–37. doi:10.1177/1077558709341065

Goldsmith, L. J., Suryaprakash, N., Randall, E., Shum, J., MacDonald, V., Sawatzky, R., … Bryan, S. (2017). The importance of informational, clinical and personal support in patient experience with total knee replacement: A qualitative investigation. *BMC Musculoskeletal Disorders*, 18. doi:10.1186/s12891-017-1474-8

Marcus-Aiyeku, U., DeBari, M., & Salmond, S. (2015). Assessment of the patient-centered and family-centered care experience of total joint replacement patients using a shadowing technique. *Orthopaedic Nursing*, *34*(5), 269–277. doi:10.1097/NOR.0000000000000177

Pruitt, Z., & Sportsman, S. (2013). The presence and roles of nurse navigators in acute care hospitals. *Journal of Nursing Administration*, 43(11), 592–596. doi:10.1097/01.NNA.0000434510.74373.40

Sherman, R., & Hilton, N. (2014). The patient engagement imperative. *American Nurse Today*, *9*(2), 1–4. Retrieved from https://www.americannursetoday.com/the-patient-engagement-imperative

STANDARDIZED WORK

Taiichi Ohno, introduced in Chapter 2, The Innovators, as the father of the Toyota Production System®, is credited with saying, "Without standard, improvement is impossible."

"Standardization" simply means to find the best, safest, fastest, least expensive way to carry out a process and make sure everybody does it that same way. Only when that way is identified, documented, and communicated can improvement become possible. This is called "standardized work" or sometimes shortened to "standard work."

Unless a process is standardized, it can never be significantly improved. Standardization does not mean "robotization," a term that suggests people are supposed to act like robots. While some people might argue that standardized work stifles creativity or critical thinking, those who have embraced it have found the opposite to be true. Standardized work eliminates guesswork when it comes to performing tasks, freeing team members' minds to focus on how to improve the work. Instead of stifling creativity, having standardized work fosters creativity.

How do you implement standard work?

There are many ways and shapes to what constitutes standard work. A checklist is a form of standardized work, whether it stands on its own or as a complement to a more comprehensive standardized work document. The important thing is that standardized work must include these three elements:

1. Well-defined sequence of steps

2. Who is responsible for each step?

3. How long should each step take?

There are many templates to write standardized work as shown in Exhibit C9.1. The more visual you can make your standardized work, the better is the outcome. The more comprehensive templates contain areas of key points and/or reason for doing this step that enable the team member following the standard work to learn or pay special attention to a critical step in the process.

EXHIBIT C9.1 Templates/forms for standardized work.

Job Breakdown Sheet for Daily Hospital Visit
Unit: Hospitalists   Date: August 2009

IMPORTANT STEPS	KEY POINTS	REASONS
Step #1 **The Welcome**	Sit down	
The Patient needs to be given Hope and wants to be Healed	My name is	
	My role is	
	My connection with your referring	
	I have reviewed your information	
	know how to care for you	
Step #2 **The Care**	Here is what I am going to do a	
The Patient needs to feel Safe and in Control	Here are the next steps	
	Ask for understanding of the Proc	
	Ask for permission to proceed	
	Ask for patient's needs	
Step #3 **The Goodbye**	Continues care: I'll be back at	
The Patient needs to know they will not be alone or forgotten	At discharge: I'll inform you	
	Your test results will be available	

Inoculate plates

Related SWS #: 1

Related documents:

Insert picture or sketch	Step #	Symb		PROCESS	
	Time		STEP	RESPONSIBLE PARTY	ACTION
	1				
	2				
	3		Move swab and plate	rotating swab to a thumb print size	BAP (uniform inoculum)
				3.1 After inoculation move swab to white throat rack in BSC and set BAP to the side.	3.1.1 Are set to the side to be put on isoplater after inoculation.
	4		Repeat steps 1–3	4.1 Repeat steps 1–3 for each throat swab in batch of 12	

CASE 10: HCAHPS and the Quiet-at-Night Measure

1. Understand patient experience measurement of the Hospital Consumer Assessment of Healthcare Providers and Systems survey.
2. Analyze root causes of sleep disturbances in a hospital setting.
3. Identify potential solutions to suboptimal patient experience performance scores.
4. Examine the connection of patient experience to patient care outcomes.

INTRODUCTION

The Hospital Consumer Assessment of Healthcare Providers and Systems (HCAHPS) survey measures patients' experiences of hospital care and publishes the results on Medicare's Hospital Compare website. The HCAHPS (pronounced "H-caps") survey results are used for the Medicare Hospital Value-Based Purchasing program, meaning that the results are used to determine how much Medicare will pay the hospital. Still, the validity of HCAHPS patient experience scores remains controversial among some clinicians (Jones, 2019).

Loma Vista Hospital is the largest of three hospitals in the WellFront Health System (WHS) located in northern New Mexico. The system includes Loma Vista Hospital, St. Mary's Hospital, and WellFront Hospital. Dr. Samuel Scroggins is the chief medical officer (CMO) of Loma Vista Hospital, whose HCAHPS scores are below state and national averages. However, Dr. Scroggins remains unconvinced that time, energy, and resources should be devoted to improvement of patient experience scores. Charles Larkley, the Loma Vista CEO, developed an unorthodox plan to convince Dr. Scroggins to engage in patient experience quality improvement initiatives, and the CEO and CMO of the other hospital, St. Mary's Hospital, have agreed to play along.

 DATA FILE FOR CASE 10

Data files for students are available by accessing the following url: https://www.springerpub.com/hqm

The data file for Case 10 provides summary HCAHPS Measures for hospital with state and national 75 percentile benchmarks.

CASE SCENARIO

The Secret Shopper

"I'm not sure what is more unbelievable, that I missed the 6-foot putt or that you are actually making me stay the night at the hospital," said the Loma Vista Hospital CMO, Dr. Samuel Scroggins.

"A bet is a bet," replied Charles Larkley, the Loma Vista CEO. "It's only one night, and acting as a Secret Shopper over at St. Mary's might do you some good."

"Nonsense! I'm not sick, so how can I evaluate the care that St. Mary's provides?" Scroggins asked.

"I am not asking you to evaluate the care as much as the patient experience. As you know, our overall hospital score is 75%, which is below the 75th percentile benchmark for HCAHPS," said Larkley. "St. Mary's HCAHPS scores are not much better, which is why their people agreed to let you act as a Secret Shopper for patient experience."

"Take a look at these scores," said Larkley as he showed Dr. Scroggins the HCAHPS summary scores compared to the 75th percentile New Mexico and national benchmarks from the last reporting period (Table C10.1).

"Charley, we've talked about this. HCAHPS scores don't measure quality of care," Scroggins insisted. "The data collected are nonrandom, slow to be collected, and create incentives for bad care that I can't abide. Catering to patient satisfaction scores might encourage

Table C10.1 Comparison of HCAHPS Measures for Loma Vista Hospital

COMPARISON OF HCAHPS MEASURES	LOMA VISTA SCORE (%)	NEW MEXICO 75% BENCHMARK (%)	NATIONAL 75% BENCHMARK (%)
Overall Hospital	75	77	78
Discharge Information	90	88	90
Nurse Communication	89	87	87
Doctor Communication	85	84	85
Cleanliness	83	79	80
Pain Control	76	75	74
Recommend the Hospital	74	78	78
Timely Help	74	74	74
Explanation of Medications	69	68	69
Always Quiet at Night	53	61	62
Understood Care Leaving ...	56	55	56

our doctors to provide unnecessary care, which would only increase our costs and probably would reduce health outcomes. One doc called it 'death by patient satisfaction.'"

"Yes, I've heard your criticisms, Dr. Scroggins. Take a look at this report, and tell me what you see. Where are we struggling?" Larkley quizzed.

Scroggins reviewed the report. "Overall, we're not rated so good. And a couple of measures are way below the benchmark, Quiet-at-Night, especially. What poppycock! Hospitals are just noisy places. What do you want the medical staff to do about it?"

"I want you to support our new chief patient experience officer. I heard that you were not very professional in your interaction with her," Larkley said looking over his reading glasses.

"I just told her that her job was meaningless. We just get dinged for things outside our control," Scroggins dismissed.

"Well, maybe. But unless you improve your putting, I'm going to continue to make my point about improving patient experience. You may pick sometime within the next month to spend the night at St. Mary's," said Larkley. "Oh, and the admitting physician will be your old practice partner. He promised to keep your identity a secret."

The Former Partner

"Good afternoon, my old friend!" said Dr. Jake Marley as he entered the St. Mary's Hospital room. "How are you feeling?" Dr. Marley was not only Scroggins's old partner but also the CMO of St. Mary's Hospital.

"You damn well know how I'm feeling," Scroggins grumbled.

"No, you have a heart condition, that's why you're here," Marley said. "Play along, now." Marley opened the electronic medical record on his tablet and made a few clicks. "Yup, says here that your symptoms include a case of the 'yips.' Still can't make 6-foot putts, I see."

"Very funny. Leave me to pay off my debt in peace," Scroggins said.

"Have you been admitted or spent time with your family in the hospital before?" Marley asked.

"No, I haven't. And you know very well that I don't have family," Scroggins snorted. "The practice of medicine is my only family."

"Yes, which is why I want to warn you," resumed Scroggins's old partner. "Listen, you will be visited by three nurses. Without their care, you won't be able to complete your Secret Shopper quality check."

"Couldn't I see them all at once and get it over with, Jake?" hinted Scroggins.

"I'm afraid not," Marley said as he backed out of the hospital room. "Sleep well, Dr. Scroggins."

The First of Three Nurses

Scroggins shared the hospital room with another patient, a young man whose family had come to visit him. Long past the end of the visiting hours, a young child trilled in response to his father's incessant raspberry sounds. Scroggins had once hoped to get a good night's rest.

A young nurse came in to check on Scroggins. She was a lovely Puebloan woman with an angelic and caring spirit. "Nurse," Scroggins complained, "Isn't it past visiting hours?"

"Yes, my dear, it is," said the nurse. "But can't we wait just a bit more? The family lives a long way away, and Mr. Fezziwig gets so much energy from the love of his family."

Scroggins harrumphed. He supposed that he once laughed like the child, full of joy and wonderment. But still, Scroggins thought, a man has to get some sleep.

Sometime later, just as Scroggins nodded off, the public address system made a bong sound followed by, "Code Orange. Unit 3A." A startled Scroggins paged the nurse.

"What was that sound, nurse?" Scroggins asked as the nurse came into his room.

"It was nothing. Just a biohazard spill that needs cleaning. Go back to sleep, Mr. Scroggins."

"It's Dr. Scroggins," he griped as he hammered his pillow into shape.

As he lay there trying to return to his slumber, Scroggins noticed how the mix of beeps and whirrs climbed to a cacophony. The cardiac telemetry electrode patches began to tingle and the lead wires started to tangle as he tossed and turned. An alarm sounded as Scroggins accidently detached a telemetry patch from his skin. The nurse did not come; instead Scroggins heard her talking on the phone at the nearby nurses' station. A phone line rang without anyone answering. Ring, ring, ring.

Scroggins couldn't stand it. He threw his cup of water against the closed hospital room door. Scroggins stared at the puddle on the floor, wondering if he should call for a nurse. He decided against it figuring he'd prefer to sleep.

The Second of Three Nurses

And yet, sleep did not come. The tick-tock of the wall clock seemed to get louder and louder. The elevator door opened and closed repeatedly. Someone kept slamming doors throughout the unit. An equipment cart with a wonky wheel bumped and thumped in the hallway.

Finally, the door opened and a flood of light entered his room. A huge shape stood in the light's glow. "Oops!" said a male nurse with dark brown curls and a big grin. "Did we have an accident? No worries. We'll clean it up for you, Mr. Scroggins."

"It's doctor ... never mind," Scroggins muttered.

The jolly giant took Scroggins's blood pressure.

"Oh, wow! Your blood pressure is really elevated," the large male nurse said. "Are you feeling okay?"

"No, I can't sleep," Scroggins whined.

"I will let the doctor know," the nurse said.

Just as Scroggins drifted off to sleep, a woman with a bucket entered the room, slopped a mop twice across the floor, squeezed the excess water, squeaked the floor with her sneaker, and then left. Unbelievable, Scroggins thought.

The Last of the Nurses

Deep into the night, Scroggins was not sure he was even sleeping when another nurse slowly, gravely, silently, approached his bedside with an outstretched hand. "What are you doing?" said Scroggins lamely. The dark figure pricked his arm to draw his blood. Scroggins, afraid and disoriented, wondered why the previous nurse had not taken blood at the same time as the blood pressure measure. Once affixed with a cotton swab and bandage across the crook of his arm, Scroggins sat quietly and listened to a conversation outside his room.

"I don't know why we're here either," said one man to another in the hallway outside Scroggins's room. "We were supposed to get this done yesterday. I was just told to replace these stained ceiling tiles and do it very quietly." As they unfolded the creaking ladder as quietly as possible, the maintenance man said, "The CMO of the hospital is coming by later this morning. We gotta make sure everything looks tip-top."

Scroggins wanted to scream, but he thought of poor Mr. Fezziwig sleeping soundly next to him. Instead, he concentrated on his breathing. In. Out. In. Out. His thoughts calmed then began to make little sense. Scroggins knew he was falling asleep.

A time later, the shadowy figure said in the dark, "Mr. Scroggins. The doctor wanted you to take this sleeping pill. Sit up now."

The Secret Shopper Quality Check Ends

As the daylight leaked through the hospital window blinds, Scroggins awoke again with his former medical practice partner, Dr. Marley, shaking his shoulder.

"Is it over?" Scroggins asked. "What time is it?"

"It's 6 a.m. I'm rounding early. How are you feeling?" Marley asked.

"I ache all over. That was my worst experience ever in a hospital," Scroggins answered.

"Even worse that our residency days?" Marley asked.

"Residency was nothing next to this nightmare!" Scroggins said. He ripped off the electrodes, kicked off the blanket, and arose from the hospital bed. He patted Marley on the chest and gave him a wry smile. "I've made a great mistake." He stripped off the gown and threw on his trousers.

"Where are you going?" Marley called to Scroggins as he ran from the hospital room.

Scroggins had no further reason to sleep at the hospital or to berate the patient experience staff at Loma Linda Hospital. "I have to apologize to our chief patient experience officer!" Scroggins said. He even became a member of the Patient Experience Governance Committee and rededicated his approach to patient healing and the power of a sound night's sleep.

DISCUSSION QUESTIONS

1. Do you think Dr. Samuel Scroggins is correct that patient experience is unrelated to patient health outcomes? Do you subscribe to the idea of "death by patient satisfaction?" Give examples.

2. How was Dr. Samuel Scroggins's behavior to the chief patient experience officer unprofessional? How could Dr. Scroggins have more positively expressed his criticisms?

3. In what way was Dr. Samuel Scroggins changed by his experience? Do you think another approach could have changed his opinion of patient experience measurement? If so, what approach would you recommend?

4. Describe the manner in which the Quiet-at-Night score is a nurse-sensitive patient experience measure. How is the measure related to physician behaviors? The healthcare administrator? Other hospital staff?

5. Describe the benefits of a Secret Shopper approach to assessing patient experience. Do you think it is a reliable and valid method to evaluate health services? Why or why not?

PODCAST FOR CASE 10

Listen to how experts approach the topic (you can access the podcast by following this url to Springer Publishing Company Connect™: https://connect.springerpub.com/content/book/978-0-8261-4514-7/front-matter/fmatter2)

REFERENCE

Jones, R. (2019, March 6). *Death by patient satisfaction.* Retrieved from https://www.kevinmd.com/blog/2019/03/death-by-patient-satisfaction.html

FURTHER READING

Giordano, L. A., Elliott, M. N., Goldstein, E., Lehrman, W. G., & Spencer, P. A. (2010). Development, implementation, and public reporting of the HCAHPS survey. *Medical Care Research and Review, 67*(1), 27–37. doi:10.1177/1077558709341065

Loden, J. C., & Frederick, R. C. (2008). Do secret shoppers have a place in medicine? *American Medical Association Journal of Ethics, 10*(5), 288–294. doi:10.1001/virtualmentor.2008.10.5.ccas5-0805

Luthra, S. (2015, August 17). *For hospitals, sleep and patient satisfaction may go hand in hand.* Retrieved from https://khn.org/news/for-hospitals-sleep-and-patient-satisfaction-may-go-hand-in-hand

Wilson, C., Whiteman, K., Stephens, K., Swanson-Biearman, B., & LaBarba, J. (2017). Improving the patient's experience with a multimodal quiet-at-night initiative. *Journal of Nursing Care Quality, 32*(2), 134–140. doi:10.1097/NCQ.0000000000000219

TOOLS AND APPROACHES

SECRET SHOPPER

There is no substitute for going to the *gemba*, "the actual place" where work happens and value is added to the customer. The *gemba* provides the greatest insight into the actual customer experience. You can look at surveys, interview people, analyze metrics or reports, but actually experiencing the customer's perspective will provide you with invaluable insights into how to improve quality.

Secret shopping has been implemented in all industries, from retail to hospitality to restaurants. A secret shopping experience is kind of an "undercover" *gemba* walk, focused on the customer. Much like a *gemba* walk, a secret shopping experience must be structured and have a stated goal or focus. Secret shopping allows for proactive identification of issues. Healthcare providers and leaders can implement secret shopping into their quality improvement initiatives to help them pinpoint areas of opportunity perhaps even before they become an issue.

To implement secret shopping into your quality management program:

1. Identify an area of opportunity in the customer experience.

2. Select the Secret Shopper (physician, nurse, pharmacist, technician, etc.).

3. Protect the Secret Shopper's identity.

4. Plan the Secret Shopper experience (hospital stay, outpatient visit, pharmacy visit).

5. Identify focus of the experience (cleanliness, friendliness of staff, clinician behavior, etc.).

6. Implement the secret shopping experience.

7. Gather input as close to real time as possible.

Armed with the information from the secret shopping experience, you will identify opportunities for improvement, uncover root causes of the problems, and build empathy with the customer.

FURTHER READING

Lazarus, A. (2009). Are "secret shoppers" an antidote for medical errors caused by physicians' arrogance? *The Journal of Medical Practice Management: MPM, 24*(5), 273–275.

CASE 11: Discharge Phone Calls (En Español)

1. Evaluate the impact of cultural competency on patient satisfaction scores.
2. Explain how to track patient experience measures in order to set organizational priorities.
3. Distinguish common cause variation from special cause variation for quality measures.
4. Identify causal associations within healthcare quality management problems.

INTRODUCTION

St. John's River Community Hospital (SJRCH) is a 253-bed acute-care hospital serving the St. John's River Valley area for over 40 years. SJRCH started as a 130-bed hospital, and it grew along with the community for the better part of four decades. The St. John's River Valley area is home to a large Hispanic community, composing about 42% of the total population.

Katrina "Kat" Vasilova is Director of Patient Experience and Service Excellence for SJRCH. Her job is to champion the organization's culture to assure the highest level of experience for patients and their families. Kat analyzes results of patient experience survey data and collaborates with senior leadership and department managers to develop and implement improvement strategies. Her position requires extensive knowledge of quality management tools and approaches, such as Lean and/or Six Sigma.

CASE SCENARIO

"St. John's River Community Hospital, how may I direct your call?"

"Oiga, ¿usted me podría explicar por qué me siguen llegando esas llamadas automáticas en inglés?" was the very agitated response on the other side of the line.

"I'm sorry, Miss, I do not understand what you are saying; is there somewhere you would like me to transfer your call to?" replied the dumbfounded call center representative.

DATA FILE FOR CASE 11

Data files for students are available by accessing the following url: https://www.springerpub .com/hqm

The data file for Case 11 provides score summary data for 24 months of HCAHPS Overall patient experience surveys for one hospital. Includes total, average, upper control limit, and lower control limit. Demonstrates creation of control charts.

"*Sorri*, sí, ¡*sorri*! Me too *sorri*, porque ya van dos meses desde que yo estuve en su hospital y me siguen llamando en inglés para *folou-op* o qué se yo ni qué. ¡Y los he llamado varias veces y nunca nadie me puede explicar cómo puedo hacer para parar estas llamadas!" continued the patient in her broken-English-and-Spanish conversation.

"Miss, please, let me try to find someone who can help me understand. Is it Spanish… uh, *español*, that I'm hearing?" replied the representative, trying to be as helpful as she could.

"¡Sí, español, sí! ¡Gracias a Dios, por fin alguien entiende español!" replied the patient.

"OK, let me put you on hold while I try to find someone; give me a minute, OK?" answered the representative and immediately placed the patient on hold.

"Mire, por favor, dígale a…" the patient stopped abruptly when she heard the hold music and message. "¡Hola! ¿Está todavía ahí? ¡Ay, por favor!" she said while hanging up the phone, feeling defeated.

Elsewhere in a meeting room at SJRCH …

"Kat, we are still not where we should be on patient experience scores." said Sylvia Sosa, COO of SJRCH, during January's staff meeting. Sylvia showed the following chart to demonstrate the patient experience average monthly score. The chart showed the Overall Rating of Hospital score according to the Hospital Consumer Assessment of Healthcare Providers and Systems (HCAHPS) survey (Figure C11.1). The HCAHPS survey allows hospitals to measure patients' perceptions of their hospital experience and to compare different facilities and organizations with one standard instrument.

"You are correct, Sylvia. Much to our dismay, we are still struggling to come back to the level we were at 8 months ago," answered Kat. She then looked around the table at her colleagues and continued, "When you look at this chart, it seems pretty evident that the average has shifted. This usually means that a process change has caused the ratings to fall. What I mean by that is that when a process is stable and standardized, you expect the data to fluctuate within certain parameters, but when you see a big shift, such as what we see here, it is a sign that we need to stop and look at the process. It appears something has changed. Therefore, I had one of the analysts on my team run some quick analyses. We are almost ready to

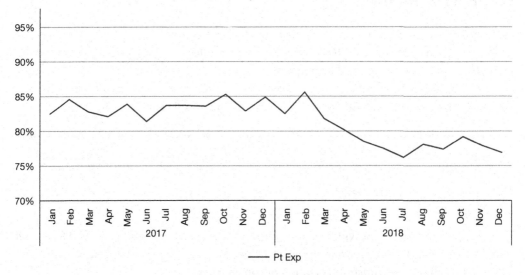

FIGURE C11.1 St. John's River Community Hospital (SJRCH) patient experience score.

give you a full debrief. It will take more than the few minutes we have now, so I will set up time for us to discuss this next week."

"Great! I look forward to it," replied Sosa.

On her way out of the meeting, Sosa went by the information desk. "We just had another one of those Spanish calls, Ms. Sosa," the representative said, handing her a sticky note. "But, by the time I was able to get someone to translate, the person hung up. I feel terrible!"

"Another one? *¡Ay, Dios mío! ¿Cómo puede ser esto?*" complained Sosa. "OK. Thank you for keeping track of this and letting me know." Sosa wondered why these calls from Spanish-speaking patients kept coming in and felt concerned that call center staff did not know what they needed. "This is unacceptable!" Sosa thought as she walked back to her office. "Here I am, a Spanish-speaking executive, leading an organization in a community with a large Hispanic population, with a call center that is not equipped to handle calls from Spanish-speaking patients! How out-of-touch are we? Oh, my God! Have I allowed myself to desensitize myself to the needs of the population, *my* people? This needs to change!"

The following week, Vasilova and her analyst, Romeo Fernández, sat down with Sosa to go over their findings.

"Sylvia, I will let Romeo run us through his analysis and feel free to stop him at any point if you need to ask any questions, and I will do the same," announced Vasilova. "OK, Romeo, take it away!"

"Thank you very much, Kat," replied Romeo. "Ms. Sosa, when Kat and I started talking about this a few weeks ago, we noticed that the run chart, shown in Figure C11.1 here, definitively shows that the mean of the process shifted. To further illustrate this, I ran some statistics and created the Control Chart for the process and you can see that here," he said as he showed a chart on the screen (Figure C11.2). "This Control Chart shows the average patient experience scores. If the metric were operating under common cause variation, we would expect that the variation in the scores would stay between the upper control limit (or UCL) and the lower control limit (or LCL)."

"What this shows us," Romeo continued, "is that something happened around April or May that caused this process to become *out of control*," he said as he stood up and pointed

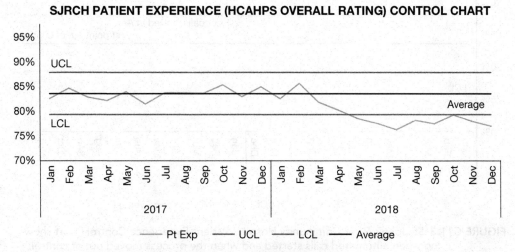

FIGURE C11.2 SJRCH patient experience score control chart.
LCL, lower control limit; UCL, upper control limit; SJRCH, St. John's River Community Hospital.

at that area on the chart. "These results show some sort of special cause variation caused by some sort of unexpected part of the process."

Sosa turned to look at Kat and was surprised to see a hint of a grin on Katrina's face. "Why are you smiling?" asked Sosa.

"Do you remember what happened in April?" asked Vasilova, looking intently at Sosa.

"Gosh, Kat, a lot of things happened in April, could you be more specific?" replied Sosa playing along.

"Sorry," replied Vasilova still smiling. "Do you remember what new process we started in April to follow up with patients after they get discharged from the hospital?"

"I got it!" replied Sosa with the excitement of someone who has solved a mystery. "Postdischarge phone calls!"

"Not just phone calls…" added Vasilova.

"Automated calls!" they both said in unison.

"Ding! Ding! Ding! The robocalls," said Romeo as he advanced his slide to show one still with the Control Chart, adding pointers to when the automated calls started and when the process moved out of control (Figure C11.3).

"Are you saying the *robocalls* are to blame for our slipping patient experience scores?" asked Sosa incredulously. "I am going to need more detail here. Why do you think that? I mean, other than the data you are showing me."

"Well, I was just as puzzled as you are right now," answered Vasilova sounding honest. "Then, I had Romeo take a deeper dive into our patient experience data. He sliced it six ways from Sunday and found some very interesting stuff. Romeo, do you want to share with Sylvia the rest of your analysis?"

"Certainly!" replied Romeo hardly able to contain himself. He proceeded to share several looks at patient experience (gender, age, language, zip code), and when he finished, Sylvia

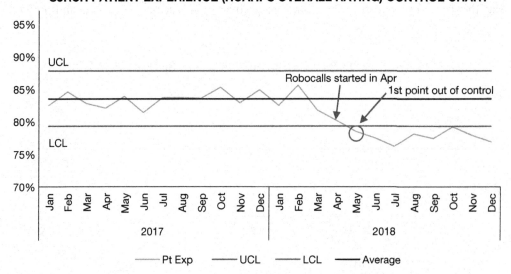

FIGURE C11.3 St. John's River Community Hospital Patient Experience Control Chart showing when automated calls started and when the process moved out of control.

LCL, lower control limit; UCL, upper control limit.

Sosa's eyes were opened wide and her jaw dropped to the floor. She looked back at Vasilova, who, at this point was grinning from ear to ear (see Case 11 Data file provided in the Instructor's and Student ancillary materials).

"Data are power, isn't it?" Vasilova asked rhetorically.

"Oh, my gosh, guys! The mysterious Spanish calls!!!" screamed Sosa, not able to hold back. Now, the puzzled faces were those of Vasilova and Romeo.

"Wait, what?" asked Vasilova. "What Spanish calls are you talking about?"

"I think you guys just solved two problems in one," replied Sosa. "I feel like hugging you guys!"

DISCUSSION QUESTIONS

1. Which of the many views of the data that Romeo provided shows the most promise to help answer the question of why the patient experience scores have slipped?

2. What do you think of Kat Vasilova's approach to data analysis?

3. Discuss the connection Sylvia Sosa found between the mysterious Spanish calls and the patient experience scores.

4. There is a difference between correlation and causation, as represented by Sylvia Sosa's incredulity that the automated calls were to blame. Discuss how data analysis helps us move beyond correlation and into causation.

5. Discuss how the degree of cultural competency of an organization can affect patients' satisfaction.

 ## PODCAST FOR CASE 11

Listen to how experts approach the topic (you can access the podcast by following this url to Springer Publishing Company Connect™: https://connect.springerpub.com/content/book/978-0-8261-4514-7/front-matter/fmatter2)

FURTHER READING

Agency for Healthcare Research and Quality. (2016, October 12). *What is patient experience?* Retrieved from https://www.ahrq.gov/cahps/about-cahps/patient-experience/index.html

Moore, T. L., Casiday, R., Cortes, C. G., Davey, K., Stoltzfus, K. M., Terry, P. H., & Robertson, A. S. (2017). An interprofessional review of cultural competency education: Approaches to strengthen healthcare management education in preparing culturally competent healthcare managers. *Journal of Health Administration Education, 34*(2), 319–343. Retrieved from https://www.ingentaconnect.com/contentone/aupha/jhae/2017/00000034/00000002/art00010

Russell, C. T. S., Augustin, F., & Jones, P. (2017). Perspectives on the importance of integrating diversity into the healthcare administration curriculum: The role of cultural humility. *Journal of Health Administration Education, 34*(3), 371–393. Retrieved from https://www.ingentaconnect.com/contentone/aupha/jhae/2017/00000034/00000003/art00003

Weech-Maldonado, R., Elliott, M. N., Pradhan, R., Schiller, C., Hall, A., & Hays, R. D. (2012). Can hospital cultural competency reduce disparities in patient experiences with care? *Medical Care, 50,* S48–S55. doi:10.1097/MLR.0b013e3182610ad1

TOOLS AND APPROACHES

CONTROL CHARTS

"Control Chart" is the short name for Statistical Process Control Chart, first introduced by Walter Shewhart, created to visually display whether a process is performing within statistical control. There are numerous types of Control Charts that can be used for different analyses, depending on the kind of data that are being studied.

Every process has inherent variation. A Control Chart helps you identify when a variation in a measure of interest is important. Is it within the normal limits of variation in the process? Or should we react to the variation with some sort of intervention?

Common cause variation is the expected variation between the control limits (lower control limit [LCL] and upper control limit [UCL]) inherent in the process. When data exceed these control limits, it indicates special cause variation. Control Charts help you distinguish between common and special cause variation in a process. People often react to the smallest changes in a metric, seeing trends where there may not be any. If the metric goes in the direction we want it to go, we immediately celebrate. If it goes in the opposite direction, some people look for someone to blame. Common cause variation should be ignored. Special cause variation must be investigated and eliminated.

As seen in Figure C11.4, a Control Chart contains a plot of the data (sometimes sample averages, sometimes individual numbers). The three lines help you identify whether a process is in control or not. These lines are the mean, the UCL, and the LCL. For repetitive processes, the control limits are generally set at ±3 standard deviations around the mean. In this example, it is not until April to May of 2018 that the process can be deemed a special cause variation requiring intervention to return the process within statistical control.

Calculating control limits requires statistical analysis and a table of Shewhart's constants. For example, to calculate the standard deviation, you must have the underlying data that result in those averages, not just averages of all the data. Furthermore, when the sample size month over month varies, constructing the Control Charts requires more advanced data analytics. Software packages, such as Minitab, SAS, or SPSS, are useful in this regard.

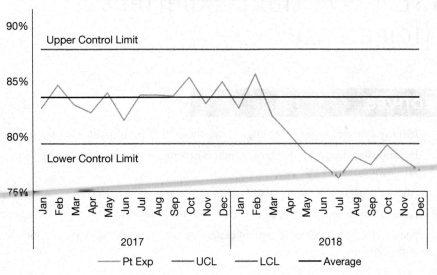

FIGURE C11.4 Statistical Process Control Chart example.

LCL, lower control limit; UCL, upper control limit.

CASE 12: Patient Experience in Home Care

OBJECTIVES

1. Identify a formal approach to engage stakeholders in performance improvement.
2. Examine how leaders hold team members accountable for high levels of patient satisfaction.
3. Apply a proactive, inquisitive attitude to problem-solving.
4. Explain how lead measures can be used to make improvements to patient experience.
5. Summarize how a failure in patient experience can create an opportunity for improvement.

INTRODUCTION

CTR HomeCare is the largest home healthcare provider in the greater Redwood metro area, with 18 offices, divided in two regions: the North and the South. All 18 offices provide approximately 70,000 home visits per month, including skilled nursing services such as wound care, infusion services and medication management, rehab services (physical, occupational, and speech therapy), and home tele-monitoring, among others. CTR HomeCare has provided services to the Redwood community for nearly 40 years.

One year ago, the retiring founder and CEO of CTR HomeCare hired Gary Mewborn as the company's new CEO. Mewborn spent 25 years running home healthcare businesses out of state. His new job presented many challenges, not the least of which was leading an executive team with the average CTR HomeCare tenure of 17 years. Entrenched in old organizational practices, the team was accustomed to running their respective operational units relatively independent of central office interference.

The newest member of the CTR HomeCare executive team was Susanna Banderas, the Director of Quality and Patient Experience. When Banderas was hired last year, she was enthusiastic and full of personality, but she's been in a bit of a funk lately. Banderas has worked extremely hard, often putting in 60-hour weeks running quality and patient experience reports and finding solutions to patient complaints and other quality issues. However, she came to resent her coworkers, feeling that they did not respect her or her role at the company. In addition, the quality scores, as measured by patient experience surveys called Home Health Care Consumer Assessment of Healthcare Providers and Systems (HHCAHPS) have shown little improvement since she began. Banderas felt she could not improve patient experience scores by herself.

CASE SCENARIO

Weekly Leadership Meeting

During the weekly leadership meetings, Mewborn sat at the head of the table and various levels of attendees sat around the room. The usual attendees included:

- Susanna Banderas, Director of Quality and Patient Experience
- Jeannette Henderson, RN, Director for the South Region
- Jaime Cruz, RN, Director for the North Region
- Gina Merced, PT, Director of Rehabilitation Services
- Philip Miller, RN, Director of Central Intake

To highlight quality and patient experience issues with the leadership team, Banderas always selected two patient letters for Mewborn to read at the beginning of the weekly leadership meeting—one from a patient with a good experience and one from a patient who had a bad experience.

"As usual, I will begin by sharing a letter from the patient who had a good experience," Mewborn began.

"Dear CTR HomeCare Employees,

I want to thank everyone at CTR HomeCare for the phenomenal care you provided my mom. She has always been a very active woman, even in her 70s, and this hip replacement has been hard on her. The compassion with which Jake and Tina (her therapists) treated her was unbelievable. I saw them a few times with her, and I could not have asked for better care. And it was not only their compassion. Just after her second session with Jake, she was very happy and excited to see improvement in her mobility! They both took great care of her, and they even informed her if they were running a bit late, which she greatly appreciated. She raves about the awesome team you guys have and I wanted to let you know. She is now able to walk (still with a cane) and is very happy she can be independent again. We owe it to you! Thank you again and keep up the good work!

Thank you,

Alexandra Jankovic Harris"

Everyone in the leadership team had big smiles on their faces, and some of them had watery eyes. "Gina," Mewborn said, as he took off his glasses and placed the letter on the table, "you make sure to let Jake and Tina know about this and tell them I appreciate them very much for taking such good care of Mrs. Jankovic."

Gina Merced, Director of Rehabilitation Services, agreed. "Oh, absolutely!" she said.

"OK," continued Mewborn, "as you probably expect, I have a different kind of letter that I also want to share with you." There was a collective groan from his captive audience. Some of them shifted their weight on their chairs, as if they were bracing for impact.

"Dear Mr. Mewborn,

I want to let you know about my recent experience with CTR HomeCare. I recently had surgery to remove a portion of my colon, and I needed wound care. Before being discharged from the hospital, when I was given the choice to select which home care company to go to, I chose CTR because you are a well-known name in our community. I was discharged on

Tuesday, and the nurse at the hospital told me that I would be hearing from you that same evening. I did not hear from you that same day, but, since I was discharged in the early afternoon, I thought that you probably could not get to me that day, so I supposed I would hear from you the next morning. When I did not hear from you by mid-morning, I was starting to worry whether you knew about my case and if I was going to hear from you or how long it would be until I heard from you. Finally, around noon on Wednesday, I got a call from the nurse that she was on her way over to my home and that she was sorry she was late, but she was lost and wanted some directions to get to my home. I thought, '*what the heck?*' I was confused and asked her if she was sure she was coming to see me, since I had not heard anything from anyone at CTR prior to that. She said, '*Yes, Mr. Alberts, right?*' I then gave her directions to get to my house.

When she came to my house, she was very professional and courteous, I will give her that. She asked me if she could see my wound, and when I showed her where the bandage was, she ripped it off immediately with no warning! I screamed in pain and asked her if she knew my wound was very fresh! To my total bewilderment, she looked at me with a scared face and apologized, adding that she did not know that and that she thought it was at least a week old. She told me she thought other nurses had already come to take care of me. She shook her head and said something like, '*I wish they gave me more notice!*' She then proceeded to take care of my wound and put a fresh bandage on it. She apologized several more times and gave me some instructions about bathing and taking care not to get it wet.

Before she left, she said that someone (could be her or could be another nurse) would come see me on Friday and asked if I had any preference on time of the day for my appointment. I told her I would rather have early morning, so I could get on with my day after that. When Friday came, guess what? I had not heard from anyone to tell me about what time they were coming! Just before 9 AM, I got a phone call from a different nurse asking me directions and told me it would be 'at least an hour' before he got to me. I thought, '*Great!*' It took him until almost 11 AM to get to my house! When he finally arrived, I let him know how frustrated I was and he apologized. He said something like, '*I am not from around here, and it is confusing to get around this neighborhood.*'

When he finally started to care for my wound, he looked at my bandage and looked at his notes and said, 'That's weird! I thought your wound was on the right side of your abdomen, I was thinking you had a whipple!' When I asked him what the heck a 'whipple' was he said, 'a pancreas resection.' I was like '*Whoa! No way!*' He said, '*no problem, I will correct that in our notes so I or whoever the next nurse is that we can have the correct information, okay?*' He added that my wound was 'looking good' (whatever that means) and that he or someone else would be by the following week.

Over the next few weeks, a varied selection of nurses came to see me, all with varying degrees of knowledge of my wound and my healing process. So many, I can't even remember their names. Some were chatty (yuck!), some were slow (sat around on my couch), and some were very good, professional, and quick!

Thank God, I am doing a lot better, and I have fully recovered from that surgery. Your team of nurses did help me get better and I appreciate that. However, not once did I get a phone call the day before to let me know what time they were coming, regardless of how many times I requested it with every one of them. Also, the glaring lack of communication made me feel uneasy and unsafe throughout the whole thing. I want to end with two things:

1) I do not feel good about recommending you to anyone, and 2) I hope this is not every patient's experience!

Disappointed,

Jerry Alberts"

Mewborn let the leadership team sit in silence for a long uncomfortable moment. This day, Mewborn's tone reflected a sense of urgency and resolve. "Every week for the last year, I have read two letters to you—one from a patient who had a good experience with us and another from a patient who did not have a good experience with us. I started this practice in the hopes that by listening to these stories, we would become more watchful, and we would dig deeper into these issues. And yet, that has not happened. In fact, nothing has changed." Mewborn said.

Jeannette Henderson, RN, Director for the South Region, spoke up in order to try and lighten the mood, "We take the bad ones with the good ones." This did not help.

"The time has come when we do not take the bad ones with the good ones anymore," Mewborn announced in a sobering tone. "Why do we have to settle for that? I, for one, am tired of receiving and reading these letters and seeing that nothing has improved. I've watched Susanna distribute the HHCAHPS scores to your teams, but things are not changing. For that reason, we are going to take a different approach. We are going to take a closer look at our operations, and we are going to find out why we still have experiences like that of Mr. Alberts."

Banderas turned on the 55-inch TV in the room, and everybody turned their attention to it. Banderas showed them the graph of the Patient Experience Score and Percentile Rank she had reviewed at the leadership meeting a few weeks before. She said, "Our Patient Experience surveys, or HHCAHPS, as some of you know them, over the last year show that, while we may have made a little improvement, our competitors are improving at a faster rate."

"As a reminder, our Net Promoter Score is the answer to the question '*Would you recommend this agency to your family or friends if they needed home healthcare?*' On this survey item, responders can give an answer ranging from 0 ('not at all likely') to 10 ('extremely likely'). People giving us a 9 or a 10 are called 'promoters,' individuals answering 7 or 8 are considered 'passives,' and individuals answering 0–6 are called 'detractors.' To calculate the Net Promoter Score," Banderas explained, "you subtract the percentage of 'detractors' from the percentage of 'promoters'" (Figure C12.1).

"Let me show you how we perform. The Patient Experience percentile rank, represented as a line in the chart, represents how we compare to the home healthcare industry in overall patient experience. As you can see, it does bounce around. However, this is correlated with our overall Net Promoter Score, represented with the bars. As our Net Promoter Score goes up, so does our Patient Experience percentile rank," explained Banderas (Figure C12.2).

"I mean, our slogan says '*Every Patient, Every Time*,'" Mewborn said pointing at the glossy poster on the wall of the boardroom. "It does not say '85% of patients' or '85% of the time.' We are not going to change our slogan. Don't you want CTR to be the kind of organization that rises to the occasion to meet the expectations set by our slogan? Do we want to rely on Susanna to improve our Patient Experience scores all by herself?" The leadership team all nodded their heads.

Mewborn said, "I have taken the liberty of scheduling a leadership meeting for later this week to kick off our Patient Experience and Operational Excellence initiative. I have a very good feeling that this will be just what we need to improve our operations and meet our customers' expectations."

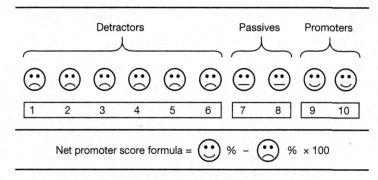

FIGURE C12.1 Net promoter score.

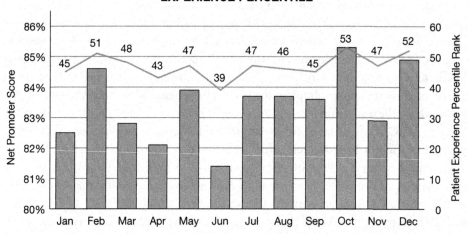

FIGURE C12.2 CTR HomeCare patient experience scores.

Patient Experience and Operational Excellence Initiative Kickoff Meeting

After Mewborn kicked off the meeting, Banderas led the leadership team with an activity. "I know that there may be other patient experience issues, but we are going to start with the letter from Mr. Alberts. Please write down on your note pad all of the causes of his poor patient experience or reasons you think he would not recommend CTR HomeCare to his family or friends." When they finished, Banderas asked them to call out the issues, and she wrote them on a flipchart at the front of the room. "Just call them out," she said enthusiastically.

"Now, we are going to use a process known as 'multi-voting' to rank how we prioritize these issues as a team," Banderas said. "Each of you gets three dots, and you are going to use them to signal which three of these have the highest priority, in your mind. You decide how you want to use your dots. You can assign all three to one issue or you can spread them among several issues. We will then count how many dots each issue gets and we will rank them."

When the team finished the exercise, they decided that the top three issues were:

1. Too many nurses/clinicians see the patient
2. No advanced notice to patient about time of visit
3. Delay in contacting patient upon admission

Banderas continued, "So, let's get to the bottom of these causes. Why are there too many nurses/clinicians seeing the patient? First of all, what is 'too many?' Why don't we know how many is 'too many'?"

Jaime Cruz, the Director for the North Region said, "Because we have never agreed on a standard of what the max should be."

Jeannette Henderson jumped in, "I think no more than four clinicians makes sense."

Cruz spoke up not wanting to lose any momentum, "So, that's it, then! Four clinicians is the maximum we should strive for."

Banderas grabbed a marker and wrote on a new flipchart, "Why are we not able to keep the number of clinicians to a maximum of 4?" while she asked "Why?"

"Because we see a lot of patients and our teams are huge," answered Henderson.

"Why are our teams huge?" was Banderas's next question.

Henderson scoffed, gave her a look as if to say, "Are you serious?" and replied, "Because every office covers a large geographic area."

There was silence and Henderson enjoyed a brief moment of victory. Her short-lived victory was shattered when Gina Merced, Director of Rehabilitation Services asked, "Why does the whole office have to cover the whole geographic area?"

"Actually," added Cruz, in a tone and with a face that lit up as he had the epiphany, "I think this is a remnant of when we were smaller, as I remember from many years ago when I ran the office on Inverness Road. Perhaps we can come up with a way in which the team of clinicians each office employs can be broken down in sub-teams or something like that!"

"Great idea!" Banderas said.

Next, they discussed how patients did not get advanced notice about the time of the home visit. They talked about some barriers such as the fact clinicians are very busy on the field, and when they get home they are trying to finish up and upload their notes, and then get ready for the following day's patients. "Could schedulers call the patients to let them know the approximate time of their visit the next day?"

When discussing "Delay in contacting patient upon admission," the conversation was focused mainly on how Central Intake always waited to have all the paperwork before calling patients to let them know they were admitted. Philip Miller, the Director of Central Intake, claimed that his team needed all that paperwork in order before they called the patients and sometimes, by the time they got it all, it was too late in the evening to call. "But, did they really need all the paperwork to call the patient?"

This and more healthy discussion took place before Banderas asked, "How often do we look at our Patient Experience metrics?"

"Once a month, as far as I know" answered Henderson.

"That is correct!" reinforced Banderas. "Furthermore, we only get our patient survey results three months after we have discharged the patients! That is why we refer to this as a lag measure. A lag measure is sometimes also called an 'outcome measure,' because we are measuring the outcome, or the result of our process. However, by the time we get the result, it is too late to change anything to improve the outcome, right? We cannot go back in time to change something we did or did not do. It is as if we were all playing a game (choose whichever sport you like) and we finish the game and go home and the score is not revealed until 3 days later. What good is that? What happens if we realize then that we lost the game? We need a way to know the score while we are playing the game, so we can make adjustments. Don't you agree?" Everyone nodded in agreement.

"So, we need lead measures," Banderas stated, driving her point home. "Lead measures are a lot more immediate than lag measures. What we need to do now is identify a few lead measures that we can all track every day so that by achieving our lead measure goals, we will then achieve our lag measure goal of improved patient experience. That is the main characteristic of a lead measure: that achieving it predicts achieving the lag measure. With the root causes and/or solutions you came up with, what are some things we could track that would become our lead measures? I suggest we agree on three to five lead measures."

"Also, one final note about lead measures. If we are going to have our teams tracking and trying to improve these lead measures, they must be within the control of the team. This is the first step in something called Managing for Daily Improvement, or MDI. MDI is a system for managing our business in a way that it fosters improvement daily by involving and engaging the frontlines. No improvement effort can succeed without input and buy-in from the frontlines who are going to have to deal and grapple with the changes. One of the main reasons why so many improvement initiatives fail is because they are conceived at a high level that does not take into account the perspective and input of frontline team members and managers. If we want our improvements to produce sustained results, we must involve frontline team members!"

There were some heads nodding as Banderas drove home her point.

"There are several components that make up the whole MDI system," she continued. "The first one is the Visual Board in which we are going to track our measures and actions and I will show you what that looks like in a second. I brought a mock one. The second component is a daily huddle. In this huddle, we are going to have as close to everyone involved, from your leadership teams at each office to the frontline team members, schedulers, clinicians, etc. This will be a quick huddle where the measures are reviewed and the team then discusses things that are preventing them from hitting their targets and what they can do about it. Actually, I thought it would be better if I show you an example."

Banderas got on YouTube and pulled up a video showing a very efficient MDI huddle that lasted just under 6 minutes. "See what I mean? Now, granted, when we first deploy this," she continued in response to some eye-rolls and deer-in-the-headlights looks, "it will probably take us longer, maybe up to 15 minutes, but we will get better, the teams will get better quick!"

"And we are going to do this daily for each of these, these lead measures?" asked Henderson. "This is going to take us all day!"

"Yes," replied Banderas, "we are going to do this for each lead measure and no, this will not take us all day. The goal is that the MDI huddle lasts no more than 10 minutes. In fact, once we have matured in our practice of this concept, we will be doing these in 4 to 6 minutes." Banderas then guided them through several mock huddle practice rounds, each with a different volunteer as facilitator. Banderas continued, "I will be there for the huddle every day for the first 2 weeks; then, a few times a week; then once a week. In the meantime, all of you, the leaders, are going to get trained on auditing MDI, and you will also go and observe the huddles, the boards, and give feedback. Within about a month, the process should be running pretty well. That's it in a nutshell!" She finished with a smile.

After the session was adjourned, team members stayed around, talking to each other, planning the next steps, taking note of some individual actions and the energy in the room was palpable! They did not want to leave!

DISCUSSION QUESTIONS

1. Gary Mewborn started the practice of reading two letters (one positive and one negative) "in the hopes that by listening to these stories, things would turn around." Why did things not improve? Why did nothing change?

2. How would you evaluate Gary Mewborn's leadership in announcing and launching the Patient Experience and Operational Excellence initiative? Would you have done something different?

3. Susanna Banderas started her job with a lot of enthusiasm and ideas, yet she had lost some of that after working at CRT HomeCare for a while. Why? How would you ensure that does not happen in your team?

4. If you were CEO of CTR HomeCare, how would you hold your leadership team accountable for improved patient experience performance without negating Susanna Bandera's authority as Director of Patient Experience and Quality?

 ## PODCAST FOR CASE 12

Listen to how experts approach the topic (you can access the podcast by following this url to Springer Publishing Company Connect™: https://connect.springerpub.com/content/book/978-0-8261-4514-7/front-matter/fmatter2)

FURTHER READING

Fikar, C., & Hirsch, P. (2017). Home health care routing and scheduling: A review. *Computers & Operations Research*, *77*, 86–95. doi:10.1016/j.cor.2016.07.019

Krol, M. W., de Boer, D., Delnoij, D. M., & Rademakers, J. J. (2015). The Net Promoter Score—An asset to patient experience surveys? *Health Expectations*, *18*(6), 3099–3109. doi:10.1111/hex.12297

Smith, L. M., Anderson, W. L., Lines, L. M., Pronier, C., Thornburg, V., Butler, J. P., … & Goldstein, E. (2017). Patient experience and process measures of quality of care at home health agencies: Factors associated with high performance. *Home Health Care Services Quarterly*, *36*(1), 29–45. doi:10.1080/01621424.2017.1320698

TOOLS AND APPROACHES

MANAGING FOR DAILY IMPROVEMENT

One of the best ways to involve and engage the frontline employees in improvement is by implementing a Managing for Daily Improvement (MDI) system. This system involves the staff in the process of finding the root causes of the problems they face every day, implementing solutions, and sustaining improvement so the problems are permanently fixed.

MDI has four major components:

- Visual Boards—These are the boards where you will track and display your metrics.

- Huddle—A team-driven stand-up meeting in which you review your lead measures, identify barriers to achieving your goals, design actions to improve, and follow up on those actions. The practice of huddling at the Visual Board is known as "working the wall."

- Gemba Walks—This is the practice by leadership of going to "the real place," as we loosely translate "gemba." It is about the leaders being part of the MDI process, not offering solutions, or trying to solve everything for the team, but rather, encouraging them, helping them find solutions on their own and removing any barriers they encounter.

- Daily—The huddles, the metric tracking and review, the action follow-up and accountability, all have to occur daily.

An MDI board contains four rows and as many columns as metrics you are tracking (Figure C12.3). The first chart, at the top, contains the lag measure you are tracking, monthly. The second chart shows your lead measure and this is tracked and updated daily. One very effective way of filling out this chart is to color how many instances you met your goal in green and the instances in which you did not meet your goal in red.

There should be a goal, for example, "four clinicians or less." For those instances in which you did not meet your goal, you have to ask why that happened and you populate the third chart, "Reasons," with this information. You see bars in this "Reasons" chart because you are going to indicate how frequently each reason repeats, essentially creating a histogram. For example, if you are asking why you did not follow up with a patient timely and the reason is "Because you did not have a valid phone number," then every time that happens you color another square above that reason. After a while, this will help you see which are your biggest opportunities, as it will become very obvious which are the causes of the issues.

Finally, the last chart at the bottom is the Action plan. There will be an action for every one of the reasons identified in the previous chart. The actions in this Action plan should be within the control of the team. Perhaps a small amount may require escalation, but you must focus on identifying actions that the team can own and execute themselves.

About the placement of these Visual Boards, the idea is to install these boards in a visible place where your team can see them continuously and a place that allows for people to gather around them for the huddles.

The second component of MDI, as explained above, is the huddle. This huddle must occur daily. There must be a facilitator for the huddle and it must be clear who the facilitator is. The job of the facilitator is to ensure the huddle runs smoothly, that the standard work is followed, and that you get some good actions and accountability out of it.

The standard work for running a huddle is provided in Exhibit C12.1.

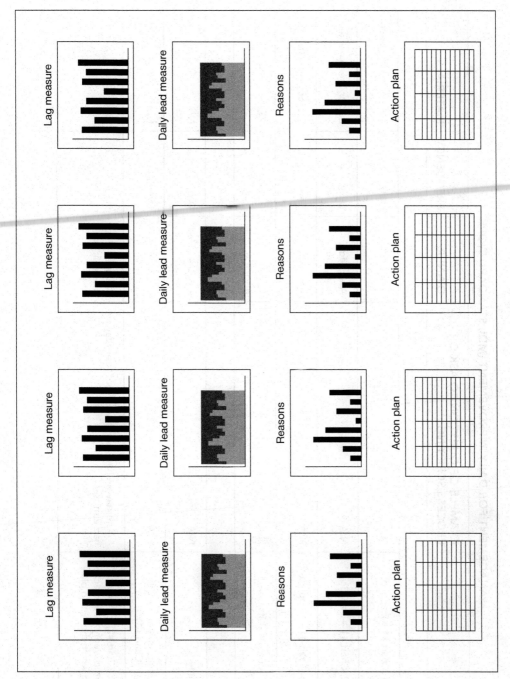

FIGURE C12.3 MDI board sketch.

Exhibit C12.1 MDI Huddle Standard Work

		MANAGEMENT FOR DAILY IMPROVEMENT (MDI) STANDARD WORK			
STEP	TASKS	EXAMPLE OF QUESTION TO ASK OR PROCESS SCRIPTING	OWNER	FREQUENCY	MATERIALS
Prior to Huddle					
1	Populate Metric 1 (Chart #1—if applicable—and Chart #2)	N/A	Assigned resource	Daily	Red or Green marker
2	Populate Metric 2 (Chart #1—if applicable—and Chart #2)	N/A	Assigned resource	Daily	Red or Green marker
3	Populate Metric 3 (Chart #1—if applicable—and Chart #2)	N/A	Assigned resource	Daily	Red or Green marker
4	Populate Metric 4 (Chart #1—if applicable—and Chart #2)	N/A	Assigned resource	Daily	Red or Green marker
During Huddle					
5	Start Huddle on time	N/A	Assigned Huddle facilitator	Daily	N/A
6	Review monthly results only at the beginning of each month (Chart #1)	N/A	Assigned Huddle facilitator	Monthly	N/A
7	Review daily chart (Chart #2) for metric 1. If no misses occurred, verify that no action items are pending within the Action plan sheet.	"Yesterday we had zero misses" or "Yesterday we had 2 misses"	Assigned Huddle facilitator	Daily	N/A

(continued)

Exhibit C12.1 MDI Huddle Standard Work (*continued*)

	MANAGEMENT FOR DAILY IMPROVEMENT (MDI) STANDARD WORK			
STEP	TASKS	EXAMPLE OF QUESTION TO ASK OR PROCESS SCRIPTING	OWNER	FREQUENCY	MATERIALS
8	If misses occurred, investigate until identifying the root cause. Continue to ask "Why" until you get to an actionable root cause.	"Why did these misses occur?"	Assigned Huddle facilitator	Daily	N/A
9	Identify the obstacles that are preventing us from meeting the metric. Document obstacles in the Reasons chart (Chart #3).	"What obstacles are causing us not to meet this metric?" "Which ones can we address now?"	Assigned Huddle facilitator	Daily	Black marker
10	Ask the team for potential solutions that would mitigate or eliminate these barriers.	"What can be done to prevent this from happening again?" "What can we try today to prevent this from happening again?"	Assigned Huddle facilitator	Daily	N/A
11	Create an action plan for each *identified solution*. Ensure to include the owner of the action, and the identified completion date.	"Who can perform this task/step?" "When can we go and see what we have learned from these actions/steps?"	Assigned Huddle facilitator	Daily	Black marker
12	If there are any open actions on the Action plan, *address those* (get updates).	"Did we try that potential solution yesterday? What did we learn?" "Did we follow up with John Q about that?"	Assigned Huddle facilitator	Daily	N/A

Patient Safety

Patient safety is a quality management category that concentrates on mitigating the risk of harm to patients. The Institute of Medicine's groundbreaking report, *To Err Is Human: Building a Safer Health System*, highlighted the U.S. healthcare system's failure to reduce medical errors (Kohn, Corrigan, & Donaldson, 2000). Despite patient safety improvements in some areas, such as reducing hospital-acquired infections, patients in the United States still experience preventable harms (National Patient Safety Foundation, 2015). Key patient safety issues in the U.S. healthcare system include diagnostic errors, patient misidentification, patient falls, healthcare-acquired infections, medication errors, and wrong-site surgeries (IHI, 2019). Consequences of patient safety errors include dissatisfaction, anger, physical and emotional pain, delayed care, worsening health condition, injury, disability, and death.

The following are descriptions of the patient safety case studies included in this casebook.

Case 13: Reducing Patient Falls: The Sleuth Resident

A hospital invested US$200 million to remodel the facility to meet modern patient safety standards. The hospital experienced significant improvements with some quality measures, but not patient falls. To a third-year physician resident working at the hospital, one patient fall is too many. Acting as a patient safety detective, the resident developed five hypotheses as plausible root causes of patient falls and then tested each hypothesis systematically.

Case 14: Sustaining Hand Hygiene

The increased surgical site infections at a multilocation ambulatory surgery center organization were likely due to hand hygiene noncompliance. A remote video auditing system records all hand hygiene opportunities with the use of video cameras and doorway motion sensors. After analyzing the hand hygiene compliance data and visiting each of the six centers, an infection prevention manager uncovered the root cause of the poor hand hygiene compliance.

Case 15: A Warning Letter From the State Regulator

The state regulator uncovered numerous patient safety violations during an investigation of Sandywood Nursing Home, as outlined in an official warning letter regarding patient misidentification issues. Sandywood needed to develop a Plan of Correction within 30 days or face the legal consequences. The Sandywood administrator forwarded the letter via email to the nursing director and the manager of quality and risk. Unfortunately, the administrator quickly lost control of the situation, and an argument about accountability ensued. How would Sandywood respond to its legal jeopardy?

Case 16: Failure-to-Rescue

An inpatient care team waited an unacceptably long time to respond to the cardiac distress of a patient, belatedly called a "code blue," and then unsuccessfully attempted a resuscitation. After the failure-to-rescue event, the patient's family decided to sue the hospital. The chief nursing officer defended the reputation of the hospital and staff during the deposition by the family's lawyer. Was an ineffective escalation system responsible for the patient's untimely death? Is the chief nursing officer liable for the death of the patient?

Case 17: CLIF's Medication Errors

In the year 2048, a health system planned to invest US$700 million into implementation of an artificial intelligence–enhanced health information technology (HIT) system, called "Clinical Learning Information Framework," or "CLIF." The intention of the technology was to improve clinical decision-making and patient outcomes. However, the hospital director of pharmacy fretted over the unintended consequences of artificial intelligence technology. Back in 2023, he experienced many HIT-related errors, including one that led to the untimely death of a patient. What could be done to prevent CLIF from harming patients?

Case 18: A Mom's Story of Sepsis

A sepsis misdiagnosis in an ED caused dire consequences for a young boy. While the clinical leaders apologized to his mother, her personal story involving this failure revealed the need for quality improvement throughout the organization. The newly formed Sepsis Response Team analyzed the problem and developed countermeasures to achieve a reduction in mortality seen in sepsis cases.

REFERENCES

Institute for Healthcare Improvement. (2019). Topics: Patient Safety. Retrieved from: http://www.ihi
    .org/Topics/PatientSafety/Pages/default.aspx"
Kohn, L. T., Corrigan, J. M., & Donaldson, M. S. (Eds.). (2000). *To err is human: Building a safer health
    system*. Washington DC: National Academies Press. doi:10.17226/9728
National Patient Safety Foundation. (2015). *Free from harm: Accelerating patient safety improvement
    fifteen years after To Err Is Human*. Boston, MA: Author.

CASE 13: Reducing Patient Falls: The Sleuth Resident

OBJECTIVES

1. Describe how generating hypotheses can support the quality management process.
2. Examine collaboration among caregivers and quality management leaders.
3. Analyze patient safety data using quality management problem analysis tools.
4. Identify causes of variation in patient safety outcomes and relevant safety-enhancing technologies.
5. Evaluate efforts to overcome complacency with current patient safety performance.

INTRODUCTION

Patient falls are a leading Sentinel Event that are required to be reported by hospitals to The Joint Commission, the accreditation organization (The Joint Commission, 2019). Thousands of patients of acute care and rehabilitation hospitals are injured in falls that cause at least some sort of injury (Bouldin et al., 2013; Oliver, Healey, & Haines; 2010). The Centers for Medicare and Medicaid no longer pays hospitals for costs related to patient falls, which they consider preventable (Centers for Medicare and Medicaid Services; 2018). For these reasons, healthcare organizations seek to identify the root causes for patient falls and develop best practices for preventing them.

Red Valley Clinic is a large academic medical center that has served the Greater Red Valley metro area for 80 years. It has three large hospitals (300–500 beds each) and 28 medical group practices ranging from primary care to specialists, such as ophthalmologists, endocrinologists, orthopedic surgeons, and physical rehabilitation. Out of the three large hospitals, St. Xavier Memorial Hospital is the one that has been in operation the longest, and it is the flagship of Red Valley Clinic. Five years ago, Red Valley Clinic invested close to US$200 million to expand and update St. Xavier Memorial to modern standards. After the renovation, St. Xavier Memorial became a 340-bed hospital.

DATA FILE FOR CASE 13

Data files for students are available by accessing the following url: https://www.springerpub.com/hqm

The data file for Case 13 provides summary data for 24 months of patient falls for one hospital by unit. Also includes total falls and averages for five hypothesized root causes (patient age, bed age, acuity, RN years of experience, and average census) for each of the 15 patient units. Ideal data for creating scatterplots.

CASE SCENARIO

"Another month, another great review!" said Dr. Sanjeep Metha, a third-year resident at Red Valley Clinic as he came out of their monthly operations review. He high-fived his friend and colleague, Dr. Carson Stanley, another third-year resident at Red Valley who begrudgingly joined his friend's hand in the air. Dr. Stanley was visibly troubled.

"What's wrong?" inquired Dr. Metha. "Did you not like that glowing review of our units? In the past year, we almost eliminated infections, reduced length-of-stay, and increased revenue for the organization. Seven more months and we will be writing our own ticket, man! Cheer up!"

"Yes, I agree," replied Dr. Stanley, "that our teams have done some great work on those fronts, but, does it not bother you how poorly we are doing on patient falls?"

"Oh, man, here we go! Why do you always insist on fixating on the negative?" asked Dr. Metha.

"Well, for one, because that is a huge patient safety issue. Plus, I know we can do better," Dr. Stanley answered.

"Man, I can't hang out with you when you are being Mr. Negative! I'll catch up with you later, OK? We'll celebrate!" said Dr. Metha as he bid farewell to his friend and went down a different hallway.

Dr. Stanley continued walking down the wide, well-lit, pristine clinic hallway, deep in thought. He did not notice the nurses coming and going, the family who came out of one of the rooms full of joy, getting ready to get Dad home today, or the environmental services tech cleaning the spill into which he almost stepped. After a few minutes walking, he realized he had no idea how he got there. He then turned around and went back to his office to review the charts of the patients on whom he had to round.

The reason troubling Dr. Stanley was that over the 3 years he has been a resident, patient falls throughout St. Xavier Memorial have remained constant at between 30 and 40 every month. Not only is this number significantly higher than the national benchmark of 3.56 falls per 1,000 patient days (Bouldin et al., 2013), but for Dr. Stanley, one fall is too many. He needed to find a way to reduce falls. He set an ambitious goal to reduce patient falls by half over the next 18 months.

Dr. Stanley knew he first needed data to try to find some opportunities to reduce patient falls. He enlisted the help of Dan Stroman, a young, wide-eyed data analyst in the Process Excellence department to get him some data. "Sure thing, Dr. Stanley," was Dan's enthusiastic response. "Just let me know what you need."

Dr. Stanley asked Dan to give him the falls data for the last 2 years by nursing unit for St. Xavier Memorial Hospital. He was delighted when, upon returning to his office that evening, he had an email from Dan Stroman with the subject, "Patient Falls data you requested." Dr. Stanley thought, "Man this guy works fast," as he smiled and opened the email (see Case 13 Data file provided in the Instructor's and Student ancillary materials).

Upon studying the data, it was immediately obvious to Dr. Stanley that some nursing units were more prone to patient falls than others. He made the decision right then to find out the differences between nursing units and determine which, if any, of those differences could explain the higher numbers of falls for some units. Like a good quality improvement sleuth, Dr. Stanley knew that there is no substitute for "going and seeing for yourself." So, the following day, he visited not only those units on which he normally rounded, but other units as well. He introduced himself and engaged with the staff there (nurses, transporters, techs). As part of his conversations with them, he always asked one of two questions, depending on the number of falls in that unit:

1. What do you think contributes to your low number of patient falls?
2. What do you think contributes to your high number of patient falls?

He listened to their many theories and set out to test them with data. Dr. Stanley generated hypotheses that could be proved or disproved using the data file. He was determined to get answers for his questions.

Hypothesis A: Older Patients Fall More Often

One day, while rounding on 4-West, Dr. Stanley asked the charge nurse, "What do you think contributes to your high number of patient falls?"

"Oh, I know exactly why we have such a high number of falls every month," she answered. "It's because we have the oldest population of patients in the whole hospital! Older patients are more prone to falls. It's that simple."

Dr. Stanley went back to his office and called Dan Stroman. "Hello Dan! It's Dr. Stanley!"

"Hello, Dr. Stanley! How can I help you today?" Dan said with his usual excitement.

"Could you pull the average age of the patients by unit for the last 2 years?" Dr. Stanley asked. He paused for a moment, and when Dan did not immediately answer, he added, "It does not have to be by month, just an average for the whole year, by unit, for the last 2 years."

"Okay, let me see what I can do," replied Dan as he started helping Dr. Stanley in his quest.

The next morning, Dr. Stanley walked in to an email from Dan. He opened and studied the data. He wanted to find out if there was positive correlation between patient age and number of falls by unit. He knew that an easy way to do that is by using a scatterplot, so he plotted the data and studied the result.

Hypothesis B: Older Beds Cause More Patient Falls

While rounding the Surgery floor another day, Dr. Stanley asked one of the staff nurses in 2-East, "What do you think contributes to your low number of patient falls?"

"Well, we have some really well-trained staff and everyone is on their toes and when there is a bed alarm, we hustle!" replied the nurse. "I think that the new beds have definitively had an impact."

"New beds? What do you mean by that?" asked Dr. Stanley.

"Yes, a few years ago, about 4 or 5 years ago, we got these new beds," she started walking toward an empty room so she could show Dr. Stanley. "They have a lot of nice features, and all the alarms work great! Bed alarms alert personnel when a patient at risk for a fall attempts to leave the bed without assistance. When I was upstairs in 4-North, half of those beds did not have alarms."

"Really?" was Dr. Stanley's response as he considered his next data request.

Dr. Stanley went back to his office and got on the phone with Dan Stroman. "Hello Dan! This is Dr. Stanley, how are you?"

"Doing great, Dr. Stanley," replied Dan. "What can I do for you?"

"Do you have any way to find out how old the beds are in each unit?" asked Dr. Stanley.

"Hmm, that, hmm, that's a new one!" replied Dan, sounding stumped.

"Do you know of anyone who could have that kind of data, short of me having to go unit by unit asking the nurse managers?" Dr. Stanley kept the conversation going.

"Well, maybe Jan from facilities could help. You could ask her if they keep that information. Would you like her contact information?" Dan asked in an attempt to get out of having to go trying to find these data.

"Well, I don't really know Jan," replied Dr. Stanley. "Do you have a good working relationship with her?"

"Man! This guy is going to make me go hunting for data for his little quest, isn't he?" was Dan's thought. He let out a sigh and responded, "Let me ask her if they keep that information or if she can point me in the direction of someone who can. Give me a few hours, or maybe until tomorrow and I will let you know what I find," Dan said.

While he waited for the data, Dr. Stanley could not help but wonder what the data would tell him. Could it be that there was a correlation between the age of beds and patient falls?

Hypothesis C: Higher Acuity Patients Are More Prone to Falls

As Dr. Stanley rounded on 5-West, he found a group of team members at the nursing station. The group included the charge nurse, two staff nurses, and a patient care tech. He asked them how their day was going and engaged them in conversation. When he got to his question, "What do you think is causing your high number of patient falls?" the group fell silent for a brief moment. One of the staff nurses broke the silence. "We have really complex patients on this unit!" she said. The others nodded in confirmation. "We probably have some—if not the highest-acuity patients in this facility. Our patients are really, really sick, and sicker patients are harder to manage in all aspects, including falls."

Dr. Stanley thanked them and went back to his office, pondering this along the way. In his office, he picked up the phone and called Sara Mullins, Chief Nursing Officer for St. Xavier. "Hello Ms. Mullins! It's Dr. Stanley. How are you?"

"I'm doing great, Dr. Stanley," replied Mullins. "What's on your mind?"

"As you may have heard, I am doing an in-depth study on patient falls in our hospital, and I have been gathering some data to try to pinpoint several areas for opportunities. I have a question for you; it's kind of a two-part question. How do we rate patient acuity? Does every patient get assigned an acuity rank? And, if so, are that data available retrospectively? I guess it was more of a three-part question" Dr. Stanley finished, smiling.

"Well, we use QuadraMed® scores," responded Mullins. "Yes, every patient should get a score assigned, based on their current condition, their present illness and things like comorbidities, among others. And, for the third part of your question, yes, the data can be pulled from the EMR. We have reports we run routinely on this. What are you thinking?"

"This is great!" replied Dr. Stanley. "One of the hypotheses I am interested in testing is whether more complex, or higher acuity, patients are more prone to falls. This came up in my conversations with some of the nurses on one of those units that have historically struggled with patient falls. How can I get my hands on these data?"

"Lindsey McAllen in Nurse Informatics is the expert and owner of these data. She should be able to help you. By the way, I am very interested in knowing what you find out, so, please, keep me in the loop! I have my own opinions about this, but I will wait and see where the data take us. Please, do not hesitate to reach out if you need anything else."

"Will do! Thank you, Ms. Mullins!"

"Lindsey?" asked Dr. Stanley on the phone.

"Yes …" answered Lindsey McAllen with a hint of a question.

"Sorry, this is Dr. Stanley, one of the residents. Sara Mullins gave me your information for some data requests I have."

"Oh, yes, Dr. Stanley! How can I help you?" replied Lindsey.

"Well, I am interested in getting the average patient acuity," continued Dr. Stanley, "the QuadraMed score by nursing unit for the last 2 years. Is it possible to pull an average for the whole year by unit?"

"I've never done that, but I don't see why it would not be possible. We can pull it weekly and monthly, so, it should be pretty straightforward to pull it for the year. You just need one number for the whole year?"

"Yes," replied Dr. Stanley. "Well, one number for the whole year, by unit, for the last 2 years."

"Right, right!" replied Lindsey. "I'm in the middle of something right now, but let me play with it and I will get back to you."

"Great! Thank you, Lindsey!" said Dr. Stanley. As they hung up, Dr. Stanley pondered whether the data would corroborate or disprove the theory that higher acuity patients are more vulnerable to falls.

Hypothesis D: Less Experienced Nurses Contribute to Higher Number of Patient Falls

Dr. Stanley's investigation took him to the third floor. While on 3-West, he went to the nurse manager's office, Rebecca Nieves, after he could not find anyone with whom to have a conversation and ask some questions. Her door was open. He peeked inside and, since she did not appear to notice him, he knocked on the door.

Rebecca turned her head down and looked at him over her glasses. "Yes, Dr. Stanley! What brings you around to this side of the tracks?" she asked, while keeping her fingers on her keyboard.

"Hello, Rebecca. How are you?" asked Dr. Stanley.

"Argh! I am working on this serious event report I have to file and the amount of data and information I need to type in is so much!" Rebecca said while her eyes went back to her computer screen.

"Oh, then, maybe I should come back when it is a better time for you," said Dr. Stanley genuinely understanding her situation.

"No, no, no, no!" replied Rebecca, taking her glasses off and motioning him to stay and come closer. "Come! Tell me. What's on your mind?"

"Thanks," added Dr. Stanley. "I'll try not to take too much of your time. I am doing an investigation into patient falls and trying to find some opportunities on which we can improve. So, I just have one simple question for you. What do you think contributes to your high number of patient falls?"

"Wow! You went straight for the jugular on that one!" said Rebecca with a smile. "No, in all seriousness, you are right. We do have a high number of falls and while there are several things we have tried with some mixed results, I think it all comes down to experience. I mean, I have one of the youngest staff in this hospital. Don't get me wrong! I love my staff, and they are all trying as hard as they can, but sometimes there is something to be said about being an old fox, like me. More experienced nurses have seen it all and can plan better and, in my opinion, are better prepared to handle different situations, including preventing patient falls. There are things that the chart does not tell you. If you just go by the fall risk score from the chart, you may miss a few things, and this is where experience comes in handy."

"I knew you would have some insight! Thank you Rebecca!" said Dr. Stanley as he left Rebecca's office. He made a few notes in his tablet and continued with his rounds.

When he came back to his office that afternoon, Dr. Stanley picked up the phone and called Sara Mullins, Chief Nursing Officer for St. Xavier. "Hello Ms. Mullins! It's Dr. Stanley. Do you have a few minutes?"

"Sure thing, Dr. Stanley!" replied Mullins. "What's on your mind?"

"I have been interviewing some more staff and had another idea. Do we track anywhere how many years of experience our nursing staff has?"

"Ooh, that's a good one!" replied Mullins with an air of mystery and a smile Dr. Stanley could feel over the phone. "You can probably start with Kevin Stanton, Director of Team Resources. They keep all those records, although I am not sure how easy it is to pull the data. Kevin can definitively tell you."

"Thank you very much, Ms. Mullins!" replied Dr. Stanley.

Dr. Stanley immediately dialed Kevin Stanton expecting to leave a message, given how late in the day it was. To his surprise, Kevin Stanton picked up the phone. "Oh, um, Mr. Stanton! I'm sorry I was expecting to leave a message on your voicemail. This is Dr. Stanley, one of the residents here at St. Xavier. May I trouble you for a few minutes, sir?"

Kevin Stanton was literally already packed up and leaving the office when the phone rang, so, he placed his laptop bag on top of the desk and sat back down. "I have a few minutes, sure!" he said with a grunt, as he sat down.

"Thank you, I will be brief. As you may have heard, I am doing a study on patient falls in our hospital, and I have been gathering some data to try to pinpoint several areas for opportunities. My latest investigations have pointed me in the direction of looking into the years of experience of our nursing staff. Do we track anywhere how many years of experience our nursing staff has? I would like to get, if possible, the average years of experience of the nursing staff on our hospital, by unit, for the last 2 years."

Kevin had both elbows on his desk, holding the phone on his left ear and stroking his forehead with his right hand.

Since there was silence, which Dr. Stanley interpreted as hesitation or confusion, he added, "Basically, I am just looking for one number by unit (the average years of experience of the nursing staff) for the last 2 years, just one number by year for each individual unit."

"Yeah, yeah …" responded Kevin. "I am thinking about this … hmm. Listen; let me have a word with Alberto, our analyst. Alberto …" (Kevin was trying to remember his last name) "Rodríguez! I'll try to talk to him tomorrow to explain what you are looking for, and I'll put him in touch with you. How's that?"

As they hung up, Dr. Stanley was excited at the prospect of getting his hands on the data and trying to find some clues as to whether nursing experience really has an impact on patient falls. He had to wait a little bit more than 24 hours to get it, however. Two days later, when he checked his email first thing in the morning, Dr. Stanley found an email from Alberto Rodríguez.

Dr. Stanley,

I hope this is the data you need. If it is not, or if you need a different pull or slice of the data, please, let me know.

Thank you very much!

Alberto Rodríguez

Dr. Stanley opened the attachment and went to work on this latest data gold mine.

Hypothesis E: Units With Higher Daily Census Are More Vulnerable to Patient Falls

Dr. Stanley went up to the sixth floor, to round the neuro units. While there, he talked to the nurse manager, the staff nurses, case managers, and patient care techs, always finding a way to ask about patient falls. When he asked, "What do you think contributes to your low number of patient falls?" he heard that floor nurses on that floor had it "relatively easy." When he continued probing, one staff nurse offered, "Well, I know in most of the floors below, the nurse-to-patient ratio could be as high as 1:5 or even 1:6 sometimes. They have units with really high daily census downstairs. Up here, it is rare if we ever get close to 20 patients, and we have five staff nurses. I would be willing to bet that those units with higher census probably have more falls, don't you think?"

"Actually, I know of a great way we can find out," he replied, already planning his next data request for Dan Stroman.

"Dr. Stanley, how can I help you now, sir? You still acting like a patient falls detective?" asked Dan with a hint of cynicism. *"Darn it! I thought I was done with this guy. I'm pretty sure he thinks I work for him,"* is what he was really thinking.

"Hi Dan! Yes, I am still on my search. I know I have made many requests from you, and I appreciate your help very much. Let's hope this is the last one. Could you get me the average daily census by unit for the last 2 years?" Dr. Stanley asked.

"Ah! I see where you are going with that, Doctor! Listen, I am working on a large simulation project for the Emergency Department. Is it okay if I get you your data by Friday this week?"

"Sure thing, Dan! I appreciate it a lot!" said Dr. Stanley, already pondering what the data would tell him. Would it corroborate or disprove the theory that higher census units are more vulnerable to patient falls? He could not wait to see the data and play with it!

As Dr. Stanley waited for the data, he could not help but notice he followed a repetitive process every time he was testing a hypothesis (Figure C13.1). He noted everything started with a theory, the hypothesis that needed to be tested. How did he test it? Gathering and

FIGURE C13.1 Hypothesis-testing process.

analyzing data, mostly through the use of scatterplots. In the end, he was able to make conclusions about each of the hypotheses with respect to their validity and identify potential interventions to attack those root causes that were uncovered as some of his hypotheses were proven correct.

DISCUSSION QUESTIONS

1. What other potential root causes might influence patient falls?
2. Equipped with the data, what would you do about the hypotheses that proved to be unsupported?
3. Based on the correctly identified hypothesis in the case scenario, what would be your course of action if you were the CEO/president of St. Xavier Memorial Hospital?
4. What do you think of the CNO's (Sara Mullins) position of "waiting and seeing what the data tell us" instead of immediately jumping to conclusions?

 ## PODCAST FOR CASE 13

Listen to how experts approach the topic (you can access the podcast by following this url to Springer Publishing Company Connect™: https://connect.springerpub.com/content/book/978-0-8261-4514-7/front-matter/fmatter2)

REFERENCES

Bouldin, E. D., Andresen, E. M., Dunton, N. E., Simon, M., Waters, T. M., Liu, M.,…Shorr, R. I. (2013). Falls among adult patients hospitalized in the United States: Prevalence and trends. *Journal of Patient Safety, 9*(1), 13–17. doi:10.1097/PTS.0b013e3182699b64

Centers for Medicare and Medicaid Services. (2018). *Hospital-acquired conditions.* Retrieved from https://www.cms.gov/Medicare/Medicare-Fee-for-Service-Payment/HospitalAcqCond/Hospital -Acquired_Conditions.html

The Joint Commission. (2019). *Sentinel event data summary.* Retrieved from https://www .jointcommission.org/assets/1/6/Summary_4Q_2018.pdf

Oliver, D., Healey, F., & Haines, T. P. (2010). Preventing falls and fall-related injuries in hospitals. *Clinics in Geriatric Medicine, 26*(4), 645–692. doi:10.1016/j.cger.2010.06.005

FURTHER READING

Fehlberg, E. A., Lucero, R. J., Weaver, M. T., McDaniel, A. M., Chandler, M., Richey, P. A.,…& Shorr, R. I. (2018). Impact of the CMS no-pay policy on hospital-acquired fall prevention–related practice patterns. *Innovation in Aging, 1*(3), igx036. doi:10.1093/geroni/igx036

SCATTERPLOT

When you suspect that one variable may be related to another—whether in a positive or negative direction—create a scatterplot. A scatterplot is a visual way to check if one variable is associated with another variable. The simplest way to construct a scatterplot is to graph the "cause" variable (that variable which you suspect might impact another) on your horizontal axis and the "effect" variable on your vertical axis. The grouping of data points in a line, whether a negative (downward) or positive one (upward), indicates an association between the two variables.

For example, if you think that sepsis bundle compliance affects your sepsis mortality, then you can use a scatterplot. If you get a result like the one in Figure C13.2 where the dots are aligned in a systematic way (note that they line up), you have a strong association between the variables.

There are two major warnings we must issue when using scatterplots. First, be mindful of the scale you use for both your variables. If you select the wrong scale, you may miss an interaction. For example, the data from the first plot (Figure C13.2) are plotted on a different vertical axis scale and look like the second plot (Figure C13.3). The scale used on this second plot hides the interaction that looks so obvious on the first plot.

The second warning when using scatterplots is that "correlation" does not mean "causation." That is, just because one variable seems to be affecting another on a scatterplot, it does not mean that one variable causes the other. You have to understand the process to know whether causation makes sense. You should always involve the people who know and understand the process before investigating causation further through more sophisticated techniques. Frontline staff can tell you whether the correlation between two variables is causation or coincidence.

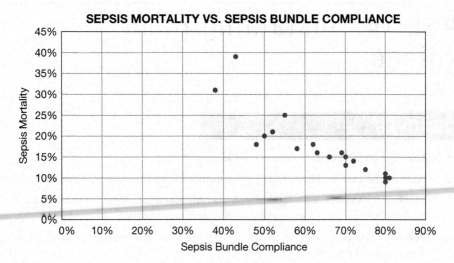

FIGURE C13.2 Scatterplot example.

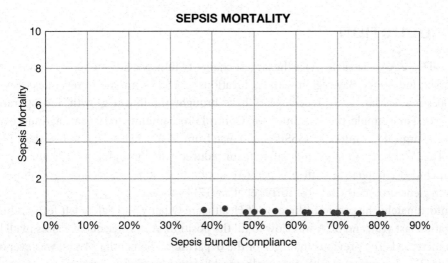

FIGURE C13.3 Bad Scatterplot (bad scale on vertical axis).

CASE 14: Sustaining Hand Hygiene

OBJECTIVES

1. Analyze hand hygiene compliance data.
2. Evaluate the performance of an organization-wide hand hygiene compliance program.
3. Examine the impact of leadership styles on sustained commitment to healthcare quality management process and patient safety performance.
4. Describe various approaches to holding people accountable for compliance with organizational policies.
5. Explain the value of mentoring high-potential leaders in healthcare quality management.

INTRODUCTION

Surgical Care Associates (SCA) is the largest chain of multispecialty ambulatory care surgery centers in the Apollo Bay region with six locations and $85.7 million in revenues from over 42,000 surgeries last year. Recent years have brought significant growth and operational successes. For example, the SCA Infection Control Program initiated 2 years ago successfully reduced surgical site infections (SSIs) incidence from 17.8% 4 years ago to less than 1% last year. The Healthcare Quality and Safety team reduced SSIs through a multifactor approach that included compliance with preoperative antibiotics, skin preparation procedures, and hand hygiene protocols (Berríos-Torres et al., 2017).

Unfortunately, the previous director of Healthcare Quality and Safety left for another organization last year, and SCA was slow to fill the position. As a consequence, SSIs in all locations increased. The previous manager of the department, Samantha Myers, was eventually promoted to director of Healthcare Quality and Safety. Myers's first priority was to examine the root causes of the elevated SSI rates. Among other issues, she found that hand hygiene compliance over the first 6 months of the year had declined significantly.

Jerry Simons, RN, BSN, MBA, CIC was promoted to manager of Infection Prevention and Employee Health last month to fill the vacancy created by Meyers's promotion. Previously,

DATA FILE FOR CASE 14

Data files for students are available by accessing the following url: https://www.springerpub.com/hqm

The data file for Case 14 provides over 4,600 lines of hand hygiene compliance data by location, staff member, and pass/fail.

Simons was an operating room circulating nurse at the highest volume and best performing center location, Stanton Street Surgery Center. Simons became responsible for the infection control programs across all six SCA ambulatory surgery centers. In his current role, he manages the ongoing analysis, development, and implementation of infection control methods and systems. He has been tasked with ensuring that evidence-based practices are implemented for the safety of patients, families, and staff. This includes new program development and management of existing improvement projects.

SCA instituted a remote video auditing system that records all hand hygiene opportunities with the use of video cameras and doorway motion sensors (Armellino et al., 2011). Every day, the off-site vendor randomly samples five instances for each of the six locations. Then, personnel called "remote video auditors" assess each opportunity for hand hygiene compliance standards. Healthcare workers are identified through a remote frequency identification device (RFID) embedded in their personnel badge. When a healthcare worker is observed performing appropriate hand hygiene protocol, the opportunity is assigned a pass; if not, a fail is assigned. Feedback metrics are automatically tabulated and reported utilizing web-based software in comprehensive periodic performance reports (see Case 14 Data file provided in the Instructor's and Student ancillary materials).

CASE SCENARIO

The afternoon before I left for the Institute for Healthcare Improvement (IHI) Patient Safety Congress in San Diego, my boss asked me to personally address hand hygiene protocol compliance at SCA. She would focus on other root causes to curtail the increasing incidence of SSIs, including preoperative antibiotic and skin preparation compliance. This initiative was my first as manager of Infection Prevention and Employee Health, and, frankly, I felt overwhelmed.

At the IHI Patient Safety Congress, I was looking forward to getting the opportunity to hear from successful people, keynote speakers, experts in the workshops, and other like-minded professionals in healthcare safety. More than anything else, though, I was excited to meet with my mentor, Edna O'Donnell, RN, MSN, MBA, CIC. Edna had been the national leader of Infection Prevention and Control for VitaNational Health Insurance for 5 years, an incredibly big job. As a fellow alum of my graduate school, Edna started working with me as a part of the formal mentorship program coordinated by the Master of Business Administration program. Since we were both nurses, the match was a great fit. Since I graduated 5 years ago, I have made an effort to stay in touch with her, and she has continued to be helpful to my career.

While Edna and I spoke multiple times on the phone and exchanged a flurry of emails—such as my resumes and cover letters—this was my first time meeting Edna in person. I knew from our phone conversations that Edna spoke with a heavy English accent, which made her sound even more brilliant to me. She told me that she originally moved from London to the United States on a Fulbright scholarship to earn her Master of Nursing degree. She had married an American, but stayed in the States after she divorced him. She retained her English identity, and was constantly using phrases that I would have to Google, such as when she told me, "I was happy to hear about your promotion, you must be chuffed!" Yes, I was very pleased to get the job.

Edna and I were scheduled to meet for coffee on the first morning of the IHI Patient Safety Congress. I arrived early at the hotel restaurant, but it was already crowded with conference goers. When Edna walked in, I knew her from her pictures. She was less than 5 feet tall but wore impossibly high, leopard print heels. In other ways, she looked the part of a healthcare executive—expensively cut, vibrantly gray hair, dark suit, and leather handbag. She recognized me, too, and surprised me with a warm hug and big smile. Since it was crowded, I suggested we take seats in the lobby. She said that this was nonsense and that someone would "bloody well budge up." She led me to a spot where we could have a "good ol' chinwag."

She placed her phone on silent and stored it away. Looking me directly in the eyes, she asked how my new job was going. I admitted I was very nervous about my new hand hygiene compliance project. She asked me if I thought I was qualified to do the job. When I answered yes, she told me "Bob's your uncle—you'll solve this problem, dear!"

Edna and I caught up and talked about some of the professors still teaching in the MBA program. Then, with equal measures of intensity and amusement, Edna asked me about my hand hygiene compliance root cause analysis. Since the project was assigned to me only the day before, I confessed that I didn't know what was leading to the declining rates of hand hygiene compliance. I showed her the chart that I had been given by my boss (Figure C14.1).

After telling me that someone had done a "botch job" on sustaining hand hygiene compliance rates, she asked a flurry of questions, starting with "How do you define the hand hygiene compliance standard?" I told her that the original hand hygiene program included intensive training in hand hygiene by using the World Health Organization (WHO)- and the Centers for Disease Control and Prevention (CDC)-supported guidelines, called the "Five Moments for Hand Hygiene." Each of the five hand hygiene opportunities, called "moments," were:

1. Before touching a patient
2. Before aseptic/clean procedure
3. After body fluid exposure risk
4. After touching a non-sterile item inside the patient zone
5. After touching patient surroundings (outside the patient zone)

"What's a patient zone?" she asked. I explained that the patient zone includes the patient and the patient's immediate surroundings (Figure C14.2). For surgery, patient zone includes the intact skin of the patient and all inanimate surfaces that are touched by or in direct physical contact with the patient, such as the instrument tray or other "high frequency" touch surfaces.

"How is hand hygiene compliance measured?" Edna asked. I explained how the remote video auditing system worked and that performance reports (Table C14.1) are presented and discussed at monthly Quality Assessment Process Improvement (QAPI) committee meetings.

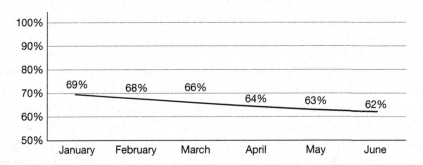

FIGURE C14.1 Average hand hygiene compliance rate.

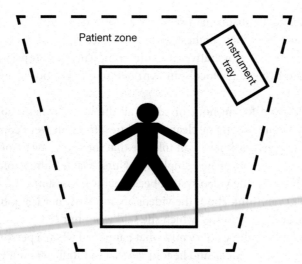

FIGURE C14.2 Diagram showing the patient zone.

Table C14.1 Hand Hygiene Compliance Performance Report Fields

DATE	LOCATION	HH_OPPORTUNITY_TYPE	PASS/FAIL	HEALTH_CARE_WORKER

Edna asked many more questions. "When was the last time the staff had training? Is there an issue with noncompliance on any particular hand hygiene opportunities in the Five Moments paradigm? Do the staff or leadership of the surgery center locations receive incentives? Are there healthcare workers who are not following the hand hygiene protocols at a higher rate than others? Are there differences among the six SCA locations? Who leads each location? Do they support the hand hygiene protocol compliance program?" I simply did not yet have the answers. Edna told me to "have a gander at the data." I promised to find out the answers using the data in the hand hygiene data report (see Case 14 Data file provided in the Instructor's and Student ancillary materials).

Edna and the IHI Patient Safety Congress inspired me with confidence. I analyzed the data in the hand hygiene compliance performance report. The data were revealing, and many of Edna's questions could be answered. The remaining answers could be found only by interviews and direct observation. I set out to visit each of the six ambulatory care center locations. I promised to keep Edna in the loop.

Stanton Street Surgery Center (Location 1)

I started at my old workplace, Stanton Street Surgery Center, which was labeled as "Location 1" in the hand hygiene compliance report. I confirmed much of what I already knew. The surgery center administrator, Amy Sanders, was an outstanding leader. She set a realistic and achievable vision for the organization. She kept her ego in check and had a way of getting the best performance from others. She was proactive in managing patient safety initiatives, including hand hygiene, by inspiring a sense of commitment and purpose. She often told staff that patient safety was their highest priority. In fact, Sanders included patient safety metrics, including SSI rates, preoperative antibiotic compliance, appropriate skin preparation procedures, and hand hygiene protocols, in her operational dashboard and discussed them at daily huddles.

I watched my old team for an hour or so. In all the hand hygiene opportunities that I observed, especially before aseptic or clean procedures, the staff were compliant with hand hygiene protocols. As I already knew, staff told me that they were aware of the remote video auditors assessing their hand hygiene compliance. Nurse Gayle Nunez told me that it didn't bother her to be watched by the video system because it was just a normal part of their work processes. She didn't even think about the videos anymore. At her last job, they had to take turns being the "handwashing police," which she said was a burden.

I asked a nurse named Philip Underwood what happened when a person was noncompliant with the hand hygiene protocol, and he told me that the staff were not punished. Instead, Sanders typically involved the staff in a root cause analysis of the instance of noncompliance and asked for ideas for improvement. Staff were encouraged to give ideas for changing patient safety processes, especially when supported by evidence. Another nurse, Ellen Fields, told me that staff all have confidence that their perspectives will be considered by Sanders.

Edna told me she thought Sanders "ran a proper good shop."

Bay Area Surgery Associates (Location 2)

I was less familiar with the Bay Area Surgery Associates (Location 2 in the report). On my first visit to the location, I learned that the administrator, Dan Graham, enjoyed holding competitions for various initiatives, such as shortening operating room turnaround time and improving patient experience scores. Graham insisted that his role as administrator was not to transform things, but to keep a "watchful eye" on the performance of all employees' specific goals discussed in their annual performance plans. When I asked him about hand hygiene, he told me that they held a big contest when the staff were trained on the Five Moments process, but that he does not include hand hygiene compliance in the staff annual performance plans.

According to several staff with whom I spoke, Graham is great at motivating them externally. Staff are rewarded for compliance with policies and procedures. Nurse Lillian Hayes told me that Graham loves to reward the staff with pizza parties. However, surgeon Dr. Melvin Goodwin told me that hand hygiene had not been the focus of a contest, at least for the year since he started at Bay Area Surgery. Dr. Goodwin was actually not aware of the video surveillance system.

Noncompliance with policy can sometimes result in being penalized. However, no one had recently been "written up" for hand hygiene noncompliance. For example, on two occasions, I saw clinical staff not wash their hands after touching patient surroundings outside the patient zone. Despite me watching them, they were not compliant with the hand hygiene protocol. According to a medical tech named Will Gray, Graham does not emphasize teamwork or seek any input from staff on ideas for improving patient safety. Gray told me that when someone makes a mistake, Graham will micromanage them. Graham tends to make all the decisions, and employees must simply follow his directives or instructions.

When I explained Graham's approach to leadership, Edna said, "Pizza parties seem a bit daft, but whatever works."

Westside Surgery (Location 3)

At Westside Surgery, I joined the center administrator, Andrea Acharya, and other leaders for a series of meetings on a variety of topics. Acharya told me that she delegated responsibility among her team to gain buy-in. According to Acharya, they hold many meetings to ensure deliberation and shared decision-making. Acharya told me that she considered herself a facilitator between members of the group to create a respectful environment for solving complex issues. She thought that consensus led to better decisions.

The staff really love the teamwork at Westside Surgery. They usually prioritize issues as a group, which really invites collective engagement. However, according to surgeon Agnes Mason, the constant deliberation makes the pace of change very slow. Still, once they commit to an issue the team pulls together to solve it. However, I learned from nurses, Tia Arroyo and Darrin Abbott, that hand hygiene has not been a discussion point for many, many months. Neither were aware of the hand hygiene video compliance assessment. This lack of awareness was apparent, as on several instances, I saw nurses not washing their hands before touching a patient.

Edna told me, "If you leave the hand hygiene leadership to Acharya, then it could take donkey's years to fix."

Premier Day Surgery Center (Location 4)

The Premier Day Surgery Center administrative assistant told me that I had to "go through the right channels" to set up a meeting with the administrator. What she meant is that I had to ask my boss to set a meeting for me. Apparently, a manager title was not sufficient, so my director had to personally request that the administrator, Bob Watson, meet with me. I learned from Watson that his staff follow rules and regulations set by the corporate office. When I pointed out that the hand hygiene compliance of Premier had declined over the last 6 months, he was very surprised, stating that "the corporate Director of Quality had not mentioned anything to him." When I mentioned the issue with increasing SSIs, he stated he was reviewing the policies and procedures with his staff, and that he planned to roll out a plan of action once he received feedback on best practices and approval from the corporate office. None of the staff would meet with me, stating that I needed to speak with their boss about these matters.

Apollo Surgery Services (Location 5)

Susan Page, the administrator for Apollo Surgery Services was not happy when I shared the hand hygiene compliance chart with her. She said that she was embarrassed at the number, blamed the previous Director of Quality and my current boss. She also wanted to know the names of the five lowest scorers for hand hygiene. After reluctantly giving her the names, Page invited all five employees (Allen French, Desiree Davis, Lloyd Alexander, Jessie Woods, and Damon Klein) into the conference room so that she could berate them in front of me. It was awkward and humiliating! Page assured me that the rates would return to compliant levels or that "certain people would not be working at Apollo much longer." I left Apollo so embarrassed that I did not get a chance to speak with the staff about hand hygiene.

Edna told me that she didn't blame me for leaving the center without interviewing staff when "Page threw a wobbly."

Whatley Surgical Associates (Location 6)

Whatley Surgical Associates administrator, Travis Stone, was surprised that the hand hygiene compliance scores were declining so far. He admitted that the staff were actually more knowledgeable than he was at patient safety issues, and that staff are expected to solve problems on their own. Because of this, Stone seemed to be blaming the staff for not complying with the hand hygiene protocols.

The Whatley staff told me that they got very little guidance from the administrator on hand hygiene initiatives or anything else, really. Nurse Dianna Garner told me that the staff were provided a set of P&P binders with all of the policies and procedures in them. However, another staff member, Christy Riley, had never heard about the P&P binders. Clark Thomas, a med tech, told me that Stone was never seen during operating hours; instead he was usually working in his office. A nurse, Kendra Byrd, told me that Stone seemed unconcerned about patient safety, compared to other organizations where she had worked. Also, if good things happen at the center, such as a patient letter of appreciation, Stone did not recognize the efforts of team members which was done at other medical centers.

When I told Edna about the administrator's leadership style, she said, "Sounds like Mr. Stone is a few sandwiches short of a picnic."

DISCUSSION QUESTIONS

1. Describe the leadership styles at each of the ambulatory surgery center locations. Are some leadership styles more effective than others at affecting patient safety?

2. What are the consequences to patient safety of creating a punitive culture? How would you recommend creating a just culture (nonpunitive) throughout Surgical Care Associates?

3. How should Samantha Myers, the director of the Healthcare Quality and Safety, and Jerry Simons, the manager, Infection Prevention and Employee Health, hold the administrators accountable for hand hygiene compliance?

4. How would you recommend collaborating with clinical staff to improve hand hygiene compliance at Surgical Care Associates?

5. Describe how the mentorship of Edna O'Donnell supports Jerry Simons's career.

 ## PODCAST FOR CASE 14

Listen to how experts approach the topic (you can access the podcast by following this url to Springer Publishing Company Connect™: https://connect.springerpub.com/content/book/978-0-8261-4514-7/front-matter/fmatter2)

REFERENCES

Armellino, D., Hussain, E., Schilling, M. E., Senicola, W., Eichorn, A., Dlugacz, Y., & Farber, B. F. (2011). Using high-technology to enforce low-technology safety measures: The use of third-party remote video auditing and real-time feedback in healthcare. *Clinical Infectious Diseases, 54*(1), 1-7. doi:10.1093/cid/cir773

Berríos-Torres, S. I., Umscheid, C. A., Bratzler, D. W., Leas, B., Stone, E. C., Kelz, R. R.,…Dellinger, E. P. (2017). Centers for Disease Control and Prevention guideline for the prevention of surgical site infection, 2017. *JAMA Surgery, 152*(8), 784-791. doi:10.1001/jamasurg.2017.0904

FURTHER READING

Laureani, A., & Antony, J. (2019). Leadership and Lean Six Sigma: A systematic literature review. *Total Quality Management & Business Excellence, 30*(1-2), 53-81. doi:10.1080/14783363.2017.1288565

McLean, H. S., Carriker, C., & Bordley, W. C. (2017). Good to great: Quality-improvement initiative increases and sustains pediatric health care worker hand hygiene compliance. *Hospital Pediatrics, 7*, 189-196. doi:10.1542/hpeds.2016-0110

Sax, H., Allegranzi, B., Chraïti, M. N., Boyce, J., Larson, E., & Pittet, D. (2009). The World Health Organization hand hygiene observation method. *American Journal of Infection Control, 37*(10), 827-834. doi:10.1016/j.ajic.2009.07.003

Sfantou, D., Laliotis, A., Patelarou, A., Sifaki-Pistolla, D., Matalliotakis, M., & Patelarou, E. (2017, October). Importance of leadership style towards quality of care measures in healthcare settings: A systematic review. *Healthcare, 5*(4), 73. doi:10.3390/healthcare5040073

Speroff, T., Nwosu, S., Greevy, R., Weinger, M. B., Talbot, T. R., Wall, R. J.,…Englebright, J. (2010). Organisational culture: Variation across hospitals and connection to patient safety climate. *BMJ Quality & Safety, 19*(6), 592-596. doi:10.1136/qshc.2009.039511

World Health Organization. (2009). *WHO guidelines on hand hygiene in health care: First global patient safety challenge clean care is safer care*. Geneva, Switzerland: Author. Retrieved from https://www.ncbi.nlm.nih.gov/books/NBK144036

THE 5-WHY? METHOD

One of the most important and useful questions in quality management is "why?". When trying to improve a process, you must first seek to understand it by asking questions. To understand why a certain process is carried out a certain way or by certain people or roles, you must ask "why?". The first reply, however, is seldom a satisfactory one, especially if you are trying to identify the root cause of the problem and solve it permanently. Asking "why?" multiple times allows you and the team members to go beyond the superficial answers (usually, just excuses) to find the real reasons why things happened.

The 5-Why? method encourages you to ask "why?" repeatedly until you are satisfied you have arrived at the root cause. It is worth mentioning that we do not mean you must ask "why?" exactly five times each time. Sometimes you might be satisfied after just four "whys" and other times, you may need to go seven or eight "whys."

Let us look at an example. Let us say that a patient's medication dose information is found to be wrong. A 5-Why? analysis of this issue might look like this:

1. Why is the patient's medication dose wrong?
   The previous nurse did not update the dose information.
2. Why did the previous nurse not change the dose?
   The doctor's order had gone to the pharmacy and the medication administration record (MAR) was not updated.
3. Why wasn't the MAR updated?
   The MAR is updated only once per day.
4. Why is the MAR updated only once per day?
   Updating the MAR more than once per day uses a lot of resources and it is not efficient to do so.
5. Why does updating the MAR take so many resources?
   Actually, this is not true anymore! The process was constructed a decade ago, when our information technology infrastructure was a lot slower. We can probably update it more often now!

It is worth noticing that the first few replies were placing blame on people. This is very often the case! Hint: If the answer is blaming someone, you have not found the root cause; keep asking "why?".

Remember to conduct your 5-Why? analysis with respect. As mentioned earlier, respect is one of the core tenets of quality improvement. When asking "why?" repeatedly, do not do it in a confrontational manner, but with a genuine desire to understand and learn.

CASE 15: A Warning Letter From the State Regulator

1. Describe the patient safety and quality improvement oversight of the government within the long-term care industry.
2. Demonstrate opportunities for patient misidentification in care processes in skilled nursing facilities.
3. Summarize a near miss reporting system and program.
4. Evaluate a just culture environment in healthcare.
5. Appraise organization's leadership effort to promote positive relationships and facilitate conflict resolution.

INTRODUCTION

Long-term care consists of a wide range of services, from providing lower acuity assistance in patients' homes to managing complex medical conditions in skilled nursing facilities (SNFs). Government regulations require long-term care facilities to comply with licensing standards, as determined by federal and state regulators, to keep patients safe from harm. SNFs obtain certification from state regulatory agencies, such as Arkansas's Office of Long Term Care (OLTC) in this case study, which conduct thorough compliance and quality of care surveys and audits of facilities. SNF certification is also subject to the Centers for Medicare and Medicaid Services (CMS) approval to provide skilled nursing services to Medicare beneficiaries. Sandywood Nursing Home is an SNF in Little Rock, Arkansas with an average daily census of 82 patients over the last 12 months.

CASE SCENARIO

The following is an email exchange between Lester Young, the Administrator for Sandywood Nursing Home, Sharon Barton, the Director of Nursing, and Tara Smith, the Quality and Risk Manager, regarding a Warning Letter from the Arkansas Department of Human Services, Division of Medical Service, OLTC.

Young, Lester

From: Young, Lester
Sent: Wednesday, April 3, 2019, 7:52 AM
To: Barton, Sharon; Smith, Tara
Subject: FW: Warning Letter from Arkansas OLTC
Sharon and Tara,

As expected, we got the warning letter from the OLTC. Fortunately, our licensure has not been revoked or suspended. However, we must create a Plan of Correction within 30 days. Please review the attached and develop our Plan of Correction immediately. Meanwhile, I will be notifying our Board of Directors.—Lester

Attachment:

Tuesday, April 2, 2019

Lester Young, CNHA, Administrator

Sandywood Nursing Home

3014 Eldersford Rd.

Little Rock, AR 72212

   Re: WL No. 24-56-RO-359 Sandywood Nursing Home, Little Rock, AR

Mr. Young,

The Arkansas Department of Human Services, Division of Medical Service, Office of Long Term Care (OLTC or Office) has reason to believe that Sandywood Nursing Home (120 licensed beds) may be in violation of the federal regulation 42 CFR 483.13 and state law Ark. Code Ann. § 5-28-101 et seq. and 12-12-501 et seq., pursuant to Ark. Code Administrative Procedures Act Arkansas Statute Annotated §5-713. This letter is not a case decision. OLTC requests that you respond within 30 days of the date of this letter with a Plan of Correction.

OBSERVATIONS AND LEGAL REQUIREMENTS

On March 17, 2019, OLTC staff conducted a formal survey of Sandywood Nursing Home (Sandywood). File and license issuance documents were reviewed. Sandywood staff interviews were conducted, and the full interview transcript is available upon request. The following describe Sandywood staff's factual observations and identify the applicable legal requirements.

   #1 Observation: Two days after admission to Sandywood, 80-year-old Leland Mayer was hospitalized after choking on solid food. Mr. Mayer was served solid rather than pureed food despite being categorized as an individual at high risk of choking. Mr. Mayer suffered from dementia, which can cause swallowing problems, and he had ceased wearing his dentures. Mr. Mayer's medical records contained all of the care instructions, including a label on his medical record that explicitly stated that he could not have solid food. The Licensed Practical Nurse (LPN) who delivered the meal to Mr. Mayer did not confirm the order with the dietetic service supervisor or Mr. Mayer. Sandywood reported this incident to OLTC within the next business day, consistent with OLTC Regulation 306.1, federal regulation 42 CFR 483.13 and state law Ark. Code Ann. § 5-28-101 et seq. and 12-12-501 et seq.

   #2 Observation: Based on interviews and chart reviews, the survey findings include thirteen (13) additional dietary errors or near misses at Sandywood over the last 12 months. Among these, three (3) dietary errors were not reported, pursuant to OLTC Regulation 306.3, as an incident involving accident or injury to residents reportable within five (5)

(continued)

(*continued*)

days after discovery. In each of these dietary-related error instances, residents experienced allergic reactions, even though their medical charts noted the patients' allergies. Neither instance resulted in apparent patient harm. Sandywood's written policies and procedures, pursuant to 42 CFR 483.13 and state law Ark. Code Ann. § 5-28-101 et seq. and 12-12-501 et seq., were developed and implemented, but not followed by staff.

#3 Observation: Based on interviews and chart reviews, the survey findings include eleven (11) medication errors or near misses at Sandywood over the last 12 months. Among these, two (2) medication errors were not reported, pursuant to OLTC Regulation 306.3, as an incident involving accident or injury to residents reportable within five (5) days after discovery. On one of these occasions, the medication of a similarly named patient was delivered to the wrong patient. In the other instance, the wrong medication was delivered to an 85-year-old Cantonese-speaking woman, instead of her 79-year-old Cantonese-speaking roommate. Neither instance resulted in apparent patient harm. Sandywood's written policies and procedures, pursuant to 42 CFR 483.13 and state law Ark. Code Ann. § 5-28-101 et seq. and 12-12-501 et seq., were developed and implemented, but not followed by staff.

#4 Observation: Based on interviews and chart reviews, the survey findings include six (6) patients wrongly transferred to radiology for diagnostic testing at Sandywood. These instances of patient misidentification were documented in the charts. In three (3) of these instances, radiological diagnostic tests were performed on the wrong patient, but were not reported pursuant to OLTC Regulation 306.3 as an incident involving accident or injury to residents reportable within five (5) days after discovery. Sandywood's written policies and procedures, pursuant to 42 CFR 483.13 and state law Ark. Code Ann. § 5-28-101 et seq. and 12-12-501 et seq., were developed and implemented, but not followed by staff.

ENFORCEMENT AUTHORITY

Violations of these regulations shall be punishable in accordance with Ark. Code Ann. § 20-10-1407 and 20-10-1408.

FUTURE ACTIONS

Please respond with a Plan of Correction in writing to OLTC within 30 days of the date of this letter. The Plan of Correction should detail the actions you have taken or will be taking to ensure compliance with state law and regulations. If corrective action will take longer than 90 days to complete, you may be asked to sign a Letter of Agreement with the Office to formalize the Plan of Correction and schedule. It is OLTC policy that appropriate, timely corrective action undertaken in response to a Warning Letter will avoid adversarial enforcement proceedings and the assessment of civil charges or penalties.

Please advise us if you dispute any of the observations recited herein or if there is other information of which OLTC should be aware. In the event that discussions with

(*continued*)

(continued)

OLTC staff do not lead to a satisfactory conclusion concerning the contents of this letter, you may elect to participate in OLTC's Informal Dispute Resolution (IDR) process with the Long Term Care Facility Advisory Board, governed by Act 1108 of 2003, codified at Ark. Code Ann. § 20-10-1901 et seq. The request for an informal dispute resolution of deficiencies does not stay the requirement for submission of an acceptable Plan of Correction within the required time frame or the implementation of any remedy, and does not substitute for an appeal. For IDR process, please ask the OLTC contact listed below or make a written request to the Arkansas Department of Health, Health Facility Services, 5800 West 10th, Suite 400, Little Rock, AR 72204 within ten calendar days of the receipt of this Warning Letter from the OLTC.

Your contact at OLTC in this matter is Jae Bender. Please direct written materials to her attention. If you have questions or wish to arrange a meeting, you may reach her directly at (501) 555-1452 or Jae.Bender@oltc.arkansas.gov.

Sincerely,

Kaitlin Parry

cc: Case File; Jae Bender

Barton, Sharon

From: Barton, Sharon
Sent: Wednesday, April 3, 2019 8:02 AM
To: Young, Lester
Cc: Smith, Tara
Subject: RE: FW: Warning Letter from Arkansas OLTC

Mr. Young—I will have to take some time to review our files to confirm the OLTC findings. As the Director of Nursing, I can say that my LPNs are following our policies and procedures. I am not really sure if the OLTC findings are correct. Maybe they are, but maybe they're not. I will get back to you ASAP. Best, Sharon

Smith, Tara

From: Smith, Tara
Sent: Wednesday, April 3, 2019 8:12 AM
To: Young, Lester
Cc: Barton, Sharon
Subject: RE: RE: FW: Warning Letter from Arkansas OLTC

Lester—We knew this was coming, so I am not surprised. As the Quality & Risk Manager, I know the P&Ps are compliant as written. If they are not being followed, then we should check with Sharon. I will need to review the data in question. Can Sharon create reports to validate these findings? Can we meet to discuss? Thanks, Tara

Young, Lester

From: Young, Lester
Sent: Wednesday, April 3, 2019 9:04 AM
To: Smith, Tara
Cc: Barton, Sharon
Subject: RE: RE: RE: RE: FW: Warning Letter from Arkansas OLTC

Tara—It is not necessary to meet. You need to take the lead on developing the Plan of Correction. Yes, Sharon should create the reports you need. Please have a draft to me by Friday. I will manage the Board of Directors.—Lester

Smith, Tara

From: Smith, Tara
Sent: Wednesday, April 3, 2019 9:12 AM
To: Young, Lester
Cc: Barton, Sharon
Subject: RE: RE: RE: RE: RE: FW: Warning Letter from Arkansas OLTC

Lester—This needs to be a team effort. I have our relevant policies and procedures, but I need the data from nursing. Also, I need to meet with LPNs who report to Tara. The responsibility for the errors lies with Sharon and her nurses. I think we should look at how we can "idiot proof" the processes.—Tara

Barton, Sharon

From: Barton, Sharon
Sent: Wednesday, April 3, 2019 9:14 AM
To: Smith, Tara; Young, Lester
Subject: RE: RE: RE: RE: RE: RE: FW: Warning Letter from Arkansas OLTC

Tara—I told you that I would give you the reports. I don't appreciate your suggestion that my nurses are idiots. I can make my staff available to your project, if appropriate. I think we should find a way to better manage the quality and risk issues. First, I suggest you review your P&Ps to confirm your assertions. Also, your department should review the request I made for wristband bar code/RFID technologies.—Sharon

Young, Lester

From: Young, Lester
Sent: Wednesday, April 3, 2019 9:17 AM
To: Smith, Tara
Cc: Barton, Sharon
Subject: RE: RE: RE: RE: RE: RE: RE: FW: Warning Letter from Arkansas OLTC

Tara and Sharon—Perhaps we should meet. I will set something up for later today.—Les

DISCUSSION QUESTIONS

1. In what way could the Administrator enhance a more collaborative relationship between the Director of Nursing and the Quality and Risk Manager?

2. How should the Administrator address the performance shortfalls to encourage accountability?

3. Could the Sandywood Nursing Home team improve its management of the quality issues addressed by OLTC? If the Warning Letter was anticipated, how could have the team prepared?

4. What could Sandywood Nursing Home do to support a just culture (nonpunitive) reporting environment for identifying unsafe practices?

5. What processes should be implemented to assure prompt reporting of potential liability by staff?

6. What role does qualitative and quantitative measurement have in identifying and improving patient safety in this case?

 ## PODCAST FOR CASE 15

Listen to how experts approach the topic (you can access the podcast by following this url to Springer Publishing Company Connect™: https://connect.springerpub.com/content/book/978-0-8261-4514-7/front-matter/fmatter2)

FURTHER READING

ECRI Institute. (2016). *Patient identification errors.* Retrieved from https://www.ecri.org/Resources/HIT/Patient%20ID/Patient_Identification_Evidence_Based_Literature_final.pdf

Rahman, M., Norton, E. C., & Grabowski, D. C. (2016). Do hospital-owned skilled nursing facilities provide better post-acute care quality? *Journal of Health Economics, 50,* 36–46. doi:10.1016/j.jhealeco.2016.08.004

Southard, P. B., Chandra, C., & Kumar, S. (2012). RFID in healthcare: A Six Sigma DMAIC and simulation case study. *International Journal of Health Care Quality Assurance, 25*(4), 291–321. doi:10.1108/09526861211221491

Ursprung, R., Gray, J. E., Edwards, W. H., Horbar, J. D., Nickerson, J., Plsek, P.,...& Goldmann, D. A. (2005). Real time patient safety audits: Improving safety every day. *BMJ Quality & Safety, 14*(4), 284–289. doi:10.1136/qshc.2004.012542

TOOLS AND APPROACHES

POKA-YOKE

Poka-yoke is a mistake-proofing device or procedure to prevent a defect from occurring (Womack & Jones, 1996). Poka-yoke is about making it impossible to make a mistake.

When we create or own processes that allow people to make mistakes, we are not showing respect for people, which is one of the core principles of quality management. When you give broken processes to team members to carry out their daily work, you are disrespecting their expertise and their passion to heal people. You should create processes that make it impossible for people to make mistakes.

A common reaction in healthcare when someone makes a mistake is to discipline them, up to and including termination. For practitioners and experts of healthcare quality management, you know that the correct action is to look at the process and see where the breakdown occurred in order to modify the process to make sure that does not happen again.

One of the more prominent examples of poka-yoke in healthcare is bar coding (Figure C15.1). Laboratories have been labeling specimens with barcodes for decades now, to eliminate mistakes in specimen identification and eliminate instances where specimens are lost or misplaced. In more recent times, admitted patients get an arm band with a barcode that is used every time medications are to be administered or procedures performed.

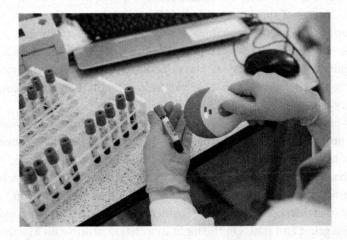

FIGURE C15.1 Specimen barcoding is an example of poka-yoke.
Source: Sergiophoto/Shutterstock.

REFERENCE

Womack, J. P., & Jones, D. T. (1996). *Lean thinking: Banish waste and create wealth in your corporation.* New York, NY: Simon & Schuster.

CASE 16: Failure-to-Rescue

INTRODUCTION

When Chief Nursing Officer (CNO) Roseann Martin was first hired to improve patient care at Lipton Regional Medical Center (LRMC), a small 150-bed community hospital in Georgia, she focused her considerable energies on decreasing the high mortality rate. Unfortunately, less than a month after Martin started her new job, a patient death occurred that should have been prevented. At first, the patient's unnecessary death angered Martin. Then, after she was summoned as a defendant in a malpractice lawsuit filed by the patient's family, she was overcome with feelings of shock and disbelief. Her resolve to conduct root cause analyses, create interventions, and study their impact was replaced by anxiety and a self-defeating impulse to blame everyone else involved in the event. Martin knew that nurses at the bedside need to recognize changes in patient status because their condition may unexpectedly intensify. Delays in response mean that the worsening condition may be recognized too late leading to injury or death (Garvey, 2015).

The 59-year-old Mary Logan was diagnosed with Stage IV Lung Cancer, which meant that the illness was probably terminal within a matter of months. When she had been admitted to LRMC the first time, she became a staff favorite. Logan believed she would "beat the damn cancer and be back at work in no time." At various times, her grown children had visited her in the Georgia hospital from all over the country, including Chicago (son and daughter), New York City (daughter), and Florida (daughter). Her children were scared, though, because she looked gaunt and frail. On the night in question, a nurse on Martin's team waited unacceptably long to respond to the serious cardiac distress of Mrs. Logan, and then the team unsuccessfully attempted to resuscitate her.

Later, the episode was classified by the investigating panel and confirmed by The Joint Commission as a failure-to-rescue adverse event. Failure-to-rescue occurs when clinicians ineffectively monitor the signs and symptoms of a worsening patient condition and fail to take proper action to stabilize the patient (Thielen, 2014). As a key quality indicator, the failure-to-rescue measure reflects an organization's overall ability to successfully "rescue" patients after complications. Failure-to-rescue is measured as the conditional probability of death after a complication or the observed ("O") divided by the expected ("E") mortality (Reddy et al., 2013).

The year Martin began as CNO, LRMC reported an unacceptably high O/E ratio of 2.5. In addition, their discharge rate for "Code Blue" alerts, 10.4 per 1,000, was far above the national benchmark of 4 per 1,000 discharges. Code Blue is the term for the announcements made over the public address system that a patient is in need of immediate attention. These out-of-line performance measures led to deep scrutiny from the Board of Trustees, local media, and community.

Almost 12 months after Mary Logan's death, Martin arrived at the law offices of Littler, Mendelsohn, and Lowe for questioning by the Logan family's attorney. A majority of medical malpractice cases are resolved before trial in a legal process known as "discovery" (Miller, 2018). In malpractice cases, the discovery phase usually serves to help each side decide how to settle the case, such as how much money in damages to negotiate. The questioning under sworn testimony to determine the facts of the case is called "deposition." Unlike questioning at trial which must adhere to the facts of the case, questioning at deposition can also pertain to all aspects of one's career and personal life (Miller, 2018).

Timothy Lowe, the attorney representing the Logan family, wore an obvious toupee and an expensive suit. The video camera was rolling and CNO Roseann Martin sat composed and elegant in the drab law firm conference room. The paralegal read the introduction of the deposition citing details, such as case number, date, address, and people present. The following documentation is the transcript of the deposition.

CASE SCENARIO

Spivey: Good afternoon, I am Joe Spivey, the paralegal for Littler, Mendelsohn, and Lowe. It is 11:04 on May 31, 2021. The case number is X52-8539. Also present for this video-recorded deposition is Timothy Lowe, partner of Littler, Mendelsohn, and Lowe, the plaintiff's attorney representing the Logan family in the medical malpractice wrongful death case against Lipton Regional Medical Center. The person being deposed this morning is Roseann Martin of Lipton Regional Medical Center. She is represented by her attorney, Jim Turley, also in attendance.

Lowe: Good afternoon, Ms. Martin. Have you ever been deposed before?

Martin: No, this is my first time, Mr. Lowe.

Lowe: You can call me Tim. That's okay, this is a relatively straightforward process. We are going to cover three basic topics then you can get back to your important work at the hospital. First, I want to get the basics on your background and education. Then, I will ask about some basic definitions regarding medical care. Finally, I want to understand the communication among team members at the hospital. Does that sound good to you?

Martin: Yes.

Lowe: Can you tell me about your background in nursing?

Martin: I am a Registered Nurse with a Bachelor of Science in Nursing degree from Texas Women's University. I also have a Master of Science in Nursing from the University of Texas at Austin. I have practiced for 32 years. I became the Chief Nursing Officer of Lipton Regional Medical Center on April 1st of last year.

Lowe: What is the role of the Chief Nursing Officer?

Martin: The CNO is in charge of all the nursing care at the hospital. I oversee the patient care programs, nursing staffing and budgets, new patient service development, quality management activities, and nursing policies and procedures. As a member of the senior management team, I report directly to the Chief Executive Officer and participate in strategic and operational decision-making. I represent nursing services in Board of Trustees meetings.

Lowe: Ms. Martin, you would agree that patient safety is your highest priority?

Martin: Yes, I would agree with that.

Lowe: Can you tell me about Stage IV Lung Cancer, the diagnosis for which the late Mary Logan was admitted to Lipton Regional Medical Center?

Martin: In Stage IV, the cancer has metastasized beyond the lungs.

Lowe: Metastasized means spread into other areas of the body, right?

Martin: Yes.

Lowe: Did you know that Mary worked in a factory when she was younger and was exposed to carcinogenic materials thus leaving her with this terminal illness?

Martin: I was aware of the prognosis, but not the cause.

Lowe: And, why was she admitted to Lipton Regional Medical Center that day?

Martin: Mrs. Logan presented to the hospital with nausea and vomiting while being treated with chemotherapy.

Lowe: Did you know Mary Logan?

Martin: Actually, I did. I got to know Mary on her previous admissions. I thought Mary was in remission. I learned later that she had restarted chemotherapy because the tumor was getting larger. I was surprised when I learned that a Code Blue had been called on Mary and that she had died.

Lowe: Let's not get ahead of ourselves, dear. To which hospital unit was Mrs. Logan admitted?

Martin: Mrs. Logan was admitted to a Medical Surgical Telemetry unit, 9 South, room 972. She was having irregular heartbeats, so her physician ordered telemetry to monitor her cardiac status.

Lowe: Mary was in good spirits when she arrived to the hospital, wasn't she? She believed she will beat cancer and soon return to work, right?

Turley: I'm going to object to the question, but you can go ahead and answer, if you know.

Martin: I don't know.

Lowe: Here's where your medical knowledge would be important to an old lawyer like me. Help me understand what ST elevations on an electrocardiogram are?

Martin: The electrocardiogram, sometimes called the ECG or EKG, records the electrical activity of the heart with electrodes placed on the skin. On the Med-Surg Telemetry unit on 9 South, we remotely monitor the heart activity data. An ST elevation refers to when the ECG shows that the electrical feedback in the contraction phase is abnormally high above the baseline. It could mean that there is clinically significant injury to the muscular tissue of the heart.

Lowe: Thank you. You explained that superbly. I can understand why you are the CNO. Let's see. What is a lethal dysrhythmia?

Martin: Cardiac dysrhythmia is an abnormal heart beat. Lethal, in this case, meant that the ST segment elevation indicated a myocardial infarction, or heart attack. This is called a STEMI, or ST segment elevation myocardial infarction. This heart attack becomes lethal when it results in cardiac arrest. The heart stops beating.

Lowe: Can you tell me about the staff caring for Mary Logan on the evening in question?

Martin: The unit Mary was admitted to is a large unit with very young, new, and enthusiastic nurses.

Lowe: By young, you mean inexperienced?

Martin: Yes.

Lowe: You already agreed that patient safety is your highest priority. Why doesn't Lipton Regional Medical Center hire more experienced nurses?

Martin: Nurse staffing can be very challenging. Hiring new graduate RNs has its benefits and drawbacks.

Lowe: What do you mean by benefits and drawbacks?

Martin: Excuse me. Jim, do I have to answer that?

Turley: Yes, you do. Mr. Lowe, I am advising my client to answer only the questions you pose.

Martin: By benefits, I mean that they are recently trained in the most current nursing care theory and practice.

Lowe: Don't you mean that young nurses are cheaper for the hospital to hire?

Martin: No, that's not what I mean.

Lowe: What do you mean by drawbacks?

Martin: Um, younger nurses often need additional supervision and training.

Lowe: I see. We'll get back to training, dear. Who was the staff caring for Mary Logan?

Turley: Mr. Lowe, my client can't be expected to cite that from memory. Surely, you have the list of personnel already provided to you by Lipton?

Lowe: Fair enough. Brenda Davidson was the Unit Nursing Director that evening?

Martin: Yes.

Lowe: Brenda Davidson told us that safety issues are related to years of experience of the nurses.

Martin: Safety issues are multifactorial.

Lowe: So you are disputing the fact presented by your unit nurse, Brenda Davidson?

Martin: No, I am disputing your oversimplification, Mr. Lowe.

Lowe: The charge nurse that night was Susan Honaker, an RN with 15 years of experience. She told us that the nightshift nurse responsible for Mrs. Logan's care, Celine Baron, was a newly hired novice nurse that had difficulty speaking up.

Martin: Celine Baron was 6 months off orientation. I am not sure about Susan's generalization, but Celine did not speak up that day.

Lowe: Dr. Christopher Rush was the third year resident physician that day, yes?

Martin: Yes.

Lowe: The Certified Nursing Assistant working that evening Howard Judson?

Martin: Yes, the Certified Nursing Assistant—we call them Patient Care Technicians or PCTs—was working that night.

Lowe: Do you remember Howard Judson's background?

Martin: I think Howard had just started with Lipton 4 months after finishing his CNA certificate.

Lowe: Okay, one last person—the Monitor Tech Simon Shaw. Can you tell me what Simon Shaw does?

Martin: A Certified Cardiac Monitor Telemetry Technician monitors the heart rhythm patterns of patients to detect abnormal variations. So, Simon's main job is to immediately notify the nurse of abnormality in heart rhythms seen on the cardiac monitor. If the nurse caring for that patient is unavailable, the monitor technician should call a Rapid Response Immediately and allow all staff to go to the patient room and identify any change in condition based on the cardiac rhythm.

Lowe: Okay, I will ask you some questions about communication at Lipton Regional Medical Center on the night that Mary Logan died. When did Simon Shaw the Monitor Tech notice the ST elevation in Mary Logan?

Martin: I learned through the course of our internal investigation that Simon called 9 South at about 11:30 p.m.

Lowe: Simon called 9 South from his remote telemetry lab. So, Simon spoke to the nurse caring for Mrs. Logan?

Martin: No. The PCT happened to be in patient room 972 at the time. So, the Monitor Tech told Howard about the ST elevation.

Lowe: Hmm, the Monitor Tech told the PCT about the abnormal heart beat. Do PCTs, or patient care technicians, have authority to make medical decisions on their own?

Martin: No, a PCT has authority to provide basic medical treatments.

Lowe: Is it the Lipton Regional Medical Center policy for the Monitor Tech to tell the nurse on duty directly?

Martin: Yes.

Lowe: I see. So Howard told the nurse, Celine Baron, about the ST elevations immediately?

Martin: No, Howard continued his work in patient room 972, then shared the information from the Monitor Tech's phone call with Celine about 20 minutes later.

Lowe: Okay. The Monitor Tech did not speak directly to the nurse. Then there was a delay of 20 minutes before the nurse was told about the change in Mary Logan's condition by the Certified Cardiac Monitor Telemetry Technician. After Celine was finally told, did she immediately go to check on Mrs. Logan?

Martin: No, Celine finished giving medications in room 976. Then it was after about a half hour that Celine stopped at Mary's room and asked from the doorway to her room if she felt okay. Mary replied that she felt fine, just tired. Celine said that she would be back in an hour to check on her.

Lowe: Okay. So another delay of 30 minutes or so?

Martin: Yes.

Lowe: Before I ask you what happened next, I want to get back to the training issue you brought up earlier. Had Lipton educated nurses about the escalation procedure?

Martin: We conduct periodic trainings in the escalation procedure. We have a policy document outlining the principles and protocols for escalating care for patients whose condition is deteriorating. Nurses are trained on this policy.

Lowe: What are escalation triggers?

Martin: Triggers are abnormalities in physiological observation measurements that require an escalation of care according to clinical protocol.

Lowe: So, the goal is to respond to a spark before it becomes a forest fire. Had Nurse Celine been trained in escalation triggers?

Martin: We have annual in-service trainings on escalations, including the trigger system.

Lowe: You are not answering my question. Had Nurse Celine been trained in escalation triggers?

Martin: I don't know. We have a schedule of in-service trainings on a variety of topics.

Lowe: Again, you already agreed that patient safety is your highest priority. Would it surprise you to learn that Celine Baron had not been trained in Lipton's escalation policy?

Martin: No. Celine was a very new hire, so it is possible that she had not yet received that in-service training topic.

Lowe: At the time of Mary Logan's death, did Lipton Regional Medical Center conduct mock Rapid Response trainings?

Martin: No.

Lowe: Mrs. Martin, what is a Modified Early Warning System or MEWS?

Martin: MEWS is the standard clinical protocol that uses routine physiological measurements and observations to identify patients at risk. Members of the care team, with the appropriate skills, knowledge, and experience, respond as soon as patients at risk are identified.

Lowe: At the time of Mary Logan's death, did Lipton Regional Medical Center have a Modified Early Warning System policy?

Martin: No.

Lowe: Mrs. Martin, what is the consequence of not having a Modified Early Warning System policy in place?

Martin: In theory, nurses would be less capable of recognizing triggers for escalation of the Rapid Response team.

Lowe: Mrs. Martin, what is the consequence of not recognizing triggers for escalation?

Martin: Lower Rapid Response rates.

Lowe: Mrs. Martin, what is the consequence of Lower Rapid Response rates?

Martin: Higher number of Code Blue alerts.

Lowe: Mrs. Martin, what is the consequence of higher number of Code Blue alerts?

Martin: A higher failure-to-rescue rate for the hospital.

Lowe: What is failure-to-rescue?

Martin: Failure-to-rescue is the failure to prevent a deterioration in patient status, such as death or permanent disability, due to a complication of medical care.

Lowe: Okay then. Back to the night that Mary Logan unnecessarily died. What time was the Code Blue called?

Martin: I don't recall.

Lowe: It was 1:15 a.m. What happened when the Code Blue was called?

Martin: The Monitor Tech called the Code Blue because the patient was having a pulseless ventricular tachycardia. All of the nurses ran to room 972, Mary Logan's room, and found her unresponsive. The nurses conducted CPR for 25 minutes. Then, the resident physician Dr. Rush, came in and tried to help resuscitate Mary, but with no result.

Lowe: Mary was pronounced dead at 1:45 a.m.

Martin: I don't recall the time, but yes, she was pronounced dead.

Lowe: Susan Honaker told us that the night she answered a Code Blue was "scary, unforgettable, and traumatizing." What was your response? Finger-pointing? Blaming?

Martin: No. Sadness and a determination to prevent this from happening in the future.

Lowe: Yes, it is sad, but Mary Logan has no future. Speaking of futures, to your knowledge, has Celine Baron worked again as a nurse?

Martin: No, not to my knowledge. Sadly, adverse events like these can have a "second victim" where those involved in the incident experience stress, anxiety, depression, denial, and withdrawal.

Lowe: Sad, yes, but cold comfort to Mary Logan's grieving family. Anything else you want to tell us about your supposed commitment to patient safety?

Martin: No.

Lowe: Thank you for your time, Mrs. Martin.

DISCUSSION QUESTIONS

1. Was Celine Baron adequately trained to be on a cardiac floor? How do you know?
2. Do you think Lipton Regional Medical Center was liable to Mary Logan's family in this case? Why or why not?
3. What is the ideal escalation process in this instance? What mistakes were made by the Lipton staff?
4. What responsibility does the CNO Roseann Martin have in this case?
5. Did the CNO demonstrate a culture of safety, also called a "just culture," value system in this case?

PODCAST FOR CASE 16

Listen to how experts approach the topic (you can access the podcast by following this url to Springer Publishing Company Connect™: https://connect.springerpub.com/content/book/978-0-8261-4514-7/front-matter/fmatter2)

REFERENCES

Garvey, P. K. (2015). Failure to rescue: The nurse's impact. *MedSurg Nursing, 24*(3), 145–149. Retrieved from https://pdfs.semanticscholar.org/b89d/b007722a609e9caf71d2851a3664e2a9f3b0.pdf

Miller, L. A. (2018). Litigation in perinatal care: The disposition process. *The Journal of Perinatal & Neonatal Nursing, 32*(1), 53–58. doi:10.1097/JPN.0000000000000304

Reddy, H. G., Shih, T., Englesbe, M. J., Shannon, F. L., Theurer, P. F., Herbert, M. A.,...Prager, R. L. (2013). Analyzing "failure to rescue": Is this an opportunity for outcome improvement in cardiac surgery? *The Annals of Thoracic Surgery, 95*(6), 1976–1981. doi:10.1016/j.athoracsur.2013.03.027

Thielen, J. (2014). Failure to rescue as the conceptual basis for nursing clinical peer review. *Journal of Nursing Care Quality, 29*(2), 155–163. doi:10.1097/NCQ.0b013e3182a8df96

FURTHER READING

Aiken, L. H., Clarke, S. P., Cheung, R. B., Sloane, D. M., & Silber, J. H. (2003). Educational levels of hospital nurses and surgical patient mortality. *Journal of the American Medical Association, 290*(12), 1617–1623. doi:10.1001/jama.290.12.1617

Chan, P. S., Khalid, A., Longmore, L. S., Berg, R. A., Kosiborod, M., & Spertus, J. A. (2008). Hospital-wide code rates and mortality before and after implementation of a rapid response team. *Journal of the American Medical Association, 300*(21), 2506–2513. doi:10.1001/jama.2008.715

Franklin, C., & Mathew, J. (1994). Developing strategies to prevent inhospital cardiac arrest: Analyzing responses of physicians and nurses in the hours before the event. *Critical Care Medicine, 22*(2), 244–247. doi:10.1016/0300-9572(95)94133-T

Gould, D. (2007). Promoting patient safety: The rapid medical response team. *The Permanente Journal, 11*(3), 26. doi:10.7812/tpp/07-101

Larson, K., & Elliott, R. (2010). The emotional impact of malpractice. *Nephrology Nursing Journal, 37*(2), 153–156.

Seys, D., Scott, S., Wu, A., Van Gerven, E., Vleugels, A., Euwema, M.,...Vanhaecht, K. (2013). Supporting involved health care professionals (second victims) following an adverse health event: A literature review. *International Journal of Nursing Studies, 50*(5), 678–687. doi:10.1016/j.ijnurstu.2012.07.006

Wu, A. W. (2000). Medical error: The second victim: The doctor who makes the mistake needs help too. *BMJ: British Medical Journal, 320*(7237), 726. doi:10.1136/bmj.320.7237.726

ESCALATION

In a healthcare environment, life-and-death situations, where patient safety is the number one priority, demand immediate and decisive action. These complex and stressful situations, however, can cause confusion or inaction. It becomes necessary, then, for healthcare organizations to standardize procedures for how to deal with these situations. Escalation is a process by which different clinicians caring for a patient are made aware of any significant deterioration of the patient's condition.

A Lean quality principle called "stopping the line" in a Toyota manufacturing plant is similar to escalation. Healthcare workers are empowered to "stop the line" or stop the process to make sure an error is not going to occur. Once escalated, the accountable leader examines and resolves the problem. This approach encourages lower level staff to communicate issues to higher level executives, not as a challenge to the work of others, but to collaboratively ensure patient safety.

Any deterioration in the patient's condition should trigger a very prescriptive process of escalation to reach a clinician who can assess the patient's condition and recommend or perform treatment rapidly to avoid physical or permanent harm to the patient. This escalation procedure should clearly state:

- When the attending physician (the physician caring for the patient) should be contacted and how long to wait for a response

- When a Rapid Response Team should be called

- When the Chain of Command should be initiated and

- Who forms part of that Chain of Command (supervisor, unit director, Chief Nursing Officer, Chief Medical Officer, Administrator On-Call, et al.)

Once in place, healthcare organizations must continuously train team members on the standardized escalation procedures to ensure patient safety.

REFERENCE

Furman, C. (2005). Implementing a patient safety alert system. *Nursing Economics, 23*(1), 42–46.

CASE 17: CLIF's Medication Errors

1. Identify common causes and contributing factors of medication errors in the hospital setting.
2. Explain how to persuade stakeholders through the use of data, concrete examples, and visual aids.
3. Defend the implementation of the latest health information technology in order to promote wellness.
4. Evaluate the positive and negative consequences of health information technologies on the practice of healthcare quality management.
5. Identify expected and unexpected risks to patient safety associated with new technologies or changes in work processes.

INTRODUCTION

Nearly 5% of all hospitalized patients experience an adverse drug event (ADE), making them one of the most common types of inpatient safety issues in U.S. healthcare (Agency for Healthcare Research and Quality [AHRQ] Patient Safety Network, 2019; Hauck & Zhao, 2011). While some medication errors do not reach the patient (called "Potential ADEs" or "near misses"), thousands of preventable errors cause patient harm each year (AHRQ Patient Safety Network, 2019). Hospital staff, including pharmacists, nurses, physicians, and trainees of all professions, are trained to enter all ADEs—near misses, ADEs with no harm, and ADEs causing harm—into an incident reporting system.

Valley Health Hospital is a 204-bed teaching hospital with 250 medical staff and faculty and almost 2,000 employees. Valley Health Hospital is a part of Sequara Health, a health system with five other inpatient facilities, a myriad of imaging centers, nursing and assisted-living centers, outpatient campuses, home health, hospice, rehabilitation services, and two medical groups. The Sequara Chief Executive Officer, at the direction of the Sequara Health Board

▦ DATA FILE FOR CASE 17

Data files for students are available by accessing the following url: https://www.springerpub.com/hqm

The data file for Case 17 provides six months of reported medication errors, including patient information, harm scale, actions, contributing factors, medication, and detailed event descriptions.

of Directors, recently announced a $700 million investment in a new health information technology (HIT) platform that features artificial intelligence (AI)-enhanced clinical decision support system (CDSS). Valley Health Hospital must implement the system within 1 year—the year 2049.

At Valley Health Hospital, the four clinical pharmacists in the centralized inpatient pharmacy dispense approximately 2.5 million doses of medications annually. The hospital pharmacists face a complex set of responsibilities, including consultations to manage pharmacokinetics and other complex therapies, dispensing medication, making purchasing decisions, monitoring drug therapy, preparing IV medication, and supporting drug administration (Hawes, Maxwell, White, Mangun, & Lin, 2014).

The Valley Health Hospital Medication Operation Safety Team (MOST) meets each month to review all reported ADE incidents, including the near misses, no harm events, and medication errors causing patient harm. The MOST committee membership includes the Medical Director for Patient Safety, Director of Pharmacy, Medication Safety Nurse Manager, Clinical Educator, and five staff nurses from selected care areas, such as surgery and the ICU. The team conducts an investigation and analysis of each incident, including determining the root cause, developing corrective actions, and preventing similar future occurrences.

CASE SCENARIO

At his annual State of the Valley Health address to employees on July 16, 2048, Chief Executive Officer Jerry Westfall made a big announcement. The CEO's words hung in the air like a speech bubble from a comic strip. "CLIF will reduce medication errors," he said. Westfall was referring to the touted AI technology called the Clinical Learning Information Framework, affectionately known as "CLIF." This new AI-enhanced system was to be implemented by 2049. "The future is now," Westfall said.

At that moment, I was transported back in time to when I became Valley Health Hospital's Director of Pharmacy 25 years ago. In 2023, we implemented medication management systems with computerized physician order entry. In my flashback, I could imagine my younger self saying, *"These technologies have great potential to combat the shortcomings of manual medication systems and improve clinical decisions and patient outcomes."* Now that it was 2048, our health system was making an enormous bet on the AI technology. I wondered if 2023 was repeating itself in 2048, which was a terrible thought. I knew I needed to act fast, speak truth to power, and risk it all to save our patients from harm of healthcare AI.

Over my two and a half decades at Valley Health, many CEOs have come and gone; some good, some not so good, and all deeply ambitious. Westfall was 10 years my junior and a self-proclaimed "straight shooter." Although well-liked by most people at Valley Health, I thought of him as the typical alpha male. He tended to dominate the room with his oversized personality and prickly sarcasm. And yet, he connected to people through his gritty, working-class demeanor, strong work ethic, and positive, encouraging message. In his first 6 months on the job, he worked in every department and every unit, immersing himself in all hospital operations. His personal mythology included regular 80-hour work weeks and bloodhound-like ability to smell "bull." I doubted both as little more than a self-perpetuated legend, but agreed with the general consensus that Westfall was a good guy.

When I requested a meeting with Westfall's executive assistant, I was surprised that I was invited to lunch the very next week. On the day of our meeting, I found boxed lunches waiting for us on the conference room table. The simple food seemed out of place among the digital boardroom technology, such as the giant wall display, video conferencing, and tabletop controls. Westfall adjusted the smart windows that adjusted opacity of the glass looking out into the hospital lobby to give our meeting a more private feel.

Westfall asked me how the hospital had changed since I joined the pharmacy staff all those years ago. I shared my wonder at all the developments—some good (new patient tower), some bad (the terrible parking), and some everlasting (bad food). He asked me why I had remained in the same position for so long, a question that seemed to doubt my ambition. I said what I always say, that I love teaching the first year postgraduate pharmacy residents. This answer let me pivot to the reason I requested the meeting. Not wanting to seem like a scaremongering Luddite, I framed my concerns with CLIF in terms of pharmacy resident training and patient safety.

Westfall pushed back immediately. "The Clinical Learning Information Framework holds great promise for improving medication safety. We are fully committed to the value that CLIF can bring to Sequara Health hospitals," he said.

"I understand the organizational commitment, I just want us to consider the unintended consequences," I said.

Westfall delivered what sounded to me like a prepared speech. "With CLIF, we are leveraging our capacity in advanced data analytics. CLIF will collect millions of data points throughout our health system to develop risk predictors and treatment algorithms that do not necessarily require clinician participation, except in only the most difficult cases," Westfall said.

I said, "It sounds like you believe that CLIF's clinical ability is superior to that of our doctors, nurses, and pharmacists? I think you overestimate the performance of these technologies to …"

Westfall interrupted, "Actually, I think you are underestimating the upside of AI. Imagine how CLIF will improve patients' outcomes by telling clinicians, 'patients with these genetic markers, co-morbidities, and lab values did perform better with these medicines.' CLIF will be a better analytical thinker than our clinicians just by the sheer number of factors that can be considered at once. Is it possible that you are afraid of creating a super-intelligent machine that will threaten your role as a pharmacist?" Westfall smiled at this, trying to soften his mockery.

I laughed. "CLIF will not replace us. CLIF will change us—probably in unintended ways."

"Then maybe you think the CLIF will turn evil?" Westfall asked with a smirk.

"Look, Jerry, I don't see artificial intelligence as evil," I said. "I just want to respectfully push back on your notion that technology is necessarily virtuous. I think the truth is somewhere in between. We have to consider how we use CLIF, because technological interventions change us physically and mentally. As English zoologist and neurophysiologist JZ Young said almost 100 years ago, 'We create tools, and we mold ourselves through our use of them.'"

Westfall leaned in close to me. "CLIF will make many medication decisions better than we can—better drug treatment decisions, better drug selection decisions, better drug dosing decisions, better decisions regarding inventory management, not to mention better medication safety practices. Imagine a model that would predict whether an individual will or will not experience some adverse drug event," Westfall said.

"You're not listening to me, Jerry. What I am saying is that CLIF raises larger questions about the vulnerability of clinical and administrative operations created by our dependence on AI. What if CLIF diminishes clinician instincts leading them to accept inaccurate artificial intelligence? We need to train people to be suspicious that CLIF's predictions may be wrong. CLIF predicts, then the clinician explains and acts."

Westfall corrected me, "No, it's: CLIF presents decision, clinician confirms or denies. Then CLIF learns."

I shook my head. "Do you recall the advent of smartphones in the 2000s, Jerry? Did you notice that people's actual memory withered? Today, our voice-controlled communicators make memorization almost a lost skill. What's next? Will we fix our poor memories by implanting computers in our heads? Won't that aggravate the problem rather than solve it? The same applies to knowledge. If CLIF makes the diagnostic, therapeutic, and patient safety judgments for us, rather than us seeking understanding ourselves, we become lazy thinkers. The ability to use CLIF to identify particular drug–drug interactions, for example, is not the same as understanding the contexts around chemistry, physiology, and pharmacodynamics: that's where real knowledge comes in."

Westfall smiled and said, "I think we are saying the same thing. Based on data captured regarding millions of clinician experiences, CLIF will identify particular drug–drug interactions based on who is and who is not likely to experience particular adverse effects from a particular drug. The pharmacist will be alerted to the potential adverse event, and a clinical decision can be made."

Exasperated, I tried a new approach. "No, you're still not understanding me, Jerry. Let me tell you a true story. Over 40 years ago, computerized physician order entry was just becoming popular. These new health information technologies overcame the problems of illegible handwriting and prevented transcription errors. The C.P.O.E. systems also checked for drug interactions and alerted physicians about known patient allergies. They made dose adjustments according to things like patient's weight or renal function. Amazing, right?"

"Not today, these advances seem as antiquated as the stethoscope," Westfall said.

"Yes, indeed," I chuckled. "I know that C.P.O.E. seems quaint by today's standards, but at the time, the advantages of such systems were revolutionary. I was a huge proponent of adoption for all the reasons you've given me today. However, I was wrong, and I want you to learn from my mistakes. Human errors associated with computers harm patients."

Westfall's communicator pinged with a message, and he said, "Silence notifications." He returned his attention to me, but I sensed I needed to move things along.

I continued, "In 2023, the Valley Health Hospital upgraded our electronic medical record platform with major enhancements to the C.P.O.E. and the clinical decision support system. Like I said, I was a big supporter. However, I did not take these technology-related errors seriously enough. What I should have realized is that the interaction between staff, technology, and their environment can actually increase the risk of disastrous medication errors."

I turned to the information display wall in his meeting room. "I brought some data from 2023 to share with you. Do you mind if we look at it?"

"No problem. I love data-informed discussions," Westfall said.

Using my communicator, I threw the data file onto the wall. With a flicker, the columns and rows of data of the first 6 months of the 2023 medication safety incident report immediately projected on the wall display (see Case 17 Data file provided in the Instructor's and Student ancillary materials).

"Back in 2023," I said, "the Medication Operation Safety Team met on a monthly basis to review patient safety incidents related to medications. This is 6 months after the implementation of the major technology enhancements. What do you think we found?"

"Okay," Westfall said, "I'll play along. I'd bet that medication-related incidents fell over the first 6 months." I ran the visualization for number of medication-related incidents reported by month (Figure C17.1).

"You're actually right," I said. "But the downward trend of incidents doesn't tell the whole story."

Westfall looked at me doubtfully, so I returned to the data table. "Look at the contributing factor field of the data table. In fact, in this period following the implementation, close to half of the incidents are related to technology and equipment."

"That's to be expected, though," Westfall said. "With any new technology implementation, there are bound to be issues. I bet after a few months, the incidents related to technology and equipment decreased."

With a few taps, I created visualization for number of medication-related incidents where technology and equipment was a contributing factor for each month after implementation (Figure C17.2).

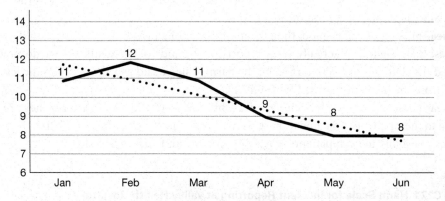

FIGURE C17.1 Medication-related incidents reported by month.

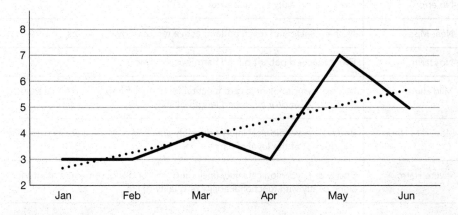

FIGURE C17.2 Medication-related incidents: Technology/equipment as contributing factors.

"That's not it," I said. "In fact, the opposite is true, and I think I can explain why. See the incident on February 17th?"

With a two-fingered slide on my communicator, I zoomed in on the description of the event field for incident number 613385432 and said, "Well, this was an issue related to our automated dispensing cabinet or A.D.C. You see, back in the day, a Pharmacy Tech was responsible for loading the A.D.C. from which nurses obtained the drugs to administer to patients. The problem was that the 'scan-on-load' option had not been enabled for refill of the machine. This meant that a Pharmacy Tech could load a package of Norco by mistake because it looked almost exactly like Percocet. In this case, once the nurse selected Percocet and got Norco, she noticed the error and reported it as a near miss. After this incident, we enabled the scan-on-load function that required the Pharmacy Tech to scan the bar codes when they loaded the machine."

"Doesn't this example prove my point that technology, if used correctly, can reduce medication errors?" Westfall asked.

"Maybe it does, but I think it showed the excellent critical thinking of the nurse to catch the potential error and her good judgment to report the 'near miss.' It turned out that the issue was pervasive in many units throughout the hospital. As should be true today, nurses in the '20s were trained in the 'Five Rights' of medication administration: right client, right route, right drug, right dose, and right time. The nurse realized that Norco was the wrong drug. She caught it and communicated it," I said.

"Near miss reporting is good, though, an indicator of a just culture," Westfall said.

"Yes, that's right. We actually want reports of all kinds of incidents. As we do now, we trained the staff on how to report using the harm scale," I said as I showed him the levels of harm from the incident reports (Table C17.1).

"Near misses mean that the clinician was thinking critically about the care they are providing to their patients. Imagine if there were a kind of mental handover to CLIF? If we shed our responsibility to keep patients safe, errors will occur. Patients will die."

Table C17.1 Harm Scale for Incident Reporting at Valley Health Hospital

LEVEL OF HARM	DEFINITION
A—No error	No error, capacity to cause error
B—Near Miss	No harm—Did not reach patient, active recovery by caregivers
C—No Harm	Event reached patient but no harm was evident
D—Mild Harm	Minimal symptoms or loss of function, or injury limited to additional treatment, monitoring, and/or increased length of stay
E—Moderate Harm	Bodily or psychological injury adversely affecting functional ability or quality of life, but not at the level of harm
F—Severe Harm	Bodily or psychological injury (including pain or disfigurement) that interferes significantly with functional ability or quality of life
I—Death	Dead at time of assessment

"Remember, there's a difference between medication errors caused by CLIF and those occurring despite CLIF," Westfall said.

"I agree with that distinction," I said, "but I think you're being naïve to think that CLIF won't make dangerous mistakes."

I returned to the data table to the wall display. Sliding down to May, I said, "Which brings me closer to my main point. Here's a day I will never forget. Take a look at May19, 2023?" I asked.

"A patient died?" Westfall asked with any hint of witty banter gone for good. I zoomed in on the event description.

I explained, "Admission medication history and reconciliation is a process of creating the most accurate list possible of all medications that a patient is taking—including drug name, dosage, frequency, and route—and comparing that list against the existing medication list in the patient record. Our newly implemented technology system contained a medication reconciliation module that retrieved medication data from many different sources, such as retail pharmacy fill records, current orders, patient interviews, and orders from previous visits. This new system was supposed to streamline the med rec process."

"I know what med rec is," Westfall said as he waved his hands for me to hurry up.

"Well, anyway, on May 19, 2023, an 84-year-old woman named Frances Nichols was admitted to Valley Health from a long-term care facility for an atrial fibrillation episode. She had a history of atrial fibrillation, chronic heart failure, hypertension, and chronic hypokalemia. So, basically heart problems and low potassium."

"The new automatic med rec system created a medication list that included digoxin 0.25 mg daily," I said. "When the nurse reviewed the med history on admission, because of how it was reported, she assumed all medications listed were current. The patient stayed in the hospital for only one night. Upon discharge, the physician prescribed the digoxin 0.25 mg daily for her to take at the long-term care facility."

"I was the pharmacist responsible for reviewing the discharge medication reconciliation. This was a challenging case, because for patients with atrial fibrillation, 0.25 mg daily is within the recommended oral maintenance dose of digoxin. However, the patient's history of kidney function problems, low potassium, and use of loop diuretics made digoxin 0.25 mg daily inappropriate."

"So you should have caught the issue on the discharge med rec?" Westfall asked.

"Yes," I said as my heart sank. "After 2 days of taking digoxin 0.25 mg at the long-term care facility, the patient's condition deteriorated rapidly. She was subsequently diagnosed with digoxin toxicity and died of a cardiac arrest. Only later was it discovered that the patient's cardiologist had discontinued the use of digoxin more than 2 years prior."

"That's really sad. I'm sorry that happened," Westfall said.

"Thank you," I said, then continued. "Over the previous months, medication reconciliation essentially had become a technology-directed process that distributed responsibility for med rec between the nurse, the discharging physician, and the pharmacist. The nurse missed it. The physician missed it. I missed it. We didn't communicate well with each other or the patient. It took only a few months for us to get lazy. Collectively, we went from catching and reporting near misses to increased patient harm, even a patient death. And the data here show this."

"So, you're saying we train clinical staff to critically think, communicate, and report? We stay vigilant?" Westfall asked.

"Yes, but I think we need to do more. Let me tell you one last story. Later that year, a researcher at the hospital flooded our whole network with large quantities of data meant for external colleagues. All of the HIT systems slowed down to a crawl—drug orders, admissions, discharges, everything. After failing to solve the problem, the decision was made to shut the entire network down. We went without the health information technology for 3 days. Three Whole Days. We resorted to manual processes, such as paper lab results, handwritten medication orders, and countless other documents. Our CEO spent his days running verified and labeled medications to the pharmacy and medication orders back to the units."

"Not good," Westfall said with wide eyes.

"No, very bad. When the system went down, we couldn't remember how to work without it. The clinicians had trouble remembering standard dosages, hospital formulary recommendations, and medication contraindications. Dependence on technology must never become so great that basic medical care cannot be provided in its absence. Even though its use can make many aspects of the medication-use system safer and more efficient, CLIF should be viewed as supplementary to our clinical judgment and communication."

Westfall just nodded slowly.

"The threat is not that CLIF will become more intelligent. It is that we will become less intelligent. Because, let me ask you, Jerry, what if something disastrous happens with CLIF? Will we be prepared? Or will everything change?"

DISCUSSION QUESTIONS

1. In what ways do you think the narrator effectively communicated the patient safety issue with CEO Jerry Westfall? How could the narrator have improved his persuasiveness?

2. Jerry Westfall correctly predicted the decline in reported medication-related incidents in the 6 months after the 2023 health information technology implementation. If the analysis had stopped at this point, what would have been the consequences to patient safety associated with CLIF implementation?

3. How can the practice of healthcare quality management enhance patient safety and minimize the negative consequences of health information technologies?

4. In the implementation of new technologies or work processes, what risk management approach would you take to monitor clinical activities to identify both expected and unexpected risks?

 ## PODCAST FOR CASE 17

Listen to how experts approach the topic (you can access the podcast by following this url to Springer Publishing Company Connect™: https://connect.springerpub.com/content/book/978-0-8261-4514-7/front-matter/fmatter2)

REFERENCES

Agency for Healthcare Research and Quality Patient Safety Network. (2019, January). *Adverse events, near misses, and errors.* Retrieved from: https://psnet.ahrq.gov/primers/primer/34/adverse-events-near-misses-and-errors

Hauck, K., & Zhao, X. (2011). How dangerous is a day in hospital? A model of adverse events and length of stay for medical inpatients. *Medical Care, 49,* 1068–1075. doi:10.1097/MLR.0b013e31822efb09

Hawes, E. M., Maxwell, W. D., White, S. F., Mangun, J., & Lin, F. C. (2014). Impact of an outpatient pharmacist intervention on medication discrepancies and health care resource utilization in posthospitalization care transitions. *Journal of Primary Care & Community Health, 5*(1), 14–18. doi:10.1177/2150131913502489

FURTHER READING

Campbell, E. M., Sittig, D. F., Ash, J. S., Guappone, K. P., & Dykstra, R. H. (2006). Types of unintended consequences related to computerized provider order entry. *Journal of the American Medical Informatics Association, 13*(5), 547–556. doi:10.1197/jamia.M2042

Cohen, M. R., & Smetzer, J. L. (2017). Understanding human over-reliance on technology; it's exelan, not exelon; crash cart drug mix-up; risk with entering a "test order". *Hospital Pharmacy, 52*(1), 7–12. doi:10.1310/hpj5201-7

Flynn, A. (2019). Using artificial intelligence in health-system pharmacy practice: Finding new patterns that matter. *American Journal of Health-System Pharmacy, 76*(9), 622–627. doi:10.1093/ajhp/zxz018

Johnson, A., Guirguis, E., & Grace, Y. (2015). Preventing medication errors in transitions of care: A patient case approach. *Journal of the American Pharmacists Association., 55*(2), e264–e276. doi:10.1331/JAPhA.2015.15509

Jones, J. H., & Treiber, L. (2010). When the 5 rights go wrong: Medication errors from the nursing perspective. *Journal of Nursing Care Quality, 25*(3), 240–247. doi:10.1097/NCQ.0b013e3181d5b948

Keers, R. N., Williams, S. D., Cooke, J., & Ashcroft, D. M. (2013). Causes of medication administration errors in hospitals: A systematic review of quantitative and qualitative evidence. *Drug Safety, 36*(11), 1045–1067. doi:10.1007/s40264-013-0090-2

Kellie, S. E., Battles, J. B., Dixon, N. M., Kaplan, H. S., & Fastman, B. R. (2008). Patient safety learning pilot: Narratives from the frontlines. In K. Henriksen, J. B. Battles, M. A. Keyes, & M. L. Grady (Eds.), *Advances in patient safety: New directions and alternative approaches* (Vol. 1: Assessment). Rockville, MD: Agency for Healthcare Research and Quality. Retrieved from https://www.ncbi.nlm.nih.gov/books/NBK43631/

Kilbridge, P. (2003). Computer crash-lessons from a system failure. *New England Journal of Medicine, 348*(10), 881–882. doi:10.1056/NEJMp030010

Korb-Savoldelli, V., Boussadi, A., Durieux, P., & Sabatier, B. (2018). Prevalence of computerized physician order entry systems-related medication prescription errors: A systematic review. *International Journal of Medical Informatics, 111,* 112–122. doi:10.1016/j.ijmedinf.2017.12.022

Long, J., Yuan, M. J., & Poonawala, R. (2016). An observational study to evaluate the usability and intent to adopt an artificial intelligence-powered medication reconciliation tool. *Interactive Journal of Medical Research, 5*(2), e14. doi:10.2196/ijmr.5462

Magrabi, F., Baker, M., Sinha, I., Ong, M. S., Harrison, S., Kidd, M. R.,…& Coiera, E. (2015). Clinical safety of England's national programme for IT: A retrospective analysis of all reported safety events 2005 to 2011. *International Journal of Medical Informatics, 84*(3), 198–206. doi:10.1016/j.ijmedinf.2014.12.003

Mutter, M. (2003). One hospital's journey toward reducing medication errors. *The Joint Commission Journal on Quality and Safety, 29*(6), 279–288. doi:10.1016/S1549-3741(03)29032-8

Verghese, A., Shah, N. H., & Harrington, R. A. (2018). What this computer needs is a physician: Humanism and artificial intelligence. *Journal of the American Medical Association, 319*(1), 19–20. doi:10.1001/jama.2017.19198

Wachter, R. M., & Howell, M. D. (2018). Resolving the productivity paradox of health information technology: A time for optimism. *Journal of the American Medical Association, 320*(1), 25–26. doi:10.1001/jama.2018.5605

RISK MITIGATION TOOL

Risk management seeks to reduce the inherent risks created by a remarkably complex healthcare delivery system. Central to healthcare quality management, risk management includes all the clinical risks of health services delivery, such as prescribing or administering potentially harmful medications, inconsistent care, wrong-site procedures, and nonclinical risks, such as double-booking appointments, divulging personal health information, gathering and storing inaccurate patient medication history, and more.

To manage these risks, organizations adopt enterprise risk management (ERM) models that encompass clinical, operational, strategic, financial, legal and regulatory, environmental, and technological domains (*New England Journal of Medicine* Catalyst, 2018). These systems allow organizations to track, manage, and mitigate risks.

An application of an ERM system is "near miss" reporting. Near misses are when mistakes or adverse events are avoided due to luck or intervention. When near misses are reported in the system, organizations can investigate the root causes, create prevention activities, and eventually learn to avoid those errors. For this risk mitigation approach to work, an organization must create an environment in which speaking up is encouraged, called a "just culture" or a "culture of safety."

However, near misses should not be viewed as evidence of safe systems but as examples of how the system could fail. That is, near misses are opportunities for improvement. A good way to learn from near misses is by categorizing them in a Near Miss Classification Matrix (Figure C17.3) based on their potential severity (from low to high) and their frequency of occurrence (from rarely to often).

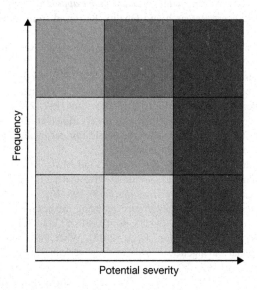

FIGURE C17.3 Near miss classification matrix.

By using this Risk Classification Matrix, quality management teams can decide where to focus risk mitigation efforts and how to prevent future occurrences of error. Because an organization cannot work on all the identified risks simultaneously, this tool helps an organization efficiently prioritize their quality management efforts.

REFERENCE

NEJM Catalyst. (2018). *What is risk management in healthcare?* Retrieved from https://catalyst.nejm .org/what-is-risk-management-in-healthcare

CASE 18: A Mom's Story of Sepsis

OBJECTIVES

1. Apply collaborative quality management approaches that enhance patient safety.
2. Analyze data to align patient outcomes with the organization's goals and objectives.
3. Examine areas of avoidable risk to patients and organizations.
4. Explain how collaborative relationships with community and business leaders can improve an organization-wide patient safety program.
5. Describe how written clinical policies and procedures should be updated in accordance with evidence-based practice.

INTRODUCTION

"Sepsis" is the body's devastating response to infection that damages a person's organs and tissue (Novosad, 2016). Common and frequently fatal, sepsis is one of the leading causes of death in the United States (Cohen et al., 2015). Patient safety depends on early recognition of sepsis and rapid administration of appropriate treatment (Lynn, Gupta, Vaaler, Held, & Leon, 2018).

However, sepsis can be difficult to diagnose (Novosad, 2016), as no rapid diagnostic tool exists. So, clinicians must rely on the identification of two or more criteria of the systemic inflammatory response syndrome (SIRS), including fever or hypothermia, elevated heart rate, rapid breathing, and an elevated white blood count. Because these symptoms can be mistaken for other common illnesses, such as influenza or respiratory infections, sepsis identification requires keen clinical judgment to uncover a potential source of infection (Gatewood, Wemple, Greco, Kritek, & Durvasula, 2015). Typically, concerns for infection—bacterial, viral, or fungal—stem from wounds, pneumonia, influenza, or urinary tract infections (Seymour & Angus, 2018).

Once the SIRS criteria have been met, care providers must act quickly to treat the suspected sepsis. Current sepsis treatment protocols (Levy, Evans, & Rhodes, 2018), referred to as the "Hour-1 Sepsis Bundle," require that the following be initiated within 1 hour of patient assessment:

1. Measure serum lactate level in the blood
2. Obtain blood cultures before administration of antibiotics

DATA FILE FOR CASE 18

Data files for students are available by accessing the following url: https://www.springerpub .com/hqm

The data file for Case 18 provides Hour-1 Sepsis Bundle summary chart for Current State. Instructor's file includes full and summary failure modes and effects analysis (FMEA).

3. Administer broad-spectrum antibiotics

4. Administer intravenous fluids and

5. Apply vasopressors medicines during or after fluid resuscitation, if the patient has low blood pressure

Compliance with this protocol saves lives (Lynn et al., 2018).

CASE SCENARIO

The following is the speech delivered by Anna Wallace, one of the founders of the Sepsis Community Action Network (SCAN), at the First Annual SCAN Awards Ceremony, the fundraiser scheduled to coincide with September's Sepsis Awareness Month. Anna Wallace received the Courage Award, an honor given to a community member who perseveres through hardship to strengthen their communities through sepsis awareness and advocacy.

Thank you very much. Thank you, SCAN. I appreciate the recognition, but I must instead insist that the credit go to my friends at Franklin Children's Hospital. Many of them are here today. Franklin's Chief Medical Officer, Dr. Sandy Wang. Hello, there! Chief Nursing Officer, Billie Hughes. Where are you, sweetheart? There, yes! Thank you. And Tom Frost, Quality Director, please stand, Tom. You all deserve a special round of applause. I think these individuals should be acknowledged for their courage to admit their mistakes.

Let's see, will the slide show work here? There. I intend to keep telling Logan's story in order to prevent other families from experiencing this indescribable pain. This was Logan, a beautiful, athletic, healthy 5-year-old boy. During Christmas vacation, he fell off the playground slide and skinned his knee. But, like all boys, he had various cuts and scrapes from playing, so we didn't think much of it. Logan woke up on the early morning on January 4th saying his heart hurt.

Now, the clinical process I will describe was not familiar to me then. I was, and still am, the Quality Manager for Prime Motorcycles, the manufacturer of electric motorcycles started by NASA engineers. We at Prime are true believers in Lean/Six Sigma quality management, but I had never thought about how these philosophies could be applied to healthcare. Tonight, I want to highlight healthcare failures. But, I want you to know this much: it's the process, not the people.

Al, my brave husband of 10 years, and I took Logan to the Franklin Children's Hospital emergency department that morning. When we arrived at the ED, the triage nurse assessed Logan within 10 minutes. I know now that many patients with sepsis experience a dangerous delay of the triage assessment upon arrival at the ED, but not Logan. The triage nurse promptly collected his vitals, including a fever and elevated heart rate.

Now, here was the first mistake. She told me that my boy probably had the flu. False negative sepsis diagnoses often happen in emergency departments. Sepsis looks like the cold or the flu. Unfortunately, the nurse did not have a sepsis protocol to follow. She had not been adequately trained to identify possible sepsis. She did not ask about Logan's recent infections. If she had, the sepsis care process could have started then, but no workup was initiated while we waited for the physician. Just a misdiagnosis and a worsening sepsis.

We waited for over an hour that morning for Logan to see the physician. When she did assess Logan, she was unable to detect the sepsis signs: fever, rapid breathing, quickened heart rate. Frankly, Logan chatted her up, so I understand how sepsis could be missed. He was lucid, although a bit diminished. But sitting still was not really Logan's thing. The physician agreed with the nurse—it was the flu. No discussion of his scraped knee.

At home later that afternoon, Logan began breathing funny, very quick and shallow. Al became very concerned, but I was more calm. The doctor said it was the flu, after all. Give him lots of fluids, they said. After some cajoling by Al, I agreed that we should take him back to the Franklin ED.

At this point, the ED was very busy. So, we waited, and poor Logan just lay in Al's lap. A nurse finally saw us, and he said the same thing. It was the flu. He told us not to bring him back for 4 or 5 days.

The next day, however, Logan could not even walk to the bathroom. He was coming in and out of consciousness. It was so ... sorry, I promised Al I wouldn't cry. Sorry, um. After a 24-hour delay in diagnosis, the infection put Logan in severe cardiogenic septic shock.

When we went to the ED a third time, only then did the nurse and doctor suspect sepsis. The nurse drew his blood to measure the lactate level. A high level of lactic acid caused by infection is an important clue for diagnosing sepsis. They also requested a complete blood count, or CBC, that measures, among other things, the level of Logan's white blood cells. A higher white blood count means infection. Unfortunately, there was a miscommunication, and there was a delay in getting the results back from the lab. There was no automatic trigger alert for sepsis. There was no Sepsis Response Team that could coordinate continual evaluation and response from nurses, physicians, lab techs, and pharmacists.

They also collected blood cultures in a few different places from Logan's veins. Here, no mistake was made. They did the exact right thing. They knew to collect blood samples before giving antibiotics. If they had started antibiotics before collecting blood cultures, then they would have reduced the chances of identifying the precise organism that caused the severe sepsis. It can take a couple of days to get the results of a blood culture to identify which antibiotic will target the exact cause of sepsis. So, they started Logan on broad-spectrum antibiotics immediately. Delaying antibiotics is a common mistake. I now know that the worry of creating antibiotic-resistant superbugs is real. For this reason, some physicians hesitate to administer broad-spectrum antibiotics when they are not certain of the source of the infection. However, giving broad-spectrum antibiotics at this point saves lives.

Later that morning, the nurse noted that Logan's heart rate had decreased dangerously low. The doctor intubated him, then later had to conduct chest compression for 30 minutes. They put him on total life support.

Nationwide, almost 22% of patients diagnosed with sepsis will die in the hospital or be discharged to hospice. Some studies show the mortality rate to be as high as 35% among older Americans. Some hospitals' sepsis mortality rates are better than others. At the time that Logan had sepsis, 28% of the Franklin's patients arriving at the emergency department died from sepsis. Sadly, Franklin was not performing well, and Logan paid the price.

Some people encouraged us to sue the hospital. A malpractice claim will motivate the hospital to improve, they told me. Do you know why we didn't sue? Because Franklin's Chief Medical Officer and Chief Nursing Officer apologized. They knew we could have sued, but they took responsibility and expressed regret for having caused Logan harm. Dr. Sandy Wang took the time to get to know me. She learned that I was a Lean-certified, Six Sigma Black Belt at Prime Motorcycles. Months later, Dr. Wang introduced me to Tom Frost, Franklin's

Quality Director. Tom and I spoke the same language, but he told me that Franklin staff were mostly suspicious of adopting quality management tools from industries outside healthcare.

I invited the team, including Tom, Dr. Wang, and the CNO Billie Hughes, to visit our operation at Prime Motorcycles. They learned about some of our quality management practices, and began imagining how they could be applied to patient care. Hesitant at first, the Franklin team eventually realized how Prime Motorcycles effectively used Lean Six Sigma methods to focus on the customer, make process improvements, and sustain the improvement over time.

Soon after that visit to the facility at Prime Motorcycles, they asked me to join a patient safety project at Franklin to address sepsis care. I am so grateful that they embraced me like this. I learned so much about the Hour-1 Sepsis Bundle, which is the sepsis care protocol that must be started within 1 hour of the patient's presentation with sepsis. The overall Hour-1 Bundle compliance at Franklin at that time was 22%.

Another slide here, yes, here we go. In each of the first three quarters of last year, the percent of compliance for each of the components of the Hour-1 Bundle for sepsis care declined (Table C18.1).

The quality management team knew we could do better. So, the team set goals to improve sepsis mortality or discharge to hospice for patients arriving at emergency department target to 20%. We set the Hour-1 Bundle for sepsis care target at 50% (Table C18.2).

We identified all the steps in the process, what could go wrong, and the causes and consequences of those failures, such as delay in sepsis care or death. The clinical staff scored likelihood of occurrence, likelihood of detection, and severity to rank all of the risks in order of priority. This was a very technical process that required clinical expertise from the staff at Franklin Children's. Luckily, the staff's effort was supported by previously published evidence.

Franklin Children's convened Sepsis Response Team with the chief medical officer and the emergency department medical director as leaders. The project team implemented countermeasures to improve sepsis mortality and compliance with the Hour-1 Bundle. The Sepsis Response Team developed a nurse-driven sepsis protocol and a training program. Together with the senior director of Medical Technology, the Sepsis Response Team created an automatic sepsis trigger that activates Sepsis Bundle when certain information is entered in the electronic medical record system.

Table C18.1 Hour-1 Bundle for Sepsis Care Before Project

	QUARTER 1 (%)	QUARTER 2 (%)	QUARTER 3 (%)
Measure serum lactate level	23	22	22
Obtain blood cultures before administration of antibiotics	60	58	55
Administer broad-spectrum antibiotics	52	41	38
IV fluids	41	36	32
Apply vasopressors, if hypotensive	55	51	49

Table C18.2 Hour-1 Bundle for Sepsis Care After Project

	QUARTER 4 (%)	QUARTER 1 (%)	QUARTER 2 (%)
Measure serum lactate level	24	30	45
Obtain blood cultures before administration of antibiotics	60	65	72
Administer broad-spectrum antibiotics	42	52	65
IV fluids	35	41	51
Apply vasopressors, if hypotensive	55	58	65

I am happy to say that Franklin is showing progress. On a monthly basis, Franklin shares this information in a new Sepsis Dashboard with the patient care team.

Back to my sweet boy, Logan. It took about a week on life support for Logan to show improvement. It was a terrible, terrible time. Eventually, the life support was decreased, but then the nurse noticed Logan's neurological change. He had a significant brain bleed. Logan was taken off life support right away. We were told that if he survived, then he would need brain surgery to save his life. Thankfully, he survived being removed from life support, and the surgeons successfully stopped the brain bleed. Logan turned 6 years old in a coma in the hospital on January 12. After weeks of a very quiet environment, we started to see signs of Logan coming back to life. He then went to Franklin's inpatient rehabilitation unit for several months to regain his strength.

Logan is a survivor. He deserves this award for his courage. Today he is 7 years old and healthy. Logan, you've sat very still while Mommy talked. Can you please stand now? We are so proud of you. You have taught us all the true meaning of living life to the fullest. I love you!

Throughout this ordeal, I met other sepsis survivors of grieving family members from hospitals around the region. It was Billie who encouraged us to found the Sepsis Community Action Network or SCAN. Together, we will raise sepsis awareness among general public and healthcare professionals. We will also provide area hospitals with a quality management tool kit to improve the care of sepsis. I am so grateful to you all for your support of SCAN.

Thank you to Franklin Children's Hospital and to SCAN. I am proud of what we accomplished so far, and I appreciate your courage to improve the quality of care for people throughout our region. Thank you!

DISCUSSION QUESTIONS

1. How would you hold clinical staff accountable for patient-safety errors? How would you support a nonpunitive reporting system for identifying unsafe practices?

2. Do you agree with the approach of the chief medical officer and chief nursing officer for apologizing in this case? Do you think this approach should always be followed in cases of patient harm or mortality?

3. Was the involvement of the mother, Anna Wallace, in the patient-safety project appropriate in the case? Are there circumstances when involvement with community members in collaborative quality management would be inappropriate?

4. What would be the best way to disseminate research findings and new clinical policies and procedures to patient-care team members?

5. What role should pharmacy, laboratory, and allied health professionals play in the patient-safety issue discussed in this case study?

 PODCAST FOR CASE 18

Listen to how experts approach the topic (you can access the podcast by following this url to Springer Publishing Company Connect™: https://connect.springerpub.com/content/book/978-0-8261-4514-7/front-matter/fmatter2)

REFERENCES

Cohen, J., Vincent, J. L., Adhikari, N. K., Machado, F. R., Angus, D. C., Calandra, T., … & Tracey, K. (2015). Sepsis: A roadmap for future research. *The Lancet Infectious Diseases, 15*(5), 581–614. doi:10.1016/S1473-3099(15)70112-X

Gatewood, M. O. K., Wemple, M., Greco, S., Kritek, P. A., & Durvasula, R. (2015). A quality improvement project to improve early sepsis care in the emergency department. *BMJ Quality and Safety, 24*(12), 787–795. doi:10.1136/bmjqs-2014-003552

Levy, M. M., Evans, L. E., & Rhodes, A. (2018). The surviving sepsis campaign bundle: 2018 update. *Intensive Care Medicine, 44*(6), 925–928. doi:10.1007/s00134-018-5085-0

Lynn, N. B., Gupta, C., Vaaler, M., Held, J., & Leon, L. (2018). Severe sepsis Hour-1 bundle compliance and mortality. *American Journal of Infection Control, 46*(11), 1299–1300. doi:10.1016/j.ajic.2018.04.228

Novosad, S. A. (2016). Vital signs: Epidemiology of sepsis: Prevalence of health care factors and opportunities for prevention. *Morbidity and Mortality Weekly Report, 65*(33), 864–869. doi:10.15585/mmwr.mm6533e1

Seymour, C. W., & Angus, D. C. (2018). Sepsis and septic shock. In J. L. Jameson, A. S. Fauci, D. L. Kasper, S. L. Hauser, D. L. Longo, & J. Loscalzo (Eds.) *Harrison's principles of internal medicine* (20th ed., Chapter 297). New York, NY: McGraw-Hill.

FURTHER READING

Alamry, A., Al Owais, S. M., Marini, A. M., Al-Dorzi, H., Alsolamy, S., & Arabi, Y. (2014). Application of failure mode effect analysis to improve the care of septic patients admitted through the emergency department. *Journal of Patient Safety, 13*(2), 76–81. doi:10.1097/PTS.0000000000000118

Hatfield, K. M., Dantes, R. B., Baggs, J., Sapiano, M. R., Fiore, A. E., Jernigan, J. A., & Epstein, L. (2018). Assessing variability in hospital-level mortality among US Medicare beneficiaries with hospitalizations for severe sepsis and septic shock. *Critical Care Medicine, 46*(11), 1753–1760. doi:10.1097/CCM.0000000000003324

Rhee, C., Dantes, R., Epstein, L., Murphy, D. J., Seymour, C. W., Iwashyna, T. J., … & Jernigan, J. A. (2017). Incidence and trends of sepsis in US hospitals using clinical vs claims data, 2009–2014. *Journal of the American Medical Association, 318*(13), 1241–1249. doi:10.1001/jama.2017.13836

FAILURE MODES AND EFFECTS ANALYSIS

A Failure Modes and Effects Analysis (FMEA) is a technique to look at a process and focus on several steps of that process to estimate the following:

1. The various ways a particular step can fail
2. The impact of that particular step failing
3. How likely it is that that step will fail and
4. How likely it is that, if that step were to fail, we would be able to detect it

By estimating these factors, we can calculate a weighted average, called a "risk priority number" (RPN) and focus on those failure modes that produce the highest RPNs to minimize the risk of the process failing.

As with many quality management and improvement tools, the best way to carry out a FMEA is to assemble a team of subject matter experts (SMEs) that includes frontline staff, mid-level managers, and even some senior leaders who have different levels of knowledge about the process and its potential failure modes and the effects of those failures.

As the team is evaluating each potential failure mode, a number from 1 to 10 is assigned to each of the elements of severity (SEV), occurrence (OCC), and detectability (DET).

The nature of an FMEA is subjective. Team members use their knowledge of the process to identify those four elements just specified. This is why it is critical that people with intimate knowledge of the process be included in the analysis.

There are several templates used for conducting an FMEA. One of the most widely used is presented in Table C18.3.

As far as the scoring scheme for severity, occurrence, and detectability, although technically any number from 1 through 10 can be assigned, it is the recommendation of the authors to utilize a discreet scale of 1, 4, 7, and 10 only. During the exercise, the team must decide what each of these levels means. For example, let us take the occurrence element of a potential failure mode. The team is advised to create some standard definition of each of the levels as presented in Table C18.4.

The team should do this for all three—Severity, Occurrence, and Detectability—prior to starting the analysis.

Table C18.3 Failure Modes and Effects Analysis (FMEA)

Process or Product Name:			Prepared by:		Page ___ of ___
Responsible:			FMEA Date (Orig) _____ (Rev) _____		

Process Step	Potential Failure Mode	Potential Effects of Failure	SEV	Potential Cause(s)/Mechanism(s) of Failure	OCC	Current Process Controls	DET	RPN	Recommended Action(s)	Responsibility and Completion Date	Action Results				
											Actions Taken	SEV	OCC	DET	RPN
The highest value process steps	In what ways might the process potentially fail to meet the process requirements and/or design intent?	What is the effect of each failure mode on the outputs and/or customer requirements? The customer could be the next operation, subsequent operations, another division, or the end user.	How severe is the effect to the customer?	How can the failure occur? Describe in terms of something that can be corrected or controlled. Be specific. Try to identify the causes that directly impact the failure mode, i.e., root causes.	How often does the cause or failure mode occur?	What are the existing controls and procedures (inspection and test) that either prevent failure mode from occurring or detect the failure should it occur?	How well can you detect cause or FM?	SEV × OCC × DET	What are the actions for reducing the occurrence, or improving detection, or for identifying the root cause if it is unknown? **Should have actions only on high RPNs or easy fixes.**	Who is responsible for the recommended action?	List the completed actions that are included in the recalculated RPN. Include the implementation date for any changes.	What is the new severity?	What is the new process capability?	Are the detection limits improved?	Recompute RPN after actions are complete.

DET, detectability; OCC, occurrence; RPN, risk priority number; SEV, severity.

Table C18.4 Standard Definitions of Occurrence (OCC) Levels

OCC SCORE	DEFINITION
1	Rarely occurs—1 time a month or less
4	1 time a week
7	1 time a day
10	Multiple times each day

Performance Improvement

In this casebook, the performance improvement category includes a variety of case studies that do not specifically relate to process improvement, patient experience, or patient safety. We conceptualize performance improvement as issues related to demands for quality improvement made by external stakeholders, such as auditors, the community, health insurance companies, and government regulators.

Financial pressures often motivate healthcare organizations to improve performance. U.S. health policy makers pay bonuses to high performers and levy fines to low performers. This value-based purchasing, also called "pay-for-performance," replaces the traditional fee-for-service payments for financing efforts intended to keep patients healthy (VanLare & Conway, 2012). In addition to government policy, market competition and community encourage performance improvement, such as market competition and community influence.

The following are descriptions of performance improvement case studies included in this casebook.

Case 19: Operating Room Recovery

After firing all of the C-suite executives at a struggling hospital, the Board of Directors hired a consulting firm to conduct an extensive audit and aggressive turnaround of the enterprise. Based on the audit findings, the director of surgical services was given 60 days to find operating room utilization improvement opportunities. He investigated thousands of lines of data from the 6 months of surgeries to identify ways to increase utilization of the operating rooms. Will enough improvement be identified in the data file to save his job?

Case 20: Opioid Overdoses in the Emergency Department

Caught unprepared, a chief executive officer (CEO) told a newspaper reporter that the hospital would conduct a community outreach plan to reduce opioid overdoses in its emergency department. After the plan was made public, the chief medical officer and chief nursing officer scrambled to devise a plan to convince the CEO to change course. Their message: conduct a root cause analysis of opioid addiction before developing any solution.

Case 21: The Lunchroom: Physician Engagement at a PCMH

The patient-centered medical home (PCMH) is an innovative model of healthcare delivery that emphasizes improved access to primary care, coordinated care, and better management of patient chronic conditions. After earning PCMH certification, a primary care practice's quality scores were still below the national averages. One of the lowest performing doctors resisted change associated with the new model of care. Can the medical practice leaders engage the reluctant physician in quality management initiatives?

Case 22: The Fulfillment Affair

Plethora.com is the second largest online retail company in the world. The company hired a managed care organization, InsuraCare, to investigate the causes for the unusually high number of employees with exceptionally high healthcare costs. The InsuraCare newly hired medical director and the brilliant but blunt director of quality conducted a site visit (gemba walk) at one of Plethora's fulfillment centers. After confronting the site management, the director of quality interviewed employees who pack products in the boxes for delivery. Using astute observation and data analysis, the problem became clear, at least to the director of quality.

Case 23: Composite Quality Score

The Centers for Medicare and Medicaid Services (CMS) Overall Hospital Star Ratings are published on the Medicare Compare website to allow consumers to compare a hospital performance across the United States. Based on a single composite score calculated from dozens of quality metrics, consumers can make informed decisions about where to obtain inpatient care. A health system CEO must lead his organization to improve the poor CMS Overall Hospital Quality Star Ratings of its hospitals. The underlying problems vary at each of the hospitals. How will they prioritize their quality management initiatives?

Case 24: Both/And Thinking in Readmission Prevention

The chief nursing officer (CNO), who oversaw the case management departments for two recently merged hospitals, wanted to improve their 30-day inpatient readmission rates. First, though, the CNO needed to collect data on the root causes of readmissions. The CNO provided the directors of case management at each—one a nurse and the other a medical social worker—with a data collection template for tracking the reasons for each patient readmission. After 30 days, the data collection effort revealed two very different professional perspectives.

Case 25: Community Collaboration for Suicide Prevention

The Affordable Care Act requires nonprofit healthcare organizations to complete community health needs assessment (CHNA) to justify their tax-exempt status. A hospital identified the need for increased access to mental health and development of suicide prevention programs.

However, suicide prevention efforts remained underfunded by the hospital. Later, the hospital CEO learned that his old friend committed suicide. Shocked and saddened, he sought the advice of a trusted doctor and social worker who inspired him to confront the challenge of suicide prevention in the community.

REFERENCE

VanLare, J. M., & Conway, P. H. (2012). Value-based purchasing: National programs to move from volume to value. *New England Journal of Medicine*, *367*(4), 292–295. doi:10.1056/NEJMp1204939

CASE 19: Operating Room Recovery

OBJECTIVES

1. Apply operating room utilization performance measures.
2. Analyze time stamp data using advanced spreadsheet calculations to identify opportunities for improvement in operating room utilization.
3. Evaluate methods of communicating workforce performance expectations.
4. Describe the importance of accountability and consequences for underperformance in healthcare quality management.
5. Identify collaborative behaviors in healthcare quality management.

INTRODUCTION

Last month, the Board of Directors for Akron Memorial, a struggling 500-bed community hospital, replaced the entire leadership team, including the chief executive officer, chief operating officer, and chief financial officer. After installing interim C-suite executives in leadership positions, the Board hired the notorious consultant firm, the Fischer Group, to develop a Performance Improvement Plan (PIP) for the hospital. The interim executives and consulting team were tasked with guiding the hospital through an aggressive organizational turnaround effort. According to the Fischer Group's agreement, the PIP assessment phase included "evaluation of data, comparison of performance to benchmarks, and dissection of system workflows in order to optimize infrastructure, consolidate resources, improve processes, and create efficiencies." Following the initial 90-day assessment, the consultants planned to make recommendations to the Board of Directors regarding potential actions to improve financial and operational performance.

Jim Phoenix is the director of Surgical Services for Akron Memorial, a position he has held for 3 years since being internally promoted from manager of Surgical Services.

 DATA FILE FOR CASE 19

Data files for students are available by accessing the following url: https://www.springerpub.com/hqm

The data file for Case 19 provides almost 5,000 lines of patient-level time stamp data for surgeries with over 30 fields, including room ready, patient-in, procedure start. Includes data dictionary with detailed instructions for writing Excel statements for analyzing potential operating room utilization opportunities. Instructor's file includes completed analysis with pivot tables and utilization calculations.

CASE SCENARIO

60 Days Until Recommendations to Board of Directors

"Hi, Jim," the assembled group replied to me in unison. The 6:30 a.m. meetings were usually well-attended, and this day was no exception. Acceptance and social support surrounded me from others in two dozen folding chairs. I usually just stared into my Styrofoam cup of coffee, but today, I made eye contact with each person as I spoke to express my gratitude. I was happy to get my 6-month chip. I would keep it with me, rubbing the dark blue chip for luck. I was fortunate to still have my family and a job. Frankly, I had been pretty lousy with both. I was still not great with either, if I was being honest. One day at a time, though.

I kept my mobile phone on vibrate, but I felt it buzz at least three times during my little speech. *Who calls at this time of the morning?* I thought. I checked my phone. It was actually one email, one text, and one voicemail, all from the same person—my new boss, Cynthia Corel. The interim chief operating officer was nothing if not thorough. I texted back: "Headed to office now. Need me?"

She replied, "Got preliminary recommendations from Fischer. We need to talk. Come to my office ASAP."

"OMW," I texted back as I walked to the community center parking lot in the pitch black morning. I started my 10-year-old Mini Cooper. *So cold out. I hope she starts*, I thought. When she revved to life, I wondered if my luck would continue. I popped a Nicorette® gum, the third of the morning.

As I pulled into the hospital garage entrance gate at 7:35 a.m., a red Maserati pulled into the automated ticket machine alongside of me. Our barrier gates lifted at the same time, and the other car screeched ahead to the physician parking area. Behind the red brake lights, I noticed the personalized license plate. "ZZZ-ZZZ," it read. *Must be an anesthesiologist. Clever,* I thought. As the physician exited his car, I made a mental note. *Dr. Pearson is running late to surgery.*

I entered the executive office suite, and rubbed my 6-month coin. I rapped on Corel's door with a confident knock that belied my true feelings. "Hi, James. Come in, sit down," she said.

Why does she insist on calling me James? I feel like I'm in trouble with the school principal, I thought.

I sat at the two-person work table next to her large uncluttered desk. Photos of her beautiful family watched us from the credenza. They all looked so happy. *I'll bet no turnaround is needed at the Corel household,* I thought. Cynthia sat and crossed her hands politely. *Is that her smile or her ultra-tight hair bun pulling her face that way?*

"James, I've received the preliminary recommendations from Fischer," Cynthia repeated. "I wanted to give you a heads-up on some of the analysis so that you are not surprised when the recommendations are given to the Board in 60 days."

"I appreciate that," I said. She held my gaze with a sympathetic look. *Was she comforting me?*

"Well, things don't look too good in Surgical Services," she said. I resisted the urge to pop another Nicorette.

"The surgical revenue is substantially below expectations," she continued. "We've reviewed the financials, and it does not seem as though it's a billing or collections issue. The per case revenue is on the low end, but not too bad. The payer mix could improve, but we don't think that's the problem either."

Again, Cynthia paused and searched my face. *Say something, Jim!*

"It's the Operating Room utilization, James," she finally said.

"I see," I said. *Stay calm, this too shall pass,* I told myself.

"Overall, your Surgical Services unit is operating substantially below the 70% utilization national benchmark. While the rate used to be close to the benchmark in the first quarter of 2017, the situation declined precipitously in the ensuing quarters. See here." She showed me the quarterly OR utilization for the "primetime" surgical hours between 7:30 a.m. and 3 p.m. over the last 2 years: 66%, 59%, 61%, 63%, 62%, 61%, and most recently, 55%.

"I see," I said again. *How did I let things get this bad?* I thought.

"It's 55%, James," she said very slowly. "With 23 ORs at Akron Memorial at 7.5 hours of primetime operation, your ORs only use about 95 hours. According to Fischer, the benchmark rate is 70% or about 121 hours per day, which is 26 hours more per day than we are currently utilizing."

I nodded pensively, trying to regain my composure.

"Here's what happens next," she said. "You have 60 days to develop a response to the Fischer Group's preliminary report. At that time, they will present their report to the Board with near-term, medium-term, and long-term recommendations."

"Cynthia, I, uh," I stammered, "I will develop a plan. What exactly do you need from me?"

"You need to find 26 hours per day in potential increased utilization opportunities across all 23 ORs. You need to develop a plan to address these opportunities. You have 60 days," she said. "And, James," she paused for effect, "unless we have a plan to turn around Surgery Services, Akron Memorial will have to go in another direction with respect to leadership. Do you understand what I am saying to you?"

"Yes, I understand," I said. "I appreciate the heads-up." *Did I sound like a suck up? It doesn't really matter,* I thought. I felt nauseous.

After I settled my nerves and chewed two Nicorettes, I went to the OR suite to think some things out. Large screen monitors lined the wall with each screen listing three different surgeries taking place. On each monitor, the patient, the active surgeries, and the pending surgeries were listed. Notably, each surgery was in "red alert," meaning that surgery was taking place behind schedule. *Okay,* I thought, *I've got 60 days. First thing's first.*

59 Days Until Recommendations to Board

I asked the Decision Support Services department to run me a report of all the surgeries for the last two quarters. The next day, I ran some basic analysis to investigate my hypothesis that Dr. Zachary Pearson was chronically behind schedule to start the day (see Case 19 Data file provided in the Instructor's and Student ancillary materials).

First, I needed to define the measure, "surgery on-time start." To calculate how many minutes early or delayed a case was, I subtracted the scheduled time from the time the patient entered the room. Time stamp data in the spreadsheet is confusing to me because the times are decimal numbers formatted to look like times. So, I Googled how to calculate the difference in times of day in minutes. I learned that after subtracting scheduled start time from patient in the room time, I multiplied by 1,440. A positive number shows that the case started late.

Exhibit C19.1 Example of a Pivot Table

Anesthesiologists

Row Labels	On-Time (%)	Count of Patient Class
Samuel Sims, MD	43.0%	458
Jordyn Farley, MD	55.8%	335
Easton Coleman, MD	46.8%	312
Emily Gates, MD	36.5%	307
Katherine Strickland, MD	51.8%	301
Alison Owen, MD	49.8%	265
Javier Bender, MD	37.5%	248
Tabitha Farmer, MD	43.9%	239
Mikayla Reynolds, MD	31.5%	203
Xavier Hodge, MD	38.5%	174
Jayden Mullen, MD	30.6%	170
Eliezer Griffin, MD	40.2%	169
Cristofer Hatfield, MD	17.9%	162
Krista Clements, MD	28.0%	157
Zachary Pearson, MD	11.0%	154
Maddox Aguilar, MD	36.0%	150
Brittany Houston, MD	32.2%	143
Paola Mcbride, MD	47.7%	130
Kylie Rowland, MD	43.6%	117
Aditya Yu, MD	56.9%	109
Asia Harris, MD	45.3%	106
Isaias Raymond, MD	50.5%	101

PivotTable Fields

Choose fields to add to report:

Search

- ☑ Patient Class
- ☐ Age (Years)
- ☐ Surgery Date
- ☐ Room
- ☐ Location
- ☑ Anesthesiologist

Drag fields between areas below:

FILTERS

COLUMNS
Σ Values

ROWS
Anesthesiologist

Σ VALUES
On-Time (%)
Count of Patient Class

But that doesn't tell me easily what proportion of Dr. Pearson's cases started late. Again, some Internet research taught me that I needed to create a column with zeros and ones to be able to calculate an average of cases that started late. That is, a calculation of the average of zeros and ones for the cases is the proportion of late surgery starts. I wrote a formula to look at the number of minutes a surgery case started late (a positive number) or started early (a negative number). In this formula, I decided to give a buffer time of 5 minutes to account for a delay in data entry. So, if the patient entered the room more than 5 minutes after scheduled time, then the surgery is not on time and gets a "0" in the On-Time (Y/N) column (see Case Study Data file Dictionary tab in the Case 19 Data file ancillary).

Then, I created two pivot tables of late starts by the anesthesiologists and surgeons. Being a bit rusty in pivot tables, I had to Google this, too. Three Nicorettes later, I examined Pearson's first-case surgery starts by showing anesthesiologist in the rows and the pivot table values as On-Time (Y/N) and a count of Patient Class formatted as a percentage. I highlighted "Zachary Pearson, MD" in the printout (Exhibit C19.1).

53 Days Until Recommendations to Board

"Dr. Pearson, do you have a minute to talk?" I asked the anesthesiologist.

"Sure, what's up," Dr. Pearson responded as he walked out of the cardiovascular operating room in his scrubs.

"Well, as you know, we are working with the consultants to identify areas for improvement, and, well, I've volunteered to examine the surgical area."

"You volunteered, huh?" he asked.

"Well, you know what I mean. Anyway, one of our issues is on-time surgery starts, and well, I've noticed that we are not performing as we should in that area," I said.

"Sometimes we start on-time, sometimes not," he said.

"Yes, well, that's the thing. I did an analysis on the last two quarters of surgeries, and I noticed that when you're the anesthesiologist of record, the surgeries almost never actually start on time," I said.

Dr. Pearson stopped walking. "Is that what the data say?"

"Actually, yes." I said handing him the summary report. "I looked at all the cases on which you were the anesthesiologist of record, and it says that out of the 154 surgeries for you in my data, only 17 started on time. That's 11%."

Dr. Pearson scanned the report. "Well, I'm not the only one with late starts. Some of the others have issues, too. A lot of these people are also cardiovascular operating room anesthesiologists. If they are going to be late, then I don't see why the rest of us should be blamed," he said.

"Sure, I bet that's true. I just thought I would check with you if there was something I could do to help."

Dr. Pearson stared at me then lowered his eyes. "Yes, actually. We're having a terrible time with our nanny. My wife has to leave the house at 7 a.m., but the nanny doesn't arrive until 7:30. So, while I live only 5 minutes away, I can't actually leave the house until the nanny gets there. The earliest I can get to the COR. is 7:45."

Ah ha! I thought. *Add that to my "opportunities for improvement" list. How many other late starts are there? And who are the physicians? Is it only anesthesiologists? Is it only the cardiovascular operating room?*

"I see," I said to Dr. Pearson. "We can work it out so that your surgeries don't start until after 8 am. Let me get back to you with the details."

51 Days Until Recommendations to Board of Directors

Next stop: Kristopher Germann, the business intelligence analyst who pulled the surgery time stamp data report for me. Germann was a compact, fastidiously dressed, and boyishly handsome young IT guy. Germann had an unusual way of speaking to nontechnical people that wasn't patronizing, exactly, but more like he was setting up a joke to which you were supposed to deliver the punch line.

"I made lists of surgeons and anesthesiologists whose surgery cases start late. It took me forever. Can you tell me if there is an issue with late starts in the various locations?" I asked.

"Sure, that's no problem. Using your spreadsheet file, I see that you defined late starts in these columns. So ..." Germann flashed through the spreadsheet to generate the pivot table before I could get my Nicorette gum out of its wrapper.

"As you can see, overall the On-Time surgery starts are 41.3% on average. And the COR—I assume that's the cardiovascular OR—is way under that average at 25.6%. But ..." Germann trailed off.

"But, what?" I asked.

"I'm happy to help you out, but can you tell me what you're trying to achieve here? I've found I can be more helpful when I understand the big picture," Germann said gently.

I sighed. *How much does this kid need to know?* I rubbed my 6-month chip and summarized my predicament.

"Well, that sucks," Germann said. I shrugged.

Germann asked, "So you really need to quantify all opportunities for improvement related to average OR utilization during the primetime hours from 7:30 a.m. to 3 p.m.? And it's gotta equal more than 26 hours more per day?"

"Yup," I answered.

"And surgeries that start late are the place to start?" he asked.

I thought for a moment. "Yeah, it probably makes sense to examine the first case of the day. If the first case is late, then, like a cascading waterfall, the rest of the cases for the day are late," I said.

"Okay. Let me calculate the delayed first case starts opportunity. Are there other potential opportunities out there?" he asked.

"Probably. Let me look into it," I said. "Begin with first scheduled cases that start late."

Germann nodded and went to work, kindly explaining as he went. I figured I might as well learn because I might need the spreadsheet skills for a new job.

To identify all of the first surgeries of the day, he sorted all the surgery data for the last two quarters by Date of Surgery (ascending), Room (ascending), and Patient in the Room time (ascending). The he wrote a formula in a new column to compare both the date and the location of the room for the current case and the previous case. A formula looked to see if both conditions were true (see Case Study Data file Dictionary tab in the Case 19 Data file ancillary). He then copied and pasted the values (not the formula) into a new column. He told me that if he skipped this step, then the results will be inaccurate if/when re-sorted.

Germann also created a column to note if a case was within the primetime hours of 7:30 a.m. to 3 p.m. Two conditions must be true for a case to be considered a primetime case. First, the scheduled start time must be equal to or greater than 7:30 a.m. *and* less than 3:00 p.m. He explained that because the spreadsheet sees times during the date as fractions of a full day (24 hours), he had to express these times as fractions (i.e., 7:30 a.m. = 7.5/24 and 3:00 p.m. = 15/24). He wrote a formula and copied the formula to the bottom on the data file (see Case Study Data file Dictionary tab in the Case 19 Data file ancillary).

Finally, Germann created columns in the spreadsheet for week of the year, month, year, day of the week, and weekday. Each of these formulas referenced the Surgery Date column. He didn't show me how to do this, but just said, "Google it" (see Case Study Data file Dictionary tab in the Case 19 Data file ancillary).

Germann then created a pivot table that filtered to include, by week of the year, only first cases that were in the primetime and weekdays. He excluded Case Classifications of "trauma" and "emergent" from the pivot table. He used the pivot table results to convert each week's total minutes delayed into hours, then per day (divided by 5). He then took the average number of delays in hours for all the weeks of the year in Quarter 1 and Quarter 2 (weeks 14–39).

"Not bad," he said.

I agreed, but it was not enough. "I'll get back to you," I said determined to find other opportunities for improvement.

35 Days Until Recommendations to Board of Directors

"Hey Kristopher, turnaround times," I said as I pulled a chair into his cubicle.

"Huh?" Germann asked.

"Turnaround time, or TAT, measures how long it takes for a room to be ready for a case, following another case," I said. "That is, TAT measures the time that elapsed between the prior patient exiting the room and the next patient entering the room. Some people call it turnover time or TOT."

"If you say so," Kristopher said.

I explained, "There's a sequential process that occurs to prepare the operating rooms, such as staff bringing the previously completed case instruments to the decontamination area, retrieving supplies for the next case, completing the room setup, transporting the next patient into OR, etcetera."

"So, you want to conduct a process improvement project? I'm not your guy for that," Germann said.

"Maybe I do. From watching the OR turnaround processes, I think there's room for improvement. We could do some parallel processing for some of these steps, but that's actually not why I'm here. Remember? I need to quantify the OR utilization opportunities using that file we worked on," I said.

"So how do you want to measure the TAT in the time stamp data file?" Germann asked.

I told him that the TAT calculation consists of subtracting the time when the previous patient left the room from when the room was ready for the current case. I also told him that I wanted to look at only the elective and urgent cases that occurred in the primetime period.

Germann gave me an animated look, then opened the data file. After sorting the data by Date of Surgery (ascending), Room (ascending), and Patient in the Room time (ascending), he worked some spreadsheet wizardry to identify the TAT for elective and urgent cases where subsequent surgeries on the same date in the same location occurred. First cases were also excluded from his TAT calculation (see Case Study Data file Dictionary tab in the Case 19 Data file ancillary). He copied and pasted those values to a new column so that it didn't get messed up when the file was resorted. Also, he noticed that there were some negative values for TAT, which is an indication of dirty data, so he manually removed those from the file.

Germann also created a new column in the spreadsheet to count the cases with a TAT calculation that also happened in primetime. He told me that this variable would be useful when calculating the average TAT opportunity per weekday (Monday through Friday) in the primetime period (see Case Study Data file Dictionary tab in the Case 19 Data file ancillary).

Germann then created another pivot table filtered by primetime cases and weekday that calculated both the sum of TAT minutes by week and sum of all primetime cases. After converting the minutes to hours, he had a total hours of the TAT per week (see Case Study Data file Dictionary tab in the Case 19 Data file ancillary).

"So, is there a benchmark that we can compare to? I mean, how long is an OR turnaround supposed to take?" Germann asked.

"Well, according to the OR Benchmarks Collaborative, the median TAT is 28.5 minutes and the 90th percentile is 22.7 minutes. Because I want to be conservative, let's use 28.5 as the comparison," I said. "So, we need to figure out what the average TAT would be if we always hit the median benchmark. That is, let's calculate the weekly hours that should have been spent in turnover."

"Right," said Germann, "Then we want to subtract that number from the actual total weekly average TAT. That will give us the average per day opportunity for TAT." Using the pivot table, Germann calculated the difference from the ideal estimated average TAT from the actual average TAT for each week, then calculated the average per day opportunity. "Boom!" Germann said.

12 Days Until Recommendations to Board of Directors

"Kristopher, whatcha doing?" I asked while blocking his exit from the cubicle.

"I was about to head to lunch," Germann said as he sat back down in his chair.

"This will only take a minute or two," I said. "I was thinking about the in-room time segments for surgical cases. I wonder how much time elapses between the patient entering the operating room and the first incision by the surgeon? This is called 'Patient in to Incision time,'" I said.

"That one's easy," Germann said. "We just subtract the Procedure Start times from Patient in the Room times." Germann then created another pivot table that filtered for primetime and weekday cases. After calculating the sum of Patient in to Incision minutes per week and the number of cases per week, he converted minutes to hours (see Case Study Data file Dictionary tab in the Case 19 Data file ancillary).

"What's the benchmark?" Germann asked.

"Again, using OR Benchmarks Collaborative data, I learned that the median Patient in to Incision time is 25.7 minutes. Let's use that," I said.

Germann spent some time setting up the pivot table and then calculating the average per day opportunity for primetime cases. "Okay. There you go. Will that do it?" Germann asked.

"Yes, I hope that saves my job," I said.

"No, I meant can I go to lunch now?" Germann asked as he slid past me.

3 Days Until Recommendations to Board of Directors

I knocked on Cynthia Corel's door. She welcomed me with a warm smile. *She's way too nice to me,* I thought.

"Hi, Cynthia. I've compiled my list of opportunities to improve the OR utilization as a response to the Fischer Group's recommendations," I said with confidence.

I rubbed my red 30-day coin for strength. *I'm not sure it will be enough, but it's out of my control,* I thought.

DISCUSSION QUESTIONS

1. In what ways can operating room utilization efficiency be measured?
2. What was the central conflict for Jim Phoenix? Why do you think he is in this position at his job?
3. What is the relationship between Jim Phoenix and Cynthia Corel? What would you recommend as an action plan to create accountability with healthcare managers?
4. What would you recommend for holding healthcare managers accountable for performance? Is there a concern in Jim Phoenix's personal life that should be taken into consideration in evaluating his performance?
5. Describe Jim Phoenix's style of collaboration? In what ways can he improve?
6. Who is ultimately responsible for the operating room utilization inefficiencies?

 ## PODCAST FOR CASE 19

Listen to how experts approach the topic (you can access the podcast by following this url to Springer Publishing Company Connect™: https://connect.springerpub.com/content/book/978-0-8261-4514-7/front-matter/fmatter2)

FURTHER READING

Balzer, C., Raackow, D., Hahnenkamp, K., Flessa, S., & Meissner, K. (2017). Timeliness of operating room case planning and time utilization: Influence of first and to-follow cases. *Frontiers in Medicine,* *4,* 49. doi:10.3389/fmed.2017.00049

Foster, T. (2012). Data for benchmarking your OR's performance. *OR Manager, 28,* 1–5. Retrieved from https://cdn.ormanager.com › 2012/01 › 0112_ORM_5.Benchmark_r.pdf

TOOLS AND APPROACHES

DATA ANALYTICS

Thanks to the digitization of the healthcare encounter, quality managers now have access to an immense amount of data. Unfortunately, many do not know how to make meaning out of all that data. Terabytes, petabytes, and exabytes of data occupy large amounts of storage space, but remain useless until you extract information out of them. As the volumes of data in healthcare become larger and larger, it is imperative that you acquire and develop data analytics skills.

While buzzwords like "big data" are well known and understood to a certain level, for healthcare leaders and organizations, "small data" holds bigger promise for translating data to actionable information (Wills, 2014). Data analytics applies analytical disciplines, such as statistics, to drive decision-making for planning, management, measurement, and learning (Cortada, Gordon, & Lenihan, 2012).

For you to be proficient in analytics, it does not mean you have to pursue a degree in computer science. Whether it is a spreadsheet tool, data visualization software, or a statistical analysis package, there are tools readily available to you that enable you to extract information out of the data. The ability to perform basic data analytics to uncover meaning in the data will enable you to perform effective quality management.

This casebook provides data files in the Microsoft Excel spreadsheet format. Some basic analytical methods can be executed using spreadsheet software, including the following:

- Use common formulas to calculate values for quality measurement, such as descriptive statistics of your data, such as central tendency (mean, median, mode) and spread (range, standard deviation).

- Write custom functions, such as VLOOKUP or IF statements, to transform data into meaningful quality measures.

- Employ pivot tables to stratify data (e.g., by location, by physician, by zip code).

- Visualize data by constructing scatterplots to identify potential correlation among variables or bar and line charts to examine potential trends.

- Construct multi-axis Pareto charts that illustrate the frequency of occurrence and allow you and your team to prioritize areas for improvement.

REFERENCES

Cortada, J. W., Gordon, D., & Lenihan, B. (2012). *The value of analytics in healthcare: From insights to outcomes*. Retrieved from https://www.ibm.com/services/us/gbs/thoughtleadership/ibv-healthcare-analytics.html

Wills, M. J. (2014). Decisions through data: Analytics in healthcare. *Journal of Healthcare Management*, 59(4), 254–262. doi:10.1097/00115514-201407000-00005

CASE 20: Opioid Overdoses in the Emergency Department

OBJECTIVES

1. Describe the responsibility of healthcare leaders to build community relationships through identification of stakeholders to improve population health outcomes, such as the prevention of opioid overdoses.

2. Identify ineffective and effective problem-solving approaches to healthcare quality issues.

3. Discuss how providing evidence to collaborators can motivate these team members to take a specific course of action.

4. Describe how an evidence-based management approach can be applied to healthcare quality management issues.

5. Describe how power relationships in an organization influence how healthcare quality management problems are solved.

INTRODUCTION

Gulf Coast Hospital, a community teaching hospital with approximately 400 staffed beds, 26 outpatient clinics, 3 urgent care centers, 2,000 employees, and an annual operating budget of approximately US$1 billion, is considered the jewel of Gulf City, the largest city in a regional area of close to 500,000 citizens. Like many regions in the United States, opioid overdoses in the Gulf City area have reached epidemic proportions. Patients overdosing on substances such as heroin and synthetic opioids (e.g., fentanyl) are overwhelming the emergency department, which strains the hospital finances, stresses the staff, and increases the waiting time for other patients.

 DATA FILE FOR CASE 20

Data files for students are available by accessing the following url: https://www.springerpub.com/hqm

The data file for Case 20 provides sixteen quarters of emergency department drug overdoses attributable to opioids that are summarized by quarter and monthly average. Data file compatible with time-based trend analysis.

CASE SCENARIO

The CEO and the VP of Marketing and Physician Relations

"Excellent interview, sir, I think you handled those questions well," said Gulf Coast Hospital's VP of Marketing & Physician Relations, Bert Simmons. The reporter of the *Gulf City Herald* just left the executive offices of Gulf Coast Hospital.

"Thank you," responded the Chief Executive Officer, Tom Smith, MHA, FACHE. "I thought she really grilled me on our emergency department opioid overdoses. Do you think I communicated my main point?"

"Yes, sir. You were quite clear about your vision for stabilizing the Gulf Coast finances for the future," Simmons reassured. As a seasoned healthcare executive close to retirement, Simmons knew to keep the CEO happy. "She seemed to understand how the emergency department's contribution margins continue to decline for us. You made your point that the current ED crowding was hurting our profitability, but she kept asking about opioid deaths."

Smith massaged his temples. "I know. She quoted some dramatic statistics. Drug overdose deaths tripled from 1999–2015. Last year 42,000 lives were lost in the United States due to opioid-related deaths. Drug overdose deaths increased by, what, 42%? Tragic," said Smith.

"Very sad," said Simmons. "This is a nationwide problem, but the reputation of the hospital is at risk. I thought your opioid community outreach initiative was great. You've got some big ideas! I can start putting a plan together today." Simmons maintained extensive relationships in the community that have served him well over the years. Simmons always wants to support new initiatives, but has a small department of three, including a marketing manager and manager of the medical staff. Even so, he was already thinking about how to make the opioid community outreach initiative happen.

The *Gulf City Herald* published the article, "Opioid Crisis at Gulf Coast Hospital" later that week. The article stated, "The opioid crisis has hit Gulf Coast Hospital emergency department particularly hard with over 1,500 and 1,700 overdoses annually. The Chief Executive Officer Tom Smith described how crowding in the emergency department is worse than ever. 'The patients taken to the emergency department for overdoses are often uninsured and consume a high number of resources when admitted to the hospital,' he said. CEO Smith plans to create an opioid community outreach initiative to address the overdoses in the Gulf Coast Hospital emergency department."

The article went on to describe the facts associated with opioid epidemic:

- Prescription pain reliever misuse occurs in 4.7 out of 100 people.

- 80% of new heroin users began by misusing prescription pain medications.

- 20% of patients who are newly prescribed an opioid will become addicted.

- Addiction is a disease. Many patients lack mental health insurance coverage to support outpatient therapies, yet the payer coverage for mental health services is poor at best.

The Chief Medical Officer and the Chief Nursing Officer

Elliott Dupont, MD, the chief medical officer (CMO), made a harrumphing sound at the coffee machine that morning. Usually warm and supportive, Dr. Dupont looked angry.

"Good morning, Dr. Dupont. What's going on?" Antonella asked hesitantly. The chief nursing officer, Caroline Antonella, PhD, started in the kitchen over 40 years ago, and eventually was promoted to the chief nursing officer role. She has the respect of the medical staff and hospital staff, because Antonella thought the alignment among the CNO and CMO produced sound organizational performance. If this relationship is strained, patient care suffers. These two clinical chiefs have to work hand in hand on a daily basis to achieve a five-star hospital rating.

"My Facebook blew up this morning over the *Gulf City Herald* article. Did you see it?" Dupont asked. Dupont explained that the CEO had promised to create an opioid community outreach initiative to address the overdoses in the emergency department.

Antonella was taken aback. She had not heard about any opioid community outreach initiative. Still, she couldn't resist teasing Dupont about his social media obsession. "Elliott, I have a solution to this problem: get off Facebook."

Dupont relaxed. "Very funny. But, we need to bring this up at Friday's executive meeting."

Antonella agreed. "Let me do some research. Can we meet Thursday afternoon to review?"

As a doctoral-prepared nurse, Antonella valued extensive research and use of best practices. So, she researched the topic and found a plethora of information regarding opioid and emergency care. Using an evidence-based management approach, here is what she found:

- According to the Centers for Disease Control and Prevention (CDC), opioids are not the recommended first-line or routine therapy for chronic pain.

- A well-educated group of providers and patients with full understanding of disease process and alternative therapies can reduce addiction and overdose.

- Opioid prescriptions should be replaced with alternatives for patient pain management and addiction.

- Physicians and patients should conduct a discussion of benefits, risks, and availability of non-opioid therapies, such as nonsteroidal anti-inflammatory drugs (NSAIDs) and acetaminophen (APAP).

CMO, CNO, and the Medical Director of Emergency Medicine

On Thursday afternoon, Antonella and Dupont met to develop a plan to address the opioid issue with the CEO the next day. Dupont invited Mary Anderson, MD, the medical director of Emergency Medicine. Anderson has lived in this community for most of her life, and is deeply rooted and committed to creating a safe healthcare environment for all citizens. Her coworkers know her as strong-willed, but empowering of her physician team. She is a leader willing to speak up during difficult conversations and to set expectations for excellence in emergency medicine with every patient. Make no mistake, Anderson is vocal about her clout with the CEO and her need to be in the forefront with the opioid initiative.

After Antonella thanked Anderson and Dupont for coming to the meeting, they stared at each other for a moment. They all sensed slight tension between them because all three wanted to lead the initiative. Then Anderson said flatly, "I read the *Gulf City Herald* article. Smith is a good guy, but he is wrong about the community outreach initiative." Antonella and Dupont exchanged a weary smile. Anderson can afford to be gruff in this meeting, but Antonella and Dupont have to be more diplomatic at the executive meeting.

"Opioids are a serious issue here and throughout the nation," Anderson continued. "That's why I learned all I could about opioid addiction at the recent Emergency Medicine Conference." Anderson recounted how attendees learned alternative pain management therapies and cleared up some common misconceptions on opioid dependence. One physician workshop helped her learn to discuss the benefits, risks, and availability of nonopioid therapies with patients. She also attended a model patient education workshop that covered opioid substitution treatments, pain management techniques, and peer support resources. She learned about some reputable web resources with more information on protocols, order sets, and power plans with alternative therapies. Resources can be found at the CDC, the National Institute on Drug Abuse, the American College of Emergency Physicians (ACEP), and the U.S. Food and Drug Administration (FDA).

"Did you know that the FDA lists several different medications to treat opioid dependence," Anderson said. "I thought that the so-called Medical Assisted Treatments substituted one drug for another, but instead they actually relieve the withdrawal symptoms and psychological cravings of opioids. I now know that there are protocols for pain management, but most of our emergency medicine staff don't know this. Some people will say that the emergency physicians will never comply with protocols, but that's a bunch of bull."

"What makes you say that?" Antonella asked.

Anderson sighed. "The *Gulf City Herald* had it right. The volume of opioid overdoses in the emergency department is pretty scary. We want to make some changes."

Antonella then shared some of the data she gathered. "First," she said, "there is clearly an increasing trend of opioid overdoses in our emergency department. Here are the quarterly numbers for the last 4 years" (see Table C20.1).

"These data were easy to pull," Antonella said. "But when I tried to dig deeper, I found out that we actually lack transparency into our opioid issues. Did you know that there is no way to identify high-risk patients within our electronic medical records system? I also found no systematic way to compare patient-reported pain levels over time. Furthermore, I had to manually calculate prescriptions for opioids and other pain medications, such as NSAIDs and APAP, out of our hospital. Frustrating."

"What proportion of opioids do we prescribe in the emergency department?" Dupont asked.

"Okay, I've got that figure for last quarter. Of all the medications prescribed, I estimate that approximately 11% of them were opioids and 15% were pain medication alternatives," reported Antonella (see Table C20.2).

"The opioids prescribing throughout the hospital seems pretty high to me," Anderson said. "And I don't think we're seeing an overall change in pain reported by patients."

Dupont asked Anderson, "Do you think we could reduce opioid prescriptions? What is the optimal proportion of opioids?"

Anderson thought for a moment and said, "I don't know. Look, reducing opioid prescriptions will help, sure. But, if we want to make a difference with overdoses in the emergency department, we have got to examine the CDC guidelines for prescribing opioids. I don't think the emergency medicine staff are following them that closely, if at all."

Table C20.1 Opioid Overdoses in the Emergency Department

QUARTER	OVERDOSES
Jan-15	223
Apr-15	218
Jul-15	234
Oct-15	241
Jan-16	274
Apr-16	266
Jul-16	281
Oct-16	295
Jan-17	311
Apr-17	296
Jul-17	322
Oct-17	331
Jan-18	348
Apr-18	361
Jul-18	376
Oct-18	423

Table C20.2 Gulf Coast Hospital Opioid Use

QUARTER	OPIOID (%)	NSAID/APAP (%)
2017 Qtr 1	6	20
2017 Qtr 2	8	19
2017 Qtr 3	9	16
2017 Qtr 4	11	15

APAP, acetyl-para-aminophenol (acetaminophen); NSAID, non-steroidal anti-inflammatory drug.

While both would like to lead this initiative, Antonella and Dupont knew to present a united front to the CEO. In addition, they both knew Anderson would likely be a key stakeholder no matter what was decided at the next day's executive meeting.

Executive Meeting

As CEO, Tom Smith was usually in a spirited mood as he looked across the large conference room table at his assembled team, including Bert Simmons the vice president of Marketing, Caroline Antonella the chief nursing officer, and Elliott Dupont the CMO. The chief financial officer (CFO) and chief operating officer (COO) were also present. Simmons shuffled his marketing papers while Antonella and Dupont awaited the right opportunity to speak up about their quality management approach. They knew to anticipate a negative response to their challenge to Bert Simmons's project.

"As you know," the CEO began, "the new Emergency Care Center planned for June should improve efficiency, increase revenue, and help improve our profitability." The CFO and COO nodded along.

Smith continued, "Based on our history, however, I am deeply concerned that the new facility will be burdened with patients with addiction seeking temporary services and treatment through opioids. The resulting crowding will place unnecessary financial burden on the new facility. That's why I've asked Bert to put together an opioid community outreach initiative. Bert?"

Clearly pleased with his central role in the project, Simmons shared his solution to what the *Gulf City Herald* reporter and CEO discussed. Simmons explained that the CEO has insisted on hosting an educational session for business leaders, community leaders, families who have suffered addiction issues, county drug-free task forces, sheriff's department, local police department, drug enforcement agency, local emergency management officials, department of health, and government officials. Simmons concluded, "I think this awareness plan will have a spectacular outcome. The community stakeholders will come together and the publicity should be very positive."

"I think that the opioid community outreach initiative is an excellent idea, Bert," Antonella said. "I just wonder if we should take a step back and look at the problem a little more closely."

"What do you mean, Caroline?" Simmons asked with suspicion.

"Well, I think your approach may work, but it might be good to put a working group together to carefully define the problem. I always think a rich discussion and thoughtful dialogue can produce better results."

"Good idea," interjected Dupont.

Continuing, Antonella said, "Besides, I know Bert has a lot of marketing initiatives currently in the works already. Some additional examination into this issue may balance the marketing team's workload more effectively. Then again, the opioid community outreach idea you and Tom brainstormed is really good."

"Well," Dupont quickly added, "From a medical perspective, I would like to get to the root cause of the emergency department overdoses. I would also like to know what the emergency medicine staff think. Of course, we should involve community providers in these quality management efforts, and any solution we develop should be communicated to the providers early in the process."

"Hold on," said Simmons. "You read the *Gulf City Herald* article. We already know that the community doesn't understand the nature of addiction. Also, there is a lack of patient awareness on addiction therapies. That's why we should go with the opioid community outreach initiative."

"And it *is* a good idea, Bert" said Antonella. "I also agree with Dr. Dupont that meeting as a team would go a long way ensuring buy-in by all stakeholders."

"But, I don't see …" Simmons said.

Smith interrupted, "Let's take a step back. There are too many competing priorities in the hospital at this time to be pursuing new initiatives without full analysis." Antonella and Dupont managed to keep their poker faces.

"There certainly may be other solutions, and I will consider your recommendations at a later time. Caroline, why don't you take the lead on this? Work with Bert and Elliot to examine the issue. Who else do we need to consult?"

"Pharmacy," Antonella and Dupont said at the same time. "And Mary Anderson, MD, the chief medical director of the emergency department," Antonella added. "She's already done a lot of thinking on this issue."

A serious discussion ensued, with a multitude of questions raised. How could the project be accomplished, given that resources are tight? Who should be the project manager for the quality management project? Whose input is needed? What might be the most impactful approach? Is this a public health problem? If so, what level of involvement is required of the community? What responsibility does the state public health department have to develop a state-wide tool kit to support the development of an opioid overdose strategic initiative?

DISCUSSION QUESTIONS

1. What mistake did the CEO Tom Smith make? How should this kind of mistake be avoided?

2. Dr. Elliott Dupont and Bert Simmons share responsibilities for relationships with community physicians. How should potential conflict regarding span of control be mitigated or resolved?

3. Characterize the collaboration between Caroline Antonella and Elliott Dupont. How could things have been contentious between them?

4. Describe the approach that Antonella and Dupont used to influence the CEO to consider their opinion.

 ## PODCAST FOR CASE 20

Listen to how experts approach the topic (you can access the podcast by following this url to Springer Publishing Company Connect™: https://connect.springerpub.com/content/book/978-0-8261-4514-7/front-matter/fmatter2)

FURTHER READING

Califf, R. M., Woodcock, J., & Ostroff, S. (2016). A proactive response to prescription opioid abuse. *New England Journal of Medicine, 374*(15), 1480–1485. doi:10.1056/NEJMsr1601307

Carroll, J. J., Green, T. C., & Noonan, R. K. (2018). *Evidence-based strategies for preventing opioid overdose: What's working in the United States: An introduction for public heath, law enforcement, local organizations, and others striving to serve their community.* Retrieved from https://www.cdc.gov/drugoverdose/pdf/pubs/2018-evidence-based-strategies.pdf

Center for Drug Evaluation and Research. (2018, April 26). *FDA opioids action plan.* Retrieved from https://www.fda.gov/drugs/information-drug-class/fda-opioids-action-plan

Centers for Disease Control and Prevention. (2019, April 17). *CDC guideline for prescribing opioids for chronic pain.* Retrieved from https://www.cdc.gov/drugoverdose/prescribing/guideline.html

National Institute on Drug Abuse. (2019, May 8). *Opioids.* Retrieved from https://www.drugabuse.gov/drugs-abuse/opioids

Vivolo-Kantor, A. M., Seth, P., Gladden, R. M., Mattson, C. L., Baldwin, G. T., Kite-Powell, A., & Coletta, M. A. (2018). Vital signs: Trends in emergency department visits for suspected opioid overdoses—United States, July 2016–September 2017. *Morbidity and Mortality Weekly Report, 67*(9), 279. doi:10.15585/mmwr.mm6709e1

FISHBONE DIAGRAM

The fishbone diagram (Figure C20.1), also known as the "cause-and-effect diagram," is used with a team to brainstorm and organize the causes of a problem. It provides a graphical view of what is known of the problem or process, assists in reaching a common understanding of the problem, and reveals the potential drivers of the problem.

To construct a fishbone diagram, draw the fishbone structure (one main branch through the center with several branches coming out of it), and write the main problem at the head of the "fish." The branches that stem from the main branch could have many names. Two well-known sets of names are the six M's and the four P's (Table C20.3).

The names of the branches, or categories, should be appropriate for the team, the process, and the issue of focus, and do not need to be the ones shown here. One could choose other themes such as "EHR," "Information Systems," "Communication," among others. With the branches labeled, the team proceeds to brainstorm possible causes of the problem and these are assigned to the different branches. When a potential cause is presented, we ask "Why does this happen?" and this new cause is added as a "subbranch" (Figure C20.2). This will help you dig deeper into the actual root causes of the issue.

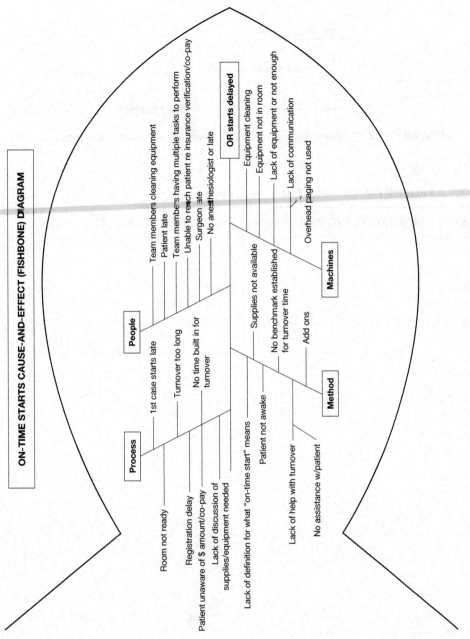

ON-TIME STARTS CAUSE-AND-EFFECT (FISHBONE) DIAGRAM

Process

- Room not ready
- Registration delay
- Patient unaware of $ amount/co-pay
- Lack of discussion of supplies/equipment needed

- 1st case starts late
- Turnover too long
- No time built in for turnover

People

- Team members cleaning equipment
- Patient late
- Team members having multiple tasks to perform
- Unable to reach patient re insurance verification/co-pay
- Surgeon late
- No anesthesiologist or late

OR starts delayed

- Equipment cleaning
- Equipment not in room
- Lack of equipment or not enough
- Lack of communication
- Overhead paging not used

Machines

- Supplies not available
- No benchmark established for turnover time
- Add ons

Method

- Lack of definition for what "on-time start" means
- Patient not awake
- Lack of help with turnover
- No assistance w/patient

FIGURE C20.1 Example of fishbone diagram.

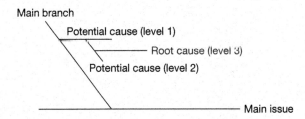

FIGURE C20.2 Fishbone diagram "subbranches" for root cause analysis.

Table C20.3 Potential Categories for Fishbone Diagram

THE 6 M'S (MANUFACTURING INDUSTRIES)	THE 4 P'S (FOR SERVICE INDUSTRIES)
Method	Policies
Mother Nature (Environmental)	Procedures
Man (People)	People
Measurement	Plant = Technology
Machine (Equipment)	
Materials	

CASE 21: The Lunchroom: Physician Engagement at a PCMH

OBJECTIVES

1. Propose interventions to improve engagement of healthcare providers in quality improvement initiatives.

2. Explain how staying current with healthcare system change can uncover opportunities for improved healthcare quality.

3. Describe how leadership can create a compelling vision for change in the processes that improve healthcare quality, efficiency, and access.

4. Analyze how healthcare staff well-being can impact organizational performance and patient care.

5. Distinguish between positive and negative responses to healthcare quality performance problems.

INTRODUCTION

The U.S. healthcare system lacks effective communication among providers and efficient coordination of patient care leading to higher costs and lower quality (Akinci & Patel, 2014). A new model of healthcare delivery, called the patient-centered medical home (PCMH), incentivizes certain innovations in health service delivery, such as coordinated care, improved access to primary care, and better management of patient chronic conditions (National Center for Quality Assurance [NCQA], 2018). The NCQA certifies PCMH model implementation in healthcare organizations, including the use of analytics to proactively identify patient care needs and the application of a physician-directed team that collectively cares for the patient (NCQA, 2018). The PCMH model of care can reduce clinician burnout and increase overall staff satisfaction (Reid, 2015).

Apollo Medical Clinic is a primary care practice with 40 providers at six locations throughout the Apollo Bay region. Although Apollo is professionally managed by healthcare administrators, the practice is jointly owned by 20 of the practicing physicians, including internal medicine doctor, Jonathan Sanders, MD. After seeing significant change in the U.S. healthcare system, Dr. Sanders perceives that he can no longer practice medicine in his ideal way, an emotional experience that follows a pattern similar to the Kübler-Ross Five Stages of Grief model of personal loss (Kübler-Ross & Kessler, 2005).

CASE SCENARIO

Denial: Reheated Fish Tacos

"None of this makes any sense," Dr. Jonathan Sanders said to no one in particular. Sanders leaned against the counter next to the lunchroom microwave completely unaware that the smell of yesterday's fish tacos had wafted into the Apollo Medical Clinic's Northside Clinic location. Supposedly a refuge for all clinic staff, people rarely joined Sanders in the lunchroom. It was a large space with a round table with seating for eight. Sanders usually ate alone.

At 6 feet, 8 inches tall, people had always asked if Sanders played basketball, but he couldn't remember how long it had been since someone had asked about his younger playing days. Or asked him anything personal, for that matter. When he began his career as a physician, Sanders spent plenty of time with his patients, educating them, taking the time to understand them, and helping improve their lives. Sanders thought he still provided his patients better care than they could get anywhere. He thought that he did not need to change the way he practiced medicine because the fundamentals had not changed—diagnosis and treatment of illness, coordination of care, and strong professional relationships with patients. These things he could control. The rest? Well, he felt like a hamster on a wheel, constantly behind, and never doing quite well enough.

"I'm sorry, Dr. Sanders. Were you talking to me? What doesn't make sense?" asked Pam Bukowski, the director of PCMH for the large, multisite, primary care practice of which Sanders was a managing partner. Bukowski breathed through her mouth hoping that whatever Sanders was cooking didn't cling to her clothes for the rest of the day.

"No, I wasn't. I'm sorry," Sanders said absentmindedly. Bukowski grabbed her bagged lunch from the refrigerator and turned to leave. "It's just that," Sanders continued, "the productivity-driven practice model does not work. The managers in this practice keep raising productivity targets, with the expectation that physicians will work faster and see more patients. It becomes a mentality for people like you, and you don't question the wisdom of it. As a physician, my goal is not simply to meet productivity targets, but to take the time to get to know my patients."

As the director of PCMH, Pam Bukowski knew better. She led the organization's PCMH certification last year. "Actually, our practices have mostly transitioned to a PCMH model, so productivity is less important than it used to be. Sure, the fee-for-service financing still dominates, but we are moving toward value-based purchasing. I mean, the number of patients we see is still important, but more and more we are paid on the quality of care we deliver."

"Who are you?" Sanders asked.

Bukowski introduced herself again explaining that she wants the PCMH initiative to improve quality of care measures through better coordination of care, improved access to services, and population health management.

"Nice to meet you," Sanders said.

"Actually, we've met before. A few times." Bukowski explained that she had visited his clinic multiple times to explain the PCMH model and her role in enabling better use of analytics and team-based care processes. She reminded Sanders about the in-service education session in which she explained how diabetes management can be improved by reporting and team-based care.

Sanders could not understand it. He did not remember meeting Bukowski before. He did not know the terms "population health management" or "team-based care."

Anger: Five-Alarm Chili

"But that's my job!" Dr. Sanders yelled with his face reddening. "As I've told you before, I control how I practice medicine. And yet you continue to ask me to work with all of these people. I don't even know what they are supposed to do."

Vanita Modi, MD, FACP, the chief medical officer of Apollo Medical Clinic, sat with Sanders at the lunchroom table. Sanders was eating his Five-Alarm Chili, a recipe that won him second place at a chili cook-off 10 years ago. (A veggie chili won first place, but Sanders dismissed that competitor because he thought that chili should not be vegetarian.) Modi ate her red lentil curry.

Modi was voted by the other partners to provide clinical leadership to the organization as the chief medical officer. Her job was to meet with the other physicians individually and discuss their performance. "Dr. Sanders, my main focus is to protect physician autonomy, and nobody dislikes productivity targets more than me, but the practice of medicine has changed. Demands required by the PCMH model mean that we have to change how we organize care delivery. Team-based care means leveraging the expertise of many individuals in our practice—case managers, patient educators, medical assistants—to deliver care so that you can provide services that only a physician with your deep expertise can provide."

"Don't flatter me," Sanders scoffed. "No wonder we're under so much financial pressure. We hire all these people we don't need."

"I hear what you are saying, Dr. Sanders," Modi said calmly, "but you are taking on too much by yourself. You are stressed trying to keep up."

"Damn right, I'm stressed!"

"And, Dr. Sanders, here's the thing, you just aren't keeping up," Modi said and then let the silence linger between them.

Modi continued, "One of the ways that our payers—Medicare included—evaluate our practice is through healthcare performance measures. We became an NCQA-certified PCMH to help us improve our quality scores. We are making progress, but we still have a long way to go. To keep things simple, I have some of the Diabetic Care Measures to review with you (Table C21.1). As you can see, compared to the national averages as the benchmark, Apollo is underperforming. On each of these measures, your scores are below the Apollo average," Modi explained.

"Quality indices are the bane of my existence," Sanders barked. "These measures do not reflect whether I deliver good care or not. These are simply what managers are able to extract from the health record system, and these data often turn out to be wrong," Sanders said.

"These measures are the nationally recognized standards for diabetic care. These process measures are related to health outcomes, such as mortality and morbidity," Modi said.

"You say you want to protect physician autonomy, but now you are asking me to spend a good part of my day collecting and reporting data on my performance?" Sanders asked irrationally.

"No, Apollo has a full-time quality director. I am asking you to let us help you improve your performance. Think about it. We can always talk about how later. Now, tell me about your chili recipe," Modi asked in a conciliatory tone.

Table C21.1 Diabetic Care Measures

	SANDERS (%)	APOLLO AVERAGE (%)	NATIONAL AVERAGE (%)
HbA1c testing	52.5	55.3	63.2
HbA1c poor control	81.9	83.5	93.5
Medical attention for nephropathy	73.5	86.3	95.6
Eye exam	59.5	66.4	70.2
Blood pressure control	62.7	65.6	63.2
Statin therapy received	62.3	67.9	70.1

HbA1c, hemoglobin A1c.

Bargaining: Arugula Salad With Avocado Citrus Vinaigrette

"Maybe I can make the best of a bad situation," Sanders said to Jacki Stevens, Apollo's quality director. Sanders was ready to make a deal with anyone. He just wanted to feel like a competent physician again. "I will start coming in earlier to tick off all the little boxes and get your records completed promptly. I will stop eating in the lunchroom. I'll eat at my desk to work on my notes from now on." Sanders was eating a salad and thinking about getting back into shape.

"Dr. Sanders, you don't have to do all that. You can get high performance scores without doing all the work yourself. With Pam Bukowski's leadership, Apollo has developed what's called "population health management protocols." Using the diabetes care as an example, we can help you identify all of your diabetic patients using our electronic medical records. Then, we can reach out to them to make sure they have appointments to see you to get the care they need, such as HbA1c testing and eye exams. These appointments don't have to be very long. They can be brief patient check-ins, but then followed up by the patient educators and clinic coordinators. We now have the technology and personnel infrastructure to improve these quality scores without you bearing all the responsibility," Stevens explained.

"Maybe there's hope. If only I understood these electronic systems and the quality measures better, I could be a better doctor," Sanders sighed.

"You are a good doctor. You care about you patients. It's just that everything's more complicated now. We can help you improve the performance measures," Stevens consoled.

Depression: Peanut Butter and Jelly Sandwich

"None of this matters anyway," said Sanders as he dismissed what the chief financial officer Henry Kaplan was saying. Sanders felt resigned to performance scoring, but the whole idea just left him feeling empty.

"It matters a great deal that Apollo remains financially stable," Kaplan said surprised at Sanders's cynical attitude. Kaplan didn't usually come to the Northside clinic location, but he was trying to increase his visibility in this important time of organizational change. Even for an executive responsible for the finances of the organization, it was good to build relationships with physicians over lunch. Usually, there were many staff in the breakroom chatting away. In Northside's lunchroom, however, just Kaplan and Sanders sat at the table. Kaplan ate a fast-food burger and fries that he had grabbed on his drive over to the clinic. Sanders ate just a single peanut butter and jelly sandwich. He's heard that some physicians in the practice were having trouble transitioning from getting paid for the number of patient visits to a model that rewarded performance on certain quality scores. Sanders certainly was having a hard time.

Kaplan tried to connect with Sanders. Kaplan admitted his uncertainty about how to transform Apollo from a fee-for-service financial model based on volume to a pay-for-performance model based on value. Kaplan asked for Sanders to provide his perspective on achieving success under these new value-based purchasing insurance contracts.

Sanders just slumped in his chair and stared at his PB&J. "I can see you're trying to do the right thing, Henry," Sanders said, "I just don't see how any of this applies to me. I can't really impact the scores. Maybe if I were younger. Not any more, though."

Kaplan tried to motivate Sanders by saying, "I think it is important for all of us to take control over our organization's strategy. If payers are paying us for increasing our quality scores, then we need to respond effectively. There's good evidence that the PCMH model and value-based purchasing initiatives can improve patient outcomes. Our financial models show their promise, as well."

Sanders sighed. "Do your financial models include all of the extra support staff we've hired—director of quality, director of PTSD—er, PCMH—and the patient educators?"

"Yes, they do," Kaplan replied. "The insurance companies are paying us bonuses if we meet the healthcare quality performance benchmarks. If we don't meet the quality standards, then we could lose money. That's why we need everyone working toward these goals."

"I guess it's always been about the money," Sanders complained to his sandwich.

"I'm sorry you feel that way," Kaplan responded, not knowing what else to say.

Acceptance: Thin Crust Margherita Pizza

"I admit that I've not really been myself," Sanders said. He had been thinking about his choice of career a lot lately. "I've talked to other physician partners, and they feel like me."

"I get it," Apollo's CEO Gina Vega said to Sanders. "I've talked to others, too. Many of you feel overwhelmed. I don't blame you for being frustrated. I know that quality measures probably seem like an unnecessary nuisance defined by some anonymous person somewhere. As a physician seeing patients, you don't think in quality measure terms," she said. "You are just doing whatever you think is the right thing and hoping that will translate into a better performance score."

"That's exactly right," Sanders said. "I think I speak for all partners when I say that we just want to be engaged in the goal setting and care redesign efforts. We don't feel you've done this adequately."

Vega heard this from the physicians at Apollo before. She led Apollo for 5 years and was the COO for a local hospital system's physician practice for 4 years before that. She knew physicians didn't want a motivational speech; they wanted to be understood. They didn't necessarily want more pay or longer vacations. More than anything, physicians want to help patients.

In the lunchroom this day, Vega brought a pizza of Sanders's choice to share with him. Sanders preferred a thin crust margherita pizza. Vega pulled a second slice from the box and asked Sanders, "Based on what you know about today's healthcare environment, what would be the ideal way for you to practice medicine?"

"I want the PCMH model to conform to how I want to practice, as opposed to the other way around," Sanders said. "This notion of one-size-fits all PCMH practice does not work."

"Makes sense to me," Vega agreed. "Ever since I first met with you, I knew that you believed that a personal physician can improve patients' lives. These are our shared values."

Sanders smiled and grabbed his third slice of pizza, feeling good that he was convincing Vega of his way of thinking.

Vega continued, "It's just that the changes in the health system have outstripped any physician's ability to coordinate care and improve quality by themselves. There's simply too much to do—patient segmentation, quality measurement tracking, medical practice redesign, all of it. That's why we invested in the management tools and staff to become a certified patient-centered medical home."

"These investments mean that I have to see more patients, right?" Sanders challenged.

"Not necessarily. What we need is for you to practice at the top of your license. You should be helping patients with things that need your highly trained expertise. If others can do a job, then you need to let them," Vega said and then paused for effect. "Frankly, to reach our goals, Apollo will need you to change your approach some."

"See, here we go," Sanders warned.

"You know what?" Vega asked. "Your patients need you to make some changes. The Diabetes Care Measures reveal that some of the basics of medical care can be addressed. Do we want to be the type of organization that tries to figure out if our diabetic patients can control blood pressure or take their statins?"

"Sure we do," Sanders agreed.

"Well, in that light, our current care processes need to improve. I think the change will be difficult for you, but if we get your ideas, we can put those to work for you. Imagine how care can be better—maybe even great—for patients," Vega said.

"So you want ideas on how team-based care could lessen my workload and improve my quality scores?" Sanders asked, maybe coming to terms with practicing medicine in the new reality.

DISCUSSION QUESTIONS

1. Describe in what ways health system changes have impacted how Apollo Medical Clinic operates. What actions have the leadership taken to respond to these performance challenges?

2. Describe how Dr. Sanders's approach to medical practice is consistent with the waste in the medical system?

3. Discuss to what extent Apollo Medical Clinic leadership has held Dr. Sanders accountable for his behavior and performance. How would you recommend holding Dr. Sanders accountable?

4. Describe how physician engagement should be approached recognizing that some physicians suffer from burnout and a feeling of loss of a career ideal associated with Kübler-Ross's Five Stages of Grief.

5. Describe what principles of physician engagement in healthcare quality management the CEO Gina Vega demonstrates.

 PODCAST FOR CASE 21

Listen to how experts approach the topic (you can access the podcast by following this url to Springer Publishing Company Connect™: https://connect.springerpub.com/content/book/978-0-8261-4514-7/front-matter/fmatter2)

REFERENCES

Akinci, F., & Patel, P. M. (2014). Quality improvement in healthcare delivery utilizing the patient-centered medical home model. *Hospital Topics, 92*(4), 96–104. doi:10.1080/00185868.2014.968493

Kübler-Ross, E., & Kessler, D. (2005). *On grief and grieving: Finding the meaning of grief through the five stages of loss.* New York, NY: Simon and Schuster.

National Center for Quality Assurance. (2018). *Patient-centered medical home (PCMH).* Retrieved from https://www.ncqa.org/programs/health-care-providers-practices/patient-centered-medical-home -pcmh

Reid, R. (2015). *AHRQ transforming primary care—Transforming primary care: Evaluating the spread of group health's medical home.* Retrieved from https://www.ahrq.gov/sites/default/files/wysiwyg/professionals/systems/primary-care/tpc/tpc-profile-reid.pdf

FURTHER READING

Edwards, S. T., Bitton, A., Hong, J., & Landon, B. E. (2014). Patient-centered medical home initiatives expanded in 2009–13: Providers, patients, and payment incentives increased. *Health Affairs, 33*(10), 1823–1831. doi:10.1377/hlthaff.2014.0351

Lee, T. H., & Cosgrove, D. (2014, June). Engaging doctors in the health care revolution. *Harvard Business Review*, pp. 104–111. Retrieved from https://hbr.org/2014/06/engaging-doctors-in-the -health-care-revolution

Reinertsen, J. L., Gosfield, A. G., Rupp, W., & Whittington, J. W. (2007). *IHI Innovation Series White Paper: Engaging physicians in a shared quality agenda* (pp. 1–48). Cambridge, MA: Institute for Healthcare Improvement.

Swensen, S., Kabcenell, A., & Shanafelt, T. (2016). Physician-organization collaboration reduces physician burnout and promotes engagement: The Mayo Clinic experience. *Journal of Healthcare Management, 61*(2), 105–127. doi:10.1097/00115514-201603000-00008

STAKEHOLDER ANALYSIS

Every quality improvement project brings about change. At the onset of every change initiative, it behooves you, as the leader or facilitator of the change, to understand all the people who will be impacted by the change, known as "stakeholders." A stakeholder analysis will help you do the following:

1. Identify all stakeholders of your project

2. Identify which of them are supporters of your project

3. Identify who are against the project or who may be doubtful of the benefits of the project

4. Understand how much interest each of them has in your project, based on how it will impact them

5. Understand how much power they have either to block your project or help you advance it

6. Devise strategies to obtain and maintain support or minimize concerns they may have

Completion of a stakeholder analysis will allow you to understand how to turn detractors (those against your project) into neutral stakeholders, neutral stakeholders into supporters, and how to keep your supporters throughout the effort. For example, an effective way to turn detractors into neutral stakeholders is to eliminate or minimize the impact the project will have on them.

Additionally, a stakeholder analysis gives you insight into how much communication you need to provide to all stakeholders in order to maximize their support throughout the life of your initiative.

While there are several versions of templates for conducting a stakeholder analysis, the simplest version is a table that enables you to analyze stakeholders based on their level of support, their motivations, and any perceived barriers they may pose to your change initiative (Exhibit C21.1).

Exhibit C21.1 Stakeholder Analysis Example

STAKEHOLDER	LEVEL OF SUPPORT	MOTIVATIONS	PERCEIVED BARRIERS	STRATEGY TO OBTAIN SUPPORT OR ADDRESS CHALLENGES
Jonathan Sanders, MD, FACP	Low	Wants to control how he practices medicine	Lack of control; overworked, exhausted, and stressed	Create a sense of shared purpose; engage in goal setting and care redesign that he controls
Pam Bukowski, Director of Patient-Centered Medical Home Initiative	?	?	?	?
Others?				

CASE 22: The Fulfillment Affair

1. Identify interpersonal communication skills that facilitate quality management activities.

2. Demonstrate information-seeking behaviors, including root cause analysis and investigating quality issues with those with firsthand knowledge.

3. Analyze medical care claims to identify underlying causes of high-cost medical conditions.

4. Understand how evidence-based employee wellness policies and procedures can improve clinical outcomes and reduce healthcare costs.

5. Describe the role of healthcare purchasers and managed care organizations in quality management.

INTRODUCTION

Plethora.com billed itself as the world's second largest online retailer with over 400,000 employees worldwide, including over 100,000 people in fulfillment centers. Plethora built a western U.S. headquarters that opened in Bay City 2 months ago. Plethora self-insured all of their employees, meaning that all of the health insurance bills are paid directly by the company, as opposed to being insured by an insurance company, such as Anthem, Aetna, Humana, or InsuraCare Health. Despite self-funding all health insurance claims, Plethora still needed a managed care organization to handle all of the back office and care management functions associated with health insurance. InsuraCare Health won the contract to manage Plethora's self-insurance functions. Plethora.com pays for all the healthcare bills, and InsuraCare Health serves as their managed care organization.

 DATA FILE FOR CASE 22

Data files for students are available by accessing the following url: https://www.springerpub.com/hqm

The data file for Case 22 provides almost 400 lines of patient-level claims data, including dates of service, diagnoses, place of service, provider type, and total dollar amount paid. Also includes a summary table with patient name and primary diagnosis for the 20 highest cost patients.

CASE SCENARIO

I didn't know it at the time, but Brenda Doyle was just what my life needed. After the accident and everything that transpired with Matt, a change was certainly in order. My obstetrics practice became unsustainable, and I could not imagine another winter digging my car out of snow. But it wasn't the neck pain or the weather that made me so miserable; I needed a new challenge.

I met Brenda Doyle on my first day on the job at InsuraCare Health, as the medical director responsible for the new Plethora.com contract. My office building in Bay City overlooked beautiful Apollo Bay, quite the change from my cramped clinic office back home. The sign affixed to my office door read, "Dr. Erin Franklin, Medical Director." My assistant, Jimmy, handled all of my administrative tasks, and on that day he reminded me that I had an 11:30 meeting with Brenda Doyle, the registered nurse responsible for the Quality Improvement department. Jimmy kindly offered to walk me to the third floor conference room. In retrospect, the bemused look on Jimmy's face—a smirk and raised eyebrows—should have tipped me off to the fact that Jimmy just wanted to witness my reaction to meeting Brenda for the first time.

In the conference room, huge floor-to-ceiling windows offered a picturesque view of Apollo Bay. Transfixed, I moved past the stately wooden conference table to take it all in. The wind blew the water into little white caps on the bay. I remembered sitting not far from that shore side spot reading a novel just the day before.

"Should we get to work? Or are you going to stand there with the dumb look on your face?" These were the first of many, many questions I would get from Brenda Doyle, the renowned registered nurse and quality management expert. I turned to see Brenda leaning back in her chair with her feet on the table. She wore dark slacks, long dark coat, white shirt, and a flowing scarf the same bright red color as her sneakers. On the table next to her were two monitors and her laptop. I wondered at the time if she had adopted the conference room as her personal office.

"Sorry," I stammered, "I'm Dr. Erin Franklin, the new medical director handling the Plethora contract. You must be the Director of Quality, Brenda Doyle."

"Yes, excellent deduction. We are, after all, scheduled to meet here," she said sarcastically with just a hint of a smile. "Now it's my turn to deduce things about you. Let me see ..." She looked me over. "A fresh start, that's what you said to yourself before you moved to Apollo Bay. After the divorce and the injury, I suppose, you took this job to get away from your old life. How mistaken you've been, Dr. Franklin. It's just geography. Now, should we get to work?"

"Of course," I replied with confidence that masked my embarrassment and astonishment. Jimmy left the conference room with a barely perceptible giggle.

I recovered a bit before I spoke. "The Plethora.com people have some concerns about some very high costs claims for the last few years," I said as I sat next to Brenda. "While they've split the U.S. into two regions—eastern and western—they want us to examine the claims for the employees throughout the U.S. to uncover the root causes of the unusually high costs. We need to determine if there are interventions we can implement for our western U.S. members. I have some theories."

"I'm sure you do, Dr. Franklin. But first shouldn't we examine the data?" Brenda asked. "It is a fatal mistake to theorize before one has data. Inevitably, one begins to twist facts to suit theories, instead of theories to suit facts."

"I guess that's true. I have two things for us to review," I said. "First, I have a report of the top 20 highest cost members over the last 3 years. I also have claims data for these individuals and their family members."

"Let's see it then," Brenda said placing her feet on the floor.

In my most authoritative voice, I explained the report to Brenda. "What this report tells us is the insured identification number (member ID), name of the patient (member name), the name of the insured (insured employee)—you can see where they are different—and their ages. There are two job categories—fulfillment, meaning they work at one of the warehouses, and corporate, which is all other jobs. It also tells us the primary diagnosis (ICD-10 code). The report lists the top 20 from highest costs to lowest costs" (see Table C 22.1).

"Oh, I see. And you have the claims data that will tell me the diagnoses for the pregnant mother, Henrietta Jones, for example?" Brenda asked.

"Yes, saved to the cloud. I have the access information for you. Here you go," I said sliding over a piece of paper with the location of the server that stored the claims data file. The claims data include the same information and claims numbers, claims date period, provider identification numbers, place of service, provider types, and the total amount paid by Plethora for the claim (see Case 22 Data file provided in the Instructor's and Student ancillary materials).

Brenda moved with blazing speed, clicking, scrolling, scanning both of her monitors. Every now and again, she made "ahh" and "uh huh" noises. Then she said, without glancing up from her work, "Are you hungry?"

"Yes, I am," I replied.

"There is a wonderful sandwich place across the street. Wonderful variety. I usually get the chicken breast sandwich on the rustic ciabatta bread with bacon, gouda, spinach, spicy aioli sauce, and a nice ripe tomato slice," Brenda said.

"That sounds great!" I admitted.

"Okay, while you're there, you should get yourself something," she said.

I sat in stunned silence as Brenda clicked and dragged, ohh'ed and ahh'ed. Feeling left out of her working process anyway, I left to get us lunch. When I returned, Brenda was gone and a lone yellow sticky note was posted where she had sat only minutes earlier. "GEMBA. CHECK WITH JIMMY FOR TRAVEL ARRANGEMENTS."

"Who's Gemba?" I thought.

Two days later, I drove Brenda in the rental car because, as I was curtly informed, Brenda does not drive. I learned later that driving distracts from her deep thinking. As we traveled to the Plethora fulfillment center, she sat in the passenger seat with her eyes closed, either sleeping or thinking, I didn't know. Either way, I could not stand the silence, and something had been bugging me since we first met. "Brenda, are you asleep?" I asked.

"If I were, I wouldn't be now," she replied.

"Can I ask you something?"

"Do I have a choice?"

"How did you know I was divorced?"

"I didn't. You could be separated. It was simply a logical inference based on careful observation."

Table C22.1 Sample Report of the Top 20 Members With Highest Claims Costs

MEMBER ID	MEMBER NAME	EMPLOYEE INSURED	AGE	JOB CATEGORY	PRIMARY DIAGNOSIS	ICD-10 CODE	TOTAL COSTS
9232556-A	David Jones	Henrietta Jones	0	Fulfillment	Preterm newborn, unspecified weeks of gestation	P07.31	$1,218,367
1923454-A	Angela Smith	Susy Smith	0	Fulfillment	Preterm newborn, unspecified weeks of gestation	P07.31	$1,216,928
1293721	Barbara Jenkins	Steven Jenkins	55	Fulfillment	Malignant neoplasm of colon	C18	$1,149,804
4582771	Kimani Williamson	Jennie Williamson	0	Fulfillment	Preterm newborn, unspecified weeks of gestation	P07.32	$1,016,683
4335689	Devin Osborne	Cindy Osborne	0	Fulfillment	Preterm newborn, unspecified weeks of gestation	P07.32	$974,083
6346789	Antonio Sánchez	Maria Sánchez	0	Fulfillment	Preterm newborn, unspecified weeks of gestation	P07.33	$919,827
1368485	Leonard Mitchell	Leonard Mitchell	49	Corporate	Liver transplant	Z94.4	$829,499
4732794	Colin O'Donnell	Bobbi O'Donnell	0	Fulfillment	Preterm newborn, unspecified weeks of gestation	P07.33	$821,285

(continued)

Table C22.1 Sample Report of the Top 20 Members With Highest Claims Costs (*continued*)

MEMBER ID	MEMBER NAME	EMPLOYEE INSURED	AGE	JOB CATEGORY	PRIMARY DIAGNOSIS	ICD-10 CODE	TOTAL COSTS
2468903	Marc Curtis	Marc Curtis	31	Fulfillment	Malignant neoplasm of brain	C71	$812,566
2578954	Alejandro Martinez	Luciana Martinez	0	Fulfillment	Preterm newborn, unspeci-fied weeks of gestation	P07.33	$759,943
2357890	Huxley Johnston	Huxley Johnston	62	Fulfillment	Malignant neoplasm of esophagus	C15	$551,663
2246789	Robyn Callaghan	Robyn Callaghan	44	Corporate	Malignant neuroendocrine tumors	C7A	$419,688
2456789	Anna Simons	Marissa Simons	0	Fulfillment	Preterm newborn, unspeci-fied weeks of gestation	P07.34	$371,455
3578643	Sean Hewitt	Sydney Hewitt	0	Fulfillment	Preterm newborn, unspeci-fied weeks of gestation	P07.33	$370,289
4678964	Isabella Melendez	Darcy Melendez	0	Fulfillment	Preterm newborn, unspeci-fied weeks of gestation	P07.34	$331,854
7864678	Laurence Baker	Laurence Baker	61	Corporate	Systolic (congestive) heart failure	I50.2	$231,966

(*continued*)

Table C22.1 Sample Report of the Top 20 Members With Highest Claims Costs (*continued*)

MEMBER ID	MEMBER NAME	EMPLOYEE INSURED	AGE	JOB CATEGORY	PRIMARY DIAGNOSIS	ICD-10 CODE	TOTAL COSTS
3467543	Aakifah Patel	Aakifah Patel	42	Corporate	Blood marrow transplant (leukemia)	Z94.81	$215,544
3565357	Gracie Brown	Ariya Brown	0	Fulfillment	Preterm newborn, unspecified weeks of gestation	P07.34	$196,888
2456325	May Rogers	May Rogers	63	Corporate	End-stage renal disease	N18.6	$148,047
3565357	Ariya Brown	Ariya Brown	27	Fulfillment	Encounter for suspected cervical shortening ruled out	Z03.75	$21,505

"How so?" I asked.

Brenda opened her eyes and sat up. "First, there was your missing wedding band. You have an indention on your ring finger where your ring used to be. You married 25 pounds ago. Naturally, you moved to Apollo Bay for the sun. I could also see the sunburn outline of your sunglasses. You really must wear sunscreen. Anyway, I guessed divorce, as you seem the type that would keep wearing your wedding ring during any marital separation period."

"And, how did you know about my bike accident?"

"Again, I didn't know you had an accident, only an injury. That was a guess, too. When you first turned to look at me, you turned your whole body, not just your head. This suggests a serious physical impairment, which would also explain the job change. You were a practicing physician, but now you work for a health insurance company. That's quite a change. I assume you couldn't practice clinical medicine anymore?"

"Yes, that's right. I had a busy obstetrics clinic. After my bike accident, I couldn't handle all the patients," I admitted.

We drove in silence until we turned into the Plethora fulfillment center parking lot. "Brenda," I said in a pleading tone. "This is a big contract for InsuraCare Health, and working for them is my only job. Can you let me do the talking to the Plethora people? We are meeting with the vice president of Fulfillment and the regional director of Human Resources."

"Of course," she told me. "I prefer that you handle the corporate types."

The fulfillment center was ginormous, probably a million square feet of warehouse. The outside walls seemed to stretch forever, and hundreds of cars sat in the parking lot. The vice president of Fulfillment, Rick Jennings, met us in the small lobby of the office area of the fulfillment center. Rick was lean and smartly dressed. He had the demeanor of a military officer, orderly and efficient. He led us to a small conference room with no windows that smelled of whiteboard markers. Larry Davison, an EMT and onsite medical representative, was waiting for us there. Larry looked like a rancher stuffed into a dark blue suit. He had a protruding belly and a very large cowboy mustache.

Reiterating what I had written to them by email, I explained to Rick and Larry that we were responsible for identifying any root causes of the high-cost medical claims. However, before getting into the details of the claims, I asked them to explain what happens at the fulfillment centers. I took copious notes, which I have reproduced here.

Meeting Notes:

Rick (VP of Fulfillment) said policies of fulfillment center ensure efficiency. Plethora ranked as seventh best place to work in the U.S. by Linkedin.com. Offers competitive pay and health insurance to its employees on "day one." Warehouses are a mix of highly sophisticated robotics and low-skilled human workers. Warehouse workers make an average of $13 an hour. There is significant employee turnover, especially during the seasonal hiring period. Shifts last 10 hours. Workers get a 15-minute break in the morning, 30-minute lunch, a 10-minute break in the evening, and no more than 6 minutes for bathroom breaks. Bathrooms are located upstairs. Water is allowed on warehouse

(continued)

(*continued*)

floor, but no food. Floor managers enforce aggressive productivity targets, tracked by surveilling employee's product scans. Productivity quotas are set for each daily quarter (2.5 hour periods). Productivity increased 20% each year for past 3 years.

Larry (Onsite Medical Representative) thinks high-cost medical claims due to socioeconomic issues of workers. No Wellness and Health Promotion (WHP) program because workers didn't sign up. Work area is safe. Very few accidents. Environment free from toxins and other cancer-causing risks. Workers' Compensation claims low. Suspects socioeconomic stresses at home for many warehouse workers. "Employees don't take care of themselves." He did an informal study … workers eat lots of processed foods, fruit juices, caffeine, and sugar. Many employees are overweight. Some smoke, even a few of the pregnant mothers. Doubts pregnant women get appropriate prenatal care. Pregnant moms not required to lift heavy objects. Noticed many employees pregnant less than 6 months after last childbirth.

During my interview of Rick and Larry, Brenda paced back and forth. While I pretended not to notice, Brenda's behavior seemed to make the men nervous. "It seems to me," Brenda finally interrupted, "that you don't understand the needs of your employees or how to support their needs. You're focused on productivity and not their well-being."

"Brenda!" I blurted.

"I'm sorry, Dr. Franklin, but this fool's limited knowledge of Women's Reproductive Health is too much to bear. If you understood the HEDIS Prenatal and Postpartum Care measures, you would know that women at Plethora actually do a fantastic job of both prenatal and postpartum care," Brenda said.

"What Brenda means is that the HEDIS scores, that's Health Effectiveness Data Information Set scores, are excellent for prenatal and postpartum care. Also, InsuraCare Health did a large chart review for Women's Reproductive Health measures and found complete evidence of an OB/GYN physical exam and appropriate prenatal care procedure for a high proportion of pregnant women," I explained. "The Post Postpartum Care at 6 weeks measures also looked good, showing sufficient documentation of pelvic exams, weight evaluations, and blood pressure scores for a large majority of cases. The issue here, though, is the high-cost claims and the unusual proportion of dollars associated with moms and babies." I don't think they heard me, since they were glaring at Brenda.

"Gentlemen, we came here for a Gemba Walk. Can we get to it?" Brenda said as she left the conference room.

Trying to comfort the two startled men, I explained what I had only just learned the day before. Gemba is a translation of the Japanese word meaning "the real place." A Gemba Walk means taking the time to watch how a process is done and talking with those who do the job. As I've learned, Brenda needs to examine the problem in the real-world, not through endless talk about the issue around a conference table.

Larry and Rick led us to the fulfillment center main area through high security scanners and turnstiles that reminded me of a prison. The warehouse floor seemed endless. Bright lights illuminated row after row of product shelving. Conveyer belts snaked around everywhere. Employees scurried back and forth picking single products from the shelves and placing them in boxes to be shipped to the customers. The warehouse smelled of boxes and packing tape. Robotic machines beeped and whirled up and down the shelves.

Brenda talked to several workers standing by a table drinking from their large water bottles. They seemed weary to talk too long with the VP of Fulfillment and onsite medical representative watching, so I suggested to Rick and Larry that Brenda and I would have more success talking to people without them around. I also eased the minds of the workers by explaining to them that I was a medical doctor here on a factfinding mission, and that Brenda was a nurse with experience in these matters.

After the "corporate types" left, Brenda began chatting with a pregnant woman standing with her co-workers. "What's your name, Love?" Brenda asked the woman. She was perhaps 6 months pregnant.

"I'm Jayla Jackson," she said while sitting down on a folding chair. She slipped off her shoes and rubbed her feet.

"My name is Brenda Doyle, and this is my colleague, Dr. Erin Franklin. Can we ask some questions about your work? We'll keep it private."

"Sure. As long as I can sit for a while," Jayla sighed.

"Of course," Brenda said as she sat next to Jayla. "Do you like your job here?"

"Not really, but with the baby on the way I need the health insurance. This place is kinda like an indoor plantation. The supervisors work us hard and gripe at us for missing our quotas, which are too high anyway. I feel like they would write me up for any small thing. Three write-ups and I'm fired."

"Do your feet usually hurt?" Brenda asked.

"You bet they do. I get tired easily, and I get dehydrated."

"Don't you have a water bottle to drink like your friends over there?"

"Are you kidding? If I had a water bottle to drink, then I would have to pee more than I already do. Then I'd definitely miss my quotas with all the potty breaks I would need. Plus, the closest restroom is way over there and up a flight of stairs. I get 6 minutes tops for pee breaks, which is not enough time for me to waddle way, way over there," Jayla laughed.

"Do you go to the doctor for check-ups?" Brenda asked.

"Yes, just had an appointment last week. Glad I went, too, because I had a UTI."

"A urinary tract infection?" Brenda asked and turned to face me with a look of satisfaction. "What did the doctor tell you?"

"She gave me some antibiotics, told me to drink six to eight glasses of water each day. And I should drink unsweetened cranberry juice. I'm supposed to take a multivitamin with vitamin C, beta-carotene, and zinc to help fight infections. Also, when I pee, I gotta empty my bladder all the way. No more skipping bathroom breaks."

"That's good advice; isn't it? Dr. Franklin." Brenda said. I nodded in agreement. "Thank you for your time, Jayla. Good luck with that baby." Brenda stood quickly and walked toward the turnstile exit.

"Are we leaving?" I asked.

"Yes," Brenda said. "I have everything I need here. Now I need a sandwich."

DISCUSSION QUESTIONS

1. Examine the claims file provided to you for this case. What did Brenda Doyle discover when examining the healthcare claims?

2. What are some of Brenda Doyle's quality management talents? In what areas could she improve as a professional?

3. What did Dr. Erin Franklin learn in this case? How can these lessons be applied to future quality management projects?

4. What would be the most effective way to interact with the Plethora.com management team to affect change in healthcare outcomes?

5. In what ways could Plethora.com management better support the employees? How would you recommend they go about this?

 ## PODCAST FOR CASE 22

Listen to how experts approach the topic (you can access the podcast by following this url to Springer Publishing Company Connect™: https://connect.springerpub.com/content/book/978-0-8261-4514-7/front-matter/fmatter2)

FURTHER READING

Bennett, W. L., Chang, H. Y., Levine, D. M., Wang, L., Neale, D., Werner, E. F., & Clark, J. M. (2014). Utilization of primary and obstetric care after medically complicated pregnancies: An analysis of medical claims data. *Journal of General Internal Medicine, 29*(4), 636–645. doi:10.1007/s11606-013-2744-2

Green, D. C., Koplan, J. P., & Cutler, G. M. (1999). Prenatal care in the first trimester: Misleading findings from HEDIS. *International Journal for Quality in Health Care, 11*(6), 465–473. doi:10.1093/intqhc/11.6.465

Gyamfi-Bannerman, C., & Ananth, C. V. (2014). Trends in spontaneous and indicated preterm delivery among singleton gestations in the United States, 2005–2012. *Obstetrics & Gynecology, 124*(6), 1069–1074. doi:10.1097/AOG.0000000000000546

Nygaard, I., & Linder, M. (1997). Thirst at work—An occupational hazard? *International Urogynecology Journal, 8*(6), 340–343. doi:10.1007/bf02765593

GEMBA WALK

Gemba (also spelled "genba") means "actual place" in Japanese. John Shook adds that "the gemba is where you go to understand work and lead. It is also where you go to learn" (Womack, 2001). Gemba Walk consists of visiting the area where the work takes place and observe and engage staff, with a clear purpose.

PREPARING FOR AND CONDUCTING A GEMBA WALK

There is no one way to do a Gemba Walk, but there are some very important things that leaders who get good results from Gemba Walks do in common. Here are the crucial steps:

1. **Communicate with the team before the Walk**
   You do not want your team to feel blindsided by a Gemba Walk—it is not a surprise inspection, rather it is a technique for working together for positive change. Therefore, it is essential to describe the purpose of the Gemba Walk.

2. **Have a purpose for each Walk**
   During a Gemba Walk, leaders usually have a specific process or task in mind that may present an opportunity for improvement. It is often associated with a specific Key Performance Indicator that merits attention.

3. **Pay attention to the handoffs**
   Handoffs between processes, peoples, or departments may yield the most potential for eliminating waste.

4. **Keep the focus on processes, not people**
   Gemba Walks are not designed for employee performance evaluation. They are collaborative efforts to understand and improve processes and work spaces. You never want your Gemba Walks to become adversarial, so provide correction and coaching another time.

5. **Document what you see**
   Because you will spend some time thinking about what you have observed before acting, it is smart to take copious notes and even augment your memory with photos if that would help.

6. **Ask lots of questions**
   A good mantra for your Gemba Walk is "assume nothing." Do not guess at why people are doing things in a certain way or in a particular sequence; ask them. Ask questions about exception handling, workspace arrangement, supplies, and other realities of getting the job done.

7. **Do not suggest changes during the Walk**
   This was mentioned above, but it is worth repeating and somewhat counterintuitive. *The Walk is a time for observation and information gathering, but not action.* Once

you have completed your observations, you can identify opportunities for improvement or ask employees to do so. Then you can decide as a team what actions to take.

8. **Follow up**
    After your Walk is over, be sure to follow up with the teams, let them know what you learned and ask for additional input. Even if you are not going to take any action as a result of the Walk, it is a good idea to close the loop so people are not left wondering about your impressions.

REFERENCE

Womack, J. (2001). *Gemba walks*. Cambridge MA: Lean Enterprise Institute.

CASE 23: Composite Quality Score

1. Assess a quantitative measurement method to evaluate overall organizational performance.
2. Evaluate a leadership approach to holding a team accountable for organizational performance.
3. Construct interventions that address specific opportunities for quality improvement and organizational performance.
4. Prioritize quality improvement interventions among competing performance requirements.
5. Discuss the advantages and disadvantages of using composite scores to evaluate overall organizational performance in healthcare.

INTRODUCTION

The Centers for Medicare and Medicaid Services (CMS) publishes its Hospital Star Ratings to show how well a particular hospital performs, on average, compared to other hospitals in the United States. The CMS Overall Hospital Quality Star Rating combines many measures with different weights to create a single number, called a "composite quality score," that is published on the Medicare Hospital Compare website for healthcare consumers to compare hospital performance (CMS, 2019). Research has found that the CMS Overall Hospital Quality Star Rating is associated with lower patient mortality and readmissions, meaning that consumers can be confident that performance ratings are valid (Wang, Tsugawa, Figueroa, & Jha, 2016).

The CMS Overall Hospital Quality Star Rating is calculated in several steps. First, CMS collects 100 measures from every hospital in the United States. All of the eligible measures are combined into one of the following seven categories:

1. Mortality
2. Safety of care
3. Readmission
4. Patient experience

DATA FILE FOR CASE 23

Data files for students are available by accessing the following url: https://www.springerpub.com/hqm

The data file for Case 23 provides CMS Overall Hospital Star Ratings for 49 hospitals, including seven separate quality measure categories and composite scores.

5. Effectiveness of care

6. Timeliness of care

7. Efficient use of medical imaging

For each of these seven categories, CMS then calculates a 1 to 5 rating based on advance statistics designed to fairly rank the hospitals. In other words, every hospital in the U.S. gets a 1 to 5 score for mortality, safety of care, readmission, and so on. CMS then combines each of these scores at different weights to provide a single summary score. For example, CMS weights the mortality category at 22% and timeliness of care at 4% of the total. Once the weights are applied and the final score is calculated, the hospital is assigned between 1 and 5 "stars," called the CMS Overall Hospital Quality Star Rating. The more stars, the better the hospital performance.

Health Care Corporation (HCC) is one of the largest for-profit healthcare corporations in the United States, managing 49 hospitals across the southern states of Alabama, Georgia, Louisiana, Mississippi, North Carolina, South Carolina, and Tennessee. Three years ago, HCC relocated its headquarters into a fancy, state-of-the art campus in Knoxville, Tennessee. While the health system stock price reached an all-time high 2 years ago, the steady decline in corporate value had shareholders and the Board of Directors increasingly concerned. Bad publicity associated with the CMS Overall Hospital Quality Star Ratings was partly to blame. At the most recent Board of Directors meeting, the Board decreed that all HCC's hospitals achieve the CMS Overall Hospital Quality Star Ratings of 3 or above within 18 months.

CASE SCENARIO

Oh, Crap!

'*Oh, crap!*' was all Leon Jackson could think of when leaving the Board of Directors meeting. He sat in his Jaguar XJ, loosened his tie, and kept thinking '*Oh, crap!*' Jackson was the chief executive officer over all HCC hospitals, and the Board just gave him an ultimatum. No longer the media darling it was before Jackson took the CEO job 18 months ago, HCC was receiving plenty of bad press, due mostly to their hospitals' CMS Hospital Star Ratings. The Board of Directors directed Jackson to achieve the CMS Hospital Star Ratings of 3 or above at all HCC's hospitals. He had 18 months. The reason for Jackson's '*Oh crap!*' moment is that currently more than half of HCC's hospitals are below that mark (see Case 23 Data file provided in the Instructor's and Student ancillary materials). He was not sure how long he sat in the parking garage of HCC's headquarters pondering his next move. But, he did not get this far in his career by sitting around, he reasoned. Resolved to act, he finally started the engine and left for home.

The mandatory meeting notice from Jackson's calendar came out that same evening to all HCC hospital presidents and chief operating officers. He requested a 2-hour meeting block from 7 a.m. to 9 a.m. Eastern on Monday. Jackson was well-respected by his staff and was known for hating last-minute scrambling. He told his presidents more than once that short notice, mandatory meetings were a sign of lack of planning, lack of awareness with the day-to-day operations, or both. When they got the meeting notice, they all knew it was warranted and made arrangements to call in or be present at the meeting.

We Owe It to Them!

Jackson had a reputation for being direct, and he despised long 'death-by-Power-Point' meetings. True to form, he greeted everyone to the meeting and showed a single chart on the screen (Figure C23.1). "This is what potential customers see when they look at our ratings from CMS," he announced as he showed the chart. "As you can see, the majority of our hospitals are to the right of the chart. For everyone on the phone, I am pointing at the very tall bars with the '1' and '2' under them." There was a lot of fidgeting and people adjusting their postures around the room. Tension was palpable, even for those on the phone.

Andrew Scott, president of Baptist Regional Medical Center, one of the largest hospitals in HCC's portfolio, spoke first. "Well, Leon, by many other measures, we are not doing so bad. I mean, at Baptist, when it comes to mortality and readmissions, we excel. Our trend over the last 12 to 15 months has been incredible. Anyway, studies show that patients don't really look at these ratings when choosing a hospital. They just go to wherever is most convenient to them. We are part of the community. We've always been there for them, they know that, and that is why they come to us when they need us." There were some mild head nods around the table.

"You are correct, Andy," replied Jackson. "Your mortality and readmissions measures are strong, and I have commended you and your team for achieving such good outcomes. Nevertheless, our patients expect that we do well not only in not letting them die in our care and keeping them out of the hospital, but also to provide safe, effective, timely, and efficient care. Ultimately, they want to have a good experience. Heck, they don't only expect it, they demand it! And, you know what? We owe it to them!"

Jackson's voice was booming across the room and on the phone, as his passion was taking over. "And that is exactly what these Hospital Star Ratings measure. And they are telling us that we are not succeeding at it. In fact, we suck! More than half of our hospitals are below the '3' mark. On Friday, the Board set the goal that all our hospitals will be at a '3' or above within the next 18 months." As he said this, he showed another chart (Figure C23.2). "Therefore, basically, in 18 months, the distribution of our Hospital Star Ratings among our hospitals should look something like this." Letting this mandate sink in, no one seemed to breathe.

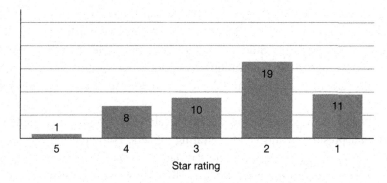

FIGURE C23.1 HCC number of hospitals by CMS Star Rating (current).

CMS, Centers for Medicare and Medicaid Services; HCC, Health Care Corporation.

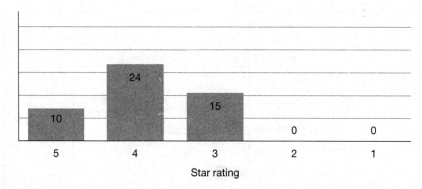

FIGURE C23.2 HCC number of hospitals by CMS Star Rating (future).
CMS, Centers for Medicare and Medicaid Services; HCC, Health Care Corporation.

"Now," Jackson continued, "I am not pointing fingers at anyone, so, please, do not think that if you are one of those hospitals currently at 3 or above that you don't have to improve. What this means is that we all have to work and shift to the left of this chart. Now, I know this feels like a daunting task and, it is, especially when you consider that CMS currently incorporates 59 metrics into their Hospital Star Ratings. Did you know that? That's right, 59. But, I do not want you all to feel like you have to go and improve all 59 of these metrics along with everything else I know you are working on."

"The good news is, as Andrew mentioned, we—not only Baptist but most of our hospitals—have really made some strides in mortality and readmissions over the last year, year and a half. Therefore, here's the plan. Over the next week, we have some of our geniuses from the Process Excellence Division crunching some numbers that are going to give us some more clarity and direction on how to choose our improvement targets and track our progress. I apologize in advance, but I am calling another meeting for early next week again to discuss the findings of this analysis. Does anyone have any questions?"

Listen to Ritu!

A week later, Jackson started the conference call. "Thank you everyone for coming together again on short notice. I promise we will not take 1 minute longer than we need from you. I am now going to hand over the baton to Ritu Reddy, head of our Process Excellence Division. As an expert in performance improvement, she certainly knows what she's talking about. Listen to Ritu!"

Ritu Reddy was a second-generation Indian in her early 50s. She had a PhD in Industrial Engineering from Purdue University and an MSHA from the University of Alabama-Birmingham. She brought Santos Torres, manager of Data Analytics to the meeting with her.

"Thank you, Leon. Good morning everyone!" Reddy, always polite, started. "What this study revealed is that we do not need to reinvent everything we are doing. There are some specific areas of opportunities, and we will give each of you an analysis specific to your hospital, highlighting the areas where you will get the biggest bang for your buck, so to speak."

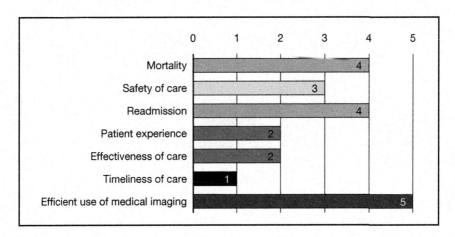

FIGURE C23.3 HCC Star Rating by category.

HCC, Health Care Corporation.

"Our data analysis experts," Reddy continued, "created a 1 to 5 rating for each of these categories to show how we rank in each of them. For the whole corporation, as shown on this chart (Figure C23.3), we are doing really well in mortality, readmission, and efficient use of medical imaging. The areas of safety of care, patient experience, effectiveness of care, and timeliness of care definitely show some opportunities, with the greatest opportunities being in the last three, patient experience, effectiveness, and timeliness."

"It is important to note, however," Reddy added, "that all these categories do not have the same weight when it comes to calculating the overall star rating. The first four categories (mortality, safety, readmission, and patient experience) are each worth 22% of the total score for each hospital. The last three (effectiveness, timeliness, and efficient use of imaging) are each worth 4% of the total score."

"Wow! That's a huge difference in weight. That makes a difference in helping us choose what we need to focus on." said Delia Washington, CEO for Springfield Memorial Hospital.

Before Reddy could continue, Jackson asked, "Ritu, I suppose it would be too easy if we all had to work on the same, say, two or three categories, wouldn't it?"

Reddy chuckled and answered, "Wouldn't that be nice?" There were a few chuckles and sighs around the room and on the phone.

Reddy continued as she motioned toward Torres, "However, Santos and his team created something they've called a composite score for each hospital, based on how each hospital performs in each of those categories, using the same weights as CMS. I will let Santos explain this part because he is the Subject Matter Expert. Santos?"

Santos, This Is Great Work!

"Thank you, Ritu. Good morning, everyone," said Torres, with a slight Spanish accent. "The way this composite score works is by creating a 1 to 5 rating for each of the categories themselves. We then ranked each individual hospital from 1 to 5 in each of the individual categories, based on their performance. Finally, using the CMS weights of 22% or 4%, as

Table C23.1 Composite Score Versus CMS Star Rating for All Hospitals

HOSPITAL	OVERALL	COMPOSITE SCORE
Southwest Alabama Medical Center	2	2
Holy See Medical Center	1	1.26
Southern Memorial Hospital	3	3.12
St. Joseph's Memorial Hospital	1	1.26
Greenriver Community Hospital	4	4.04
St Vincent's East	2	1.98
Dekalb Regional Medical Center	2	2.04
Baptist Medical Center East	2	2.14
Kaplan Regional Hospital	1	1.26
HK Memorial Hospital	3	3.06
Dale Community Center	1	1.3
City Medical Center	4	3.92
Baptist Regional Medical Center	2	1.96
Jackson Hospital	2	2.04
Northern Alabama Medical Center	2	2
Tanner Medical Center	3	2.86
University Hospital	2	2.04
Community Hospital Inc	3	2.96
St. Zachary's Community Hospital	2	2.04
Knoxville Health	4	4
Springfield Memorial Hospital	3	3
City Center Hospital	2	1.82
St. John's Regional Medical Center	2	1.78
East Lake Community Hospital	5	4.74
Fayette Medical Center—West	1	1.3

(continued)

Table C23.1 Composite Score Versus CMS Star Rating for All Hospitals (*continued*)

HOSPITAL	OVERALL	COMPOSITE SCORE
Lakeview Regional Medical Center	4	4
Sebastian Medical Center	3	3.14
Gillespie County Medical Center	1	1.26
Greene County Medical Center	1	1.3
Lake Cochise Community Hospital	2	1.9
General Hospital	3	3.08
St. Vincent's Children Hospital	4	4
C Smith Medical Center	1	1.26
Livermore Medical Center	1	1.26
Redlands Medical Center	1	1.3
Sawgrass Medical Center	3	2.74
EPR Medical Center	1	1.3
Medical Center North	2	2.04
Neverland County Hospital	4	3.78
Northeast Regional Medical Center	2	1.9
Holy Trinity Hospital	4	3.78
Delta Regional Medical Center	3	2.82
College Station Community Hospital	2	2.26
Northwest Regional Medical Center	4	3.92
University Medical Center	3	2.74
St. Paul's Medical Center	2	2
Sandy Cove Community Hospital	2	1.86
Crescent Bay Memorial Hospital	2	1.94
ZCE Regional Medical Center	2	2

CMS, Centers for Medicare and Medicaid Services.

appropriate, we aggregate the scores to one composite score." While he was explaining this, he showed a slide that contained only the following text:

"Composite Score = Mortality (.22) + Safety (.22) + Readmission (.22) + Patient Experience (.22) + Effectiveness (.04) + Timeliness (.04) + Imaging (.04)"

Torres continued, "We then validated our approach by comparing this composite score to the CMS Overall Star Rating for each hospital, and we got pretty close, as we can see on this table (Table C23.1)."

"Now, getting back to your question, Mr. Jackson," Torres added, "while it would have been nice if everyone was challenged in the same categories, we have the next best thing. By creating this composite score, we can pinpoint the category or categories in which each hospital should improve and by how much. Look at this example. Now, I am not picking on Springfield, this is just an example." As he said this, he showed a slide with the following information:

HOSPITAL	MORTALITY	SAFETY	READMISSION	PATIENT EXPERIENCE	EFFECTIVENESS	TIMELINESS	IMAGING	OVERALL	COMPOSITE SCORE
Springfield Memorial Hospital	3	2	3	4	2	3	4	3	3

"Now, what are these data telling me?" asked Torres, now showing his pride in his team's analysis.

Before anyone answered for her, Delia Washington answered, "That we need to work heavily on our safety rating. Obviously, we will have to continue watching and working on the other categories, but safety is our main challenge."

Jordan Kent, CEO for ZCE Regional Medical Center asked, "And you have one of these for each of our hospitals?"

"That's correct, sir," replied Torres scanning the room for reactions.

Reddy added, "Our plan is to meet individually with each of you over the next week or so to go over your scores. We will also update and share these data monthly on the intranet so you can all access it on-demand."

"And we will go over these data every month on our staff meeting from now until the end of time, so, you have to be prepared to talk about your scores and your action plan to improve," interjected Jackson. "Santos, this is great work! I cannot believe you pulled all this together in less than a week. I know this will be a huge help to me and the whole executive team on our journey of improvement. Ritu, thanks to you and your team for helping each of our hospitals improve their Star Ratings."

This Is One of Those Times!

Jackson then turned to everyone else around the table. "One last thing. For the staff meeting next month, each of the presidents is responsible for creating an action plan to improve the one, two, or three categories that you decide to target for improvement. Now, as you are probably tired of hearing me say this, but sometimes less is more. This is one of those times! I do not want more than two," he said as he raised his right hand showing just two fingers, "actions that you will complete in order to improve each category. Thank you everyone and please, let me know what you need from me."

DISCUSSION QUESTIONS

1. It is not uncommon in big corporations to have one CEO for several facilities, depending on their geographic location and size. If you were the CEO for Sawgrass Medical Center, University Medical Center, and Delta Regional Medical Center, what does the composite score tell you about your operations at your facilities?

2. Discuss how composite scores can be used to identify specific opportunities for improvement, but also to track the overall performance of all hospitals.

3. Discuss the advantages and disadvantages of using composite scores to evaluate overall organizational performance in healthcare. Do the advantages justify CMS's use of Hospital Star Ratings to evaluate overall performance of hospitals?

4. Evaluate Andrew Scott's comment that "by many other measures, we are not doing so bad" and Leon Jackson's answer to Andrew.

5. What is your opinion of Leon Jackson's mandate that they launch only two actions/initiatives to improve each category? How can this be beneficial or detrimental for any particular hospital president?

 ## PODCAST FOR CASE 23

Listen to how experts approach the topic (you can access the podcast by following this url to Springer Publishing Company Connect™: https://connect.springerpub.com/content/book/978-0-8261-4514-7/front-matter/fmatter2)

REFERENCES

Centers for Medicare & Medicaid Services. (2019). *Hospital Compare overall hospital rating*. Retrieved from https://www.medicare.gov/hospitalcompare/About/Hospital-overall-ratings.html

Wang, D. E., Tsugawa, Y., Figueroa, J. F., & Jha, A. K. (2016). Association between the Centers for Medicare and Medicaid Services hospital star rating and patient outcomes. *JAMA Internal Medicine*, *176*(6), 848–850. doi:10.1001/jamainternmed.2016.0784

TOOLS AND APPROACHES

COMPOSITE SCORES

Composite scores provide an effective way to make simple comparisons. There are many examples of composite scores currently being used in healthcare:

- CMS Overall Hospital Quality Star Rating

- Leapfrog Hospital Safety Grades

- Consumer Assessment of Healthcare Providers and Systems (CAHPS) scores

In most cases, a composite score combines several different metrics into one by assigning different weights to each of the metrics. For example, if you want to look at a "total health" score for your institution, you may want to combine your scores in mortality, readmissions, length-of-stay (LOS), and days cash on hand into one composite score that you can monitor daily, weekly, or monthly, as you deem appropriate.

Furthermore, you can assign different weights to each of these scores, or dimensions, such that mortality, readmissions, and LOS account for 30% of the total score each and your days cash on hand accounts for only 10% of your total score. That is:

My Facility Total Health = Mortality (.30) + Readmissions (.30) + LOS (.30) + DCOH (.10)

You should note that composite scores may mask vital information. Composite scores hide trends in the individual metrics that make up the score. Your composite score might be staying steady or even improving, but your mortality score may be degrading. For this reason, healthcare leaders must resist the temptation to blindly simplify complex information using composite scores. Composite scores are useful, but they do not tell the whole story.

FURTHER READING

Agency for Healthcare Research and Quality. (2016). *Combining measures into composites or summary scores*. Retrieved from https://www.ahrq.gov/talkingquality/translate/scores/combine-measures.html

CASE 24: Both/And Thinking in Readmission Prevention

OBJECTIVES

1. Appraise an evidence-based management approach to readmission prevention.
2. Describe how interprofessional teams can work cooperatively, as opposed to competitively, to improve healthcare quality.
3. Analyze root causes of inpatient readmissions from the perspective of nursing and social work case management perspectives.
4. Explain how leaders can facilitate team interactions using various techniques, including conflict resolution.
5. Formulate a new organizational structure for an integrated inpatient case management team.

INTRODUCTION

The Centers for Medicare and Medicaid Services (CMS) created the Hospital Readmissions Reduction Program (HRRP) value-based purchasing program to link payment to the quality of hospital care by reducing payments to hospitals with "worse than expected" 30-day readmission rates (CMS, 2019). Under HRRP, CMS withholds up to 3% of Medicare payments to hospitals if they have high readmission rates within 30 days of discharge for six conditions:

1. Acute myocardial infarction (AMI)
2. Chronic obstructive pulmonary disease (COPD)
3. Heart failure (HF)
4. Pneumonia
5. Coronary artery bypass graft (CABG) surgery
6. Elective primary total hip arthroplasty and/or total knee arthroplasty (THA/TKA)

Two hospitals of New Hampshire's Merrimack Valley Region, Irving Hospital and Wheelwright-Owen Hospital, recently merged to become Merrimack Health System. This

 DATA FILE FOR CASE 24

Data files for students are available by accessing the following url: https://www.springerpub.com/hqm

The data file for Case 24 provides inpatient readmission tracking sheet with diagnoses, discharge location, and reason for readmission. Includes 49 patient-level readmissions.

merger sought to create a larger network that could increase operational efficiencies and improve negotiating power against commercial insurance companies. Irving is the larger of the two hospitals with 205 beds, compared to Wheelwright-Owen's 119 beds.

Susy Dayton, PhD, RN, FAAN, is the chief nursing officer and now oversees nursing for both hospitals of Merrimack Health System. Her job is to assure consistent and evidence-based delivery of nursing care, lead the nursing function in executive management activities, set annual strategic goals for nursing units, facilitate nursing workforce education, and approve clinical and functional protocols (Hader, 2011). One function of particular importance to Dayton is the integration of case management operations of both Irving Hospital and Wheelwright-Owen Hospital.

CASE SCENARIO

Irving Hospital's Director of Case Management

Jorge Fernando, RN, CCM, is the director of case management for Irving Hospital. Fernando—ambitious, self-promoting, and extremely hardworking—viewed the merger as an opportunity for promotion. Fernando told Dayton that he heard that postacute facilities do not want to accept patients from Wheelwright-Owen Hospital due to poor transition in care planning, medication reconciliation, and lack of relationship building with primary care physicians. Fernando said, "You should let me run case management for both hospitals. I can bring effective case management practice to all of Merrimack Health System."

Dayton thanked Fernando for his interest and commitment to the company, but she informed him that before considering making an organizational change, she needed to address the 30-Day Readmission Reduction Measures for Medicare patients for each hospital (Exhibit C24.1). These rates showed that both hospitals were performing similarly—poorly, but similarly. While Irving has more measures below the CMS Expected Readmission Rate (AMI and CABG), the hospital-wide rates are very close: 16.92% for Irving vs. 15.23% for Wheelwright-Owen.

Exhibit C24.1 Merrimack Health System Quality Readmission Reduction Dashboard

	30-DAY READMISSION REDUCTION MEASURES (MEDICARE)						
	HOSPITAL-WIDE (%)	AMI (%)	CABG (%)	COPD (%)	HEART FAILURE (%)	HIP AND KNEE (%)	PNEUMONIA (%)
Irving Hospital	16.92	**16.28**	8.65	21.07	23.72	7.94	18.33
Wheelwright-Owen Hospital	15.23	**13.98**	20.93	19.47	25.56	4.49	20.91

AMI, acute myocardial infarction; CABG, coronary artery bypass graft; COPD, chronic obstructive pulmonary disease.
Note: Bold values indicate measure is below the CMS Expected Readmission Rate. Italic values indicate measure is above the CMS Expected Readmission Rate.

Fernando asked Dayton if he could see the data. He reviewed the numbers for a moment, then said, "Our patients are sicker." Dayton smiled and explained that the due diligence for the merger of the two hospitals contradicted that opinion. In fact, one of the motivating factors of the merger was that the hospitals seemed to be caring for similar patient populations. In fact, the risk scores that calculated the acuity of the Medicare patients showed that Irving and Wheelwright-Owen were almost identical over time. "You can assume that your patients are not sicker," Dayton told Fernando.

Dayton then showed Fernando the Hospital-wide Readmission rates dashboard chart (Figure C24.1) for Irving Hospital for the last 12 months. She said, "As you can see, the rates are variable, but usually unacceptable overall."

Dayton then requested that Fernando and his Irving Hospital case management team track all inpatient readmissions for Medicare patients for the six HRRP conditions for the next 30 days. Dayton supplied the report format with predetermined fields for Fernando (Table C24.1).

Also, based on the nursing literature for readmissions, Dayton put together a list of potential causes for Fernando to classify the readmissions (Box C24.1).

Wheelwright-Owen Hospital's Director of Case Management and Social Work

Petra Sheldon, MSW, LCSW, CCM, C-ASWCM, was a master's-prepared licensed social worker and certified advanced social work case manager who ran the Wheelwright-Owen Hospital Case Management department. Sheldon was affable and eager to gain the confidence of Dayton, whom she met only after the merger of the hospitals. Sheldon explained that her team of case managers addressed the individual client's biopsychosocial state as well as the state of the social system. Mostly staffed with social workers, her team addressed aspects that transcend the symptom–disease–treatment medical model, to incorporate client self-care skills and social networks that support recovery and transitions of care. They work hand in hand with the nurses on the units who perform the discharge planning. Sheldon told Dayton that her team specializes in connecting patients to social care organizations in the community. "Patient health suffers when we isolate the medical and social care systems," Sheldon said.

Dayton shared the readmissions dashboard with Sheldon, and explained that both Irving and Wheelwright-Owen experienced similar Medicare readmission rates (Figure C24.2). Dayton told Sheldon what she told Fernando. The hospital case management teams were to track the causes of readmissions for Medicare patients originally admitted for HRRP conditions.

Sheldon reviewed the list of possible readmission causes. Uncertain of what else to say, Sheldon simply asked, "So I put 'other' when the cause is none of these categories already on the list?"

Merrimack Health System Case Manager Leadership Meeting

After the month of tracking Medicare patients readmitted within 30 days for the HRRP conditions, they compiled the causes of readmission data in the tracking sheet with predetermined fields provided by Dayton. The two case management directors met with Dayton in her office to review the report together.

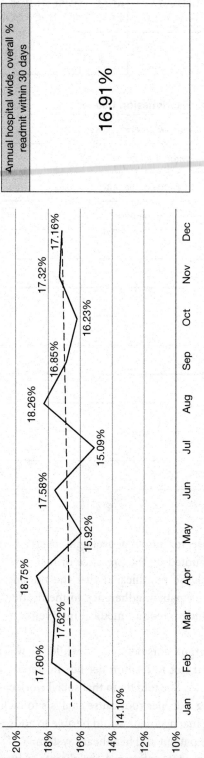

FIGURE C24.1 Irving Hospital's hospital-wide readmission rates dashboard.

Table C24.1 Medicare Patient HRRP Readmission Causes

HOSP	ADMITTING DX 1	ADM. DATE 1	ADMIT- TING DX 2	ADM. DATE 2	DISCHARGE TO LOCATION	READMISSION CAUSE	NOTES
IRV						See list below.	If needed

Box C24.1 Report Options for Readmission Causes

Discharge plan: no goals set for patient with serious illness
Discharge plan: poor coordination with OP provider
Discharge plan: patient unaware whom to contact after discharge
Discharged too soon (e.g., dyspnea not managed)
ED decision: admission not needed
ED decision: patient delayed ED visit
Infection/surgical complication
Medication: adherence
Medication: adverse effect
No PCP follow-up
Patient fall
Wrong home services ordered
Other

PCP, primary care provider.

Fernando pressed his case for nursing oversight over all of Merrimack Health System case management, undaunted by the presence of his new social work colleague from Wheelwright-Owen Hospital. He pontificated that the nursing profession improved care transitions and achieved better patient adherence to medications and treatment protocols. Highly ill patients, he expounded, require medical interventions best coordinated by those with medical expertise.

Sheldon had heard these arguments before, and while she was annoyed at Fernando's aggressive attitude, she resolved not to let him get her flustered. Sheldon leaned back, purposely showing an open posture. She told them that social work case management focuses on the whole person, conducting a deeper root cause analysis to include social determinants of health. She stressed that case management would be able to address social needs, which may be more cost-effective for the patient and healthcare system.

Sensing rising tensions, Dayton refocused the directors' attention to the readmission cause report. Clearly, there was a philosophical difference in approach to case management.

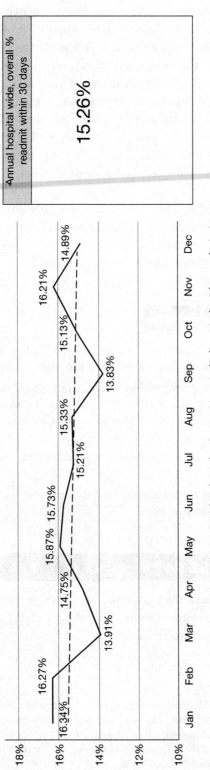

Annual hospital wide, overall % readmit within 30 days

15.26%

16.27%

16.34%

15.87% 15.73%

14.75%

13.91%

15.33%

15.21%

13.83%

16.21%

15.13%

14.89%

18%

16%

14%

12%

10%

Jan Feb Mar Apr May Jun Jul Aug Sep Oct Nov Dec

FIGURE C24.2 Wheelwright-Owen Hospital's hospital-wide readmission rates.

By breaking down the analysis of the report, Dayton pinpointed the problem (see Case 24 Data file provided in the Instructor's and Student ancillary materials).

Dayton recognized that hiding behind their shows of professional pride were misunderstandings of the other's strengths and unacknowledged fears of their weaknesses. As a nurse, she understood that sometimes nurses rely on medical interventions at the expense of psychosocial needs. Even more, a lack of knowledge about the social care system suggests a larger ethical issue of nurse case management: If nurses uncover patient social need, but have no resources to meet that need, then what? Also having worked with many social workers over the years, Dayton knew that sometimes they misjudged medication and treatment protocols. At the very least, they lacked the confidence in their medical knowledge, which interfered with their effective collaboration with medical professionals.

Finally, Dayton said, "I've heard both of you state your strengths and describe each other's weaknesses, and you've each made some excellent points. But perhaps we are looking at this the wrong way. Maybe it's not 'either/or,' but 'both/and.' If we integrated your approaches, could we achieve outcomes that neither could reach alone?"

DISCUSSION QUESTIONS

1. Dayton used the evidence-based management approach to develop the readmission root cause tracking sheet. In what ways was her effort effective? How was it ineffective?

2. How were the causes of readmission different for Irving Hospital than they were for Wheelwright-Owen Hospital? What does this evidence reveal about the case management approaches of the hospitals? How could the data collection process be changed?

3. Wesorick (2015) suggests that "either/or" thinking impedes successful interprofessional practice. How can the "both/and" approach enable achievement of professional integration?

4. How would you recommend that Dr. Dayton reorganize the case management function at Merrimack Health System?

 ## PODCAST FOR CASE 24

Listen to how experts approach the topic (you can access the podcast by following this url to Springer Publishing Company Connect™: https://connect.springerpub.com/content/book/978-0-8261-4514-7/front-matter/fmatter2)

REFERENCES

Centers for Medicare and Medicaid Services. (2019, January 16). *Hospital readmissions reduction program (HRRP)*. Retrieved from https://www.cms.gov/medicare/medicare-fee-for-service-payment/acuteinpatientpps/readmissions-reduction-program.html

Hader, R. (2011). The role of the corporate chief nursing officer. *Nursing Management, 42*(6), 45–47. doi:10.1097/01.NUMA.0000397922.26714.a5

Wesorick, B. (2015). *Polarity thinking in healthcare: The missing logic to achieve transformation.* Amherst, MA: Human Resource Development Press.

FURTHER READING

Auerbach, A. D., Kripalani, S., Vasilevskis, E. E., Sehgal, N., Lindenauer, P. K., Metlay, J. P., ... & Williams, M. V. (2016). Preventability and causes of readmissions in a national cohort of general medicine patients. *Journal of the American Medical Association Internal Medicine, 176*(4), 484–493. doi:10.1001/jamainternmed.2015.7863

Calvillo-King, L., Arnold, D., Eubank, K. J., Lo, M., Yunyongying, P., Stieglitz, H., & Halm, E. A. (2013). Impact of social factors on risk of readmission or mortality in pneumonia and heart failure: Systematic review. *Journal of General Internal Medicine, 28*(2), 269–282. doi:10.1007/s11606-012-2235-x

De Alba, I., & Amin, A. (2014). Pneumonia readmissions: Risk factors and implications. *The Ochsner Journal, 14*(4), 649–654. Retrieved from https://www.ncbi.nlm.nih.gov/pmc/articles/PMC4295742

Emechebe, N., Amoda, O., Taylor, P. L., Pruitt, Z. (2019). Passive social health surveillance systems may identify individuals at risk of inpatient readmissions. *American Journal of Managed Care, 25*(8), 294–301. Retrieved from https://www.ajmc.com/journals/issue/2019/2019-vol25-n8/passive-social-health-surveillance-and-inpatient-readmissions

Feigenbaum, P., Neuwirth, E., Trowbridge, L., Teplitsky, S., Barnes, C. A., Fireman, E., ... & Bellows, J. (2012). Factors contributing to all-cause 30-day readmissions: A structured case series across 18 hospitals. *Medical Care, 50*, 599–605. doi:10.1097/MLR.0b013e318249ce72

Navathe, A. S., Zhong, F., Lei, V. J., Chang, F. Y., Sordo, M., Topaz, M., ... & Zhou, L. (2018). Hospital readmission and social risk factors identified from physician notes. *Health Services Research, 53*(2), 1110–1136. doi:10.1111/1475-6773.12670

Zuckerman, R. B., Sheingold, S. H., Orav, E. J., Ruhter, J., & Epstein, A. M. (2016). Readmissions, observation, and the hospital readmissions reduction program. *New England Journal of Medicine, 374*(16), 1543–1551. doi:10.1056/NEJMsa1513024

PERFORMANCE DASHBOARD

If you have ever played a sport, you value the importance of the scoreboard. Without the scoreboard, how can anyone on the team know whether they are winning or losing? The strategy of the game changes whether you are winning or losing. Imagine if you played a game without a scoreboard, then, at the end of the game went home and had to wait a month to know whether you won or lost that game! At that point, there is nothing you can do to change the outcome of that game. As irrational as that may sound, many organizations today approach performance management in this way, playing the game not knowing whether they are winning or losing until they get a monthly report, at which point there is very little that can be done or learned.

In order to make significant improvements in quality and performance, healthcare quality management teams need to know whether they are winning or losing.

One way to achieve this is through the use of real-time performance dashboards (Figure C24.3). These dashboards offer a visual way for teams to monitor and manage their performance on the key metrics they choose, allowing them to react and do course corrections much more quickly. Performance dashboards can have an infinite number of looks. The important characteristics are that they do the following:

1. Present up-to-date data (as close to real time as possible)

2. Present accurate data (one source of truth)

3. Are simple to interpret

4. Track both lead and lag measures

FURTHER READING

Few, S. (2013). *Information dashboard design: The effective visual communication of data* (2nd ed.). El Dorado Hills, CA: Analytics Press.

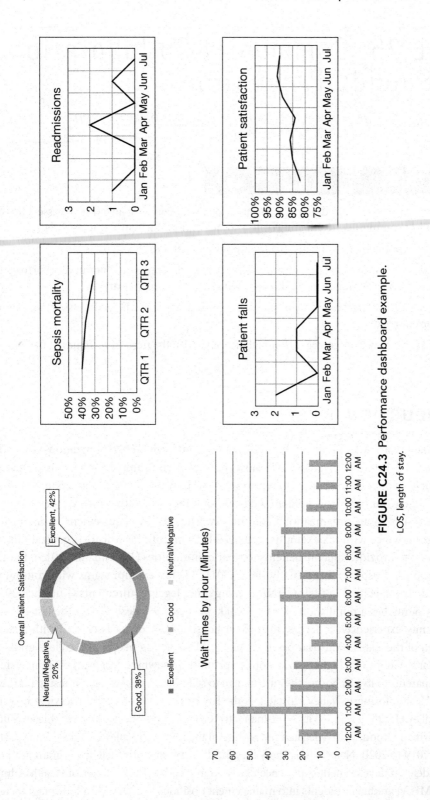

FIGURE C24.3 Performance dashboard example.

LOS, length of stay.

CASE 25: Community Collaboration for Suicide Prevention

Anthony Kovner, PhD, MPA and Zachary Pruitt, PhD, MHA, CPH

OBJECTIVES

1. Describe the legal requirement for nonprofit healthcare organizations to assess the status of community health and create a strategy for performance improvement.
2. Analyze the root causes of suicide among aging adults.
3. Evaluate a healthcare organization's efforts to collaborate with community partners for the purpose of improved health and wellness of their service areas.
4. Assess the ethical dilemma healthcare organizations face when addressing community health needs.
5. Explore how to align organizational priorities with the needs and values of the community.

INTRODUCTION

The Affordable Care Act mandated that certain nonprofit healthcare organizations covered by §501(c)(3) of the Internal Revenue Code must conduct a community health needs assessment (CHNA) at least once every 3 years. A report of the CHNA implementation strategy, updated annually, should be based on epidemiological data and qualitative interviews that assess the health issues in an organization's community. The CHNA requirement is intended to promote compliance with tax exemption enjoyed by nonprofit healthcare organizations that are supposed to provide valuable benefits to their communities (Rosenbaum, 2015). In other words, nonprofit hospitals must justify their §501(c)(3) tax-exempt status with community benefit activities specified in their CHNA, among other legal requirements (Kutscher, 2015).

Valley County has a population of over 540,000 people, a 9% decline over the last 10 years. Valley County experienced a decline in median household incomes associated with a steady contraction of the state's industrial-based economy. Many young people and college graduates have left Valley County for higher paying job opportunities elsewhere, leaving their aging parents and grandparents to live in homes they are unable to sell due to the slumping housing market.

Valley Health, formerly Valley Hospital, is the largest provider of hospital services in Valley County. Valley Health developed its ACA-mandated CHNA under the guidance of chief executive officer, Norman Drood, who delegated the writing of the report to Valley Health's administrative fellow for 2019 to 2020, Neil Maisel. The Valley Health administrative fellow program is a prestigious leadership development experience designed to transition top Master of Health Administration (MHA) graduate students into management positions at Valley Health through focused mentoring. Maisel won the coveted postgraduation job, mostly because of his excellent qualifications but also because he graduated from the same MHA program as the Valley Health's CEO.

CASE SCENARIO

The Administrative Fellow's Presentation

Maisel based his CHNA report findings on assessment of the local health metrics and feedback from community stakeholders, including patients and leaders of community-based social care organizations. Maisel identified numerous community health needs and strategies for addressing these needs through community collaboration. At his first big meeting as an administrative fellow, Maisel presented his CHNA report to the CEO, the chief financial officer (CFO), and the director of Community Health Partnerships. The Valley Health CFO, Sim Peters, made him especially nervous. Peters had a reputation for intimidating people, especially the administrative fellows. After a nerve-rattled start, Drood put Maisel at ease with encouragement and humor. "Don't worry; you're doing fine," he said. "We don't bite. Well, Peters bites, but he's had his shots."

Every 3 years, Drood gave the job of writing the CHNA to the new administrative fellow. In his opinion, understanding the community was invaluable to up-and-coming leaders of Valley Health. As Drood looks to retirement—he will turn 70 next year—his interest in developing young talent has deepened. Plus, Drood explained, he viewed the CHNA to be a regulatory obligation, not a strategic imperative. Therefore, the CHNA made for a good assignment for the administrative fellow.

Maisel eventually gained confidence speaking to the executives near the end of his presentation. "Finally," Maisel said, "the last community need is 'Lack of access to mental health and suicide prevention programs.' Although the *Healthy People 2020* targeted a reduction in suicide rates to 10.2 per 100,000 by 2020, suicide rates have steadily increased in recent years, and Valley County is no different." Maisel presented the line chart of the trends of suicide ranks from 2010 to 2017, the latest national data available (Figure C25.1).

"Furthermore," Maisel continued, "suicides rank as the seventh leading cause of death in Valley County. This is also higher than national rankings" (Table C25.1).

"Interestingly, suicides are not equally distributed in our community. Men—especially older men—are more likely than women to commit suicide. This fact is especially pronounced in Valley County" (Table C25.2).

"In summary, Valley County faces a variety of health needs documented in our report," Maisel concluded. "For each of these top priorities, the team recommends a community

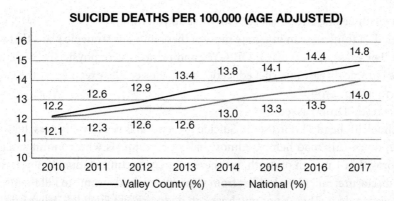

FIGURE C25.1 Suicide mortality, Valley County and national.

Table C25.1 Leading Causes of Death, Valley County Rank and National Rank

VALLEY COUNTY RANK	NATIONAL RANK	CONDITION	VALLEY COUNTY (%)	NATIONAL (%)
1	1	Heart disease	22.9	23.1
2	2	Cancer	21.6	21.8
3	3	Accidents	6.1	5.9
4	4	Lung disease	5.5	5.6
5	5	Stroke	5.0	5.2
6	6	Alzheimer's	4.1	4.2
7	10	Suicide	3.0	1.6
8	7	Diabetes	2.8	2.9
9	8	Influenza and pneumonia	1.8	1.9
10	9	Liver disease	1.6	1.8

collaboration strategy. Any questions?" Maisel presented a summary table of community health needs (Table C25.3).

"I have a question," Peters said. "You say these are top priorities, and yet you have, what, ten of them? Why so many 'priorities'?"

Maisel stuttered an answer that was mostly equivocation. After letting the young man struggle on his own for a while, Drood stepped in. "Thank you, Neil," Drood said. "The CHNA looks good. Let Mr. Peters and me discuss the budget. We will let you know the next steps soon." He dismissed Maisel and the director of Community Health Partnerships.

After the CHNA Presentation

Once alone with Peters, Drood asked, "So, what do you think?"

Peters said, "I think we can integrate most of these into our strategic plans that we already developed. For example, recruiting OB/GYN and primary care physicians is already in the works. The chronic disease and diet education programs can be executed by the Community Health Partnerships group."

"And the rest?" Drood asked.

Peters shook his head, "I don't see it. Suicide prevention is not our business. It loses money. We've been down this road before. Almost half of individuals who commit suicide visited their doctor within 1 month of death, yet there is rarely documentation of physician inquiry or patient disclosure. Suicide is hidden from view. If somebody wants to kill themselves, they will find a way to do it. There's not much we can do to prevent suicide," Peters said.

Table C25.2 Suicide Rates (Per 100,000), by Sex and Age Group, Valley County and National (2017)

SEX AND AGE GROUP	VALLEY COUNTY	NATIONAL	DIFFERENCE
FEMALE			
10–14	1.6	1.7	−0.1
15–24	5.9	5.8	0.1
25–44	6.9	7.8	−0.9
45–64	9.9	9.7	0.2
65–74	7.3	6.2	1.1
75 and over	5.4	4.0	1.4
MALE			
10–14	3.4	3.3	0.1
15–24	22.5	22.7	−0.2
25–44	27.3	27.5	−0.2
45–64	30.9	30.1	0.8
65–74	32.9	26.2	6.7
75 and over	44.1	39.7	4.4

Table C25.3 Top Ten Valley County Community Health Needs and Strategies

PRIORITIZED COMMUNITY HEALTH NEED	COMMUNITY COLLABORATION STRATEGY
1. Growth of chronic illnesses, such as heart disease, stroke, diabetes	1. Chronic disease prevention and management education programs
2. Need for more substance use/addiction programs	2. Substance abuse treatment and prevention programs
3. Lack of public transportation options	3. Subsidized medical transportation program with ride-sharing services
4. Food insecurity among low-income populations	4. Subsidize mobile food pantry provided by America's Harvest
5. Growing obesity and associated conditions, including diabetes	5. Develop and market "5 a Day for Better Health" diet education program

(continued)

Table C25.3 Top Ten Valley County Community Health Needs and Strategies (*continued*)

PRIORITIZED COMMUNITY HEALTH NEED	COMMUNITY COLLABORATION STRATEGY
6. Need for more women's healthcare services, specifically breast care	6. Recruit OB/GYN physicians and expand breast imaging service line
7. Need for more community-based long-term care for an aging population	7. Partner with Area Agency on Aging on existing programs
8. Lack of access to exercise opportunities	8. Membership to Valley Health Wellness Center for patients enrolled in weight control program
9. Growing rate of social isolation among aging adults	9. Create "Senior Companions," a volunteer program for 65+ at the hospital
10. Lack of access to mental health and suicide prevention programs	10. Develop and implement program to train community facilitators (e.g., clergy, police, postal service, barbers) to identify people at increased risk for suicide

"I know, I know. Over the last few years, we've had an exchange of letters with the Valley County Health Department. We all acknowledge the challenge of suicide prevention. We commit to help, but performance expectations are never set. The Health Department is so underfunded, that we just …" Drood said.

"Can't invest our resources?" Peters asked.

"Yes," Drood admitted.

The Sad News

Months later, Drood received an email from his cousin Tom, who lives out of town. The email read, "Norman, it pains me to tell you that our old friend Vince committed suicide 2 months ago. I happened to see his sister yesterday, and she told me. Apparently, his death was unexpected. He did not show any warning signs, but I really think his family had fallen out of touch with him. I'm sorry that no one reached out to you before now. I know that you were once very close."

Drood was shocked. In fact, he had been in touch with Vince a while back emailing reminiscences of a backpacking trip to Europe they made together after college. Norman wondered if there was anything he should have done to try to save Vince.

Good Advice

Drood decided to seek advice from people he respected. First, he talked with Dr. Al Woods, who has a large general medicine practice and sees many Valley Health aging adult patients. Usually a good listener, Woods did most of the talking because Drood struggled to speak about his old friend's suicide. Woods gave some simple advice, "I know that thinking about suicide is common among the aging adult men I take care of," he said "Suicide is particularly high among those with poor physical health, depression, and anxiety and even higher among those with drug and alcohol addiction or severe mental illness. However, restricting screening to those patients who present with these conditions may miss individuals at risk for suicide. Why don't you extend awareness and outreach for universal suicide screening by clinicians?"

Next, Drood sought the advice of Wanda Letts, a social work professor at Valley State College who has served on the board of a local social services agency. Letts said, "Other than access to firearms, killing yourself is related to people living alone. Late-in-life suicide has been linked with social isolation, such as living alone, loss of spouse, disconnection from friends and family, lack of mobility and transportation, and low social support. Imagine if you're broke, widowed, and alone. You lack meaning in your life and you feel like a burden on your family. It's terribly sad."

Letts continued, "Interventions have a greater chance of success if they utilize existing community resources and aim to build community capacity. I work with social agencies and churches, and they have the skills to create meaning and social connectedness among those in later life. We know these things prevent suicide, but no social care organization is focused on suicide prevention. What's more, these agencies are weakly linked and sparsely supported. There is no overarching entity with the wherewithal to lead a focused suicide prevention effort. Why not Valley Health?"

Community Collaboration

Drood asked himself what he should do next. He wanted to respond to the challenge and improve mental health in the county, but didn't want to raise expectations that Valley Health cannot meet. He could launch a community awareness program, convening a committee of hospital board members and local citizens. Drood thought that he could talk to the other two hospital CEOs serving Valley County and see if the hospitals can work together on this. He should ask whether any organization or a philanthropist in the county would be interested in working on suicide prevention.

After considering his options, Drood called Maisel and told him to get some more data about the extent of the problem and to conduct a literature search on the evidence-based practices in suicide prevention. He told Maisel to ask about potential volunteers from the local college and to interview the local newspaper editor and emergency room and primary care physicians. Maisel should learn more about what the community is doing now and how money is being spent on suicide prevention.

Drood also knew that he needed to convince the hospital leaders about the importance of suicide prevention. Certainly, nonprofit hospitals face increased pressure from the government to demonstrate that they're reinvesting in their communities. He knew that retaining their federal tax-exempt status was crucial. However, this perspective will not motivate his team. He needed to align their organizational priorities with the needs of the community. Perhaps he needs to make the story more personal? Shouldn't Valley Health do the right thing for people like Vince?

DISCUSSION QUESTIONS

1. What is the most important challenge Norman Drood faces in deciding what to do next about suicide prevention in Valley County?

2. Does Valley Health have a responsibility for preventing suicides? What is Norman's own responsibility as an ethical healthcare professional to do something about suicide prevention in Valley County?

3. Should Drood consider revising the Valley Health CHNA to focus more on suicide prevention?

4. Why are the social care organizations in Valley County poorly coordinated? Why don't social care organizations dedicate specific resources to meeting the challenge of suicide prevention? What organization or individuals might make suicide prevention a priority?

5. The Valley Health community health needs assessment identified many "priorities." How would you recommend the management team identify the most important needs? How many strategic priorities are too many?

PODCAST FOR CASE 25

Listen to how experts approach the topic (you can access the podcast by following this url to Springer Publishing Company Connect™: https://connect.springerpub.com/content/book/978-0-8261-4514-7/front-matter/fmatter2)

REFERENCES

Kutscher, B. (2015). *Hospitals broaden scope of community-benefit work*. Retrieved from https://www.modernhealthcare.com/article/20151121/MAGAZINE/311219988/hospitals-broaden-scope-of-community-benefit-work

Rosenbaum, S. (2015). *Health Affairs Blog: Additional requirements for charitable hospitals: Final rules on community health needs assessments and financial assistance*. Retrieved from https://www.healthaffairs.org/do/10.1377/hblog20150123.044073/full

FURTHER READING

Ahmedani, B. K., Simon, G. E., Stewart, C., Beck, A., Waitzfelder, B. E., Rossom, R., ... Operskalski, B. H. (2014). Health care contacts in the year before suicide death. *Journal of General Internal Medicine, 29*(6), 870–877. doi:10.1007/s11606-014-2767-3

Centers for Disease Control and Prevention. (2011). *Strategic direction for the prevention of suicidal behavior*. Retrieved from https://www.cdc.gov/ViolencePrevention/pdf/Suicide_Strategic_Direction_Full_Version-a.pdf

Centers for Disease Control and Prevention. (2018). *Suicide mortality in the United States, 1999–2017* (NCHS Data Brief No. 330). Retrieved from https://www.cdc.gov/nchs/products/databriefs/db330.htm

Conwell, Y. (2014). Suicide later in life: Challenges and priorities for prevention. *American Journal of Preventive Medicine, 47*(3), S244–S250. doi:10.1016/j.amepre.2014.05.040

Hofstra, E., Van Nieuwenhuizen, C., Bakker, M., Özgül, D., Elfeddali, I., de Jong, S. J., & van der Feltz-Cornelis, C. M. (2019). Effectiveness of suicide prevention interventions: A systematic review and meta-analysis. *General Hospital Psychiatry*. doi:10.1016/j.genhosppsych.2019.04.011

Horowitz, L. M., Roaten, K., & Bridge, J. A. (2018). Suicide prevention in medical settings: The case for universal screening. *General Hospital Psychiatry*. doi:10.1016/j.genhosppsych.2018.11.009

Rossom, R. C., Coleman, K. J., Ahmedani, B. K., Beck, A., Johnson, E., Oliver, M., & Simon, G. E. (2017). Suicidal ideation reported on the PHQ9 and risk of suicidal behavior across age groups. *Journal of Affective Disorders, 215*, 77–84. doi:10.1016/j.jad.2017.03.037

Turecki, G., & Brent, D. A. (2016). Suicide and suicidal behaviour. *The Lancet, 387*(10024), 1227–1239. doi:10.1016/S0140-6736(15)00234-2

U.S. Department of Health and Human Services. (2010). *Healthy People 2020: Mental health status improvement*. Retrieved from https://www.healthypeople.gov/2020/topics-objectives/topic/mental-health-and-mental-disorders/objectives

Windle, K., Francis, J., & Coomber, C. (2011). *Preventing loneliness and social isolation: Interventions and outcomes* (pp. 1–16). London, UK: Social Care Institute for Excellence.

BAR CHARTS AND HISTOGRAMS

Bar charts and histograms are excellent tools for data visualization. When tackling quality management problems, teams are sometimes overwhelmed by all the issues that contribute to the problem. It is important to realize that you cannot fix all of these issues at once. First, you need to know which of these issues are occurring more frequently, so you can decide which issues to address first.

A bar chart that helps you visualize the frequency of occurrence of certain categories of events helps you prioritize your quality management efforts. In Figure C25.2, the bars represent the frequency of occurrence of lab specimen label issues. The lab team can easily identify addressing the alignment of the label (the most frequent issue) as their most pressing issue.

There is another type of bar chart, which is widely used in quality management: the histogram. A histogram visually presents the counts of a continuous variable, enabling you to show the underlying frequency distribution of the quality management issue. In Figure C25.3, you can see that the bars are connected, indicating that the categories are numerical.

Finally, a clustered column chart shown in Figure C25.4 is useful when you have several stratifications (slices) of the issue that you want to compare, such as when comparing year-over-year data or benchmarking against national standards.

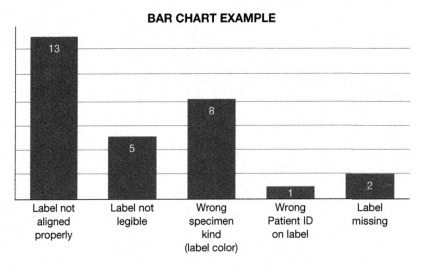

BAR CHART EXAMPLE

Value	Category
13	Label not aligned properly
5	Label not legible
8	Wrong specimen kind (label color)
1	Wrong Patient ID on label
2	Label missing

FIGURE C25.2 Lab specimen label issues.

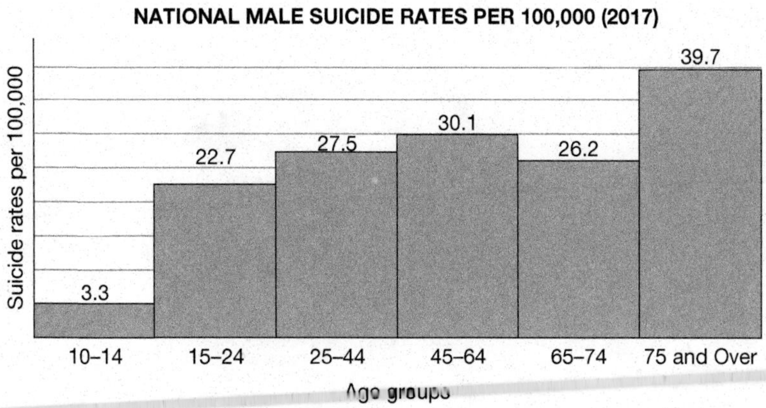

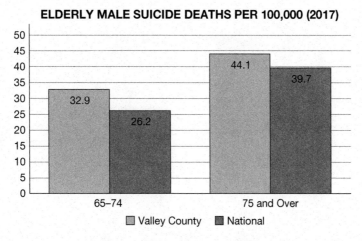

NATIONAL MALE SUICIDE RATES PER 100,000 (2017)
Suicide rates per 100,000
3.3
22.7
27.5
30.1
26.2
39.7
10–14
15–24
25–44
45–64
65–74
75 and Over
Age groups

FIGURE C25.3 Histogram example.

ELDERLY MALE SUICIDE DEATHS PER 100,000 (2017)
50
45
40
35
30
25
20
15
10
5
0
32.9
26.2
44.1
39.7
65–74
75 and Over
Valley County
National

FIGURE C25.4 Clustered column chart example.

Glossary

TERM	DEFINITION
ADKAR® model	Stands for Awareness, Desire, Knowledge, Ability, and Reinforcement. A change management model developed by Jeffrey Hiatt to describe the five phases through which people go as they experience change.
Background	Description of the context of a problem or issue included in the A3 Problem-Solving Template.
Baseline	The starting point from which the quality improvement effort is judged.
Batches	The process of producing more than one piece of an item before they are needed by the customer.
Berwick, Don	Physician, author, researcher, and founder of the IHI.
CAHPS®	Consumer Assessment of Healthcare Providers and Systems is a series of patient surveys rating healthcare experiences in the United States developed by the AHRQ. Pronounced "caps."
Case Application Exercise	The casebook activities associated with completing the A3 Problem-Solving Template for each case study.
Case method	A form of problem-based learning that involves complex written scenarios designed to engage students in problem-solving process.
Change management	Any action or process taken to move from how things currently are to how they need to be.
Clancy, Carolyn M.	Physician, researcher, former head of the AHRQ, and current leader of the Veterans Affairs health system focusing on innovation, research, and development.
Codman, Ernest Amory	Early 20th-century physician who advocated measuring the outcomes of patient treatment.
Common cause variation	A source of fluctuation inherent in the process itself caused by unknown, but steady factors in the system.

(continued)

TERM	DEFINITION
Consequence	Something caused by something else. One of the four common mistakes in the problem definition stage of problem-solving.
Control chart	Short name for Statistical Process Control Chart. Used to visually display whether a process is performing within statistical control. See also common cause variation and special cause variation.
Control Plan	Details what measures to monitor, at what frequency, and how to react when failure to work as planned.
Countermeasure	A short-, medium-, or long-term intervention, solution, or action defined in the A3 Problem-Solving Template intended to solve the defined problem.
Crosby, Philip B.	Businessman and quality expert who defined four absolutes of quality management in the book *Quality Is Free*.
Current State	Describes or illustrates how things exist right now in the A3 Problem-Solving Template.
Cycle time	The total elapsed time from the beginning to the end of a process.
Deming, W. Edwards	Quality management expert widely credited with starting the quality revolution of industrial manufacturing.
DMAIC	Stands for Define, Measure, Analyze, Improve, and Control. A Six Sigma-related continuous quality improvement cycle.
Donabedian, Avedis	A health services researcher who created the first conceptual framework for measuring healthcare quality—structures, processes, and outcomes of care.
Evidence-based management	The management practice of using evidence to empower better decision-making.
Flexner Report	A report on medical education in the early 20th century that revealed inconsistent and substandard quality in American medical schools.
Flexner, Abraham	An early 20th-century educator who audited the quality of medical schools finding inadequacies in scientific rigor. See Flexner Report.
Flow	Movement of items or people from the first step to the last step in a process.
Follow-up and Lessons Learned	A reflection on the problem-solving process documented in the A3 Problem-Solving Template.
Ford, Henry	Early 20th-century industrialist responsible for applying the assembly line concept to automotive manufacturing. Ford proved an influential innovator for efficiency, quality improvement, and waste reduction.
Gawande, Atul	Surgeon, author, and CEO of Haven, the healthcare company formed by Amazon, Berkshire Hathaway, and JPMorgan Chase.
Gilbreth, Frank	Early 20th-century quality management practitioner who applied the scientific method and standardization to healthcare.

(continued)

TERM	DEFINITION
Harry, Mikel	Motorola psychologist credited with codeveloping Six Sigma in the 1980s.
Healthcare quality management	Application of systematic practices that guide the formation of reliable processes in healthcare organizations in order to increase the likelihood of delivering evidence-based care and achieving the health outcomes expected by patients, their families, and their caregivers.
HEDIS	A widely adopted set of performance measures in the managed care industry developed by NCQA.
Huddle	Brief stand-up meetings that facilitate collaboration and improved quality management communication among team members.
Imai, Masaaki	Japanese founder of the Kaizen Institute who introduced the concepts of kaizen and gemba in industrial manufacturing.
Institute for Healthcare Improvement	A nonprofit, nongovernmental organization dedicated to improving healthcare by publishing best practices and training modules for quality management professionals.
Interprofessional	Collaborative teamwork between members of clinical and nonclinical profession on health-related work.
The Joint Commission	A nonprofit, nongovernmental organization that accredits or certifies 21,000 healthcare organizations and programs in the United States.
Jones, Daniel	Coauthor of *The Machine That Changed the World* that introduced the idea of Lean thinking based on the Toyota Production System®.
Juran Trilogy	Defined by Joseph M. Juran as (a) quality planning, (b) quality control, and (c) quality improvement.
Juran, Joseph M.	Quality management expert best known for writing the book, *Quality Control Handbook*.
Just culture	A healthcare environment that encourages open dialogue, elimination of fear, and the ability to escalate problems or concerns.
Kaizen	Japanese word that means "a change to make things better." The act of rapid experimentation for quality improvement.
Kotter's Eight-Step Process for Leading Change	A change management model developed by John P. Kotter that promotes organizational transformation by engaging individuals through an urgent and compelling vision for change.
Kübler-Ross Change Curve™	A change management model, based on the five psychological stages of grief (Denial, Anger, Bargaining, Depression, Acceptance) developed by Elisabeth Kübler-Ross that describes the typical emotions when people react to significant change at work.
Lag measure	The target for ultimate improvement. See Lead measure.

(continued)

TERM	DEFINITION
Lead measure	A measure that predicts achievement of the lag measure.
Lean	A mindset, a way of thinking, a set of ideas, or a philosophical approach to quality improvement, and a term first used in the book *The Machine That Changed the World* to describe Toyota Production System® of manufacturing.
Leape, Lucian	Physician, researcher, professor, member of Institute of Medicine's Committee on Quality of Health Care in America, who focuses on patient safety issues.
Measurement System Analysis	The process of determining the accuracy of data for measurement of quality improvement activities.
Muda	A Japanese word meaning "waste" which are inefficiencies that consume resources, such as people, time, equipment, space, money, but do not create value for the customer.
National Committee for Quality Assurance	A nonprofit organization that develops HEDIS measures and accredits healthcare organizations.
National Quality Forum	A nonprofit, nongovernmental organization that develops healthcare quality measures for public reporting.
Nightingale, Florence	A 19th-century British nurse who improved hospital living conditions through improved sanitation and innovative quality management practices.
Non–value-added	Activities that are unnecessary and can be eliminated from a process.
Ohno, Taiichi	Japanese executive recognized as the father of the Toyota Production System®.
Operational definitions	Definition of ambiguous concepts in tangible, measurable, quantifiable, and scientific terms.
Operationalization	Practice of defining quality measures in objective, precise, and scientific terms.
Organizational culture	A social system of human relations with shared norms, values, and assumptions.
Outcomes	The end result of healthcare services, such as recovery, restoration of function, and survival.
Patient experience	Judgment, attitude, or perception of all interactions in a healthcare environment, usually assessed through survey.
Patient safety	Issues related to mitigating the risks of harm to patients.
PDSA	Stands for Plan-Do-Study-Act. The structured continuous quality cycle characterized by objective measurement, goal setting, small-scale tests, and the iterative implementation of successes.
Perfection	The final principle of Lean thinking, which means never being satisfied with the Current State because opportunities to improve always exist.

(continued)

TERM	DEFINITION
Performance improvement	A variety of quality management topics related to demands for quality improvement made by external stakeholders.
Plummer, Henry	An early 20th-century physician, engineer, scientist, and inventor at Mayo Clinic who developed the first modern medical records system, among other innovations.
Problem statement	A formalized expression of the concern requiring improvement documented in the A3 Problem-Solving Template.
Process	A collection of steps that, when carried out in a specific order, produce results.
Process improvement	Proactive, ongoing practice of observing, identifying, describing, analyzing, diagnosing, and correcting suboptimal processes.
Pull	A system that links steps in a process so that each subsequent step is not started until the one before it is finished.
Push	A system that creates a product or starts a service process before the customer needs it.
Rapid Improvement Cycle	Quick experimentation quality improvement event lasting typically no more than a week. See Kaizen.
Root cause analysis	The approach to identifying the underlying problem.
SBAR	A communication method that stands for Situation, Background, Assessment and Recommendations and is designed to assure clear, concise, and organized message.
Scope	Size of the problem to be solved. One of the four common mistakes in the problem definition stage of problem-solving.
Semmelweis, Ignaz	A 19th-century Hungarian obstetrician who championed the importance of handwashing in medical care.
Shewhart, Walter A.	Influential quality management expert credited with developing the concept of statistical control and the Plan-Do-Study-Act cycle of quality improvement.
Six Sigma	A quality improvement mindset designed to reduce defects and variation in processes to assure a reliable product or service is delivered every time.
Smith, Bill	Motorola engineer credited with codeveloping Six Sigma in the 1980s.
Solution	An action intended to solve a problem. One of the four common mistakes in the problem definition stage of problem-solving. See Countermeasure.
Special cause variation	An unpredictable source of fluctuation that usually indicates that the process is beyond the statistical control limit.
Standard work	Precise procedures for work processes.

(continued)

TERM	DEFINITION
Statistical control	The monitoring of process variation to determine when interventions are necessary.
Structure	Settings, qualifications of providers, and administrative systems through which care takes place.
Symptom	An indication that the problem exists.
Taylor, Frederick Winslow	Early 20th-century efficiency expert who sought to obtain maximum output from a process or operation through the application of the scientific method. See Taylorism.
Taylorism	Application of scientific management techniques developed by early-20th-century efficiency expert, Frederick Winslow Taylor.
Time-and-motion study	A method for measuring and improving the timing and mechanics of work systems.
Triple Aim	A framework introduced by the IHI that calls for improved experience of care and population health while reducing per capita costs.
Value	The needs of the customer, which in healthcare are the patient, family, or caregivers.
Value stream	The set of activities, without waste, that meet the needs of the customer.
Value Stream Analysis	A beginning to end depiction of activities that compose the delivery of a service to a customer. Also called "Value Stream Mapping."
Value-added	An activity in the delivery of a product or service that meets the customer's needs; not waste.
Visual management	An approach comprising the use of the various illustrative tools for monitoring operations and supporting quality improvement efforts.
Voice of the customer	The opinion of the customer about the quality of the product or service.
Waste	Inefficiencies that consume resources, such as people, time, equipment, space, money, but do not create value for the customer.
Welch, Jack	Chief executive officer of General Electric Company between 1981 and 2001 who adopted Six Sigma quality methodology throughout his organization.
Womack, James	Coauthor of *The Machine That Changed the World* that introduced the idea of Lean thinking based on the Toyota Production System®.

AHRQ, Agency for Healthcare Research and Quality; HEDIS, Health Effectiveness Data Information Set; IHI, Institute for Healthcare Improvement; NCQA, National Committee for Quality Assurance.

Case Study to Data File Matrix

#	TITLE	DATA FILE DESCRIPTION	CATEGORY
1	A Summer Internship Journal	Patient-level inpatient discharge data, including data dictionary, 344 lines of time stamp data, and calculated discharge turnaround times.	Process Improvement
6	Emergency Department Heroes	Over 8,500 lines of emergency department patient encounters with length of stay and Emergency Severity Index acuity level designations for each patient discharge.	Process Improvement
8	The Cowboy Doctor's Patient Experience	HCAHPS patient experience surveys with 29 questions from 80 patients. Includes data dictionary.	Patient Experience
9	Patient Navigation at the Orthopedic Clinic	Publicly reported Outpatient and Ambulatory Surgery CAHPS facility-level data for over 1,200 ambulatory surgery centers (655 facilities with "linear mean scores"). Includes instructions on how to create Percent Rank in Excel.	Patient Experience
10	HCAHPS and the Quiet-at-Night Measure	Summary HCAHPS Measures for hospital with state and national 75 percentile benchmarks.	Patient Experience
11	Discharge Phone Calls (En Español)	Score summary data for 24 months of HCAHPS overall patient experience surveys for one hospital. Includes total, average, upper control limit, and lower control limit. Demonstrates creation of control charts.	Patient Experience
13	Reducing Patient Falls: The Sleuth Resident	Summary data for 24 months of patient falls for one hospital by unit. Also includes total falls and averages for five hypothesized root causes (patient age, bed age, acuity, RN years of experience, and average census) for each of the 15 patient units. Ideal data for creating scatterplots.	Patient Safety
14	Sustaining Hand Hygiene	Over 4,600 lines of hand hygiene compliance data by location, staff member, and pass/fail.	Patient Safety

(continued)

#	TITLE	DATA FILE DESCRIPTION	CATEGORY
17	CLIF's Medication Errors	Six months of reported medication errors, including patient information, harm scale, actions, contributing factors, medication, and detailed event descriptions.	Patient Safety
18	A Mom's Story of Sepsis	Hour-1 Sepsis Bundle summary chart for Current State. Instructor's file includes full and summary failure modes and effects analysis.	Patient Safety
19	Operating Room Recovery	Almost 5,000 lines of patient-level time stamp data for surgeries with over 30 fields, including room ready, patient-in, procedure start. Includes data dictionary with detailed instructions for writing Excel statements for analyzing potential operating room utilization opportunities. Instructor's file includes completed analysis with pivot tables and utilization calculations.	Performance Improvement
20	Opioid Overdoses in the Emergency Department	Sixteen quarters of emergency department drug overdoses attributable to opioids that are summarized by quarter and monthly average. Data file compatible with time-based trend analysis.	Performance Improvement
22	The Fulfillment Affair	Almost 400 lines of patient-level claims data, including dates of service, diagnoses, place of service, provider type, and total dollar amount paid. Also includes a summary table with patient name and primary diagnosis for the 20 highest cost patients.	Performance Improvement
23	Composite Quality Score	CMS Overall Hospital Star Ratings for 49 hospitals, including the seven separate quality measure categories and composite scores.	Performance Improvement
24	Both/And Thinking in Readmission Prevention	Inpatient readmission reason tracking sheet with diagnoses, discharge location, and reason for readmission. Includes 49 patient-level readmissions.	Performance Improvement

CMS, Centers for Medicare and Medicaid Services; HCAHPS, Hospital Consumer Assessment of Healthcare Providers and Systems.

APPENDIX C

Case Study to Healthcare Setting Matrix

#	CASE STUDY NAME	SETTING	TYPE
1	A Summer Internship Journal	Inpatient; Academic Medical Center	Process Improvement
2	Claims Payment Processing	Managed Care Organization	Process Improvement
3	Return-to-Work at a Home Healthcare Agency	Home Health	Process Improvement
4	The Ophthalmologist Who Could Not See (The Waste)	Ambulatory Surgery Center	Process Improvement
5	Building a New IR Suite	Inpatient; Interventional Neuroradiology Department	Process Improvement
6	Emergency Department Heroes	Inpatient; Emergency Department	Process Improvement
7	Hurricane Mia Hits the Patient Access Call Center	Outpatient; Call Center	Patient Experience
8	The Cowboy Doctor's Patient Experience	Inpatient; Rural Hospital	Patient Experience
9	Patient Navigation at the Orthopedic Clinic	Outpatient; Orthopedic and Spine Clinic	Patient Experience
10	HCAHPS and the Quiet-at-Night Measure	Inpatient	Patient Experience
11	Discharge Phone Calls (En Español)	Inpatient	Patient Experience

(continued)

#	CASE STUDY NAME	SETTING	TYPE
12	Patient Experience in Home Care	Home Health	Patient Experience
13	Reducing Patient Falls: The Sleuth Resident	Inpatient; Academic Medical Center	Patient Safety
14	Sustaining Hand Hygiene	Ambulatory Surgery Centers	Patient Safety
15	A Warning Letter From the State Regulator	Skilled Nursing Facility	Patient Safety
16	Failure-to-Rescue	Inpatient; Small Community Hospital	Patient Safety
17	CLIF's Medication Errors	Inpatient; Pharmacy	Patient Safety
18	A Mom's Story of Sepsis	Inpatient; Emergency Department	Patient Safety
19	Operating Room Recovery	Inpatient; Surgical Department	Performance Improvement
20	Opioid Overdoses in the Emergency Department	Inpatient; Emergency Department	Performance Improvement
21	The Lunchroom: Physician Engagement at a PCMH	Outpatient; Physician Practice	Performance Improvement
22	The Fulfillment Affair	Managed Care Organization	Performance Improvement
23	Composite Quality Score	Inpatient; Multihospital Health System	Performance Improvement
24	Both/And Thinking in Readmission Prevention	Inpatient; Case Management Departments	Performance Improvement
25	Community Collaboration for Suicide Prevention	Inpatient; Community Health	Performance Improvement

HCAHPS, Hospital Consumer Assessment of Healthcare Providers and Systems; PCMH, patient centered medical home.

APPENDIX D

Quality Management Tools and Approaches Matrix

#	CASE STUDY NAME	TOOLS/APPROACH	TYPE
1	A Summer Internship Journal	Checklist	Process Improvement
2	Claims Payment Processing	Process Map	Process Improvement
3	Return-to-Work at a Home Healthcare Agency	Swimlane Diagram	Process Improvement
4	The Ophthalmologist Who Could Not See (The Waste)	Value Stream Map	Process Improvement
5	Building a New IR Suite	Spaghetti Diagram	Process Improvement
6	Emergency Department Heroes	Kaizen	Process Improvement
7	Hurricane Mia Hits the Patient Access Call Center	2 × 2 Matrix	Patient Experience
8	The Cowboy Doctor's Patient Experience	Pareto Chart	Patient Experience
9	Patient Navigation at the Orthopedic Clinic	Standardized Work	Patient Experience
10	HCAHPS and the Quiet-at-Night Measure	Secret Shopper	Patient Experience
11	Discharge Phone Calls (En Español)	Control Chart	Patient Experience
12	Patient Experience in Home Care	Managing for Daily Improvement	Patient Experience

(continued)

#	CASE STUDY NAME	TOOLS/APPROACH	TYPE
13	Reducing Patient Falls: The Sleuth Resident	Scatter Plot	Patient Safety
14	Sustaining Hand Hygiene	The 5-Why? Method	Patient Safety
15	A Warning Letter From the State Regulator	Poka-Yoke	Patient Safety
16	Failure-to-Rescue	Escalation	Patient Safety
17	CLIF's Medication Errors	Risk Mitigation Tool	Patient Safety
18	A Mom's Story of Sepsis	Failure Mode and Effects Analysis	Patient Safety
19	Operating Room Recovery	Data Analytics	Performance Improvement
20	Opioid Overdoses in the Emergency Department	Fishbone Diagram	Performance Improvement
21	The Lunchroom: Physician Engagement at a PCMH	Stakeholder Analysis	Performance Improvement
22	The Fulfillment Affair	Gemba	Performance Improvement
23	Composite Quality Score	Composite Score	Performance Improvement
24	Both/And Thinking in Readmission Prevention	Performance Dashboard	Performance Improvement
25	Community Collaboration for Suicide Prevention	Bar Charts and Histograms	Performance Improvement

HCAHPS, Hospital Consumer Assessment of Healthcare Providers and Systems; PCMH, patient centered medical home.

APPENDIX E

A3 Problem-Solving Template

NAME:	DATE:	CASE:
DEFINE AND ANALYZE THE PROBLEM		**DEVELOP, IMPLEMENT, AND CONTROL SOLUTION(S)**

Problem Statement:
Be specific. Is the focus of improvement appropriately scoped to be described to sufficient detail within this A3? Avoid defining a problem as its consequence, symptom, or solution. A sentence or two describing Where, When, What, How Much, How Do You Know, and What is "The Pain"?

Background:
What is the context of the issue? Who are the key players and what are their view points? Are there conflicts to be resolved? Briefly explain the history. How does the problem fit within the organization's goals? Why is this problem important to the patient/organization? What are the consequences of the problem? Why is a change needed? What are the symptoms of the problem?

Current State:
What is going on? Use facts. Be visual—Use Pareto charts, pie charts, sketches. Draw a diagram of what happens now. Identify problems explicitly in the diagram. What are the key measures or metrics that can describe the current state?

Problem Analysis:
Use the simplest problem-analysis tool that will suffice to find the root cause of the problem: Five whys, fishbone diagram, FMEA, etc. Does the problem above contain multiple root causes? Do causes align explicitly to illustrated problems in the current state section? Prioritize problems.

Future State/Target Condition:
Draw a diagram of a new way to work. Create measurable targets for new ways to work. What are the success factors? Define requirements of future state.

Identify, Test, and Implement Countermeasures:
What will be done to test and validate those countermeasures? (Think PDSA).
Countermeasure #1.
Countermeasure #2.
Countermeasure #3.
Implementation Plan: Must include consultation of all who are impacted.

ITEM	WHAT	WHO	WHEN	STATUS

Verify and Sustain Results:

PRIMARY METRIC	BASELINE	TARGET	CURRENT

Define operational effectiveness. Chart, as appropriate. These data become the new Current State in the Continuous Quality Improvement cycle.
Define verification plan. Define plan to sustain and control changes. Develop Control Plan.
Follow-up and Lessons Learned:
What issues remain that need to be closed? What worked? What could be improved?

PDSA, Plan-Do-Study-Act; FMEA, failure mode and effects analysis.

INDEX